Transforming the Prairies

The Nature | History | Society series is devoted to the publication of high-quality scholarship in environmental history and allied fields. Its broad compass is signalled by its title: *nature* because it takes the natural world seriously; *history* because it aims to foster work that has temporal depth; and *society* because its essential concern is with the interface between nature and society, broadly conceived. The series is avowedly interdisciplinary and is open to the work of anthropologists, ecologists, historians, geographers, literary scholars, political scientists, sociologists, and others whose interests resonate with its mandate. It offers a timely outlet for lively, innovative, and well-written work on the interaction of people and nature through time in North America.

General Editor: Graeme Wynn, University of British Columbia

A list of titles in the series appears at the end of the book.

NATURE | HISTORY | SOCIETY

Transforming the Prairies

Agricultural Rehabilitation and Modern Canada

SHANNON STUNDEN BOWER

FOREWORD BY GRAEME WYNN

UBCPress · Vancouver

© UBC Press 2024

All rights reserved. No part of this publication may be reproduced, stored in a retrieval system, or transmitted, in any form or by any means, without prior written permission of the publisher, or, in Canada, in the case of photocopying or other reprographic copying, a licence from Access Copyright, www.accesscopyright.ca.

Printed in Canada on FSC-certified ancient-forest-free paper (100% post-consumer recycled) that is processed chlorine- and acid-free.

UBC Press is a Benetech Global Certified Accessible™ publisher. The epub version of this book meets stringent accessibility standards, ensuring it is available to people with diverse needs.

Library and Archives Canada Cataloguing in Publication

Title: Transforming the prairies : agricultural rehabilitation and modern Canada / Shannon Stunden Bower.

Names: Stunden Bower, Shannon, author

Series: Nature, history, society.

Description: Series statement: Nature, history, society | Includes bibliographical references and index.

Identifiers: Canadiana (print) 20240428129 | Canadiana (ebook) 20240428153 | ISBN 9780774870399 (hardcover) | ISBN 9780774870405 (softcover) | ISBN 9780774870412 (PDF) | ISBN 9780774870429 (EPUB)

Subjects: LCSH: Canada. Prairie Farm Rehabilitation Administration — History. | LCSH: Agriculture and state — Prairie Provinces — History.

Classification: LCC HD1790.P7 S78 2024 | DDC 338.1/871 — dc23

UBC Press gratefully acknowledges the financial support for our publishing program of the Government of Canada, the Canada Council for the Arts, and the British Columbia Arts Council.

This book has been published with the help of a grant from the Canadian Federation for the Humanities and Social Sciences, through the Scholarly Book Awards, using funds provided by the Social Sciences and Humanities Research Council of Canada.

UBC Press is situated on the traditional, ancestral, and unceded territory of the xʷməθkʷəy̓əm (Musqueam) people. This land has always been a place of learning for the xʷməθkʷəy̓əm, who have passed on their culture, history, and traditions for millennia, from one generation to the next.

UBC Press
The University of British Columbia
www.ubcpress.ca

For Alison and Danica

Contents

List of Illustrations / ix

Foreword: "The best-laid schemes … / go oft awry," The Prairie Farm Rehabilitation Administration in Time / xi
Graeme Wynn

Acknowledgments / xxii

List of Abbreviations / xxiv

Introduction: Rethinking the Prairie Farm Rehabilitation Administration / 3

1 Contexts and Mistakes: The Early Years of the PFRA, 1935–46 / 18

2 Delimiting the Public Good: Irrigation, Racism, and Sugar Beets in Alberta, 1890s–1940s / 42

3 Intensification and Simplification: The PFRA's Community Pastures, 1930s–60s / 61

4 Construction and Change: Negotiating the South Saskatchewan Regional Plan, 1940s–50s / 81

5 Rehabilitation and Colonialism: The PFRA and Prairie Indigenous Peoples, 1930s–60s / 100

6 The PFRA Overseas: Remaking Water Patterns in Northern Ghana, 1965–70 / 120

7 Hope and Disappointment: The PFRA in the 1960s and 1970s / 144

Conclusion: The Prairie Farm *Transformation* Administration / 160

Notes / 175

Bibliography / 240

Index / 278

Illustrations

0.1 Dark-grey, black, dark-brown, and brown soils of the Canadian Prairies / 12

1.1 The Great Plains of North America / 21

1.2 Area of activity under the Prairie Farm Rehabilitation Administration, 1937 / 27

1.3 Location of District Experimental Sub-Stations and Dominion Experimental Farms and Stations, 1939 / 28

1.4 Aerial image of strip farming at the Nobleford District Experimental Sub-Station, 1945 / 29

1.5 Soil surveys undertaken by the Prairie Farm Rehabilitation Administration to 1939 / 33

1.6 The wheat stem sawfly / 37

2.1 Irrigating a field of sugar beets near Raymond, Alberta, early 1900s / 45

2.2 An Indigenous family working on a sugar beet farm near Raymond, c. 1905 / 46

2.3 Historical map of southern Alberta showing existing and anticipated irrigation developments, 1938 / 52

2.4 Japanese people working on a sugar beet farm, mid-1940s / 55

3.1 Prairie Farm Rehabilitation Administration community pastures, 1942 / 65

3.2 Prairie Farm Rehabilitation Administration community pastures, 1960 / 66

3.3 Change over time in the number of PFRA community pastures, 1938–61 / 67

3.4 Change over time in the total acreage in PFRA community pastures, 1938–61 / 67

3.5 Cattle by a barbed wire fence during summer roundup / 69

3.6 Annual meeting of Beaver Hills Community Pasture patrons / 70

3.7 A sample of crested wheatgrass / 77

4.1 The location of Lake Diefenbaker within the Saskatchewan River watershed / 82

4.2 The South Saskatchewan River early in the construction of the Gardiner Dam, 1959 / 98

5.1 Ste. Madeleine, Mistasiniy, and the Saskatchewan River Delta in relation to the Saskatchewan River watershed / 101

5.2 The Saskatchewan River Delta, showing the location of The Pas and the main population centre of the Cumberland House Cree Nation / 112

6.1 Ghana and neighbouring countries along the Gulf of Guinea / 121

6.2 A Canadian family prepares to travel to Ghana / 128

6.3 A Ghanaian takes measurements / 130

6.4 A Canadian and two Ghanaians at work over a desk / 134

7.1 Placing fence posts / 152

7.2 Cattle arriving for summer grazing / 153

Foreword

"The best-laid schemes .../ go oft awry," The Prairie Farm Rehabilitation Administration in Time

Graeme Wynn

At first glance, a book on a Canadian government agency mandated to address agricultural problems on the Canadian Prairies would seem to promise all the excitement of watching grass grow. But don't be fooled. This is no boring institutional biography. Although there is much here about the complexities and challenges of government and administration in a federal system – in which relations between and among agencies, bureaucrats, and staff often shifted and where initiatives, sometimes uncertain, seem on occasion to be at cross-purposes – *Transforming the Prairies* offers a critical re-examination of the ways in which the Prairie Farm Rehabilitation Administration (PFRA) impacted land and life in Canada's prairie region. A lot happens in these pages. In Shannon Stunden Bower's capable hands, the PFRA becomes the centre pivot of a surprising story that irrigates understanding and nourishes insight across a wide swath of ever-changing ground.

Making sense of what is afoot here requires both an appreciation of the ways in which Stunden Bower fathoms the work of the PFRA at a number of scales and recognition of her concerted effort to slough off the blinkers of any single disciplinary approach. These two commitments are closely intertwined. Together, they make this book more intricate – and way more interesting – than is suggested by the thumbnail characterization of the opening sentence above.

In discussing questions of scale, we commonly adopt a loose, tiered framework, encompassing ever more expansive limits. In geographical discussions, the most common rungs in the progression might be local, regional, national, continental, and planetary. In discussions about ecosystems, scholars might identify spatially tiny procaryote and fungal communities, patches (< 10 metres^2), ecosystems (0.1–10 hectares), landscapes (10–100 hectares), and biomes (> 100 hectares). In ringing scale changes, Stunden Bower works, loosely, with an informal geographical hierarchy. The PFRA draws the narrowest focus, which allows consideration of its (evolving) purposes, the shifting ways that it was perceived, and its role as a conduit for the application of what (broadly following sociologist Bruno Latour) might be called the "immutable mobiles" of scientific knowledge to the prairie landscape.[1]

Having lived much of her life in Manitoba and Alberta, and having written previously about the paradox of wetlands and associated drainage problems in a region widely perceived to be drought-prone, Stunden Bower is well aware of the intricate variety of the prairie scene.[2] Changing the register of her analysis slightly from that used in considering the agency, she shifts her gaze to what we might think of as the local scale. Three chapters are given to discussion of particular parts of the prairie landscape where PFRA involvement was especially transformative: in early irrigation schemes for sugar beet production, in the development of community pastures, and in the works associated with the South Saskatchewan Regional Plan (SSRP). These interventions were quite different in their magnitude, intentions, approaches employed, results, and implications for the region, and engagement with them begins to reveal the welter of factors that impinged on the lives of prairie dwellers in the half century after the PFRA's foundation in 1935.

Because all of these factors affected the lives and livelihoods of Indigenous prairie residents, Stunden Bower is concerned (in the fifth chapter and more broadly throughout) to address imbalances in the ledger of earlier scholarship by demonstrating how the PFRA (and government officials more generally) "operated as a vector of colonialism in the Prairie West" (p. 102). An examination of the peremptory displacement of a Métis community to facilitate the development of a community pasture and an account of how ecosystem disruption by the SSRP impacted traditional foodways and Indigenous livelihoods provide strong evidence of PFRA activities undertaken to benefit white farm families heightening poverty and food insecurity among Indigenous peoples.

Then attention shifts to Africa for detailed consideration of the PFRA's involvement in a water conservation program in Ghana. Part of Canada's commitment in the late 1960s to overseas development assistance, this project elevated the PFRA's influence to the international scale – although it is clear throughout that PFRA leaders consistently brought scientific models, techniques, and approaches from abroad to bear on the rural Prairies. In Stunden Bower's telling, the Ghana initiative was a less than stellar venture: several of the Canadians abroad suffered low morale, and colonialist and racist attitudes shaped their interactions with Ghanaians. On balance, aid commitment appears to have been an unfortunate misstep, attributable to misplaced confidence in the universal applicability of abstract expertise. The dozen PFRA employees on the project were strangers in a foreign land. Sent there to provide technological know-how, they found their understanding of local environments inadequate. Detailed scientific data, on which they would normally base their decisions, were wanting. Their engineering calculations often rested on guesswork, and the integrity of the structures that they built depended on the inclusion of a large safety factor in their calculations (p. 132). Some material and humanitarian gains were made as food production increased, but the loftier goal of training locals was mostly stillborn, and unanticipated diseases spread from the conservation works into the local population.

Throughout the seventy-four years of its existence, the PFRA necessarily grappled with shifting circumstances. During the agency's first half century, the Depression gave way to war, and war was followed by an economic boom. Governments changed, and policy directions shifted. Farming itself was transformed by advances in scientific understanding and by successive "revolutions," both mechanical and chemical, that recast the nature of farm work and, substantially, what it meant and what was required to be a farmer. The Prairies and the country were radically different places in 1985 than they had been in 1935. Through all of these changes, the PFRA evolved. In tracing these developments, Stunden Bower's book significantly enhances our understanding of a surprisingly understudied topic: agricultural change on the Prairies in the mid-twentieth century. During these years until its closure in 2009, the PFRA also operated, in some sense and in Stunden Bower's neat phrase, as "a laboratory for experiments in federalism" (p. 158). Although its focus and actions were regional and local, it served, through trial and error and practical politics rather than through explicit design, as a testbed for the implementation (and withdrawal) of state-driven environmental change in Canada. Here, too, *Transforming the Prairies* sheds light beyond its immediate focus by engaging the larger story of change (particularly in policy and ideology) in urbanizing Canada. In broad terms, successive governments moved from assisting farmers in their hours of need, to addressing economic disparities at a regional scale, to fostering development through investment in (urban) growth poles, and embracing neoliberal convictions that favoured market-driven and user-pay philosophies over direct government intervention. Prairie farmers, and Canadians more generally, live with the consequences to this day.

Keeping all of these dimensions in focus and grappling with the many questions that they raise requires a multi-faceted approach, and the scope of Stunden Bower's curiosity is wide. Her analysis is rooted most firmly in the fields of environmental history and historical geography, but she draws insights from the literatures of agricultural history, labour history, the history of science, new political history, the history of "development," and environmental justice studies. Reflecting current emphases in historical and humanities scholarship more generally, this book places Indigenous experiences near the centre of its story and asserts the "importance of understanding the PFRA within the frameworks of settler colonialism and white supremacy" (p. 9). To do otherwise, the author insists, would be to "profoundly misunderstand both the PFRA and the history of the Canadian Prairies" (p. 9). This is a revisionist study, one that properly and helpfully challenges older interpretations and lays out new ways of looking at, and thinking about, past circumstances.

All history is written out of and into the moment of its creation. So the foundational story of the PFRA – created in the depths of the Depression and the Dust Bowl during the lost years of hunger and hardship that drove tens of thousands of settlers from prairie farmsteads within a generation of their arrival on the land – was lodged in the crisis of these years.[3] As Stunden Bower notes, the agency was created to rehabilitate, and its mandate to fix the mistakes of settlement became a mantra in writing about the agency, a refrain that lingered into the 1980s. This was a comforting view and not one devoid of evidence to sustain it.

The scale and extent of prairie settlement in the thirty-some years or so after 1896 had been astonishing. Railways, settlements, and farmsteads, the trappings of what prairie historian W.L. Morton called "a firm and confident expression of a way of life," had been brought into being.[4] This was a landscape, thought Morton, shaped to human aspirations by human effort. Later, it would be seen as evidence of the triumphal march of historian Ian McKay's "liberal order framework" across the western interior.[5] But in 1935, this edifice, an incarnation of the liberal dream of individual freedom and prosperity, was crumbling. Rather than admit its structural flaws, and risk (as it were) a demolition order that might call the wisdom of the wider liberal program into doubt, the expedient, politic, and in many ways inescapable response was to fix the identifiable muddles and missteps that had caused the structure to wobble on its foundations. Ignorance could be overcome. Summerfallowing, a perhaps fortuitously discovered adaptation to insufficient rainfall, exacerbated soil erosion; this problem could be addressed with the following new farming techniques: strip farming and trash cover.[6] Unlearning old ways could make the future better. In the great rush of enthusiasm to settle the Prairies, farmers had sometimes occupied unsuitable land. Now, they could be helped, and their errors could be corrected by unsettlement (pulling back from the most unsuitable lands) and/or by adding stock to farm operations (facilitated by community pastures); even more ambitiously, the progressive settlement dream could be sustained by fixing nature to better serve human needs. The natural order of things could be unmade by hydrological-engineering schemes designed to water dry land. None of these strategies was more than a Band-Aid applied to a particular manifestation of a deeper structural problem, and none was entirely efficacious. But in context they seemed to make sense. In pragmatic terms, they were feasible and signalled action in a time of crisis. In ideological terms, they helped to sustain the liberal progressive narrative and the conviction that scientific knowledge and technological expertise could advance human dominion over the earth.

Very different parameters shape Stunden Bower's perspective on the PFRA. Formulated in the third decade of the third millennium, it responds to the concerns and scholarship of our time. This response requires a longer, more critical evaluation of the agency than can be found in the "Mr. Fix It" story favoured by those engaged with the PFRA in the mid-twentieth century. In Stunden Bower's view, it is important to see the agency's establishment in 1935 as an episode in the larger, more protracted story of Indigenous dispossession in North America. From this perspective, its work was less about correcting errors in the settlement process than about consolidating white dominion. Again, there is ample evidence in support of this argument, and Stunden Bower marshals a good deal of it. Her local case studies offer many instances of Indigenous communities being "by turns ignored, inadequately assisted, and harmed by the PFRA" (p. 8). Perhaps the most poignant single example is the eviction of a Métis community to create a community pasture in Ste. Madeleine on the Manitoba Saskatchewan border. But there were others. In Stunden Bower's telling, the PFRA became party to the (long-established) discriminatory, racist behaviour of farmers and beet factory owners toward Indigenous, Chinese, Japanese, and other racialized workers when it became involved in irrigation for sugar beet farming in the 1930s. Certainly, work in beet fields and factories was onerous and poorly remunerated. In endorsing government-funded irrigation as a public good, the PFRA undoubtedly drew a tight circle of fairness and entrenched inequalities on the southern Prairies – but such issues lay beyond its mandate, and the patterns of power, privilege, and social and environmental inequality perpetuated by these arrangements were of less concern at the time than they are today.

In his lyrical book on conserving the prairie landscape, in which he discusses Ste. Madeleine, nature writer Trevor Herriot reflects on the forgotten stories of Indigenous loss and suffering "too quickly lacquered over" by settler tales of pioneer adventure and resilience. "We have learned too late," he laments, that colonialism "is an utterly unreliable narrator."[7] Indeed, these forgotten stories must be resurrected and honoured, and *Transforming the Prairies* makes important strides in this direction. In the process, it helps readers to recognize the distinctiveness of Indigenous experiences, casts new light on the PFRA as an agent in the negotiation of state-driven environmental change in Canada and sharpens our understanding of the state's support for settler colonialism in general and for small householders in particular.

In doing so, it seems to me, *Transforming the Prairies* also points beyond its immediate concerns to a question of some importance for those who study the past. For generations, historians aimed to understand – as fully and as closely as the evidence and their perspicacity would allow – people, events, and actions in context. Recognizing that neither the paths of individual lives nor the course of history are pre-ordained, they sought to uncover intentions and motivations, to grasp the reasons why people acted as they did, and to comprehend what people believed the results of their actions would be. Their challenge was to explain – in the fine phrase of New Zealand–born legal historian Paul McHugh – the play of "bygone contingency."[8] Knowing the twists and turns and the outcomes of the story with which they were engaged, historians of this ilk obviously thought and wrote with the benefit of hindsight, but they endeavoured to respect the limits of their historical protagonists' understandings. Although these historians' interpretations were inflected with contemporary concerns – most hoped, after all, to make the past speak to interested readers – they would generally avoid arranging evidence from historical times in the service of contemporary convictions. Their ambition was to understand "a phenomenon in all of its complexity and, especially, within the context of its own evolution," and they eschewed condemnation of historical actors for failing to live by the standards of "our" times, not theirs.[9]

Recent decades have seen a shift away from these commitments. By several recent lights, it matters little what those in the past thought; it is the (perhaps unwitting) legacy of their actions that counts. In this view, intentions matter less than outcomes; the effects of actions, choices, and policies are more important than the reasons that ostensibly lie behind them; and systemic patterns become more important than particular acts. From his base in Australia, the interdisciplinary scholar Patrick Wolfe was at the forefront of this shift.[10] His "piercing search for the real structures of colonial rule" characterized settler colonialism as a structure rather than an event and associated ongoing processes of invasion, dispossession, and settlement with a logic of elimination.[11] Historical studies undertaken for legal purposes are often similarly marked by the "desire to categorize a historical situation" and are inclined toward a "retroactive reading of history, in which the past is apprehended and questioned in light of the law."[12] These developments have certainly heightened concern for questions of discrimination and (in)justice, and this outcome is a good thing. There can be no doubt that taken-for-granted assumptions embedded in popular belief, law, ideology, and official policies were consequential determinants of development (and of how people lived) in twentieth-century Canada. These "structures" conditioned economic and social behaviour, structured individual and group prospects of advancement or restriction, shaped the contours of everyday lives, and did much to dictate the fate of nonhuman nature in northern North America. But the compelling simplicity of Wolfe's thesis – "that settler colonialism is premised on a 'winner take all,' zero-sum contest of native removal and replacement by settlers" – leaves little space for fluidity, hybridity, and nuance.[13] In assessing Wolfe's contribution, his close colleague Ben Silverstein also added the important caveat that "identifying structural complicities is not the same as castigating for malevolent intent."[14] Similar caution has not always been evident in the use of these ideas.

Listening "properly and seriously" to Indigenous accounts of the past is a fundamental scholarly responsibility; with it comes the obligation to account for (but not necessarily to adopt) these accounts. As we wrestle with the challenge of interpretation, we must recognize that stories have many facets and that most people have struggled to make lives in circumstances not entirely of their own choosing (as many continue to do). As historian Béatrice Craig demonstrates in her probing microhistory of settlers in the remote reaches of the Upper Saint John River Valley, settlers there "stumbled towards modern capitalism," worrying less about the different forms of that economic system, its close association with liberal individualism, and its overarching commitment to capital accumulation than about "trying to solve the concrete, mundane problems of everyday life, from putting a roof over their head and food on their plate, to raising their children, improving their quality of life, supporting their pastor, or ensuring the security of their old age."[15] In this respect, they were far from alone, and reductionism should not – as historian E.P. Thompson reminded us with regard to the English working class – condemn their struggles to the condescension of posterity.[16]

Both structure and agency are important, and it is part of Stunden Bower's achievement to hold them equally in hand in these pages. Although she is at pains to set her account of a consolidation of white dominion apart from the mistake-fixing tale favoured in the 1930s, it is worth pondering whether the differences here are of degree rather than kind, of emphasis rather than import. Attuned to its particular conjuncture, each interpretation highlights certain facets of a complicated story. Neither is categorically "right" nor "wrong" (for that is in the nature of historical scholarship); might they, perhaps, be complementary and cumulative? As variant accounts of the same developments, they reflect different sensibilities, remind us that there are usually different facets to any story, and in conjunction provide a fuller understanding of the work of the PFRA and the circumstances of life on the Prairies than either does alone.[17] Together, the fixing and the consolidating accounts point to the conclusion, outlined also in Herriot's *Towards a Prairie Atonement* (2016), that abuses of lands and their peoples are substantially attributable to the colonial and liberal-capitalist interests of newcomer society, but they acknowledge the limiting contexts, partial understandings, varied situations, and diverse aspirations of those caught up in these developments.

Among the many other interpretive and substantive contributions found in the pages that follow, there is space only to mention a few. One such contribution is Stunden Bower's innovative insistence on treating the PFRA – for all the range and variety of its activities – as an organization built upon the high-modernist conviction that "expert-led, state-driven undertakings could improve the human condition" (p. 34) and then refusing to simplify or reduce the organization to this function. Although many Canadian scholars have drawn insights from anthropologist James C. Scott's classic work on high modernism and although others have sought to nuance the bold strokes of his interpretation, Stunden Bower breaks new ground on this front.[18] She recognizes that the agency's structure and organization reflected high modernism's abstracting, big-picture, technocratic faith in expert knowledge and top-down decision making and that some of its projects, such as the South Saskatchewan Regional Plan, were fully congruent with its precepts. Yet she hastens to demonstrate that much of the PFRA's quotidian activity rested on the dispersed, practical wisdom of local people rather than on the formal learning of certified authorities. Here, she borrows the concept of "low modernism" from American rural sociologist Jess Gilbert to signal the importance of the PFRA's commitment to working with crisis-ridden farmers in their own fields – in decentralized, interpersonal, collaborative ways that honoured the lived experience and local knowledge of farmers and that gave them meaningful ways to contribute to bettering their circumstances.[19] Agricultural Improvement Associations, run by farmers and funded from the public purse, were created to promote soil conservation; by 1941, there were more than 200 such groups with 33,600 members. There were tensions, and a degree of paternalism, in virtually all such arrangements, as PFRA employees set out to improve the morale, as well as the success, of dejected farmers. But then there were policies with contrary effects and tensions aplenty as governments, institutions, agencies, and individuals scrambled to deal simultaneously with socio-economic and ecological crises and to lay the groundwork for a more stable future.

The second notable contribution of this book is found in Stunden Bower's discussion of the unanticipated ecological consequences of settlement and development on the Prairies and of the PFRA's efforts to address the challenges of rehabilitation. The list of things that went wrong in the course of a few decades – environmental initiatives that led to unfortunate ecological consequences and efforts to improve the human condition that ended up worsening it – is disturbingly long. Taken together, they remind us of the limits of human/scientific understanding at any point in time, of society's tendency to favour immediate "solutions" over long-term adjustments, of the hubris wrapped up in human claims to manage nature, and of the ever-shifting orientation of society's moral compass.[20] Consider three examples. First, bare summerfallowing seemed to improve prospects of a decent crop in dry marginal areas. But tilling to remove weeds broke down soil structure and enhanced erosion. Worried about degraded soils being carried aloft? Well, advised the Agricultural Improvement Associations, reduce the fetch of the wind and lessen its power by cultivating narrow strips of soil perpendicular to the prevailing wind direction. But this tactic increased the proportion of sown edges in the landscape. Because these areas were favoured by the wheat stem sawfly, efforts to reduce soil loss reduced the harvest. And so it went. Early in the 1940s, prairie farmers lost $18 million a year to the ravages of this insect.[21] Second, marginal lands that were turned into failing farms during "the great land rush" (pp. 12–13) of the early twentieth century could be reclaimed for community pastures, returning areas to grass and increasing the viability of small-scale livestock raising, or similar strategies could be applied to hitherto untilled lands. Fencing, water supply, and management arrangements needed to be put in place. Whether through rehabilitation of the land or through intensification of its use, such initiatives promised greater stability and productivity for the rural economy. Within a decade, the PFRA had 1,250,000 acres in community pastures, almost all of them sown in introduced crested wheatgrass. Thirty years later, however, critics were comparing wheatgrass-dominated pastures with the native prairie to lament their ecological impoverishment. Third, high-profile and costly projects such as the SSRP failed to return anticipated benefits, and their deleterious effects on human and nonhuman nature suggest – to borrow from Scots poet Robert Burns – that "foresight may be vain."[22] When such deleterious consequences fall unequally on particular groups or accumulate unevenly in certain places, questions of social and environmental injustice (inadvertent or otherwise) need to foregrounded. Given the massive engineering and scientific resources poured into the construction of major dams, both in Canada and elsewhere after the Second World War, it is hardly credible to suggest that the downstream impacts of the SSRP on the Saskatchewan River Delta were impossible to foresee. A cause of regret or outrage today, they were, at the time, wilfully overlooked – or accepted as the price of "progress," to be borne, substantially, by Indigenous peoples who secured very few of the project's benefits.

The book's third noteworthy contribution is a lesson of sorts – or at least an invitation to think hard about the past, and the present, and about the value of history in contemplating the future. Intriguingly, Stunden Bower identifies a recent uptick in scholarly interest in the PFRA driven by contemporary anxiety about human-generated climate change and a wider concern about the impact of the Anthropocene. The reasons seem self-evident. The 1930s were a time of environmental disaster on the Prairies. The PFRA was established by the government to ameliorate the consequences. Adjustments were made, and the persistence and relative prosperity of prairie farms and prairie dwellers into the twenty-first century are taken by some as signs of successful adaptation and resilience. Might the PFRA provide a model for government intervention in the climate-driven challenges of our times? Stunden Bower is rightly dubious. On her account, the PFRA was not an instrument of adaptation but a driver of environmental transformation that perpetuated, entrenched, and exaggerated socio-environmental inequalities. It also produced, as well as mitigated, environmental problems. This is not, she rightly insists, a history to be repeated.

Going further, I question the underlying notion that the past is something to be used, in instrumental fashion, to address current concerns. History offers many messages, even warnings, but its most fundamental lesson lies in the value of humility. We live (as did those who preceded us) in a world of change, the parameters and implications of which we can but dimly comprehend. The Prairies (and the PFRA) of 1935 were not the Prairies (or the agency) of 1985 or 2009. Neither Canada nor the world was a constant in this span. As historians, and as citizens, we need to understand as fully as we possibly can the evolving, convoluted, contested realities of our pasts, to recognize that then was not now, and to appreciate the circumstances, limitations, aspirations, and anxieties of our predecessors. It is relatively easy to identify and to be critical of the inadequacies of the politicians, bureaucrats, leaders and followers, rich and poor, oppressors and even oppressed – in short, almost everyone – who came before us. It is more difficult to understand them in the intellectual contexts and material circumstances of their times and places. But that is what we must do as we wrestle with the challenge of surmounting our own, and our society's, shortcomings to build a future free of at least some of the stains of the past.[23] This is no easy task. Utopias are elusive – and impermanent.

Perhaps Burns knew something of this challenge 250 years ago – and left us an appropriate lesson in humility beyond the reminder that even the best of plans go oft awry. Addressing the mouse startled by the ploughman's destruction of her nest, he cast himself as "your poor, earth-born companion/ And fellow mortal," before reflecting on the implications of the human sense of time. Assuming that the mouse lived solely in the present, unburdened by history or portent of the future, he lamented, "Och! I backward cast my e'e,/ On prospects drear!/ An' forward, tho' I canna see,/ I guess an' fear!"[24]

Acknowledgments

Big projects never really end – they just arrive at new stages. I'm really pleased to be at the point in this project where I can share my findings broadly. I'd like to take the opportunity to thank some people who have helped me to get here.

I've lived most of my life as a settler on the Prairies in Treaty 1 and Treaty 6 territories, areas that are Métis homelands and that have long been tended by multiple Indigenous nations. I continue to learn what it means to live carefully and responsibly on the Prairies, and I'm grateful to the many teachers who have helped me to better understand these matters.

My earliest research on the Prairie Farm Rehabilitation Administration (PFRA) took place in the context of two postdoctoral fellowships at the University of Alberta. First as a Grant Notley fellow and then as a fellow of the Social Sciences and Humanities Research Council of Canada, I was fortunate to benefit from the guidance of adviser Gerhard Ens. After that, I spent a few years as research director at the University of Alberta's Parkland Institute, learning a great deal about public-interest research. In 2015, I started an academic appointment in the History program at the University of Alberta. My PFRA project has benefited from the financial assistance of the Support for the Advancement of Scholarship program in the university's Faculty of Arts and from the financial assistance of the university's Kule Institute for Advanced Study. I'm grateful to my kind and generous colleagues in the Department of History, Classics, and Religion at the University of Alberta, as well as to colleagues in Indigenous, Canadian, agricultural, and environmental history and related fields at other institutions and outside academia. In particular, I'm grateful for Sean Gouglas's expert work on the maps in this book.

I'd like to thank the journal *Agricultural History* and Duke University Press, the journal's copyright holder and present publisher, for permission to republish portions of Shannon Stunden Bower, "Irrigation Infrastructure, Technocratic Faith, and Tunnel Vision: Canada's Prairie Farm Rehabilitation Administration in Ghana, 1965–1970," *Agricultural History* 93, 2 (2019): 311–40. I'd also like to acknowledge that some material appeared in an earlier form in "Strip Farming and the Wheat Stem Sawfly on the Canadian Prairies, 1930s–1960s," *Folklore* 41, 3 (2020): 4–8. This piece also appeared on the website of the Network in Canadian History and Environment.

I'm indebted to archivists and staff at numerous institutions but particularly at the Provincial Archives of Saskatchewan and at Library and Archives Canada's Regional Service Centre in Winnipeg. Librarians and interlibrary loan staff at the University of Alberta have been very helpful. Additionally, nonacademic staff at the University of Alberta have helped me to do my job to the best of my abilities, even while enduring a great deal of turmoil and uncertainty related to university restructuring. I'm grateful to them.

Teaching at the University of Alberta has allowed me to engage with many talented and hard-working students. It is my privilege to work and learn with them.

I've been fortunate to work with the expert editors and staff at UBC Press, as well as with series editor Graeme Wynn. I'm grateful to the anonymous reviewers who provided helpful and challenging feedback on my project, as I am to audiences who have listened to me and shared their responses when I've presented preliminary interpretations at conferences, workshops, and talks over the past number of years.

I'd like to thank everyone who, over many decades, has thought hard about the PFRA. Our shared interest in this public institution indicates the importance of finding creative ways for people to work together and to engage responsibly with nonhuman nature, as well as the need to carefully assess the outcomes of such efforts. I hope that this work is a useful contribution to ongoing conversations.

I'm grateful to friends and family who have been my heart and my community over the years that I've spent working on this project. Thanks are due in particular to my parents and my sisters, as well as to my sisters' families. Thanks to the fur beasts who have shared our homes. And above all, thanks and love to my kids and to my partner, Sean. You make it all possible, and you make it all worthwhile.

Abbreviations

AIA	Agricultural Improvement Association
ARDA	Agricultural Rehabilitation and Development Act
CCF	Co-operative Commonwealth Federation
CIA	Central Intelligence Agency
CIDA	Canadian International Development Agency
DIAND	Department of Indian Affairs and Northern Development
DREE	Department of Regional Economic Expansion
EAO	External Aid Office
FAO	Food and Agriculture Organization
LIFT	Lower Inventories for Tomorrow
LNID	Lethbridge Northern Irrigation District
LUB	Land Utilization Board
PFAA	Prairie Farm Assistance Act
PFRA	Prairie Farm Rehabilitation Administration
RCARL	Royal Commission on Agriculture and Rural Life
SRDA	Saskatchewan Rivers Development Association
SSRP	South Saskatchewan Regional Plan

Transforming the Prairies

Introduction
Rethinking the Prairie Farm Rehabilitation Administration

The Prairie Farm Rehabilitation Administration (PFRA) was eliminated by the Canadian federal government in 2009 but continued to make the news for more than another decade. In 2021, two national political parties referenced it in the run-up to a federal election. The Green Party promised to restore it.[1] The incumbent Liberal Party echoed an earlier pledge to create a new Canada Water Agency, which was described as a resurrected PFRA.[2] References to the PFRA were also common beyond politics. The agency figured large in a 2019 report by the National Farmers Union that identified "high-output, high-input agriculture" as a major driver of the climate crisis. The report urged the creation of a new entity – the Canadian Farm Resilience Administration – characterized as a "super PFRA."[3] In 2020, amid the devastation and disruption of the COVID-19 pandemic, Richard Florizone, president of the International Institute for Sustainable Development, offered the PFRA as an example of emergency assistance by government that had long-term benefits.[4] These years also saw activists urging revival of the agency and newspaper columnists calling for its resurrection.[5] Invoking the PFRA has become a means through which politicians signal and advocates demand robust commitments to state action on agricultural, environmental, and societal problems.

The Prairie Farm Rehabilitation Administration was created in 1935 by the Canadian federal government amid perceived agricultural collapse on the Canadian Prairies. Much of south-central Manitoba, Saskatchewan, and Alberta were experiencing an environmental reckoning, one exacerbated by an international economic depression that significantly suppressed prices for wheat, a commodity produced by many prairie farmers. Over the following decades, the PFRA operated under both Conservative and Liberal governments and within various federal departments. In 2009, the agency was incorporated into Agri-Environment Services, a new branch within the Department of Agriculture and Agri-Food Canada.[6] A few years later, its remaining functions were eliminated as part of what became known in some quarters as Conservative prime minister Stephen Harper's "war on science."[7] In this book, I examine the PFRA's history between its foundation and the mid-1980s to identify the agency's enduring consequences and to reckon with recent valorizations of the PFRA.

The PFRA's persistently positive press rests on the idea that the agency was involved in fixing settlement mistakes that had disadvantaged individual settlers, the prairie provinces, and the region at large. The understanding that prairie settlement involved significant mistakes became established through efforts to secure the transfer of natural resources, including land, from Ottawa to the prairie provinces. Historian Chester Martin argued in 1920 that Ottawa's retaining of control over natural resources amounted to a wrong-headed deviation from British principles of responsible self-government.[8] In a later contribution to the Canadian Frontiers of Settlement series, Martin pointed to the federal government's failure to ensure that available prairie lands were environmentally appropriate for farming and to guard against settlement by newcomers ill-positioned to succeed in creating productive farms.[9] He also noted that problematic farming techniques degraded prairie soils.[10] Martin urged the federal government to collaborate with farmers in addressing these failures and pointed to the PFRA as an example of what was needed.[11]

For early PFRA leaders and supporters, presenting the agency as a remedy for past errors enabled them to tap into an understanding of prairie history that was already prevalent and that offered a ready justification for agency activities. This view of the PFRA proved enduring. Variants on the notion of the PFRA as a fix for settlement mistakes showed up in the correspondence of federal and provincial governments,[12] and it was invoked by civil servants describing their activities and those of their colleagues.[13] It also appeared in federal and provincial royal commissions focused on prairie problems,[14] and it echoed like a refrain throughout various PFRA reports and communications,[15] both those intended for internal government purposes and those aimed at broader audiences. The anchor word in the agency's name – rehabilitation – functioned as shorthand for the notion that the PFRA was reparative: to rehabilitate meant to fix mistakes.

Scholars adopted, adapted, and perpetuated the theme. Political economist George Edwin Britnell, in *The Wheat Economy* (1939), described federal government policy of the 1930s as focused on "correction of the most glaring mistakes of settlement."[16] So consistent was the work of Britnell with the PFRA's own rhetoric that, in November 1939, PFRA director George Spence wrote to thank Britnell for another publication that offered "particularly good publicity for our work."[17] In *Canadian Agricultural Policy: The Historical Pattern* (1946), economic historian Vernon Fowke portrayed the PFRA as a federal government effort to salvage the beleaguered agricultural economy of western Canada.[18] A decade later, in *The National Policy and the Wheat Economy* (1957), Fowke described the PFRA as engaged in "correcting the mistakes of the homestead period."[19] A joint publication by Britnell and Fowke, *Canadian Agriculture in War and Peace, 1935–1950* (1962), was largely consistent with the pair's earlier publications, at least in the attention that it accorded to the PFRA.[20]

The most influential published account of the PFRA remains James H. Gray's *Men against the Desert* (1967), which detailed a range of state-sponsored efforts to respond to 1930s agricultural difficulties.[21] This volume followed the publication of Gray's first book, *The Winter Years: The Depression on the Prairies* (1966), a description of the Depression-era Prairies based largely on Gray's own experiences, which included difficult years of unemployment.[22] *The Winter Years* expresses Gray's frustration with governments that offered little assistance to hard-hit prairie dwellers. This frustration helps to explain *Men against the Desert,* in which Gray lauds a range of actors (identified as agricultural engineers, university researchers, soil scientists, entomologists, plant breeders, stock raisers, and farmers) whom he viewed as having responded to the crisis with vigour, in part through their work with the PFRA.[23] As a newspaper reporter in the mid-1930s, Gray was what he termed "a spectator at the birth of PFRA," and Gray's admiration for the agency is clear in his assertion that the experience left him "with memories to last a lifetime."[24]

Men against the Desert surveys a range of ways that the 1930s prairie crisis was addressed, including population movement out of the hardest-hit areas and the development of more appropriate farm machinery. Gray positioned the PFRA at the centre of the crisis response, which Gray called "the greatest Canadian success story since the construction of the CPR."[25] Given the focus on the agency and Gray's compelling prose, *Men against the Desert* amounted to a particularly heroic rendering of the PFRA's role in fixing the mistakes of settlement. Experts from multiple fields have lauded Gray's work. A history of the Saskatchewan Institute of Agrologists proposed that it should be "required reading for all agrologists."[26] Gray's book won an award from the Historical Society of Alberta, and in 1987 historians John Herd Thompson and Ian MacPherson called it the best nonacademic work on Canadian prairie history.[27] PFRA leadership was equally enthusiastic, feeling that Gray's interpretation operated to their benefit. They incorporated Gray's title into their own publicity work, using the phrase "Men against the Desert" to headline a mid-1980s photograph display commemorating the PFRA's fiftieth anniversary.[28] Also in the 1980s, likely based at least in part on the publicity that Gray offered the agency, the PFRA became an important touchstone in elementary school history textbooks.[29]

Later scholars, despite making valuable contributions to broader understandings of prairie history and adding nuance to prior interpretations of the PFRA, have not challenged the general conclusions of early analysts. Gerald Friesen, author of an innovative volume titled *The Canadian Prairies: A History* (1984), saw the PFRA as an effort to "correct the tragic mistakes" of farming unsuitable areas such as southwestern Saskatchewan and southeastern Alberta.[30] In *Empire of Dust: Settling and Abandoning the Prairie Dry Belt* (1987), David C. Jones lauded key figures within the PFRA for their work to "save the vile heart of the desert," as Jones termed the effort to reclaim degraded prairie areas.[31] Barry Potyondi's *In Palliser's Triangle: Living in the Grasslands, 1850–1930* (1995), despite concluding prior to the creation of the PFRA, expands our understanding of settlement's mistakes by focusing on underlying capitalist imperatives.[32] In *Places of Last Resort: The Expansion of the Farm Frontier into the Boreal Forest in Canada, c. 1910–1940* (2006), David Wood refers to the PFRA as a government-driven effort to correct problems with prairie settlement.[33] In *Happyland: A History of the "Dirty Thirties" in Saskatchewan, 1914–1937* (2011), Curtis McManus argues that the PFRA contributed to shifting prairie agriculture from exploitation to adaptation, which he sees as an important conceptual fix.[34] Gregory P. Marchildon sheds light on the PFRA's political dimensions, proposing that the agency should be understood as a political calculus as well as "an evidence-based policy response to socio-environmental disaster."[35] Although valuable for its emphasis on the PFRA's political dimensions, Marchildon's article echoes and entrenches the remediation-of-mistakes narrative. Murray Knuttila's recent analysis of national agricultural policy and transnational economic processes touches briefly on the PFRA, but it does not include sustained analysis of the agency's activities and their effects.[36]

The often told story of the PFRA's role in fixing the mistakes of settlement should be revisited. The need for a re-examination of the agency is made clear through a careful assessment of Gray's *Men against the Desert,* which since its publication has anchored the prevailing interpretation of the PFRA. Notwithstanding its acclaim and influence among professional historians, Gray's work is unfootnoted, making it challenging to evaluate the basis for his interpretations. It predates much contemporary environmental and agricultural science that now permits a reassessment of PFRA activities. *Men against the Desert* considers the PFRA only amid the 1930s crisis, although the agency continued to operate for many additional decades. Given the PFRA's importance within common understandings of prairie history, it is time for an up-to-date assessment that accounts for the agency over a longer period.

The broadest argument in this book is that the PFRA was intended to drive forward transformation in the prairie region, not simply to correct past mistakes. This interpretation is clear when the varied activities of the agency are considered in aggregate and over decades, an approach not taken by prior scholarly analysts. The PFRA aimed to profoundly transform prairie environments and prairie agriculture. The agency also contributed to change in how politicians and technical experts understood the role of the state. Yet the PFRA's ambitions were never completely realized. Change did not always take place as intended, and the agency lacked the capacity to implement some of its most transformative plans.

Over many decades, the PFRA's broad array of activities ranged from on-farm engagements with an individual farmer to the construction of massive hydroelectric infrastructure affecting multiple communities and ecosystems. Despite the diversity of these activities and their difference in scope, three common features mark the agency's work. First, the PFRA was engaged in state-driven environmental transformation that reflected what anthropologist James C. Scott described as a high-modernist ideology.[37] High modernism is defined by faith in the capacity of experts to improve the human condition. Flowing from this ideology are practices that emphasize the activity of experts and the production of expert knowledge. Historians focused on Canada have ably engaged with Scott, working to shed light on various aspects of the Canadian past and also to critique Scott's ideas. Key contributions to this literature have focused on infrastructure construction, with radically disruptive undertakings such as water-engineering projects and roads or freeways providing particularly powerful representations of high modernism.[38] Other contributions have referenced the influence of high modernism in diverse historical contexts, tracing its influence in northern and rural spaces, international relations, and urban governance, for example.[39] Positioning the PFRA in relation to high modernism offers a new way of understanding the agency.[40] Additionally, study of the PFRA brings something new to our understanding of state-driven environmental change in mid-twentieth-century Canada. Much existing literature takes a project-focused approach, with scholars drawing on Scott's conceptualization to help explain particular state undertakings. Because the PFRA undertook a range of activities over decades, the agency reflects high modernism as a process rather than an event. Studying the PFRA suggests how high modernism found purchase in Canada, how it resonated with a range of state imperatives that included conservation and development, and how it was influenced by political considerations within Canada's federal system. In this way, my study of the PFRA sheds new light on the various ways that state-driven environmental change was negotiated in Canada.[41]

The significance of the transnational context is a second characteristic feature of PFRA activities. The agency was a vector through which transnational scientific models, techniques, and approaches were brought to bear on the rural Prairies. In turn, the PFRA engaged transnationally in various ways, with the work of the agency's administrators, scientists, engineers, and economists effectively coupling the Prairies to global contexts. In emphasizing the significance of the transnational dimension, I follow in the wake of earlier scholars who have examined the influence of transnational forces on the Prairies, including empire, ecological processes, and communications technologies.[42] I also connect my work to a recent trend in the historiography of the mid-twentieth-century Prairie provinces. Scholars Erika Dyck, Alex Deighton, Valerie Korinek, and Esyllt Jones have conceptualized prairie history not as a subset of the Canadian nation-state (a region alongside other Canadian regions like Atlantic Canada and the North) but as something defined in key ways by historical processes that are transnational in scope.[43] Although our respective topics differ widely – with my colleagues attending to mental health treatment, the experiences of queer peoples, and the emergence of Medicare – we share an inclination to situate the modern Prairies transnationally, recognizing it as a region of the world.[44]

A third feature common across many PFRA activities was the agency's role in consolidating the dispossession of prairie Indigenous peoples. Many Indigenous communities were by turns ignored, inadequately assisted, and harmed by the PFRA. The PFRA also contributed to entrenching racism and colonialism within and beyond the Prairies, with consequences for other groups subject to oppression as well as Indigenous peoples. In recognizing these processes, my rendering is in tune with scholarship that demonstrates how, globally, state-driven responses to agricultural drought or aridity often entrench prevailing inequalities.[45] There is much still to learn about interactions between the PFRA and prairie Indigenous peoples, as well as other disadvantaged groups. In what follows, I aim to make clear the importance of understanding the PFRA within the frameworks of settler colonialism and white supremacy. To do otherwise would be to profoundly misunderstand both the PFRA and the history of the Canadian Prairies.

The PFRA, an agency of the federal state, envisioned and undertook transformative activities that were defined by transnational contexts and that consolidated the ongoing process of settler colonialism. In this way, the PFRA was engaged in an ambitious project of regional refashioning aimed at producing a more stable prairie agriculture sufficiently profitable to afford an acceptable quality of life for those the agency served. Although forged amid the volatility and hardship of the 1930s, this broad organizational goal persisted for decades. It was made manifest in the agency's promotion of small-scale stock raising, which agency advocates thought would bolster the ability of farm families to endure economic and environmental ups and downs. The PFRA's broad organizational goal, the pursuit of agricultural stability to ensure rural quality of life, was also evident in the agency's contributions to intensifying prairie agriculture, which involved efforts to increase regional agricultural productivity by realigning land use and land capacity as well as by facilitating access to water.

The PFRA's effort at regional refashioning played out amid changes in agriculture that were global in scope and radical in effect. In North America in the 1910s and 1920s, farming was reshaped by new technologies such as tractors and by new ideas about efficiency.[46] These forces of change intensified during the Second World War, when labour shortages combined with improved farm incomes to increase reliance on machinery such as tractors and combines – what Ian MacPherson and John Herd Thompson termed a "mechanical revolution for grain growing."[47] This mechanical revolution was, in the postwar years, complemented by a chemical one, as herbicides, pesticides, and fertilizers increased in type and availability.[48] In the words of historian Grant MacEwan, new agricultural chemicals kindled "enthusiasm, scepticism, and fear" among prairie farmers even as these chemicals shifted the bounds of agricultural possibility.[49]

New machines and new chemicals, many of which relied on or were derived from petrochemicals, knit agriculture into the fossil fuels industry in unprecedented ways.[50] They also drove shifts in the agricultural and human landscapes of the region. Prairie farms increased in size, and rural population dropped, with significant consequences for those who remained on the farm and for their governments.[51] As historian Royden Loewen puts it, mid-twentieth-century agricultural change "shook the foundation of rural North America."[52] Ongoing processes of agricultural industrialization meant that even as the PFRA sought to transform the Prairies, the ground was shifting beneath the agency's feet.

Historical and Environmental Contexts

Although enmeshed in processes playing out globally, the PFRA was oriented to the human and environmental circumstances of the mid-twentieth-century agricultural Prairies, the south-central section of the Canadian Prairies today dominated by capitalist farming. These circumstances were defined by the accelerating processes of resource exploitation and land colonization that were spurred by non-Indigenous newcomers. Resource exploitation and land colonization had catastrophic effects on Indigenous communities, and they also had significant effects on regional ecologies.

Before substantial numbers of colonizers settled in northwestern North America, the area that would become the agricultural Prairies was a profoundly multicultural space. Among the Indigenous peoples most substantially affected by the agricultural colonization of the Prairie West were Anishinaabeg and Inninewak in eastern prairie areas, along with Métis, Nakawe, and nēhiyawak extending westward.[53] The Dakota, Lakota, and Nakota were concentrated in central prairie landscapes, and the Siksika, Kainai, and Piikani extended from central to western prairie areas. The îyârhe Nakodabi also spanned central and western areas, and the Tsuut'ina were concentrated in the western Prairies. Affected groups living farther north included the Nehinuwuk.[54] Changes in the names used by Indigenous groups often reflect efforts to specify and reclaim identities that have persisted despite generations of colonial oppression, and these shifts signal the continued vitality of Indigenous communities. Historically, the Indigenous peoples of the Prairie West often organized themselves into multicultural bands united by kinship ties.[55] These communities engaged in significant and sustained ways with the environments that they lived in, moved through, tended, used, and altered.

Soil is one of the fundamental components of any system of agricultural production. Plants root in it, and they extract nutrients and water from it. Soil creation is defined by the geological, climatological, and historical processes playing out in any particular landscape. In a material sense, soil is long-term local history.[56] The history of the soils of the Prairie West extends back in time at least to the last glaciation, with glacial retreat and deposition bearing on the region's landscapes. The development of prairie soils continued across the millennia during which Indigenous peoples lived in and moved throughout the region, with burning practices being among the various ways that Indigenous peoples affected their environment. Over this long period, driven in part by climatic conditions, prairie soils came to catalogue the accumulating effects of human, plant, and animal life across the region. Distinct soil zones emerged: the brown soils characteristic of the drier grasslands, the dark-brown and black soils of the moister grasslands, and the dark-grey soils typical of the transitional area between grasslands and boreal forest.[57] The differences in these soil zones relate to the quantity and quality of the organic matter that accumulated in the topsoil prior to the establishment of colonizer agriculture, with less organic matter in the semi-arid brown region and more in the sub-humid black region. The dark-grey soil zone is distinguished by the inclusion of forest vegetation in the soil along with grassland vegetation. According to the Government of Canada's 2017 ecological classification, the agricultural areas of Manitoba, Saskatchewan, and Alberta fall within the Prairies ecozone, which includes the Aspen Parkland ecoregion along the northerly limits of the agricultural Prairies.[58]

By the late nineteenth century, the linked processes of colonial expansion and capitalist exploitation had transformed the environments and societies of northwestern North America. Fuelled by demand in Europe and eastern North America, beaver and bison as well as other animals had been pursued so voraciously as to radically shrink their numbers. The fur trade was transformative on numerous fronts, including its impact on the significance of the waterways of northern North America. The prairie region includes rivers and streams of many sizes. Some, like the North Saskatchewan River, flow east from the Rocky Mountains (along Alberta's western border) and combine with other waterways before eventually draining into Hudson Bay as part of the Nelson River system. The northward-running Red River flows into Lake Winnipeg after bisecting

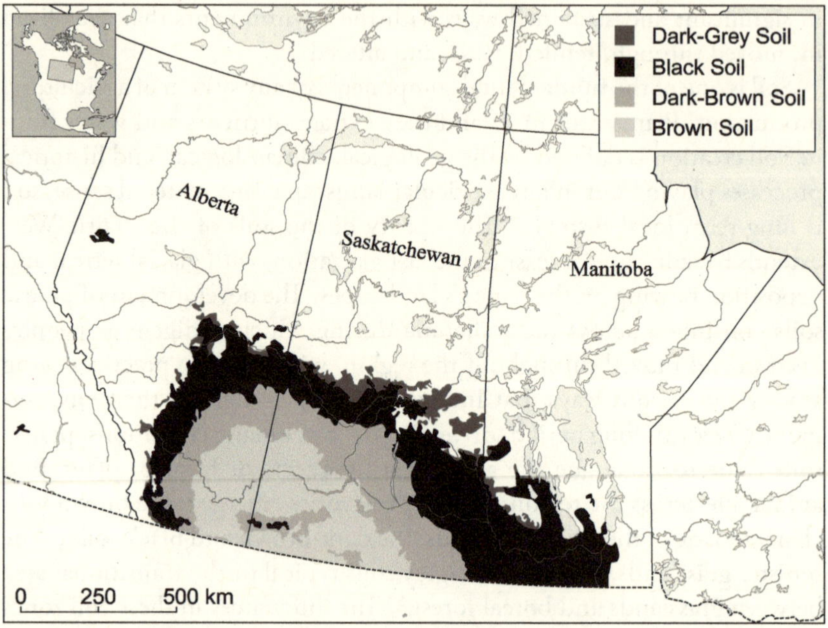

FIGURE 0.1 Dark-grey, black, dark-brown, and brown soils of the Canadian Prairies. *Adapted from W.M. Drummond and W. Mackenzie,* Progress and Prospects of Canadian Agriculture, *ed. Royal Commission on Canada's Economic Prospects (Ottawa: Queen's Printer, 1957), 253; Les Fuller, "Chernozemic Soils of the Prairie Region of Western Canada,"* Prairie Soils and Crops Journal *3 (2010): 37–45; and* CanVec Series [Admin., Land, Hydro] *(Ottawa: Natural Resources Canada, 2019).*

southern Manitoba. Other rivers like the Qu'Appelle and the Assiniboine are both locally significant and important as tributaries to larger rivers. Compared to the Canadian Shield landscape to the north and east as well as the mountain ranges to the west, there are few substantial lakes on the agricultural Prairies, a circumstance that heightens the importance of rivers as well as smaller streams. Rivers and lands adjacent to rivers were of longstanding importance to Indigenous peoples.[59] During the fur trade, rivers continued to serve as key routes of transportation, and they also became important vectors within an exchange process that affected both people and nonhuman nature.

As the fur trade declined and agricultural colonization increased, the Indigenous peoples of northwestern North America suffered displacement and dispossession. These processes were part of what historian John Weaver has termed "the great land rush," in which empires expanded overseas and established private property regimes.[60] On the agricultural Prairies, Indigenous peoples made treaties with the Canadian state, but inequities in the treaty-making process were compounded in subsequent years by Canada's failure to live up to treaty terms.[61] Epidemic diseases such as smallpox, oppressive legislation such as the 1876 Indian Act, and genocidal apparatus such as the Indian Residential Schools system bore heavily on the Indigenous peoples of the Prairie West, further advancing the state-sponsored project that historian James Daschuk has called "clearing the plains."[62]

The Canadian federal government promoted the agricultural colonization of the Prairie West both to claim territory and to develop western markets for goods produced in the industrializing East. Railway construction, policing, and land surveying were publicly sponsored efforts to create conditions more amenable to the production of private profit. State legislation, particularly the 1872 Dominion Lands Act, was intended to attract settlers to the Prairie West. This legislation enabled individuals to access a quarter-section of land (160 acres) for a fee of $10. Provided that they fulfilled certain criteria – namely cultivating a specified amount of land, erecting buildings, and living on the homestead – they could after a number of years receive title.[63] Notably, not all people were always able to access a homestead. Women and Indigenous peoples were among those often excluded from doing so under the changing policies and practices governing prairie settlement, so the process of imposing a private property system in the Prairie West entrenched gendered and racialized inequalities.[64]

The provisions of the Dominion Lands Act were a poor fit for environmental conditions across much of the Prairie West, with quality of soil and supply of water being among the key factors. Precipitation records reveal that the Saskatchewan River watershed, which extends across much of the agricultural Prairies, is Canada's most variable in terms of rates of precipitation.[65] Making more land available to individual homesteaders through the pre-emption system and providing farming guidance through the Experimental Farms Service were some ways that the Canadian state sought to improve the odds for colonizer farmers. Abetted by both the Canadian government and an unusually large quantity of rain, in the final years of the nineteenth century and the early years of the twentieth century, newcomers came to the Prairies in large numbers and sought to establish farms.[66] They did not necessarily arrive in one place and stay there. The settlement period was characterized by a significant degree of churn in human populations, with people moving out of, as well as into, the region and from one farm to another.[67]

Temporarily elevated precipitation around the turn of the century helped many new prairie farmers. Some parts of the Prairies had persistent difficulties with excess water.[68] But over the longer term and at a regional scale, large areas of the Prairies often fail to receive precipitation at rates meeting the requirements of common farm crops, a circumstance known as agricultural drought.[69] The shortfall of water is typically most severe in an area extending from southwestern Saskatchewan to south-central Alberta. Characterized by a mixed grassland ecosystem and situated within the brown soil zone, this area was sometimes termed Palliser's Triangle in reference to John Palliser, a British agent who deemed the area too dry for successful farming.[70] But agricultural drought is an ever-present risk on the Prairies even beyond this particularly dry area. Scientists Dave Sauchyn and Samantha Kerr explain that precipitation rates that are at best borderline for agricultural production are so common on the Canadian Prairies as to "define the region ecologically."[71]

The PFRA was created amid the agricultural drought of the 1930s. In those years, blowing dust was visceral evidence of farming crisis, a vivid sign of the precipitous erosion of prairie soils that had accumulated over millennia. Dust storms were seen to demand efforts at fixing what many observers – farmers, governments, and scholarly analysts alike – understood as the mistakes of prairie settlement.

Reckoning with the PFRA

By situating the PFRA in historical and environmental contexts, this book sheds light on the agency, the region, and the nation, as well as on the mid-twentieth-century global context. It is primarily a work of environmental history and historical geography, but the analysis draws from a range of historical sub-fields, including labour history, agricultural history, the history of science, new political history, aid history, environmental justice, and the history of Indigenous peoples.

My approach is thematic. Although the book progresses from addressing the agency's emergence in the 1930s (Chapter 1) to dealing with key events of the 1960s and 1970s (Chapter 7), with the Conclusion describing some important changes in the mid-1980s, there is no steady chronological progression throughout the pages to come. Traditional institutional biographies have their merits, but the PFRA is best understood critically and analytically. The chapters that follow reach backward and forward in time in perhaps unexpected ways in order to situate the agency and its activities in timelines defined by colonial processes and ecological change.

Chapter 1 locates the agency in large-scale historical processes, including the environmental changes associated with colonizer agriculture and conservationist concerns about natural resources degradation. It engages directly with the question of how the PFRA sought to fix the mistakes of settlement, as the agency framed them. This chapter deploys sociologist Jess Gilbert's notion of low modernism as a counterpoint to James C. Scott's high modernism.[72] Both modes of state action figure large in the PFRA's first decade. Finally, the chapter situates early PFRA activities in environmental context by examining an unintended consequence of strip farming, a soil conservation technique heavily promoted by the PFRA. Strip farming helped to guard against blowing soils, but it also exacerbated infestations by the wheat stem sawfly, an insect that damaged crops. Reckoning with the early PFRA means taking account not just of protected soils but also of sawfly problems.

Chapter 2 locates the PFRA's contributions to Alberta irrigation within longer and broader histories of colonialism and racism beginning prior to the 1905 creation of the province. The focus is on efforts to grow sugar beets, a potentially lucrative crop requiring both abundant water and intensive cultivation. On the Prairies, beet farmers relied on irrigation infrastructure and on labour from Indigenous peoples, Asian peoples, and other disadvantaged groups. By the mid-1930s, it was clear that public money was necessary to underwrite irrigation infrastructure, and the PFRA helped to validate this investment by maintaining that irrigation served the public interest. This notion of the public interest failed to include the people labouring in the beet fields. And so the sugar beet landscape casts into relief some of the racist and colonial frameworks that the PFRA helped to perpetuate.

The Community Pastures Program is the subject of Chapter 3. This was an important area of PFRA activity from 1937 onward. Publicly administered pastures played a key role in the unsettlement of the Prairies, the PFRA-led effort to move farmers away from unsuitable lands and to promote raising livestock. This chapter picks up on earlier discussion of high and low modernism, finding both in the PFRA's Community Pastures Program. This chapter also addresses the political constraints on and the environmental consequences of the program, particularly the reduction of ecological diversity due to the intensive seeding of crested wheatgrass. The chapter illustrates that the effects of the great land rush, which helped to create the 1930s crisis on the Canadian Prairies, were not easily reversed.

Chapter 4 examines what George Spence, first director of the PFRA, viewed as the ultimate resolution of the mistakes of settlement: the South Saskatchewan Regional Plan (SSRP). This was a typical high-modernist undertaking. The SSRP involved the construction of dams and a reservoir that were intended to transform Saskatchewan by making available additional water and hydroelectricity. Focusing on the process of planning the SSRP, this chapter foregrounds the tension between expertise and politics underlying many PFRA undertakings. The chapter also explores the evolution of conservationism in a Canadian context, elaborating on what contemporaries saw as important connections between the wise use of resources and improvements in human well-being. These connections took on particular significance in light of concerns about quality of life in rural Saskatchewan, concerns that underwrote the decision to move ahead with the SSRP.

Chapter 5 details how a number of PFRA activities had significant negative consequences for Indigenous peoples and communities, underlining that the agency should be understood within the framework of settler colonialism. Three case studies suggest the diversity of Indigenous peoples' encounters with the PFRA. They also demonstrate how mid-twentieth-century state-led efforts at conservation and development prioritized the needs of settlers, often without considering harms to Indigenous peoples.

Chapter 6 follows the PFRA to Ghana, where the agency became involved in a water conservation project in the north of that country. As wealthy nations of the Global North and the West undertook so-called international development, the Canadian government turned to the PFRA for technical expertise in order to supplement other overseas activities. Whereas previous chapters make clear how PFRA agents were situated within global communities of experts, this chapter examines one of the agency's own transnational undertakings. The chapter elaborates on the significance of colonialism and racism within the work of the PFRA and documents the tragic consequences of deploying technical expertise in the absence of local knowledge.

Chapter 7 addresses key aspects of PFRA activities in the 1960s and 1970s. In the 1960s, the PFRA helped to inspire various federal agricultural and regional development initiatives that bore on the nation at large. The agency engaged directly with prairie Indigenous peoples in these years but failed to establish programs that effectively served Indigenous communities. By the 1970s, changes in prevailing ideas of development and shifts in federal government practices disadvantaged the PFRA, and the agency diminished in power and influence.

The 1980s began amid widespread political and public alarm about a serious agricultural drought on the Canadian Prairies, and prairie drought fears resonated with growing global concerns about soil degradation. The book's Conclusion considers the changed regional and transnational contexts within which the PFRA came to be seen, once again, as an effective agent for grappling with important problems. This 1980s redemption underlies early-twenty-first-century invocations of the agency by political parties like the Liberal Party and the Green Party as well as by advocacy organizations like the National Farmers Union and the International Institute for Sustainable Development.

Recently, scholars from disciplines across the social and natural sciences have directed new attention at the PFRA. Concerned about anthropogenic climate change, researchers have examined the 1930s PFRA, as well as the broader environmental crisis that defined the agency's earliest years, for clues to how governments might successfully intervene in the contemporary context.[73] Researchers have also explored the PFRA as an example of government success in promoting resiliency, a virtue that they attribute to a range of prairie actors.[74] This research on the PFRA is important in a number of ways, most significantly for its direct engagements with the pressing challenge of promoting human well-being amid a changing climate. But this body of work risks perpetuating an understanding of the PFRA that is inconsistent with what emerges from an evidence-driven historical examination of the agency's activities from the mid-1930s to the mid-1980s. Recognizing the PFRA as a driver of environmental transformation on the Canadian Prairies complicates the prevailing understanding of the agency as an example of successful agricultural adaptation. Further, using the PFRA as an example of government success fails to reckon with the agency's history of perpetuating environmental inequalities derived from settler colonialism and white supremacy. Finally, valorization of the PFRA does not take account of the agency's profoundly mixed environmental legacy, one marked by the creation and exacerbation of problems as well as by their solution or mitigation. Ultimately, the PFRA is not a useful shorthand for present-day solutions to the linked challenges of environmental justice and environmental change on the Canadian Prairies. I hope that the chapters to follow convincingly explain why not.

1
Contexts and Mistakes
The Early Years of the PFRA, 1935–46

Early in 1939, George Spence set out on a cross-country speaking tour. Newly appointed as director of the Prairie Farm Rehabilitation Administration (PFRA), Spence spent the next few months speaking to various groups, mostly outside the Prairies.[1] At these meetings, using lantern slides and a text prepared through intensive consultation with scientific experts, Spence described the challenges facing prairie agriculture and how these challenges were being met.[2] He began with a rendering of regional history, one that opened with colonization by non-Indigenous newcomers keen to establish farms. He explained how misapprehension of the regional environment set the stage for mistakes of settlement by government and settlers alike, mistakes that led to the problems of the 1930s. Spence then described the PFRA, emphasizing what he presented as its practical and economical approach to addressing these mistakes. His talk was peppered with references to the efforts of individuals, supported by PFRA programs, to respond to the regional emergency in constructive ways that would improve both their present circumstances and their future prospects. And he was careful to make clear how improved circumstances for individuals on the Prairies would benefit Canadians nationwide. At least some of the meetings at which Spence spoke were very well attended, including a Vancouver event that attracted a crowd of over 1,000.[3]

Spence's presentations drew on his background as a farmer. He had migrated from the Orkney Islands in the early years of the twentieth century and had established a farm in southern Saskatchewan about a decade later. Spence also drew on the oratorical skills that he had honed as a politician. He was first elected to the Saskatchewan legislature in 1917 and went on to win both provincial and federal elections. He held a series of ministerial appointments in the Saskatchewan legislature between 1927 and 1938, when he resigned his provincial position to become the federal government's director of rehabilitation.[4] Spence's presentations the following year were effectively campaign speeches intended to rally support for the PFRA. They were calibrated to convince Canadians at large that expenditures on fixing the mistakes of prairie settlement were justified, appropriate, and likely to pay dividends.

Spence's speaking tour reminds us of the depth of crisis in the prairie provinces in these years. Many contemporaries wondered, as stated by Prime Minister William Lyon Mackenzie King, whether the Canadian Prairie West would "be of any real use again."[5] More than this concern, Spence's lectures reflected the careful crafting of a particular understanding of the PFRA and its work. By promoting to audiences across Canada the notion of fixing the mistakes of settlement, Spence was laying groundwork for an influential historical interpretation that would later be elaborated by Vernon Fowke, James H. Gray, and others.

This chapter offers a PFRA origin story that differs from the one propagated by Spence. It operates at three scales of analysis to explain the PFRA's emergence and early operation. The first section is relatively expansive, encompassing transnational contexts and the decades preceding the creation of the PFRA. It situates the agency not just within a narrative of prairie agriculture but also within a broader history of dryland landscapes, soil erosion, and the North American conservation movement, a politically influential effort to, as advocates saw it, adopt more efficient resource use and guard against resource degradation. The agricultural and economic crises of the 1930s, described by Spence on his 1939 speaking tour, are necessary but not sufficient to account for the emergence of the PFRA.

The chapter's second section considers the PFRA's activities during its first decade of operation. The early PFRA, both before and after Spence was appointed to head it up, was as much a big-picture, technocratic undertaking as a small-scale, on-farm program. This section elaborates on the dual nature of the early PFRA by examining some of the agency's signature activities. Here, the notions of high modernism and low modernism are useful. Framing low modernism as a counterpoint to James C. Scott's influential concept of high modernism, rural sociologist Jess Gilbert seeks to highlight what he sees as inadequately appreciated aspects of key American New Deal programs. For Gilbert, low modernism is a mode of state-led action that turns on "decentralized programs that involved local citizens in substantive, meaningful ways."[6] Low modernism is defined by faith in the ability of average people to meaningfully contribute to improving their circumstances. Flowing from this ideology are practices that foreground lived experience, collaboration between experts and non-experts, and decentralized activity in accessible locations. Situating early PFRA activities along a spectrum extending from low-modernist to high-modernist offers a fuller understanding of the agency's activities.[7] Early PFRA activities were also inflected by the role that patronage played in the agency's operations.

The third section focuses on the wheat stem sawfly, an insect that farmers and experts alike saw as an agricultural pest. Here, we see that strip farming, a soil-saving technique heavily promoted by the PFRA, actually contributed to worsening agricultural circumstances for some prairie farmers. By tracking unintended consequences, as environmental histories often do, this chapter makes clear how efforts by PFRA agents to fix the so-called mistakes of settlement in fact contributed to new problems.

Contexts for the PFRA

The landscape now widely known as the Canadian Prairies includes the northern reach of the North American Great Plains, which are part of the world's drylands. Drylands are estimated to make up between 35 and 50 percent of the globe. They are located in Africa, Asia, Australia, and South America as well as North America, and they include both arid and hyper-arid lands as well as semi-arid lands like those in key agricultural areas of the Canadian Prairies.[8] Drylands support diverse ecosystems made up of plants and animals adapted to heat and aridity, and the climatic variability of the Canadian Prairies is characteristic of dryland areas.[9] The PFRA was conceived to buttress colonizer agriculture in the drylands of the Canadian Prairies, but it expanded its mandate over time to encompass more humid areas of the Prairies and to operate nationally and transnationally.

Over centuries, European affinity for forested landscapes generated unfavourable views of drylands as well as hostile and dismissive perspectives on societies that lived in dryland regions.[10] These perspectives were intensified through processes of colonialism, where drylands were taken as particularly in need of the improvement that Europeans purported to bring to the lands that they claimed. On the northern Great Plains, the conflicting assessments of regional agricultural prospects made by nineteenth-

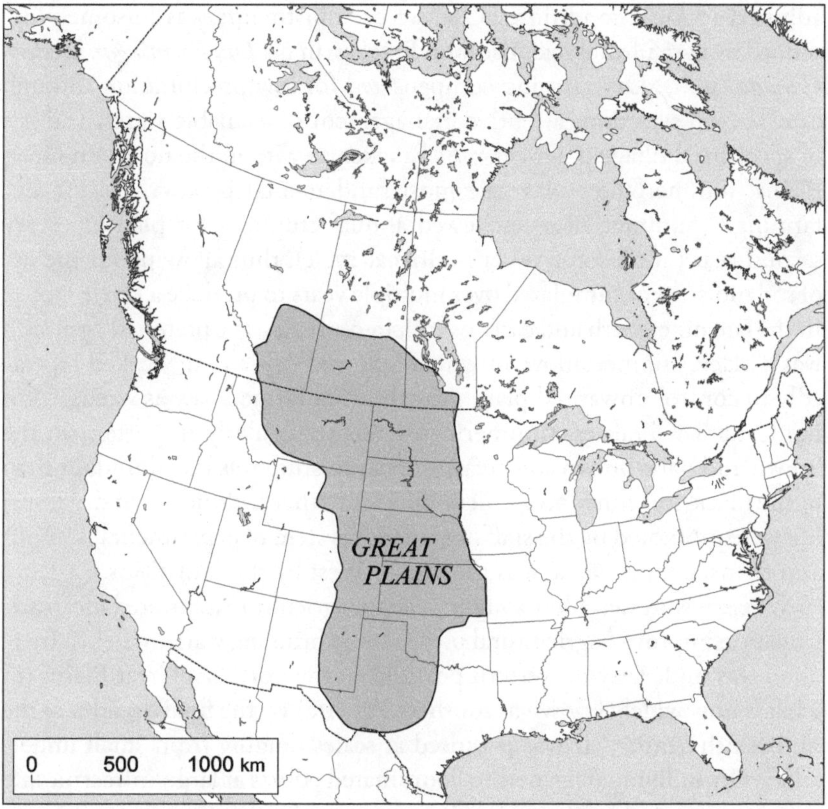

FIGURE 1.1 The Great Plains of North America. The Canadian Prairies are part of the North American Great Plains, one of the world's dryland landscapes. *Adapted from David J. Wishart, ed.,* Encyclopedia of the Great Plains *(Lincoln: University of Nebraska Press, 2004), xiv.*

century scientists and state agents reflected not just the variability inherent in dryland environments, with optimistic assessments made in particularly wet years, but also the ambiguous European view of drylands as places of both waste and potential.[11]

The northern Great Plains fit into a global dryland history characterized by radical environmental transformation. The colonization of the Prairie West advanced rapidly in the final years of the nineteenth century and the early years of the twentieth century. This process depended on the dispossession of prairie Indigenous peoples, as well as state-led efforts to establish a new political and economic regime across the Prairie West. The central role of agriculture in this new regime required that farming practices be adjusted to local conditions. One set of adjustments was fulsomely described by agricultural scientist John Bracken in his *Dry Farming in Western Canada* (1921). Dry farming compensated for low precipitation through careful crop selection, attentive management of available water, and use of specialized tillage practices.[12] As Bracken saw it, on the northern Great Plains, summerfallow was "the most fundamental practice" within dry farming.[13] Summerfallow eschewed annual cropping for planting every second year (or on some other multiyear cycle), thus allowing for the use of soil moisture accumulated over multiple years to produce a single crop.[14] In the late nineteenth and early twentieth centuries, the preferred approach was a black summerfallow, in which fallowed fields were worked repeatedly to control unwanted plant growth, what farmers saw as weeds.[15] On the Canadian Prairies, summerfallow was particularly important in the brown and dark-brown soil areas, where moisture was less abundant than in the black-soil zone.[16] Summerfallow and other techniques of dry farming were promoted by the staff of Canada's system of experimental stations and farms, established across the Prairie West by the mid-1880s.[17]

Whereas summerfallow sought to adapt agriculture to limited moisture, irrigation improved agricultural prospects by bringing water to fields. Irrigation was underway in western portions of the northern Great Plains (in what is now widely known as southern Alberta) by the final decades of the nineteenth century. It was practised at scales ranging from small undertakings by individual farmers to coordinated efforts at large-infrastructure construction, and it reflected various motivations. Farmers and communities were eager to bolster their odds of agricultural success through irrigation, and capitalist speculators bankrolled irrigation projects to generate profit from land sales and from increased economic activity. Initially, the Canadian government worried that acknowledging the need for irrigation would dissuade potential settlers, but it soon sought to attract investment in irrigation.[18] Key elements of these government efforts were favourable legislation (including the 1894 Northwest Irrigation Act) and a variety of material supports, such as absorbing the costs of survey work. Early irrigation created opportunities for the wealthy and powerful. Alexander Galt, for instance, was a central figure in negotiating Canadian Confederation and an investor in early irrigation.[19]

By enabling agricultural expansion, irrigation and dry farming drove radical alterations to prairie landscapes.[20] These transformations underwrote the widespread understanding of the Prairie West as a landscape of agricultural riches and signalled the success of federal government policies that were intended to advance the linked processes of Indigenous dispossession and agricultural colonization. They also triggered worry about the degradation of prairie soils. Emerging concerns among Canadian agricultural experts resonated with those of conservationists, who sought to promote what they understood as the efficient and responsible use of natural resources.[21] Scholarship on conservationism in Canada has focused on the management of wildlife and forests and on the development of parks and hydroelectric infrastructure, with some attention to the contributions of key thinkers and leaders.[22] Yet the Commission of Conservation, established by Ottawa in 1909 to undertake investigatory and advisory work, included a Committee on Lands alongside other committees focused on forests, water power, and wildlife.[23] Over the 1910s, the Committee on Lands gathered information about the state of land management across Canada, with significant attention to agriculture.[24] The committee's findings were worrying. As chair James W. Robertson explained, particularly in the Canadian West, farmers were failing to safeguard the soil resource. Rather, in unsustainable fashion, prairie farmers "live on the capital stored up in the soil."[25]

The soil degradation detected by the Committee on Lands reflected well-established global patterns. Environmental historians J.R. McNeill and Verena Winiwarter have documented soil degradation over long periods of time and at a global scale, in dryland as well as other environments, associating it with the intensification of agriculture.[26] The situation on the Canadian Prairies was not just a product of agricultural intensification but also part of what sociologist Hannah Holleman terms "a global problem of soil erosion associated with capitalist colonial expansion."[27] By the 1910s, this global problem was manifest on the Canadian Prairies. Declining precipitation, combined with problems caused by agricultural pests, crop diseases, hail, and short growing seasons, created a particularly difficult period.[28] As historian Curtis McManus explains in his study of southern Saskatchewan, there was an agricultural crisis playing out, with farms failing and people moving out of the region.[29] For his part, historian David C. Jones has documented a similar process in southern Alberta.[30]

The worrying findings of the Committee on Lands, combined with the agricultural difficulties of the 1910s, led the Commission of Conservation to convene a conference on soil conservation. Although nationwide in scope, the conference paid particular attention to prairie circumstances.[31] Participants at the conference included John Bracken, who acknowledged that summerfallow remained "the most important farm practice in the dry region" before pointing to its drawbacks.[32] Summerfallow caused soil erosion by reducing the organic matter that gives structure to soils, as well as soil depletion by eliminating nutrients essential for plant growth.[33] The conference also examined the different, but no less substantial, problems of prairie irrigation. It was becoming clear that irrigation was unlikely even to pay for itself, let alone generate profit. Conference participants called for the increased government investment in irrigation that they considered essential for appropriate management of the region's water and soil.[34]

By the 1920s, the Governments of Alberta and Saskatchewan were scrambling to address emerging agricultural difficulties.[35] Saskatchewan's 1921 Inquiry into Farming Conditions (which included John Bracken and George Spence as commissioners) called for "immediate action" and prescribed changes in farm practice that led to it becoming known as the Better Farming Commission.[36] Alberta's 1922 investigation examined circumstances in particularly dry areas of the province. As commissioners saw it, the issues turned on government policy as much as on environmental conditions: should dry areas be abandoned or should they be extended state supports?[37] By the late 1920s, Alberta was amending the structure of local government in newly designated Special Areas to facilitate economic transition.[38] Despite these actions, settlers continued to leave the driest regions of the Prairies throughout the 1920s.[39]

In the 1930s, the effects of lower rates of precipitation were exacerbated by economic crisis. Catalyzed by events in the United States, the Great Depression stemmed from problems in the global economy, including shifts in political and economic power structures, the overproduction of key commodities, and the lingering consequences of the First World War.[40] Nationally, Canada's economy suffered a major downswing in the summer of 1929. An uneven recovery began in the spring of 1933, but then recession marked 1937–38. Canada's dependence on the production of primary resources meant that the country was more severely affected than more economically diversified nations.[41] The reluctance of Canada's politicians to deviate from ineffective, even harmful, budgeting and public administration practices only redoubled the hardships.[42]

Prairie farmers felt squeezed between problems associated with the global economy and difficulties inherent in the regional environment. A global wheat surplus was suppressing prices by the late 1920s.[43] In the eight years before 1930, wheat sold, on average, for 98 cents per bushel; for the next eight years, the price was 60 cents a bushel.[44] As rates of precipitation dropped, wheat yields fell to shocking lows. In 1937, Saskatchewan produced 37 million bushels and the prairie provinces 159 million, compared with 1928 peaks of 321 million and 544 million bushels respectively.[45]

Grasshoppers rendered the situation even more dire. In parts of Saskatchewan in the mid-1930s, 40 percent of the wheat crop was damaged by these insects.[46] Wheat rust was another significant problem. Saskatchewan lost over 56 million bushels to this agricultural plague in 1935.[47]

The scale of these economic and environmental problems overwhelmed prairie provincial governments. By 1934, the federal government was becoming more involved in providing relief.[48] In January 1935, Prime Minister R.B. Bennett pledged broader federal government action through the Canadian New Deal.[49] Bennett's initiatives included the Prairie Farm Rehabilitation Administration, intended to "provide for the rehabilitation of drought and soil drifting areas in the provinces of Manitoba, Saskatchewan, and Alberta."[50] An additional piece of legislation, the 1935 Supplementary Public Works Construction Act, earmarked $500,000 for water conservation projects.[51] This fund would underwrite some PFRA activities. Neither piece of legislation received the same attention as the others that Bennett passed at this point, some of which were perceived as egregious federal incursions on provincial jurisdiction.

After the federal government's passage of enabling legislation, the PFRA was positioned for a rapid launch because of cooperation from Ottawa's Experimental Farms Service.[52] Staff of the service were enlisted to jump-start PFRA programs, and many welcomed the assignment, perceiving the PFRA as new support and funding for much-needed conservation activity. Tree planting provides a good example of the relation between experimental farms and the PFRA. The Forest Nursery Station at Indian Head, Saskatchewan, operational since the early 1900s, established that shelterbelts protected crops and gardens.[53] A second Forest Nursery Station was launched at Sutherland, also in Saskatchewan, in the mid-1910s.[54] By the early 1930s, both Forest Nursery Stations were administered by the Experimental Farms Service. On the PFRA's 1935 creation, tree planting became a rehabilitation activity.[55] Over the agency's first two years of operations, prairie farmers accessed over 13 million trees, with just under 7 percent of these facilitated by the PFRA.[56]

The crisis of the 1930s on the Canadian Prairies was significant not just because of the hardship that it brought to the lives of families and communities but also as part of a larger and longer story of dryland degradation and attempted agricultural responses.[57] John Bracken's career illustrates the ways that the PFRA built on earlier efforts at soil conservation. As an agricultural scientist, Bracken contributed his expert perspective to the Commission of Conservation. He was a member of Saskatchewan's Better

Farming Commission. Bracken's career swung from science to politics when he agreed to serve as premier of Manitoba in 1922 (a position that he held until 1943). And in the midst of the 1930s crisis, Bracken the politician called for efforts to conserve the soil and water of the agricultural Prairies.[58] The actions that he called for had been explored in the Better Farming Commission and refined through the work of farmers seeking to improve the use of their lands.[59] These actions became defining features of the PFRA's early work, and they signal the PFRA's position amid efforts by many governments globally, both historically and in the present day, to reckon with what are seen as deficient and problematic dryland environments.

The Early Years

The PFRA was created by a Conservative federal government, but within months of the agency's creation, Prime Minister R.B. Bennett's administration fell. The Liberals under William Lyon Mackenzie King took over in Ottawa, and James Garfield Gardiner was appointed minister of agriculture. Born in Ontario in 1883, Jimmy Gardiner had headed west early in the new century and had taught school before embarking on a political career. First elected to the Legislative Assembly of Saskatchewan in 1914, he served as minister of highways and became premier in 1926. After a five-year hiatus, Gardiner returned to the premiership in 1934 and was involved in provincial efforts to secure federal action on drought before joining King's Cabinet in 1935. His term as minister of agriculture extended for twenty-two years.[60]

Once in power, the Liberals quickly amended the PFRA's governing legislation. In 1937, "land utilization" and "land settlement" were added to the agency's responsibilities, expanding the PFRA's capacity to take on projects benefiting entire communities rather than individuals.[61] The amendment underpinned the PFRA's Community Pastures Program, which involved the creation of grazing areas on lands that could not be farmed successfully. The number of expert advisory committees guiding the agency's work was increased, and caps on PFRA funding were eliminated.[62] The agency clarified its focus on the Prairies ecozone by endorsing a geographic boundary on core PFRA activities.[63] In March 1939, the government lifted the original five-year limit on the PFRA's existence.[64] In various ways, under King and Gardiner, the PFRA was expanded and made more permanent.

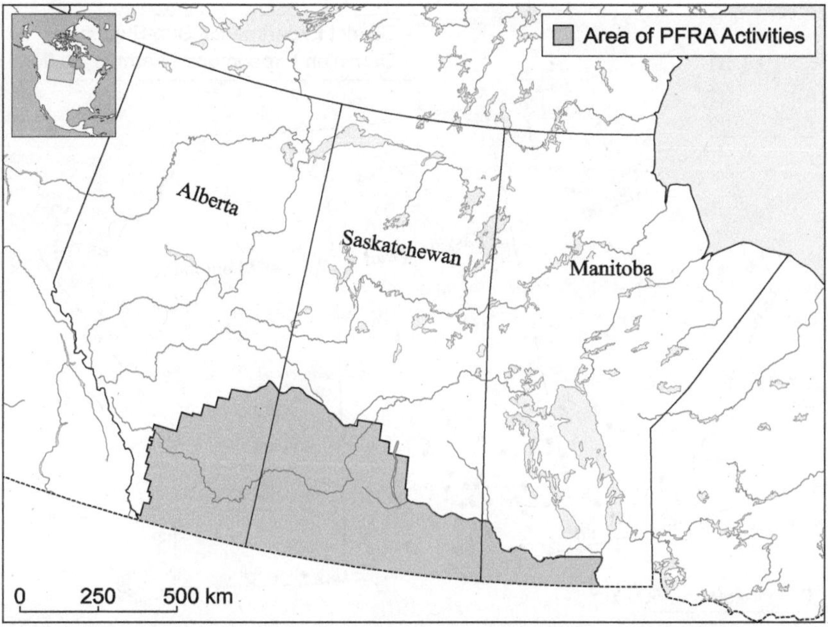

FIGURE 1.2 Area of activity under the Prairie Farm Rehabilitation Administration, 1937. In its early years, the PFRA concentrated its activities in the marked area, an arrangement understood to provide useful focus for agency undertakings. *Adapted from E.W. Stapleford,* Report on Rural Relief in the Prairie Provinces Due to Drought Conditions and Crop Failures in Western Canada *(Ottawa: Minister of Agriculture, 1939), 99; Prairie Farm Rehabilitation Administration,* Report on Proceedings under the Prairie Farm Rehabilitation Act for the Fiscal Year Ending March 31, 1938 (*Ottawa: Department of Agriculture, 1938*), *1; and* CanVec Series [Admin., Land, Hydro] (*Ottawa: Natural Resources Canada, 2019*).

By the late 1930s, PFRA projects focused on three main types of activity: cultural work, land utilization, and water conservation.[65] Cultural work, which pertained to farming techniques minimizing risks of soil drift and drought, was conducted by the Experimental Farms Service as an enhancement to long-standing activities. Land utilization and water conservation went ahead under the auspices of the PFRA's director of rehabilitation. By situating these various early PFRA undertakings along a spectrum extending from low-modernist to high-modernist, it is possible to appreciate the agency in more robust terms, ones that underline the need to look beyond the "mistakes of settlement" narrative.

District Experimental Sub-Stations were an integral part of the PFRA's earliest activities. These farms were privately owned, usually 640 acres, and

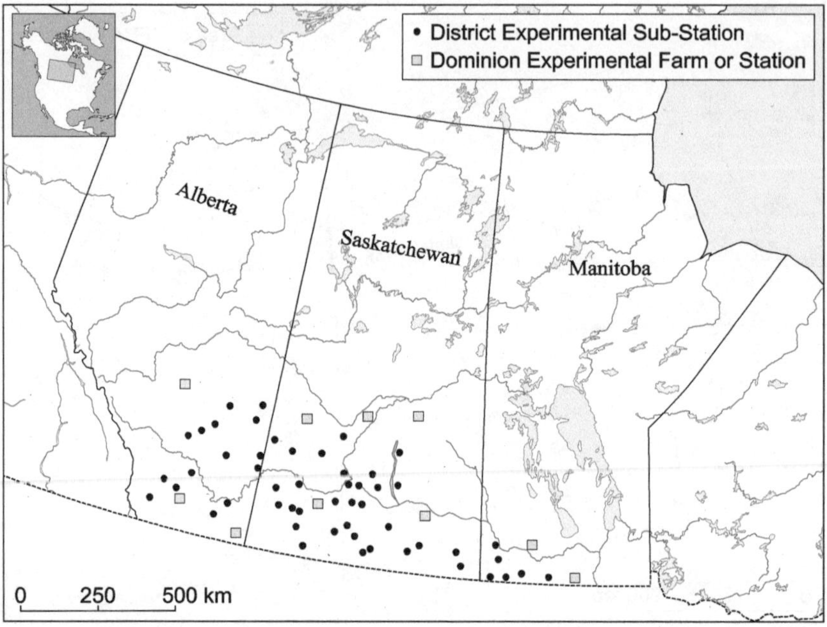

FIGURE 1.3 Location of District Experimental Sub-Stations and Dominion Experimental Farms and Stations, 1939. Placed in the spaces between experimental farms and stations, District Experimental Sub-Stations helped to ensure that a fuller scope of agriculturally relevant environmental variation was accommodated in PFRA activity. *Adapted from J.C. Moynan and M.J. Tinline, "Sub-Stations and Their Relation to Rehabilitation,"* C.S.T.A. Review *23 (December 1939): 84; and* CanVec Series [Admin., Land, Hydro] *(Ottawa: Natural Resources Canada, 2019).*

operated by private farmers with expert input.[66] They extended an earlier network of Illustration Stations established by the Experimental Farms Service and run by agricultural scientists with the aim of investigating and demonstrating locally appropriate farming techniques.[67] District Experimental Sub-Stations were grafted onto this network because it was not logistically or economically viable to expand the number of Illustration Stations even though there were too few of them to adequately address agriculturally significant environmental variation on the Prairies. Also, expert-run Illustration Stations were criticized for employing techniques and resources beyond the reach of most farmers.[68] With comparatively modest involvement from experts, District Experimental Sub-Stations were intended to address both issues. Their number expanded rapidly from thirty-nine in 1935 to fifty-one in 1938.[69] A short year after the sub-station

FIGURE 1.4 Aerial image of strip farming at the Nobleford District Experimental Sub-Station, 1945. Strip farming was intended to help anchor soils in place. A view from above makes clear the distinctive crop patterns that result. *University of Lethbridge Library Digitized Collections, Agriculture and Agri-Food Canada, Lethbridge Research Center Photo Collection, P24-21.1. Contains information licensed under the Open Government Licence – Canada.*

program began operation, it was noted as a successful and important PFRA activity.[70]

District Experimental Sub-Stations were particularly important in improving the practice of summerfallow, which continued as a valued technique of weed and water management even as it was widely recognized as a contributor to soil erosion. Farmers operating sub-stations investigated the use of a trash cover to limit soil erosion on fallowed fields.[71] Better known in the United States as a stubble mulch, a trash cover is produced by avoiding or minimizing cultivation on a fallow.[72] The retained plant material helps to protect the soil. Although the use of a trash cover had been under investigation in Canada from the late 1910s, District Experimental Sub-Stations popularized this technique and refined its use according to local conditions.[73] District Experimental Sub-Stations also popularized and refined the practice of strip farming, another technique that had been under consideration for a number of years.[74] Strip farming involved interspersing strips of fallow and cultivated land running perpendicular to the prevailing winds with the aim of interrupting soil blowing. Typically, strips ranged in width from 20 to 80 metres.[75] By 1937, a quarter of the cultivated land in southwestern Saskatchewan was strip-farmed.[76] Through their various activities, District Experimental Sub-Stations demonstrated two forms of low-modernist cooperation between PFRA experts and farmers: decentralized activity in locations across the Prairies and farmer-expert collaboration in generating new knowledge.

Agricultural Improvement Associations (AIAs) were another low-modernist PFRA project. AIAs were formed when local farmers sharing common agricultural or environmental circumstances banded together to exchange knowledge and to promote the adoption of locally appropriate agricultural techniques. Typically, these were techniques validated through the work of the District Experimental Sub-Stations or the broader Experimental Farms Service. AIAs reflected farmers' commitment to mutual aid in times of hardship, as well as their recognition that many of the environmental difficulties that they faced were area-wide in scale. As described in the 1938 PFRA annual report, the "essential characteristic" of AIAs was that members agreed "to adopt as uniformly as practicable such measures for drought and soil drifting control as seem suitable under local conditions."[77] Strip farming, trash cover, and the like were more effective if implemented widely rather than as "uncoordinated efforts of individual farmers."[78] Serving as what James H. Gray called the "shock troops" of rehabilitation, AIAs countered through cooperative action a key disadvantage of the private property system imposed on the Prairie West.[79]

Four strip-farming associations emerged before the first AIA as hard-hit farmers came together in response to their plight.[80] These early associations were quickly incorporated into the AIA program. By March 1936, over 2,600 farmers were participants in 31 AIAs spread over the three prairie provinces, with the majority in Saskatchewan.[81] By 1940, there were 210 AIAs involving more than 33,000 farmers, or almost 20 percent of those in the PFRA area.[82] The 1943 PFRA annual report described AIAs as "the largest farm organization actively engaged in soil conservation and in maintaining a stable agriculture."[83] AIAs were eligible for a small amount of direct funding, as well as other forms of support, including visits from experts and free distributions of seeds and trees.[84] From a PFRA perspective, AIAs helped to secure "the co-operation of prairie farmers."[85] Like

District Experimental Sub-Stations, they promoted decentralized activity in which farmers were supported by agency experts.

The small water-development program similarly involved collaboration between PFRA officials and prairie farmers. The PFRA offered financial and logistical support with the construction of dugouts and stock-watering dams intended to provide water year-round, as well as with small irrigation projects. Projects could serve individual farms or a cluster of neighbouring farms. Dugouts were typically built on the eastern Prairies, and stock-watering dams were erected on the western Prairies.[86] Both collected precipitation and snowmelt to smooth out variation in the seasonal and annual availability of water. Household, garden, forage, and stock needs were all met this way. By 1937, farmers could receive 4.5 cents per cubic yard of earth moved, the maximum being $75 for each dugout and $150 for a stock-watering dam.[87] By 1941, some 15,246 small water projects had been completed on the Prairies, over 10,000 of them dugouts.[88] Small water projects made a real difference to farm families. A PFRA-built dugout meant that Viola Calder's family, located near Bow Island in Alberta, could garden successfully. Garden produce helped to see the family through grasshopper-decimated crops, and Calder noted that the garden made her "feel as if life is worth living after all."[89]

The small water-development program required both farmer initiative and expert knowledge. The agency urged farmers to get engineering advice before undertaking a project. Construction typically involved large, specialized earth-moving equipment such as a backhoe, which required farmers to pay for rental and operation.[90] The PFRA established certain specifications for small water-development projects intended to ensure their utility and to guard against hazards, with particular attention given to the slope of the sides, depth of the excavation, and character of the surrounding soil. Only after an engineering inspection confirmed that specifications had been met would financial assistance be provided. Here, expertise held a somewhat perverse position. The PFRA recommended that farmers secure expert advice, but if farmers did the work themselves and managed to meet the standards, they were still eligible for financial assistance. On at least one occasion, Minister of Agriculture James Gardiner objected to the small water-development program's transfer of government funds to engineering firms or equipment operators, preferring that farmers do the work themselves so as to retain the money.[91]

Early PFRA initiatives included important activities that turned on low-modernist cooperation between agency officials and prairie farmers. Yet such collaborations did not always proceed smoothly. Consider the case of Alfred Rawlins, who arrived in southern Alberta in 1906. Rawlins established a farm and remained actively involved in various farmers' organizations for decades, including serving as secretary in the Retlaw Agricultural Improvement Association, which was formed in 1938.[92] Rawlins grew frustrated with what he took as the PFRA's focus on rhetoric over action. As he put it, "Since I drank my first bottle of milk I have never read so much self praise from an organization that was really doing so little compared to the work it should do."[93] Rawlins also objected to what he viewed as the inadequate financial assistance that the PFRA made available to farmers and critiqued what he saw as the agency's lack of genuinely meaningful cooperation with farmers in his district. Rawlins's views reflect real frustration and dissatisfaction with the PFRA, demonstrating that not all farmers felt that the agency fully achieved the ideal of low modernism.

Alongside its low-modernist efforts, the PFRA also facilitated expert undertakings focused on gathering and analyzing information. These efforts did not intersect in any direct or immediate way with the concerns of farmers. Many of the undertakings were called "fundamental research" and understood as complementary to but distinct from other PFRA endeavours.[94] These research efforts were central to the development of what James C. Scott calls tools of statecraft – tools that allowed experts to see the agricultural Prairies in new ways.[95]

Soils were a major focus of PFRA-involved expert research. Federal government money allowed the agency to accelerate soil survey work, much of which was undertaken collaboratively with provincial governments and prairie universities.[96] The aim was to extend the soil survey into previously neglected terrain and to deepen knowledge about prairie soils. Three kinds of soil surveys were undertaken: reconnaissance, detailed reconnaissance, and detailed surveys, with robustness and specificity increasing from the former to the latter.[97] Figure 1.5 illustrates the extent of these three types of surveys across the PFRA area to 1939.[98] The information generated by surveys was tailored to the needs of scientists and administrators responsible for regional administration, not to the concerns of farmers, whose focus was primarily on their own farm or the local community. New technologies facilitated soil survey work. Aerial surveys were undertaken from 1937 onward to supplement existing sources of information about topography, land use, and the human and physical geography of the region.[99] These aerial surveys were conducted in conjunction with the Department of National Defence, with 7 million acres in Alberta covered in 1937.[100]

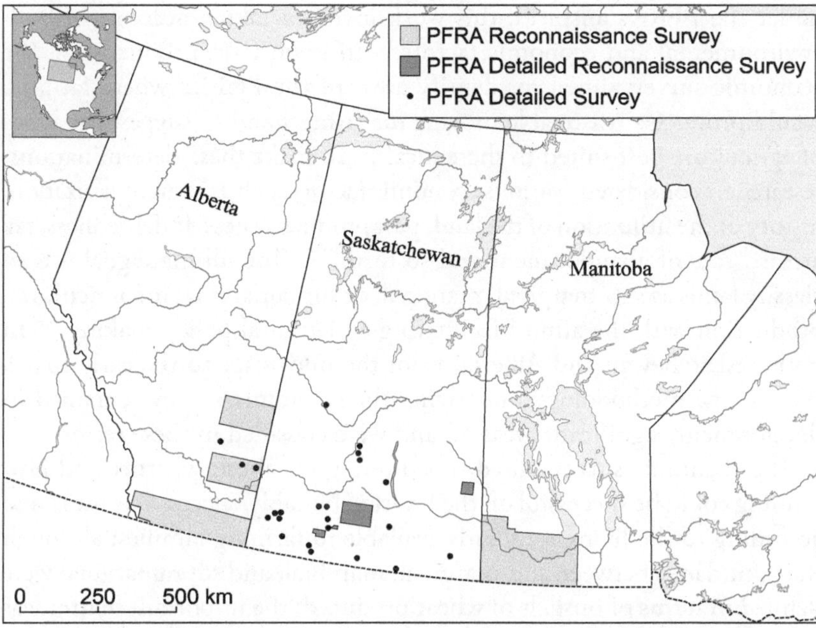

FIGURE 1.5 Soil surveys undertaken by the Prairie Farm Rehabilitation Administration to 1939. Soil surveys reflect PFRA efforts to generate new specialized knowledge about the prairie environment, knowledge intended to facilitate improved management of regional agriculture. *Adapted from A. Leahey, "Soil Surveys and Soil Research,"* C.S.T.A. Review *23 (December 1939): 12; and* CanVec Series [Admin., Land, Hydro] *(Ottawa: Natural Resources Canada, 2019).*

Water was another focus of expert research sponsored by the PFRA. The federal government had conducted hydrometric surveys prior to the 1930s, but the transfer of natural resources to the provinces had interrupted the work.[101] This interruption was damaging because, as noted by L.C. Charlesworth, director of Alberta's Water Resources Branch, a "long term program of stream and run off measurement" was very important for water management.[102] The absence of hydrometric records was a major barrier to the PFRA's water-development work.[103] By the summer of 1935, with PFRA prompting, efforts to resurrect hydrometric metering were underway.[104] These efforts culminated in revitalization and expansion of the hydrometric-gauging network, as well as substantial investment in the analysis of water data.

The leading example of research in a high-modernist vein was an economic survey. Initiated at the University of Saskatchewan but expanded under the PFRA's auspices, this work involved taking account of both environmental and economic factors bearing on farm productivity. The economic survey aimed to identify areas of the Prairies where farming would produce a reasonable income for farmers and to suggest the types of agriculture best suited to these locales. To make these determinations, researchers considered "various economic factors such as farm organization, history of the utilization of the land, past productiveness, indebtedness, tax arrears, rate of abandonment and so forth."[105] The ultimate goal was to classify lands as sub-marginal, marginal, or supramarginal for agricultural production with the aim of facilitating agricultural policy-making.[106] In both Saskatchewan and Alberta, from the mid-1930s to the early 1940s, even as the methodology underlying the economic survey remained in development, significant areas of land were classified in these terms.

The economic survey raised broad questions about whether and how farming could be successful on the Prairies. Notably, success was measured according to the living standards available to farming families: although the boundaries between sub-marginal, marginal, and supramarginal were defined in terms of bushels of wheat produced, the important matter was how agricultural productivity underwrote quality of life. The aim of the economic survey was to marshal expert knowledge in order to position government to develop policies and practices that would allow farming communities "a new era of stability and economic well-being."[107] The PFRA's efforts at land classification connect the agency to what historian Sarah T. Phillips terms the new conservation in the 1920s and 1930s in the United States, which turned in part on efforts to improve rural land use so as to ensure reasonable living standards for rural people.[108]

The PFRA was involved with the economic survey for only a few years, and not all those associated with the agency were convinced of its value. But the economic survey had an enduring impact. In its attention to quality of life, the economic survey helped to flesh out a more robust vision of PFRA activity. Over decades, across a range of agency undertakings, PFRA leaders focused on improving the stability and profitability of prairie agriculture to secure an acceptable quality of life for those the agency served. This enduring agency goal reflected what James C. Scott describes as the ideology of high modernism – a belief in the prospect that expert-led, state-driven undertakings could improve the human condition.[109]

Over its first decade, the PFRA adopted both low-modernist and high-modernist approaches. As historian Venus Bivar notes in her study of mid-twentieth-century France, these two approaches could work in tandem in the agricultural sphere.[110] For PFRA officials, low-modernist practices were necessitated by the character of the 1930s crisis. In the midst of an agricultural disaster attributable in part to problematic farming techniques, it seemed vital to engage farmers in their fields. Agency leaders, politicians, civil servants, and scientific experts also took a paternalistic view of farmers as people in need of encouragement and assistance. Similar attitudes were reflected in government efforts to bolster the spirits of the urban unemployed during the Great Depression.[111] Emphasizing farmers' important roles in rehabilitation, particularly by means of published materials for public circulation, could help with what the PFRA's annual report of 1940 termed "the toning-up of morale" among dejected farmers.[112] Jess Gilbert discusses the idealism that fuelled the low-modernist approach of US New Deal agricultural agencies, with American experts fundamentally committed to engaging farmers' expertise and working in cooperation with them.[113] PFRA experts also looked on farmers with great regard. However, in these early years, the PFRA's engagements with prairie farmers seem to have been driven by pragmatism and paternalism as well as idealism.

From its 1935 creation, the PFRA also pursued high-modernist strategies that depended on expert knowledge, thus helping to gird the power and authority of experts. These activities were rarely touted publicly by the agency, but they took up significant time and effort. Between the agency's creation and March 1937, about half of its budget went to activities that privileged expertise over farmer-expert cooperation.[114] These activities laid the foundation for the PFRA's later activities. The information generated by agricultural and hydrometric surveys underpinned regionally transformative undertakings, such as large-scale dam building. Information from the economic survey prepared the ground for a broader notion of rehabilitation, one that included attention to rural quality of life. Even in early years, when PFRA leaders described an agency oriented to fixing the mistakes of settlement, the agency sought to better the lives of prairie farmers. As historian Ronald Rudin puts it in his study of the Maritime Marshland Reclamation Administration, which was in some ways a PFRA spin-off, the notion of rehabilitation applied "to the transformation of both specific environments and the people who inhabited them."[115]

Patronage was an important feature of the PFRA's first decade. As the so-called prairie general for the federal Liberal Party,[116] Jimmy Gardiner was responsible not just for putting forward regional concerns in Cabinet but also for safeguarding the Liberal Party's interests on the Prairies.[117] The PFRA was useful in this work.[118] PFRA staff were initially excluded from the permanent civil service because the agency was considered temporary, which meant that the PFRA was not bound by civil service practices in place to minimize patronage.[119] This situation presented opportunities to manage hiring and contracting in ways that served partisan ends, and the short-term nature of these appointments put pressure on employees to remain loyal to Liberal interests.[120] Because some of the PFRA's work required little more than the agricultural experience possessed by most rural prairie dwellers, party loyalists could readily be hired as reward for faithful service.[121] The broad need for the agency's services across the Prairies meant that there were ample opportunities to spend money on useful rehabilitation work in localities where votes could be assured or where voters could be swayed. Materials prepared to support the federal Liberal Party's election planning in 1950s Saskatchewan include a list of PFRA contracts by electoral district, reflecting how patronage remained a hallmark of the PFRA's operations for decades.[122]

Mistakes

Over its first decade, the PFRA operated in the conservationist tradition, promoting techniques intended to bolster capitalist agriculture, including trash cover and strip farming. But unintended consequences ensued, particularly the rapid increase of the wheat stem sawfly (*Cephus cinctus*).

Mature wheat stem sawflies are approximately a centimetre in length. Black with distinctive yellow bands, they have in appearance been likened to wasps.[123] In the early summer, sawflies lay eggs in the stems of hollow grasses or grains. Larvae feed inside the plant stems over the summer months, then move downward to girdle the stems slightly above the level of the soil. Affected plants fall over in minimal wind, rain, or hail, a circumstance known as lodging. The larvae then overwinter in the plant stub before emerging as adults in the late spring or early summer and beginning the cycle once more.[124] The wheat stem sawfly's lifecycle hinders plant development.[125] Lodging reduces crop value and yield. Sawfly-infested crops can often still be harvested but only with costly modifications that complicate the process. Returns are better if infested crops are harvested before lodging occurs.

From early on, prairie settlers recognized the sawfly as a threat to farm success. Entomologist Norman Criddle documented losses of several million bushels to the sawfly in Manitoba and Saskatchewan in 1921.[126] By his account, the expansion of cereal agriculture had given the sawfly "practically a free hand."[127] The insect favoured popular hollow-stemmed varieties of wheat and flourished along field edges, which were more common

FIGURE 1.6 The wheat stem sawfly. This insect thrived in the strip-farmed prairie landscape, complicating efforts at soil conservation. *Public domain image, Insects Unlocked Project, University of Texas at Austin, https://hdl.handle.net/2152/69920.*

in landscapes transformed by large-scale agriculture than in expanses of prairie grasses. Also, farmers planting rust-resistant wheat unintentionally protected sawflies from the catastrophe of having a host plant destroyed by rust.[128]

Although the sawfly menace seemed to abate somewhat during the mid-1920s, the situation worsened with the increase in strip farming as farmers sought to counteract the soil drift problems of the 1930s.[129] As G.D. Matthews of the Experimental Farms Service told a PFRA-sponsored meeting in 1939, strip farming "greatly aggravated" the sawfly problem because it created additional field edges.[130] A landscape remade to counter the scouring wind was a landscape conducive to epidemic populations of sawflies.[131] This posed an intractable conundrum. The sawfly constituted, as entomologist H.L. Seamans put it, "one of the most serious stumbling blocks in the path of successful soil drifting control operations."[132]

The pros and cons of strip farming had long been understood.[133] Some PFRA experts warned early of the need to guard against sawfly infestation.[134] Despite this warning, in the context of the 1930s emergency, strip farming was often promoted by government agents and adopted by prairie farmers without significant efforts to prevent sawfly infestation.[135] But increasing sawfly populations could be ignored for only so long. In 1937, C. Shirrif, agricultural adviser at the Dominion Experimental Station in Swift Current, Saskatchewan, reported that some farmers were edging their fields with strips of brome, a grass thought to attract sawflies while stymying the development of the eggs and larvae.[136] By 1940, brome was the second most widely distributed of the grasses made available by the Prairie Farm Rehabilitation Administration, largely because of its value as a trap crop.[137] Agricultural Improvement Associations, initially formed to counter soil drift, began including techniques of sawfly management in their educational programming.[138]

Dozens of government agricultural experts wrestled with the sawfly problem. At the federal government's agricultural research station in Alberta's Nobleford district, agents worked to determine how to maximize the effectiveness of trap crops.[139] Over years of research, some government experts grew skeptical about brome's usefulness in this respect due to its uncertain growth patterns.[140] Farmers were increasingly encouraged to combat the sawfly by modifying the dates of key farm operations.[141] Later seeding might make vulnerable crops unavailable during the period in which sawflies were looking to deposit their eggs. Earlier harvest might allow farmers to get an infested crop off the field before it fell over. Still, the sawfly problem failed to abate. In 1941, the situation was so severe that 75 percent of the wheat crop suffered damage in some areas.[142]

The battle to control sawflies and soil drift could be finessed by precisely sizing crop strips to protect against drift and to reduce vulnerability to the sawfly.[143] But especially because the optimal strip width varied from place to place, this approach complicated farming work to the point that at least one agricultural leader worried that farmers would become discouraged.[144] Some farmers encountered such severe sawfly problems that they abandoned strip farming altogether.[145] For his part, Saskatchewan's deputy minister of agriculture, F.H. Auld, argued that research should focus on efforts to better balance soil conservation and insect control.[146]

It proved hard to bring down sawfly numbers. In both 1942 and 1943, sawflies were responsible for crop losses of $18 million.[147] Federal government entomologist C.W. Farstad declared that, over the past few years, "the wheat stem sawfly has been one of the most serious problems of wheat production."[148] Worsening infestations in Saskatchewan led the federal government to plan an emergency sawfly-control campaign. The program urged modifications in dates of planting as well as the use of trap strips and resistant crops.[149] These practices were promoted through various means, including educational publications, media work by agricultural experts, and public meetings targeting farmers. The campaign also involved the appointment of so-called sawfly-campaign supervisors, enthusiastic farmers given some specialized training and expected to promote sawfly control among their peers. A lot of effort was invested in this emergency campaign. Forty-seven public meetings attracted over 2,000 farmers, and fifty-four sawfly-campaign supervisors worked directly with 4,000 farmers in planning sawfly control on some 15,000 quarter-sections.[150] Although mid-twentieth-century efforts at pest control often sought the annihilation of the insect enemy, the emergency sawfly campaign was different.[151] It aimed at "quickly reducing infestations to a point where a normal control program could be expected to keep them in check."[152] But no real détente was achieved.[153]

Satisfactory resolution of the sawfly problem would require the development of a sawfly-resistant wheat cultivar, one with a solid stem that would protect it from the insect.[154] Despite the long history of controlled plant breeding on the Canadian Prairies and elsewhere, it was not easy to develop a solid-stemmed wheat that performed well through milling and baking and resisted shattering and rust. To speed research, crops were grown in California during Canada's snowy winter months.[155] In 1946, the aptly named Rescue Wheat was licensed. Distributions to needy farmers soon began. Over following years, other resistant wheats like Chinook (licensed in 1952) and Cypress (licensed in 1962) increased the options available to farmers facing sawfly problems. Still, these cultivars were in some ways inferior to their hollow-stemmed counterparts, and so the sawfly problem was not completely resolved.

Chemical pesticides and herbicides played increasing roles in agriculture after the Second World War. The sawfly was not itself vulnerable to chemical control.[156] But various agricultural chemicals facilitated the adoption of new tillage practices. Weeds could be controlled by herbicides rather than by working the soil in ways that made it more vulnerable to drift. This diminished the importance of strip farming, shrinking the sawfly niche. Other agricultural changes raised the stakes for farmers. Sawfly-infested crops could not readily be harvested by combine, a machine favoured for its labour-saving features.[157] So infestations disrupted farm work or made harvest more expensive. In this changed context, sawflies remained an agricultural problem. The wheat stem sawfly continued to be "one of the most damaging pests of wheat in some parts of the Canadian prairies."[158]

Conclusion

This chapter describes the origins and early work of the PFRA in a manner that differs from the approach taken by George Spence in his 1939 cross-Canada speaking tour. Situating prairie circumstances within global histories of dryland agriculture and soil conservation positions us to understand the PFRA in relation to broad processes of social and environmental change. The PFRA was an emergency effort to safeguard what settler colonialism and capitalist agriculture had produced on the Canadian Prairies. This interpretation is in line with the tendency of conservationist activity to benefit people and groups already possessed of political and economic power.[159] It is also consistent with historical analysis of other Canadian New Deal programs. As both John Herd Thompson and historian Ian McKay have emphasized, this suite of programs was intended to save capitalism, not to replace or substantially reform it.[160]

The PFRA's early undertakings included both low-modernist and high-modernist activities. Insofar as they ensured the ongoing viability of regional agriculture, even low-modernist undertakings perpetuated and consolidated the agricultural transformation of the Canadian Prairies. High-modernist information-gathering activities were intended to underwrite further state-sponsored efforts to bolster prairie agriculture. These high-modernist undertakings were not conceptualized in relation to immediate goals such as halting the soil drift emergency. Rather, they emerged from and helped to frame a longer-term and more ambitious endeavour: creating a stable and prosperous agriculture that would provide a reasonable quality of life to those farm families and rural communities served by the PFRA. As the coming chapters illustrate, making progress on this endeavour involved further transformation of the prairie environment.

Telling a new story about the early PFRA, one that differs from the version offered by George Spence and perpetuated and elaborated by many other commentators, has meant taking account of the wheat stem sawfly. Honing in on this insect positions us to appreciate how, even while the PFRA protected and supported prairie farming, the agency contributed to new farming problems. The sawfly demonstrates that PFRA-led transformation had agricultural consequences that were sometimes equivocal at best. Historical understanding of the PFRA should accommodate this insight alongside the view that the agency contributed to stabilizing agriculture in ways that benefited those the agency served. Buttressing regional agriculture was not always a straightforward endeavour.

At the end of its first decade, the PFRA was remade. Cultural work was removed from the agency, to be continued under the auspices of the Experimental Farms Service, a branch of Ottawa's Department of Agriculture, which had long been involved with work of this character.[161] Among the areas of activity transferred away from the PFRA were District

Experimental Sub-Stations, soil and economic surveys, and tree planting. Agricultural Improvement Associations were also transferred, although these bodies had already declined in significance, for reasons including renewed agricultural prosperity, new labour pressures related to the Second World War, and cessation of the formerly available government grants.[162] With cultural work excised, the PFRA focused on infrastructure projects related to water development and to the management of community pastures.[163]

2
Delimiting the Public Good
Irrigation, Racism, and Sugar Beets in Alberta, 1890s–1940s

Asael E. Palmer came to the Canadian Prairies in 1903 as an adolescent. Building on substantial prior experience with irrigation in the United States, the Palmer family acquired irrigated land near Raymond, Alberta. The family initially grew sugar beets, a highly labour-intensive crop. Within a few years, the Palmer family abandoned beets to take up ranching and grain farming. As Asael E. Palmer recalled it, the work was much more pleasant than with beets.[1] Palmer travelled to the United States in 1912 to study agricultural science at an institution headed by Dr. John A. Widstoe, an eminent irrigation authority. In the early 1920s, having returned to Alberta, Palmer became the assistant superintendent at the Dominion Experimental Station in Lethbridge, where he studied both dryland and irrigated farming. In the mid-1920s, partly due to Palmer's connection, Widstoe investigated Alberta irrigation and recommended that financial difficulties be alleviated through government investment. In the 1930s, Palmer worked with the Prairie Farm Rehabilitation Administration (PFRA), and he has been celebrated as an advocate for strip farming and trash cover.[2] But it is his early personal experiences that point toward key issues in Alberta irrigation: the problem of agricultural labour and the challenge of infrastructure funding.

Early Alberta irrigation works were developed as investment opportunities for well-positioned capitalists or as farmer cooperatives. Under the first model, capitalists bore the costs of infrastructure construction, anticipating a return on investment in the form of land sales and local economic development. Under the second model, farmers shared the expense among themselves through a system of irrigation districts, anticipating that improved agricultural prospects would defray the cost. Neither model proved viable, and so by the 1920s, Alberta irrigation was in crisis. This chapter considers a significant transformation in the funding of irrigation, one that involved the PFRA in important ways. This transformation hinged on the understanding that irrigation was a vehicle for ensuring the stability and prosperity of prairie agriculture, which would improve the lives of prairie residents and benefit the province and the nation.

But not everyone benefited from irrigation-driven improvements. This disparity is clearly shown through a focus on the southern Alberta irrigated areas where sugar beets were cultivated, primarily in the agricultural lands around Lethbridge, Taber, Raymond, and Magrath.[3] In the mid-1930s, sugar beets were grown on about 2 percent of irrigated farms across Alberta.[4] Despite this relatively small acreage, sugar beets were central to efforts to improve the financial viability of irrigated farms because of their high value per acre.[5] Growing beets in southern Alberta required both irrigation infrastructure and, as Asael E. Palmer's family learned, a cohort of labourers. Over decades, much of Alberta's sugar beet labour has come from groups subject to discrimination, including Indigenous peoples, Asian peoples, and migrants from central, southern, and eastern Europe as well as elsewhere. Prisoners of war have been another source of labour. Considering Alberta's sugar beet landscape from the perspectives of both environmental history and labour history contextualizes the significant change in irrigation funding that the PFRA facilitated and advanced.

This chapter situates the PFRA in relation to the longer history of prairie irrigation, a style of agriculture that furthered settler colonialism and capitalist agriculture in suitable dry areas. My analysis builds on historical studies that foreground the role of racism in the colonization and development of the agricultural Prairies.[6] It is also informed by scholarly attention to the significance of ideas of race in water-development work underway globally in the late nineteenth and early twentieth centuries.[7] While operating within its mandate to address regional agricultural problems, the PFRA perpetuated the racialized character of stability and prosperity in Alberta's sugar beet landscape.

Alberta's Early Sugar Beet Industry

The period from the late nineteenth century to the mid-1910s has been described as the commercial phase of Alberta irrigation, a time when capitalists were supported by the federal government in constructing irrigation infrastructure.[8] Multiple private corporations, including the Canadian North West Irrigation Company and the Canadian Pacific Railway, were involved in developing irrigation along southern Alberta waterways like the Bow and St. Mary Rivers.[9] These investments reflected Ottawa's belief that irrigation would ensure the success of agricultural settlement in southern Alberta, as well as investors' convictions that irrigation would generate profit through land sales at premium prices and local economic development.[10]

But irrigation was very expensive. The costs of initial infrastructure construction and year-to-year maintenance created problems for investors and farmers, particularly when irrigation did not immediately generate the anticipated returns in improved crops. The economics of irrigation were more promising when irrigation water was used to grow high-value crops like sugar beets. In Alberta, capitalizing on irrigation involved the establishment of an industry for sugar beet processing that would buy the sugar beets produced by local farmers. In the early years of the twentieth century, assisted by federal government concessions and the Canadian Pacific Railway, Jesse Knight established a plant for sugar beet processing some 30 kilometres south of Lethbridge.[11] The Knight Sugar Factory was in operation by 1903. Some three years later, the factory processed over 36 million pounds (over 16 million kilograms) of beets, producing some 3 million pounds (over 1 million kilograms) of sugar.[12]

Despite the establishment of the Knight Sugar Factory, the first decade of the twentieth century was disappointing for Alberta's sugar beet enthusiasts. There was limited understanding of how best to cultivate sugar beets in local environmental conditions. Asael E. Palmer recalled that farmers "had a fallacious idea that in order to get the beets to go down and make a long root we should let the beets get dry."[13] Early beet producers also did not understand that sugar beets benefited from the intensive use of fertilizer. Reflecting back on this period, Palmer described the establishment of the Knight Sugar Factory as worryingly ahead of "the development of our knowledge" of beet growing.[14]

The onerous character of beet work was a further complication. Only multigerm beet seeds were available until the mid-twentieth century, so significant thinning was required to ensure the growth of a single strong plant.[15] Because beets grew low to the ground, failing to rise above weeds, repeated weeding was necessary. Harvesting was also labour-intensive. Beets were pulled by hand, knocked together to remove dirt, and then had their leafy tops lopped off with large knives.[16] Harvesting an acre of

FIGURE 2.1 Irrigating a field of sugar beets near Raymond, Alberta, early 1900s. A farmer directs irrigation water through furrows between sugar beet plants, providing the moisture necessary for robust plant growth. *University of Calgary Digital Collections, CU1177276.*

beets required about 115 hours, ten times what was required for an acre of grain.[17] Early beet farmers confronted both the challenge of maximizing production amid limited agricultural knowledge and the difficulty of tending to their laborious crop.

In meeting their on-farm labour needs, beet farmers often turned to newcomers from China and Europe as well as Indigenous peoples.[18] Workers were also needed within the Knight Sugar Factory. The factory drew on residents of nearby Kainai Blood Reserve No. 148 as well as labourers of Japanese ancestry, with some recruited from Utah and some coming directly from Japan.[19] Kainai labourers, like other Indigenous peoples in similar positions, were motivated by the chance to earn money at a time when discrimination and government policy limited opportunities to do so.[20] Few people of British, American, or western European origin were interested in employment on beet farms. Historian W. Keith Regular explains that, at the time, many political and social leaders saw

FIGURE 2.2 An Indigenous family working on a sugar beet farm near Raymond, c. 1905. Indigenous peoples were an essential source of labour for many sugar beet farmers, taking on the difficult work of thinning, weeding, and harvesting the crop. It was common for men, women, and children alike to participate in this work. *John Woodruff, Library and Archives Canada, C-007819.*

beet work as unsuitable for the people described by Regular as white because of the work's rigour and tedium.[21] Benefiting from the unearned privileges of whiteness in what historian Howard Palmer has explained was early Alberta's profoundly racist society, workers with origins in Britain, the United States, or northern or western Europe had more options available to them.[22]

Many sugar beet workers encountered the prejudices that were common at the time among more privileged members of Alberta society. Racist ideas about Indigenous peoples informed the thinking of sugar beet farmers and factory operators, with Indigenous workers understood as lazy and unreliable.[23] Asian beet workers also encountered racism, with some members of the broader Alberta community expressing opposition to any efforts to support more Japanese people in becoming permanently established in southern Alberta.[24] Field and factory labour by Indigenous and Asian peoples was essential to the success of the sugar beet industry, but this necessity did nothing to counter prejudice. Rather, by circumscribing the economic prospects of workers from these groups, racism helped to ensure a ready supply of beet workers with few other options.

By the mid-1910s, notwithstanding the development of the local sugar beet industry, the commercial model for Alberta irrigation was in crisis. Investors had come to understand that when undertaken "simply for land speculation," irrigation "led to disaster."[25] Only a small number of prospective settlers were willing or able to pay a premium for irrigated land, making it hard for speculators to capitalize on their investment. Over the coming years, outcomes were little better for farmers who undertook irrigation on a cooperative basis under Alberta's 1915 Irrigation District Act.[26] In some places, infrastructure was inadequate, hampered by poor design, compromised by inexpert construction, or plagued by muskrat activity.[27] Farmers new to irrigation faced a steep learning curve. Salinity was evident in some locations and had begun to reduce agricultural production. The vagaries of weather and agricultural prices introduced additional sources of uncertainty. Increased costs for materials and labour throughout the First World War only exacerbated matters. For those invested in Alberta irrigation, the future must have looked especially bleak after the closure of the Knight Sugar Factory, a closure attributed to unreliable beet supply and difficulties in securing sufficient labour.[28]

The Role of the State

The 1920s saw various state-led efforts to reckon with irrigation in southern Alberta. The provincial government, with input from American experts, examined irrigation financing. The federal government, through its authority over immigration, helped to relieve labour shortages that hampered the sugar beet industry. In both instances, state action was fuelled by the powerful association between irrigation and improvements in the lives of prairie residents. But this understanding of irrigation's transformative power failed to account for the experiences of sugar beet workers, which continued to be defined by exploitation and uncertainty.

The Taber, Magrath, and Raymond Irrigation Districts were all formed under the provisions of Alberta's 1915 Irrigation District Act.[29] These districts extended irrigation infrastructure already put in place by the Alberta Railway and Irrigation Company. The Lethbridge Northern Irrigation District (LNID), formed in this same period, was not integrated into existing infrastructure and so faced more substantial construction costs.[30] The financial difficulties encountered by this district, although particularly severe, became symptomatic of the money problems bedevilling many irrigation projects.[31] Grappling with financial challenges induced government administrators and irrigation farmers to rethink irrigation more broadly.

In the 1920s, faced with intractable problems with irrigation, the Alberta government consulted American experts. Dr. John A. Widstoe was commissioned to investigate the troubled LNID. Prominent internationally, Widstoe held various academic appointments and spent time with the Federal Bureau of Reclamation, the American agency responsible for irrigation development. Widstoe's 1925 report on the Alberta situation recommended changes to irrigation financing, infrastructure, farming practices, landholding arrangements, and crop selection.[32] On financing, Widstoe recommended that the province assume a greater share of the cost of irrigation and accept financial liabilities that had previously rested on irrigators. Widstoe also recommended renewing efforts to foster the sugar beet industry.[33] To Widstoe's mind, additional investment in irrigation was justified by the positive changes that irrigation would bring to the community at large, including higher agricultural yields, denser settlement allowing for greater social interaction, and the more successful cultivation of flowers and gardens as well as crops.[34]

By the time Widstoe submitted his 1925 report, efforts to reinvigorate the sugar beet industry were already underway. The Experimental Farms Service took a lead role in finding ways to produce superior crops of sugar beets in southern Alberta. Results were encouraging. Researchers determined that excellent beet harvests could be secured through the application of about 50 centimetres of water during the growing season and through the use of phosphate fertilizer.[35] Optimistically, local advocates sought to secure a new sugar factory.[36] The Utah-Idaho Sugar Company established a factory in Raymond in 1925, near the site of the former Knight operation.[37] In its first year, in the face of unfavourable weather, the company manufactured 7 million pounds (3 million kilograms) of sugar from 83 million pounds (37 million kilograms) of beets.[38]

Over the coming years, the new factory struggled to realize its potential as declining rates of immigration to the Canadian Prairies contributed to broad labour shortages. To address the shortages, Ottawa authorized the Canadian Pacific and Canadian National Railways to facilitate immigration from southern, eastern, and central Europe, so-called nonpreferred regions, provided that migrants took up employment in agriculture or domestic service.[39] By 1929, over 1,200 Europeans admitted through this program were working in beet fields, and reliable and adequate labour supply underwrote an expansion of beet farming.[40] What became known as the Railways Agreement pleased the Sugar Beet Growers Association, a group led by prominent beet growers who were primarily British, Scandinavian, and American.[41] Most smaller beet growers, many of whom were Mennonite or eastern European, performed their own labour.

As Howard Palmer saw it, the Railways Agreement was necessary for the beet industry's success because the migrants it made available "would do work no one else would do."[42] They were, as historian Cecilia Danysk has pointed out, under the constant threat of deportation or imprisonment.[43] Whereas beet growers celebrated the Railways Agreement, many in Canada objected to any effort to facilitate migration from so-called nonpreferred regions. Amid prejudice toward people from south, central, and eastern Europe, the Railways Agreement was understood as a potential threat to the character and identity of the prairie provinces.[44] Additionally, Alberta labour activists were concerned about the Railways Agreement as a source of increased competition that might disadvantage Alberta workers.[45] Migrant workers in the beet industry were caught in a double bind. On one side, their vulnerable position and limited options left them susceptible to employer exploitation. On the other, they faced the hostility of some Albertans who would have preferred that they not be in Canada at all.[46]

Still, economic prospects for Alberta irrigators remained uncertain, and provincial officials felt that additional expert guidance might help. Late in the 1920s, American agricultural scientist M.L. Wilson (who would go on to serve as undersecretary in the United States Department of Agriculture) was appointed to investigate prospects for the LNID and other irrigation districts.[47] His commission not only examined conditions in Alberta's irrigated landscape but also considered lessons learned in American irrigation, particularly those related to financing. Wilson noted that federal public funds had been used to advance American irrigation with the expectation that irrigators would repay the costs over a period of years. But repayment did not take place as anticipated because irrigation failed to generate the anticipated profit. This outcome had prompted a significant change in "the whole public policy of the reclamation of the United States," one that had led the government to take on more responsibility in irrigation financing.[48] Wilson's discussion of American circumstances amounted to an argument for more substantial public involvement in funding Alberta irrigation. Public investment in irrigation was appropriate, Wilson argued, because "all portions of the community" benefited from "the stabilized agricultural production and increased productivity" that resulted from irrigation. These community benefits meant that "the cost of the reclamation should not be borne only by those farmers who operate the lands."[49]

Public money had long had a place in Alberta irrigation. In the early decades, when corporate investment or cooperative financing was supposed to cover infrastructure costs, governments nevertheless offered supports and incentives. They did so in various ways, including by funding preliminary work like surveying and guaranteeing irrigation district bonds. By the 1920s, according to historian Lawrence B. Lee, the "public in western Canada had fostered irrigation development to the tune of millions of dollars."[50] But in the early decades, public investment in irrigation amounted to compromise on the two normative funding models. By arguing that Alberta should standardize public funding of irrigation, Wilson proposed to remake the financial framework for Alberta irrigation.

Wilson's recommendations were delivered in 1930 as Alberta confronted a regional agricultural crisis derived from environmental and economic factors. That same year saw the culmination of long-running efforts by the prairie provinces to secure control over their natural resources, previously administered by Ottawa. Although desired by the prairie provinces, the transfer of control over natural resources created new problems and expenses, with consequences for Alberta irrigation.[51] In the face of these challenges, Wilson's report, if sympathetically received, did not spur immediate action.

Rehabilitation and Fairness

M.L. Wilson's ideas about how to remake irrigation financing found purchase among the experts and officials associated with the Prairie Farm Rehabilitation Administration. At a May 1935 meeting only months after the agency's creation, the PFRA expert advisory committee concerning water development affirmed the consensus view that further irrigation development was essential to the long-term goal of "establishing safe and permanent agriculture" on the Prairies.[52] Considering this finding, committee members felt that "the cost of building irrigation work [was] properly chargeable to the whole community served and should not be charged entirely to the land actually irrigated."[53] This perspective emphasized the value of irrigation to local communities, the province, and the nation. From this angle, it was only appropriate that the state have a substantial role in irrigation funding.[54]

The PFRA's sympathy for publicly funded irrigation was evident in September 1935 when the chair of the Board of Trustees of the Magrath

Irrigation District wrote to the PFRA. In his letter, Christian Jensen explained that falling crop prices were making it hard for local farmers to pay infrastructure costs. Jensen acknowledged that farmers had perhaps been overly optimistic in developing irrigation, but he was quick to indicate that it had been a mistake to "charge the whole cost of the development to the land." Instead, he endorsed the Wilson commission's "sound principle" that costs should be charged to all who benefit, not just to farmers directly involved in irrigation.[55] The PFRA water-development committee recommended that the Magrath Irrigation District be granted the financial assistance that it requested.[56] The PFRA also extended assistance to other irrigation undertakings like the Bow River Project.[57]

A few months later, in December 1935, Augustus Griffin, chief engineer with the Canadian Pacific Railway's Department of Natural Resources, addressed his fellow members of the PFRA's expert advisory committee on water development. In a presentation titled "The Relation of Irrigation to Community Development," Griffin justified public funding of irrigation with reference to the ways that irrigation served surrounding communities and the nation at large as well as irrigators. Investments in irrigation, he argued, would improve the quality of life for thousands of Canadians, including by providing them with nourishing and palatable foodstuffs such as "fresh, crisp golden bantam corn, green peas!"[58] Griffin was born in California and trained under Elwood Mead, commissioner of reclamation with the United States Bureau of Reclamation from 1924 to 1936.[59] Griffin came to Alberta in 1918 and immediately took up work in irrigation. Central to Griffin's claims was the notion that irrigation was an important opportunity for what he called community development, meaning government-led efforts to establish more stable and prosperous communities. Community development seemed particularly important in the difficult 1930s, when stability and prosperity remained elusive for many prairie farmers.

For all that Griffin's position paralleled M.L. Wilson's, Griffin credited Walter Packard (1884–1966), an American soil scientist and economist, as his inspiration.[60] This influence was notable because Packard was as concerned to address what he saw as unfairness in the economic system as he was to irrigate dry land and to drive community development. Packard's approach to irrigation funding was based on the work of American political economist Henry George (1839–97).[61] George had advocated redressing economic inequality through changes to prevailing practices of landholding and taxation.[62] Canadian historian Ramsey Cook places George among

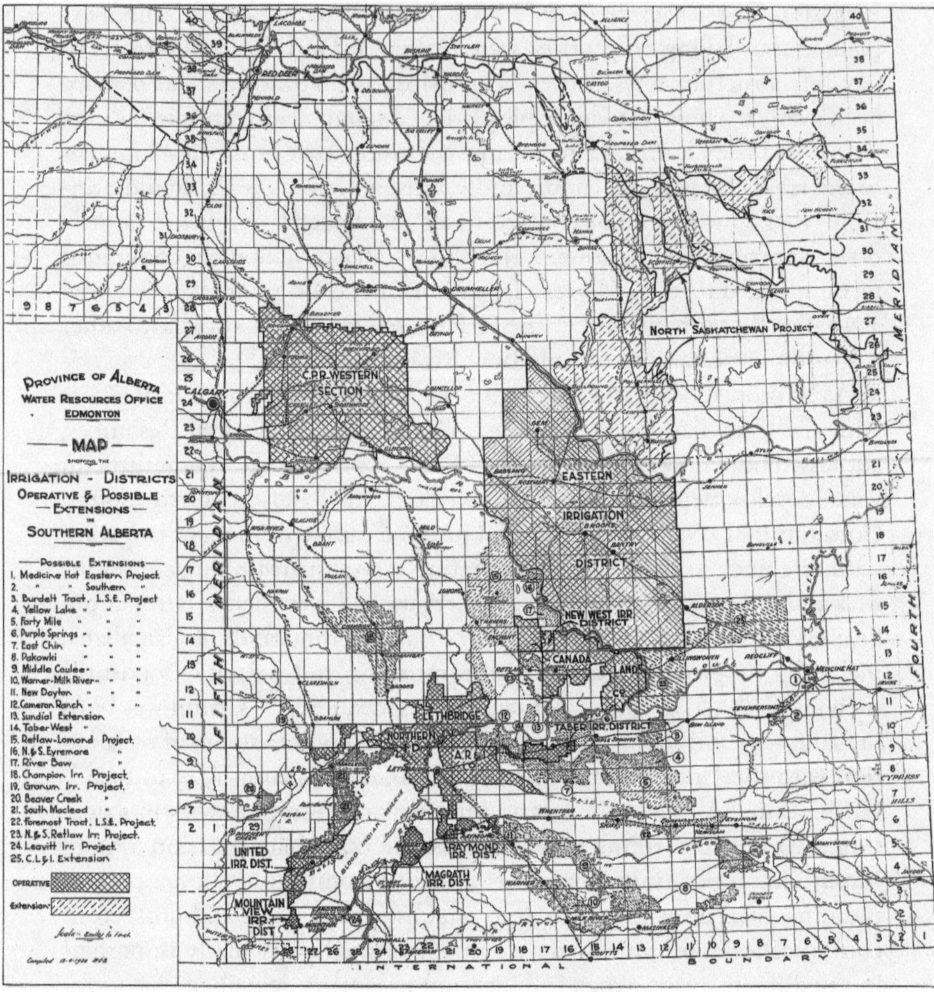

FIGURE 2.3 Historical map of southern Alberta showing existing and anticipated irrigation developments, 1938. The inclusion of both present and future projects underlines the momentum behind ongoing efforts to redesign regional water and farming patterns. *Provincial Archives of Alberta, GR1976.0206.0259.*

those he calls "regenerators" for their commitment to remaking society along what they saw as more ethical grounds.[63] Griffin was a strong supporter of George's proposals for taxation of what George had called unearned increments. In relation to irrigation, these increments were the gains realized by all those who benefited from irrigation-fuelled economic prosperity without contributing to the cost of irrigation infrastructure.

From this perspective, paying for irrigation through public funds raised from the population at large established greater fairness by ensuring that all those who benefited from irrigation helped to fund it.

At much the same time, Justice Albert Ewing of the Supreme Court of Alberta was commissioned to investigate irrigation in the province. His terms of reference were broader than those of the Widstoe or Wilson inquiries, prompting him to engage with issues like land values and water contracts. The Ewing report confirmed that leaders and experts in both Edmonton and Ottawa understood irrigation development as an investment in the public good, bolstering the logic for substantial public funding.[64] Figure 2.3, a map documenting envisioned as well as operating irrigation districts in mid-1930s southern Alberta, conveys the transformative ambition that animated irrigation in the province at this time, an ambition that persisted despite decades of mixed success.

In Alberta's irrigated landscape, public funding of irrigation promised relief for farmers struggling to pay infrastructure and maintenance costs. However, even as the PFRA advocated for financial relief for irrigators, the exploitation of sugar beet labourers became more acute. Global economic circumstances and disappointing harvests led the Utah-Idaho Sugar Company to cede control of its Alberta sugar beet plant to B.T. Rogers's B.C. Sugar.[65] In an effort to ensure profitability, Rogers dropped the price paid to farmers for beets, leading farmers to lower pay to labourers.[66] Between 1931 and 1934, labourers' pay declined by nearly 20 percent.[67]

Deteriorating pay, in conjunction with the persistently difficult character of beet work, prompted labourers to form the Beet Workers Industrial Union and to increase advocacy for improved working conditions. Efforts in 1935 were fairly successful, with labourers winning a pay increase of $2 per acre, but a renewed effort in 1936 proved fruitless.[68] Although the union had sought to establish solidarity between labourers and growers in opposition to B.C. Sugar, growers typically sided with Rogers in opposition to labourers.[69] Rogers cultivated this alliance by making concessions to growers, offering better terms for beets, and promising to erect a new beet factory.[70] Government sided with capital throughout these years, recruiting strikebreakers and offering tax concessions in support of a new beet factory. Historians John Herd Thompson and Allen Seager understand racism as a key factor in these events, with the prospect of an alliance between labourers and growers rendered less likely by the fact that many growers enjoyed the privileges of whiteness, whereas labourers did not.[71]

Juxtaposing improved public funding for irrigation with intense labour strife in the sugar beet industry helps to situate the PFRA in the uneven landscape – human as well as environmental – of the Canadian Prairies. The PFRA gave new legitimacy to the idea that government should fund irrigation by emphasizing how this investment would promote greater fairness and positive transformation in prairie agriculture. But the PFRA's mandate did not account for the experiences of beet workers, who suffered under oppressive working conditions defined by discrimination. In this way, PFRA-led rehabilitation served to reinforce existing social, economic, and environmental inequalities.

The Challenges and Opportunities of the 1940s

Wartime disruptions to global sugar supplies meant new pressure to ramp up domestic sugar beet growing in Canada.[72] At the same time, the widespread labour shortages characteristic of the war years complicated the operations of Canadian beet growers. In Alberta, the beet workers who in the 1930s had pressed for improved working conditions were keen to try again in this more favourable labour market.[73] The Sugar Beet Growers Association was concerned about these labour market changes, which seemed to tip the balance in favour of beet workers.[74] But just as wartime circumstances created what beet growers saw as labour problems, so too did the war allow for particular sorts of solutions. Over the following years, beet growers met their labour needs in part through reliance on informally interned Japanese people and prisoners of war.[75]

Following Japan's late 1941 attack on the United States naval base at Pearl Harbor, Hawaii, the Canadian federal government grew alarmed at the potential risk to national security posed by the concentration of people of Japanese origin along Canada's West Coast. The following months and years saw the ratcheting-up of state-sponsored oppression directed at Japanese people, the majority of whom held Canadian citizenship. Measures included the confiscation of property and the displacement of 22,000 people from coastal British Columbia.[76] As historian Jordan Stanger-Ross has it in a recent volume examining Japanese wartime experiences, "race was the foundational ideology of the dispossession" to which Japanese people were subject.[77]

Over the war years, some 4,000 Japanese people travelled to beet fields in Alberta, Manitoba, and Ontario, with about 3,000 going to Alberta.[78] Amid limited and unattractive options available to those subject to displacement, many of which entailed family separation, beet farms offered the prospect of keeping families together.[79] But beet labour remained

FIGURE 2.4 Japanese people working on a sugar beet farm, mid-1940s. During the Second World War, informally interned Japanese people worked on Alberta's sugar beet farms while enduring difficult material and social conditions. Amid such hardships, Japanese people were heartened by the opportunity to remain with family. *University of Calgary Digital Collections, CU193570.*

unrelentingly difficult. Japanese people were initially prohibited from seeking alternative or additional work, even during the seasons when their labour was unneeded in the beet fields.[80] As a result, many had difficulty purchasing sufficient food or other necessaries. Some Japanese families endured unsuitable accommodations, including year-round residence in buildings intended for only summer use.[81] Whereas sugar beet growers actively sought Japanese labour, many in wider Alberta society expressed concerns about informally interned Japanese people, concerns related both to pre-existing racism and to the wartime context.[82] Once it was clear that these concerns would not impede beet growers' access to Japanese labour, prevailing prejudices served growers' interests by precluding widespread sympathy for exploited Japanese beet workers.

Beet growers also relied on labour from prisoners of war. Between 1940 and 1947, about 35,000 prisoners of war were interned in Canada.[83] Internment Camp No. 133, near Lethbridge, was designed to accommodate over 12,000 prisoners.[84] The experience with informally interned Japanese people, deemed a success from the perspective of sugar beet growers, led the federal government to consider the use of prisoners in beet fields.[85] The use of prisoners of war as farm labour was approved in time for the 1943 sugar beet season.[86] Over 400 prisoners of war worked in Alberta's beet fields that year.[87] Fears that insufficient labour could scuttle a harvest overshadowed concerns about any risks, whether to national security or to the local community, of employing prisoners in the fields. Through the end of the war, beet growers relied on Japanese Canadians and prisoners of war, as well as on a small number of conscientious objectors, to meet their labour needs. In 1945, these three groups harvested over 18,000 acres of Alberta's 20,000 acres of beets.[88]

By the 1940s, it was established that optimal sugar beet growth required a steady application of water throughout the summer and into the fall.[89] There was a mismatch between the southern Alberta seasonal pattern of spring rains and the water needs of sugar beets, and this problem exacerbated growers' concerns about water supply. The sugar beet industry pressured the federal government to improve water availability year-round. J.N. Pollock, vice-president of the Sugar Beet Growers Association, estimated that water shortages in Alberta's irrigation districts caused annual agricultural losses totalling $400,000 and urged the federal government to construct a storage reservoir along southern Alberta's St. Mary River.[90] Members of the Engineering Institute of Canada were on side, favouring infrastructural solutions to southern Alberta's water-management problems.[91]

Large-scale water-management infrastructure had the potential to address difficulties related not just to water supply but also to the transboundary character of southern Alberta waterways. The St. Mary and Milk are among the rivers that cross and criss-cross the international border with the United States. The 1909 Boundary Waters Treaty, signed between Canada and the United States, was the culmination of years-long efforts to develop diplomatic tools with which to govern the allocation of waters flowing across the international border.[92] In effect, the treaty created a new management entity made up of the St. Mary and Milk Rivers, in which the total flow along both rivers was apportioned between the two nation-states.[93]

American leaders soon expressed dissatisfaction with the Boundary Waters Treaty, particularly with the provisions bearing on the St. Mary and Milk Rivers. For its part, Canadian leadership worried that revisiting these provisions would result in a settlement that was less satisfactory to Canada.[94] To members of the PFRA advisory committee attuned to the importance of securing water rights, this was "a dangerous situation."[95] By the early 1940s, it seemed that favourable aspects of the 1909 arrangement might be preserved by constructing large-scale infrastructure that would put most of Canada's apportionment to productive use.[96]

In February 1941, Ottawa charged Victor Meek with determining what further infrastructure would be necessary to "utilize fully Canada's share of international streams in southern Alberta."[97] Meek was the controller and chief engineer of the Dominion Water and Power Bureau. He was joined in his task by commission members William E. Hunter (with the federal government's Department of Finance) and George Spence (director of the PFRA). Together, they were also charged with finding ways to address problems in Alberta irrigation, including insufficient water in developed areas and insufficient development in areas suitable for irrigation.

The Meek Commission operated in the wake of the earlier inquiries led by Widstoe, Wilson, and Ewing. Commissioners understood that they were not only to propose specific infrastructure but also to articulate a perspective on irrigation that would emphasize the appropriateness of public funding, and they duly asserted that irrigation would render many benefits to a broad community. The list of benefits assembled by the Meek Commission included protecting Canada's right to international waters, meeting anticipated postwar demand for irrigated farms, promoting agricultural stability and prosperity, and stimulating transportation and manufacturing across multiple economic sectors. The commission's report proved compelling. By 1946, the construction of the St. Mary Dam was moving ahead, and it would be completed in 1951.[98] The reservoir behind the St. Mary Dam was anticipated to flood 11,600 acres of land, including 5,800 acres of Kainai Blood Reserve No. 148 and 5,785 acres forming part of two Hutterite communities.[99]

In correspondence with Victor Meek in January 1947, George Spence called the Meek report "a textbook on irrigation in the prairie provinces."[100] Its utility was formalized in June of that year by an order of the privy council that took the Meek report as the model for the financial arrangements underlying other major water-infrastructure projects. Under this order, the federal government committed to funding, constructing, operating, and maintaining major works.[101] Provinces would be involved through the provision of necessary smaller-scale infrastructure. In the postwar period, much Alberta irrigation proceeded according to these terms, although there was variation in how they were interpreted and applied.[102] After years in which the question of how to fund irrigation was persistently problematic in Alberta, the Meek report established a new format for irrigation financing by affirming the connection between investment in irrigation and the public good.

In the sugar beet landscape, where grower prosperity depended on sufficient labour as well as water, it is particularly clear how this notion of the public good operated in racist terms. The beet industry continued to rely on labour from social groups ill-positioned to demand appropriate pay and working conditions. In the immediate postwar period, migrants displaced by the war were a key labour source.[103] By the 1950s, Indigenous peoples from communities in Saskatchewan and Alberta had a growing role in sugar beet labour. The state used a range of coercive tactics to ensure this labour supply, including pausing welfare payments to Indigenous peoples when the need for sugar beet labour was greatest.[104] Exploitative labour practices enabled expansion of the area planted with sugar beets. Whereas beets had occupied roughly 20,000 acres of Alberta cropland before the Second World War, 60,000 acres were producing beets in 1950.[105] By the 1970s, workers from Mexico were labouring in the sugar beet fields.[106] Through these various shifts in workforce, the exploitative conditions in the beet fields persisted.[107]

Conclusion

The Meek report was not just an argument for the St. Mary Dam. It was also an argument for the Prairie Farm Rehabilitation Administration. The report was completed when the PFRA's future role was unclear. Precipitation increased on the Canadian Prairies in the 1940s, and it seemed that the emergency that had given birth to the PFRA had passed. But the agency should not be wrapped up, insisted its director. Rather, George Spence argued, the PFRA should be empowered to focus on "problems that are the natural and ever-present hazards of Western agriculture" within "a comprehensive program of post-war rehabilitation."[108] Even as efforts to improve farming techniques diminished in significance and were made entirely the responsibility of the Experimental Farms Service, Spence maintained that the work of rehabilitation would take on new importance.

Efforts to recalibrate the PFRA were particularly successful when they intersected with outside pleas to expand the agency. Within a few years of the PFRA's creation, such calls became a chorus. Prairie governments wanted the PFRA to encompass all agricultural lands in the provinces.[109] Central British Columbia had agricultural and irrigation concerns that PFRA expertise might solve. Prince Edward Island and Nova Scotia called for the establishment of PFRA-like institutions in these provinces.[110]

Federal government bodies, including the sub-committee responsible for agricultural aspects of postwar reconstruction, took the PFRA's postwar expansion almost for granted.[111] Consideration was given to renaming an expanded PFRA, with the moniker "Canadian Farm Rehabilitation" a frontrunner.[112] The PFRA was widely, if certainly not universally, perceived as successful: it was an entity to expand and a model to emulate, as demonstrated by the 1948 establishment of the PFRA-like Maritime Marshland Reclamation Administration in New Brunswick and Nova Scotia.[113]

The PFRA's good reputation derived from its efforts to promote agricultural stability and prosperity. Irrigation was a means to this end. The PFRA became involved in irrigation amid an ongoing expert dialogue emphasizing the appropriateness of public investment because of irrigation's positive effects on communities both local and farther flung. From this perspective, public funding of irrigation was justified and necessary; it was unfair to rely only or primarily on irrigation farmers to pay costs. Although this expert dialogue was specific to irrigation, it had the effect of positioning the state as a powerful actor in producing desired community outcomes. Calls to expand the PFRA reflect an optimistic view of the state as a vehicle of positive transformation, a view that was established in part through the agency's place within the longer history of irrigation in Alberta.

Yet the PFRA served the public good unevenly. As literary scholar Jenny Kerber puts it, "the sugar beet serves as a useful index of the Canadian government's hierarchy of interests along the southern Alberta border."[114] Concentrating on Alberta's sugar beet landscape allows the area's distinct labour pattern to reveal the limits implicit within irrigation's purported widespread benefits. Considering the experiences of those who, over many decades, did hard labour in the sugar beet industry exposes racist dimensions of the PFRA's rehabilitation efforts and of the approach to community development that would underlie future PFRA activity.

On the Canadian Prairies, the PFRA intervened in a human landscape that already reflected the operation of systems of oppression. The agency endorsed government funding of irrigation to save involved farmers from unfairly bearing the financial burden for irrigation projects with wider benefits. As the PFRA had neither mandate nor capacity to intervene in questions of agricultural labour, the sugar beet industry's reliance on workers from disadvantaged groups did not come up for consideration by the PFRA, even as the agency carefully weighed other questions of fairness in the irrigated landscape. In this way, the PFRA provides an example of how racism operated on the agricultural Prairies. A significant conceptual transformation promoted by the PFRA – that government should fund irrigation because of its contribution to the public good – perpetuated existing patterns of power and privilege. In advancing rehabilitation efforts, the PFRA contributed to entrenching environmental inequality in the irrigated landscape.

3
Intensification and Simplification
The PFRA's Community Pastures, 1930s–60s

In 1937, recently appointed federal minister of agriculture James G. Gardiner described the Prairie Farm Rehabilitation Administration (PFRA) Community Pastures Program as an "unsettlement plan," one conceived to undo settlement mistakes by facilitating a pull-back from areas not suitable for farming.[1] Also intended to make better use of these sub-marginal lands and to encourage farmers to raise stock alongside their crops, community pastures were PFRA-administered areas where nearby farmers could pasture livestock, primarily cattle. Farmers typically deposited their stock on a pasture in spring, and the animals were combined into a larger herd and managed by PFRA staff through the grazing season. Occasional roundups allowed for careful monitoring and health care. In the fall, farmers collected their stock and overwintered them on their own land. The Community Pastures Program reflected the PFRA's belief in small-scale stock raising as a means to achieve greater stability and prosperity for prairie grain farmers.

Community pastures were a type of commons where land was reserved for public use and managed cooperatively. Scholars from a range of fields have studied the operation of commons. Some have concluded that commons are likely to lead to resource degradation, whereas others have understood them as potentially successful approaches to environmental management.[2] For the PFRA, community pastures were both a solution to the mistake of agricultural settlement on sub-marginal lands and an effort to put these lands to sustainable use in a way that would benefit the local agricultural community. PFRA community pastures were not an extension of the longer history of ranching on the Canadian Prairies, in which the landscapes of southern Alberta played a central role.[3] Rather, they were based on cooperative grazing precedents on the Canadian Prairies and in the United States, with PFRA officials reaching out to their Montana counterparts for inspiration and guidance.[4]

The Community Pastures Program fostered ambitious efforts to adjust both land use and agricultural practices across Saskatchewan and, to a lesser extent, Manitoba. Creating community pastures required the federal government to establish control over appropriate locations for pastures. But the great land rush had played out with vigour across the Canadian Prairies. Before 1930, Ottawa had already disposed of more than 88 percent of surveyed lands across the three prairie provinces. The rate in Saskatchewan alone was even higher, with about 95 percent of surveyed lands having passed out of government control.[5] For provincial government officials, it proved difficult to resolve the varied private claims bearing on potential pasture areas. As illustrated in the first substantive section of this chapter, it was not so easy to put the great land rush into reverse.

The chapter's following section describes the physical infrastructure and day-to-day practices framing low-modernist cooperation between prairie farmers and the PFRA's Community Pastures Program as well as efforts by PFRA leadership to use community pastures to transform the prairie livestock industry, a thoroughly high-modernist endeavour. The next section focuses on the Prairie Farm Assistance Act (PFAA), a federal government agricultural program established in the 1930s that compensated farmers for low farm productivity. The PFAA and the PFRA pulled prairie farmers in opposite directions, which complicated the Community Pastures Program. The final substantive section considers PFRA-led efforts to regrass the Prairies, including by establishing grazing-tolerant grasses on community pastures. The heavy use of crested wheatgrass in this effort harmfully simplified prairie ecosystems by reducing ecological diversity.

The Failure of Unsettlement

Community pastures had to be put in the right places. The Community Pastures Program targeted sub-marginal lands that were unlikely to produce reasonable agricultural returns even in favourable periods, not lands suffering from resolvable difficulties related to low precipitation and inappropriate farming techniques. The economic survey, one of the PFRA's earliest high-modernist activities, was underway prior to the commencement of the Community Pastures Program. But once the PFRA was expanded to include rehabilitation on a community basis, the economic survey was understood to have laid essential ground work for community pastures by systematically identifying sub-marginal lands. Reflecting this understanding, the 1938 PFRA annual report referred to community pastures as a "practical result" of the economic survey.[6]

Due in large measure to the economic survey, agreement was readily achieved between the federal and provincial governments over where community pastures should be created. But governments differed on the question of whether authority over community pasture lands should be held federally or provincially. Until 1930, Ottawa retained authority over the lands and resources of the Prairie West, which distinguished Manitoba, Saskatchewan, and Alberta from other Canadian provinces.[7] Even after the transfer of natural resources to the prairie provinces, jurisdictional matters remained fraught. Scholars Gregory P. Marchildon and Daniel Balkwill have noted the significance of jurisdictional tensions to the operation of the PFRA.[8] The three prairie provinces held different views of community pastures but all resisted federal incursions on provincial jurisdiction. In the context of reluctance on the part of Alberta's political leaders and given Manitoba's more modest supply of sub-marginal lands appropriate for pasture, the Community Pastures Program moved ahead most rapidly and robustly in Saskatchewan.

Saskatchewan's Land Utilization Board (LUB) had been created by the province in the mid-1930s with the aim of managing land deemed unsuitable for agriculture. The LUB soon took up the related task of resolving competing claims to those lands unsuitable for intensive cropping that were appropriate for the creation of community pastures. The work was challenging because lands could be encumbered by unpaid tax bills and other debts, bisected by school-district and municipal boundaries, subject to grazing leases or reserved to help fund schools, and controlled by private or Crown corporations.[9] Because addressing these varied circumstances demanded a broad range of experience and expertise, the LUB included representatives from provincial departments like Agriculture, Municipal Affairs, and Natural Resources, as well as academics and representatives from the Association of Rural Municipalities and the Local Government Board. When it became clear that the LUB would be working closely with the PFRA, the director of the PFRA was added.[10] The LUB had broad powers: it could purchase land, spend money to improve land, or remove occupants through expropriation.[11] But still it encountered difficulties at every turn.[12]

Dealing with individual settlers was the most sensitive work undertaken by the LUB.[13] In 1938, when the Community Pastures Program was in its infancy, the PFRA's superintendent of land utilization, O. Freer, estimated that ten to twenty families probably needed to be removed from each area where a community pasture was to be created.[14] Settlers were encouraged to re-establish themselves elsewhere and offered assistance to this end.[15] But these inducements were not always sufficient. Farmers and government officials sometimes disagreed on the meaning of sub-marginality, with some farmers keen to persist in what officials saw as unsuitable locations. The PFRA sought to avoid the forcible displacement of farmers, even when doing so involved additional difficulty and expense, like fencing out areas that otherwise would have been included in pastures.

The first year of the Community Pastures Program saw fourteen pastures created.[16] They encompassed almost 190,000 acres and accommodated 3,231 livestock units, meaning one head of cattle, one horse, or five sheep. The PFRA felt that 15,000 to 20,000 acres was necessary in a pasture, or potentially in two nearby pastures, in order to ensure economical operations.[17] There were impressive increases in community pastures over the program's early years. By 1943, there were forty-five pastures in operation, encompassing over 1,261,000 acres and accommodating over 51,000 livestock units.[18] But despite rapid growth, PFRA officials worried about what they saw as the program's most serious problem: persistent difficulty in securing control over sub-marginal agricultural lands targeted for pasture development.[19] So concerning were the resulting delays that officials were prompted to revisit the prospect of forcibly moving reluctant settlers to free up more land for pasture development.[20]

The contrast between the rapid expansion of the Community Pastures Program and the worries of PFRA officials is revealing. Although the program had grown, it was not functioning as an unsettlement program facilitating what James Gardiner had envisioned as a pull-back from lands that should not be farmed intensively. The early expansion of the Community Pastures Program was rapid because it took place for the most part not on sub-marginal farms but on undisturbed Crown land. Of the 1,148,780 acres included in community pastures by December 1942, less than 250,000 acres had ever been cultivated.[21]

Although community pastures were proving an ineffective means of unsettlement, PFRA officials remained optimistic that pastures would succeed in encouraging grain farmers to raise a small quantity of livestock. This initiative had long been proposed as a means of countering the volatility of farming, yet many prairie farmers were resistant to becoming

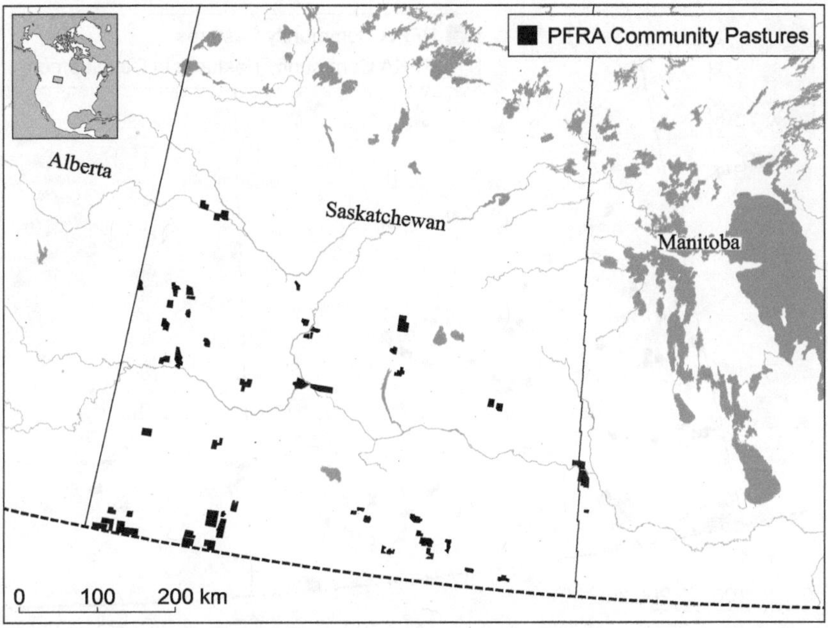

Figure 3.1 Prairie Farm Rehabilitation Administration community pastures, 1942. *Adapted from Prairie Farm Rehabilitation Administration,* Report on Activities Conducted under the Prairie Farm Rehabilitation Act for the Fiscal Year Ending March 31, 1942 *(Ottawa: Department of Agriculture, 1942), 50; and* CanVec Series [Admin., Land, Hydro] *(Ottawa: Natural Resources Canada, 2019).*

involved or to expanding their involvement with livestock. Historian Paul Voisey reports that in southern Alberta, for instance, although farmers heard about the virtues of this approach, not many took it up because, in years of high prices and good harvests, focusing on wheat paid more.[22] Voisey also emphasizes the complications of what he calls mixed farming, including additional expenses and longer working hours. Government policy was another factor, with policies like the Crow Rate, which discounted the price of grain transportation, incentivizing a focus on grain.[23] Ongoing farm mechanization was also at play, as expensive machinery purchases compelled farmers to maximize their returns on this investment by specializing in grain growing.[24]

PFRA officials believed that small-scale livestock raising would help to ensure greater farm stability and productivity. This outcome would benefit both farm families and the prairie region at large by ensuring a vigorous agricultural economy and by safeguarding against the need for additional government supports to prairie farmers. From the early days of PFRA

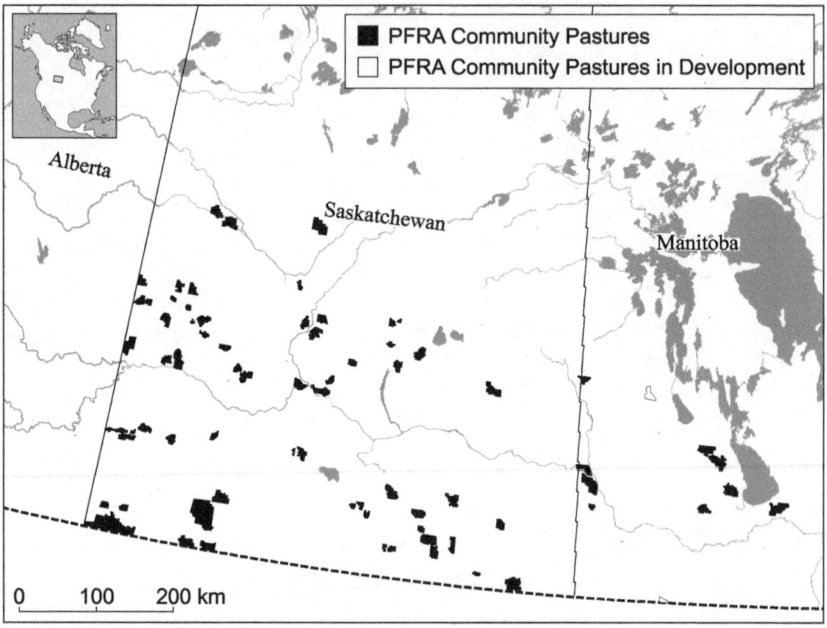

FIGURE 3.2 Prairie Farm Rehabilitation Administration community pastures, 1960. *Adapted from Prairie Farm Rehabilitation Administration,* Annual Report on Prairie Farm Rehabilitation and Related Activities, 1959–1960 *(Ottawa: Department of Agriculture 1960), 11; and* CanVec Series [Admin., Land, Hydro] *(Ottawa: Natural Resources Canada, 2019).*

community pastures, the promotion of small-scale livestock raising was, alongside unsettlement, a major program aim. In the early 1940s, global economic circumstances underlined the value of livestock. The Second World War closed many global markets for wheat and increased demand for meat and dairy, seeming to validate the recommendations for greater agricultural stability that the PFRA was offering.[25] Livestock raising remained important to the PFRA even after the war years. L.B. Thomson, newly appointed as PFRA director, told attendees at a 1948 field day in Lethbridge that the effective conservation of natural resources did not necessarily involve growing two blades of grass where one had grown before. Rather, it could mean replacing the blade of grass with a superior one and then using that blade to maximize beef production.[26] This twist on a common definition of conservation reflects the significance of livestock raising to the PFRA's vision of conservation on the agricultural Prairies.

The creation of community pastures slowed considerably after 1943. After establishing forty-five pastures in the program's first five years, the

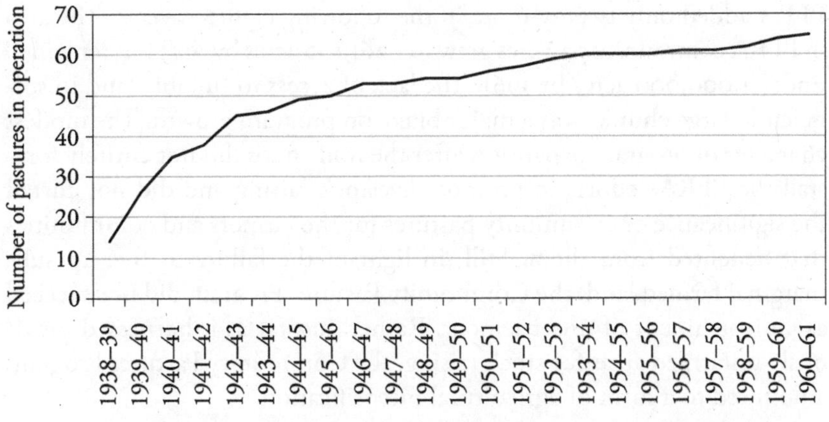

FIGURE 3.3 Change over time in the number of PFRA community pastures, 1938–61. Note that the values are not entirely consistent with those listed in the individual annual reports, though the general trends are parallel. *Department of Regional Economic Expansion, "Appendix J: Financial Analysis of PFRA Community Pasture Program," in "PFRA Pasture Program Growth," Library and Archives Canada (LAC), RG 17, acc. 1991-92/86, box 5, file 520.8, vol. 01(S); Department of Regional Economic Expansion, "PFRA Small Water Development and Community Pasture Programs: A Consolidated Report," 30 March 1972, LAC, RG 17, acc. 1991-92/86, box 5, file 520.8, vol. 01(S).*

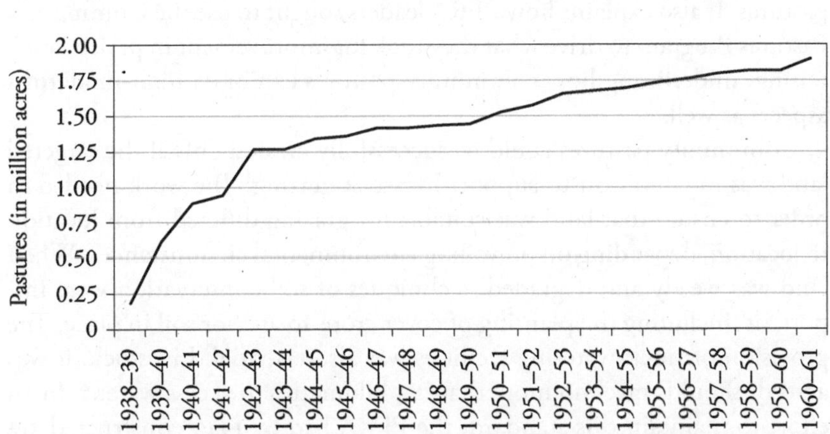

FIGURE 3.4 Change over time in the total acreage in PFRA community pastures, 1938–61. Note that the values are not entirely consistent with those listed in the individual annual reports, though the general trends are parallel. *Department of Regional Economic Expansion, "Appendix J: Financial Analysis of PFRA Community Pasture Program," in "PFRA Pasture Program Growth," Library and Archives Canada (LAC), RG 17, acc. 1991-92/86, box 5, file 520.8, vol. 01(S); Department of Regional Economic Expansion, "PFRA Small Water Development and Community Pasture Programs: A Consolidated Report," 30 March 1972, LAC, RG 17, acc. 1991-92/86, box 5, file 520.8, vol. 01(S).*

PFRA added only twenty more in the following eighteen years. The area in PFRA community pastures grew to 1,261,100 acres by 1943 but remained under 2,000,000 acres by 1961. The lack of access to suitable land in sufficiently large chunks was a major brake on program growth. The modest character of program expansion after the mid-1940s did not entirely forestall the PFRA's efforts to promote livestock raising and did not curtail the significance of community pastures for the farmers and communities that benefited from them. Still, in light of the failure to free up submarginal farmed land, the Community Pastures Program did not succeed as an instrument of unsettlement. Rather, insofar as it harnessed previously unfarmed areas for stock raising, the Community Pastures Program amounted to a form of agricultural intensification.

Pasture Operations

Community pastures were sites of meaningful engagement between PFRA employees and prairie farmers. They were examples of PFRA-administered low modernism on the agricultural Prairies. The following section describes the infrastructure and practices that defined the operation of community pastures. It also explains how PFRA leaders sought to use the Community Pastures Program to drive what they took for improvement in prairie stock raising, underlining how community pastures exhibited high-modernist aspects as well.

Community pastures could be successfully created only if the targeted land was in condition to support livestock grazing. The work needed in order to ensure that land was suitable for grazing differed from location to location, depending on prevailing environmental circumstances. When land was weedy and degraded, techniques of soil conservation were important, including the planting of cover crops to anchor soil in place. The provision of stock-watering facilities was also essential. Livestock, it was agreed, should travel no more than 2.5 kilometres to access water.[27] In an effort to maintain this standard, the PFRA had by 1940 constructed 312 water-access points within community pastures, including dams, dugouts, and wells.

Community pastures required fences to manage cattle movement and to ensure the well-being of both livestock and grass. Most commonly, fences consisted of four or more strands of barbed wire strung between posts.[28] A perimeter barrier kept pastured animals in and unauthorized users out. Interior fencing created breeding, summer, winter, and reserve

FIGURE 3.5 Cattle by a barbed wire fence during summer roundup. A large number of cattle stand along a typical fence during roundup, when cattle in community pastures were gathered for monitoring and care. *Provincial Archives of Saskatchewan, Accession 1382 (Photo R), R-B8299.*

pastures, making it possible to manage grazing with greater precision.[29] Fencing was of a high standard; fences were to last for twenty years with very little maintenance, reflecting how pastures were intended to be long-term sites of cooperation between the PFRA and the farmers who used the pastures.[30] The Community Pastures Program was popular with users from early on. For instance, in 1939, farmer T.L. Shepherd wrote to PFRA administrators that he and his brother were "very well pleased with the results of our stock in your pasture this last summer." He went on to note that "the whole pasture plan is a wonderful idea."[31]

When employment was in short supply during the Great Depression of the 1930s, the paid work, like fence building, that was involved in pasture creation amounted to a local boon.[32] But the Second World War interrupted supplies of barbed wire and produced labour shortages.[33] Late in the war, displaced Japanese people were involved in fencing work.[34] One pasture manager found these arrangements entirely satisfactory, noting that, as he saw it, the Japanese workers "are performing their duties well and not causing trouble."[35] Involuntary labour from a group subject to discrimination played a role in compensating for the wartime labour

FIGURE 3.6 View of an annual meeting of patrons of the Beaver Hills Community Pasture in the yard outside the pasture headquarters. The operation of community pastures included annual meetings at which patrons and PFRA staff engaged with each other, as seen on this eastern Saskatchewan pasture. *Provincial Archives of Saskatchewan, Accession 1382 (Photo R), R-B8306.*

shortages that threatened to retard the construction of community pastures infrastructure.

Grazing on community pastures was initially made available to stock raisers in the immediate vicinity of a pasture.[36] Users paid fees to access pasture, with these fees roughly equivalent to the costs of pasture operations and maintenance. In 1940, typical fees for cattle were 35 cents per head each month, with a reduction for a full season's grazing.[37] By 1953, the principles guiding access to community pastures were further elaborated. Grazing was offered first to farmers displaced by the community pasture who had re-established themselves nearby, then to farmers within the municipality where the pasture was located, and finally to farmers in adjoining municipalities.[38] Cooperation among farmers using a community pasture, termed patrons by the PFRA, was formalized through the creation of a pasture-grazing association that met annually, typically on the pasture itself. Each grazing association elected a decision-making council of five members.[39] The council's chief responsibility was to determine how many cattle each patron could put on the pasture according to the total carrying capacity specified by the PFRA.[40] Although established by councils in relation to local circumstances, grazing caps on individual farmers were typically kept low to ensure that many users could be accommodated.[41] Grazing associations, especially their elected councils, were important means through which local needs and concerns helped to shape the operation of community pastures.[42]

Pasture managers employed by the PFRA lived on community pastures and were responsible for day-to-day pasture operations. They spent time in the field managing livestock and grass, they interacted frequently with the pasture's elected council and with other farmers at key moments in the annual grazing cycle, and they engaged with PFRA officials and other pasture managers. The work of raising cattle has been characterized as "inherently creative," with those in charge "constantly improvising" in relation to variables outside their control.[43] For pasture managers, such variables included weather, grass quality, instructions from the PFRA, and input from the patrons and council. Pasture managers cared for cattle (which were owned by pasture patrons) while safeguarding the grass resource (which was under the authority of government), and they were responsible for finessing any tension between these objectives.

Pasture management was understood to be men's work due to the physicality of the job and the manager's authority over stock raisers. Still, the wives and children of pasture managers often lived on-site and took on necessary chores and tasks.[44] Wives also performed duties seen as consistent with their gender roles, such as hosting visiting patrons and cooking for those engaged in roundup. Women's work was uncompensated but essential to pasture functioning, and it was particularly important in facilitating the annual meetings and roundups that brought patrons and PFRA staff into close collaboration.

By the 1930s, most prairie cattle were being shipped east at the yearling stage for fattening and slaughtering in Ontario.[45] This was the trajectory even for cattle from Alberta, which would not see a significant expansion of feedlot operations until the 1960s.[46] But PFRA officials looking to bolster prairie livestock production realized that the quality of prairie livestock made it relatively unattractive to eastern buyers.[47] As PFRA director George Spence was informed by a colleague, "something will have to be done to improve this situation if we are ever going to get livestock production on a satisfactory and paying basis."[48] Governments, both provincial and federal, had long been involved in efforts to improve the quality of cattle.[49] The PFRA's Community Pastures Program provided new impetus to improvement efforts, and positive relations with pasture administration helped to make patrons receptive.

At the launch of the Community Pastures Program, PFRA officials felt that introducing more purebred cattle would improve the quality of prairie livestock. But good purebred bulls were expensive to purchase and maintain, particularly considering that their services were needed only a few weeks a year.[50] And so the PFRA made purebred bulls available to community pasture patrons for a small fee through a publicly facilitated breeding program. By 1940, there were fifty-three Herefords, thirty-one Shorthorns, and five Angus bulls in service.[51] These were all beef breeds with origins in the United Kingdom that were already well established in eastern Canada and the United States.[52] Although Herefords were considered particularly well adapted to conditions in the Prairie West, the major aim of the PFRA's breeding program was to satisfy eastern buyers.[53]

The PFRA sought to further facilitate buyers' work by concentrating desirable breeds in particular geographic areas.[54] The idea was that community pastures would choose the breed of bull that they preferred to use, with buyers then knowing where to look for that particular breed. Additionally, community pastures were to undertake breeding on a common cycle with the aim of aligning cattle growth.[55] These various tactics, being intended to standardize the cattle on pastures in terms of breed and age, were adopted in pursuit of better integration between small-scale stock raisers on the Prairies and easterners who purchased cattle.[56] Although PFRA community pastures in some ways reflected low modernism, the agency's breeding program underlines that community pastures were also influenced by expert-led high-modernist efforts to drive change in the prairie livestock industry.

Adopting the insights of evolutionary history, we might understand prairie cattle as a biotechnology, one that the PFRA sought to manipulate in order to help remake prairie farming.[57] But over time, perspectives on livestock quality shifted. The view that purebred cattle were superior waned, with an experiment conducted on a PFRA community pasture contributing to this shift in thinking.[58] By the mid-1950s, many in the Canadian livestock industry believed that crossbreeds were hardier and so more likely to thrive in Canadian conditions.[59] Although the PFRA's breeding program continued on community pastures, the transformative ambition of program leaders abated. A reckoning with the realities of the community pasture system may have been a factor in this process. By this time, PFRA community pastures represented only a relatively small proportion of grazing lands on the Prairies. In Saskatchewan, the province proved willing to create community pastures even on parcels of land that the PFRA considered too small for economical pasture operations.[60] Across the

Prairies, some farmers leased grazing land from provincial governments.[61] In this context, PFRA leaders recognized that their agency's community pastures could drive only relatively modest change in the prairie livestock industry. There were limits to the PFRA's ability to realize its ambitions.

Conflicting Policy

After an early rush of rapid development, the Community Pastures Program entered a period of comparatively slow growth. The early 1940s were wet years, and agricultural prices improved. Fewer landowners were inclined to abandon their farms, which limited lands available for pasture development.[62] Increasing use of chemical weed control meant less frequent tillage. This change diminished the risk of soil drift, even on vulnerable fields that might previously have been seen as suited only for pasture. For various reasons, the line between sub-marginal and better lands was proving mobile. The resulting uncertainties in the Community Pastures Program were exacerbated by federal government policy.

The Prairie Farm Assistance Act, adopted by Ottawa in 1939, has been described as an early form of crop insurance.[63] It promised payments to farmers in areas stricken by drought, flood, hail, or some other calamity. The program was partially funded by a 1 percent levy on marketed grain, with the federal treasury making up any shortfall. Eligibility was defined by agricultural productivity; in any given year, farms in townships or collections of townships producing less than an anticipated amount were eligible to access assistance payments. The PFAA was intended to help farmers through a few difficult years, during which they would learn how to farm their lands more effectively.[64] Government proponents of the PFAA saw it as a means to regularize the payment of relief, which had been distributed on an unsatisfyingly ad hoc basis throughout the 1930s.[65] Between 1939 and 1954, the 1 percent levy collected on marketed grain accounted for 57 percent of payouts to farmers.[66]

Both the PFAA and the PFRA originated in Ottawa's acknowledged responsibility for hardships experienced by prairie farmers and the prairie provinces.[67] They were among the various forms of assistance that Canadian governments made available to farmers in the mid-twentieth century.[68] In a 1942 analysis, E.C. Hope, professor of farm management at the University of Saskatchewan, catalogued numerous federal initiatives in agriculture (including the Experimental Farms Service and the Wheat Acreage Reduction Administration, as well as the PFRA and the PFAA) and several operated by the provincial government (including the Department of Agriculture, the Land Utilization Board, the Northern Areas Branch, the Department of Natural Resources, and the Saskatchewan Assessment Commission).[69] Government bodies active on the agricultural Prairies in this period also included those focused on tourism, environment, natural history, wildlife, mineral resources, and law.[70] Hope pointed to what he called "interlocking directorates," where people from one agency were involved in the governance of another, as well as to the commonality of goals among senior government administrators, in explaining how state entities typically managed to work well together.[71] But the coordination of policy between these entities was not always smooth. Over time, serious cross-purposes became evident between the PFRA and the PFAA.[72]

Early on, PFRA officials thought that the two programs might work together reasonably well. In the late 1940s, for instance, PFRA director L.B. Thomson used the PFAA as a metric for the PFRA, citing lack of PFAA payments as evidence for the PFRA's success in promoting soil conservation.[73] As Thomson saw it, the PFRA was helping farmers to maximize the productivity of their lands, which minimized the draw on the PFAA program. But problems with the PFAA soon became apparent. The allocation of PFAA payments came under fire. Eligibility was determined by productivity rates across a township or group of townships, even though growing conditions within them might vary substantially. Hard-hit farms in reasonably productive areas might be out of luck, and productive farms in hard-hit areas might be eligible for support that they did not need.[74] Problematically, the PFAA was not calibrated to the scale of agriculturally significant environmental variation on the Canadian Prairies. There was also a question of interprovincial equity. Between 1939 and 1958, Saskatchewan farmers received nearly $139 million in PFAA payments while contributing $61 million through the 1 percent levy. In Manitoba over the same period, farmers received just under $14 million in payments while contributing more than $16 million.[75]

For government officials concerned with agricultural adjustment, a further issue was the PFAA's practice of annually paying money to areas of low agricultural yield. A policy intended to help farmers through occasional tough times effectively became a funding stream that kept them on lands offering little prospect of productivity – a subsidy enabling farmers to persist on precisely the sort of sub-marginal lands that otherwise might have been incorporated into community pastures.[76] As Hope perceived early on, the PFAA was perpetuating "the very thing the PFRA is trying to rectify."[77] The Royal Commission on Canada's Economic Prospects confirmed this assessment, determining that the PFAA served to prop up nonviable farms.[78] If both the PFAA and the PFRA were oriented to fixing what policy makers perceived as the mistakes of settlement, it became clear that they held very different ideas about how best to do so. Tensions between the two agencies remained largely unresolved until the late-1950s creation of a federal government crop insurance program rendered the PFAA redundant.[79]

Other mid-twentieth-century government policies also limited the unsettlement of the Prairies. Wealthy nations led by the United States and including Canada introduced relief policies and price supports aimed at their agricultural sectors.[80] These programs subsidized agricultural viability with public funds. The director of Saskatchewan's Land Utilization Board wrote in 1942 to the director of the PFRA to share the worry that "the Dominion's agricultural programme of guaranteed prices for wheat, oats, barley and flax (with attractive prices for cattle and hogs) is inducing farmers to undertake the cultivation of abandoned lands."[81] Such inducements served to "reverse the government's rehabilitation programme."[82] By the late 1980s, policies that helped to perpetuate cropped agriculture all across the Prairies had proven more powerful than those, like the PFRA, that promoted land-use changes in needy areas.[83]

From its earliest days, the PFRA attempted to reckon with variations in the quality of land used for agriculture. The economic survey amounted to a high-modernist effort to distinguish between land worth farming and sub-marginal land. Experts involved with the economic survey recognized the importance of considering factors beyond the environmental. Other considerations mattered too, including agricultural markets, transportation, and farming techniques. The PFRA did not, however, anticipate the emergence of multiple government programs that protected farmers from the risks and disadvantages of farming sub-marginal lands. If the first section of this chapter illustrates the difficulty of putting the great land rush into reverse, this section demonstrates that part of the problem derived from government unwillingness to do so.

What looks from one angle like government unwillingness looks from another angle like government concern with the well-being of farm families. Jess Gilbert's work on agricultural experts in the mid-twentieth-century United States marks the genuine concern that low-modernist agricultural leaders exhibited for the American farmers and farm families that they served. Many PFRA officials felt this same duty of care toward prairie farmers, a feeling that for some was linked to their own family backgrounds in farming. They recognized that government policy forestalling agricultural adjustment underwrote improved standards of living for farm families and that the absence of such policies would create hardship. There was a tension between the PFRA's responsibility for advancing agricultural adjustment and the agency's desire to ensure the stability and prosperity of prairie farmers. At least in the short term, these two imperatives could seem to be in fundamental contradiction.

Crested Wheatgrass

Successful community pastures required grass suitable for intensive grazing. Regrassing efforts depended heavily on one plant: crested wheatgrass (*Agropyron cristatum*), a hardy bunch grass with stems standing between 50 and 100 centimetres. Seed heads measure up to up to 7 centimetres and are distinguished by their fan-like pattern, with spikelets extending outward from the main stem.[84] Crested wheatgrass became thoroughly established across the agricultural Prairies through the work of the Prairie Farm Rehabilitation Administration.

Crested wheatgrass is native to the Eurasian Steppe. It was introduced to North America in the late nineteenth century by the United States Department of Agriculture.[85] The plant proved particularly well suited to the landscape of the northern Great Plains, being hardy in dry conditions and cold temperatures. Intrigued Canadian agricultural scientists obtained samples first from the United States and then directly from Russia. John Bracken, while still an agricultural scientist at the University of Saskatchewan, worked alongside his graduate student L.E. Kirk to produce the fairway strain of crested wheatgrass.[86] Leafier and more procumbent than other strains, this variety of crested wheatgrass became the most common on the Canadian Prairies.[87]

Fairway crested wheatgrass produced excellent hay and pasture.[88] By the late 1920s, the Dominion Range Experiment Station at Manyberries, Alberta, had made it a focus of research.[89] In the mid-1930s, Kirk and others with the Canadian Department of Agriculture described crested wheatgrass as "the best grass we have for the re-seeding of depleted range lands in semi-arid districts."[90] Readily established even in dry conditions, crested wheatgrass was also planted to reduce soil blowing or drifting. As many parties both within and beyond government came to recognize, crested wheatgrass "excels for binding soil."[91] It was not the only non-native grass used in this way; brome was also deployed to address the conditions of the 1930s. But crested wheatgrass was preferred because it proved easier

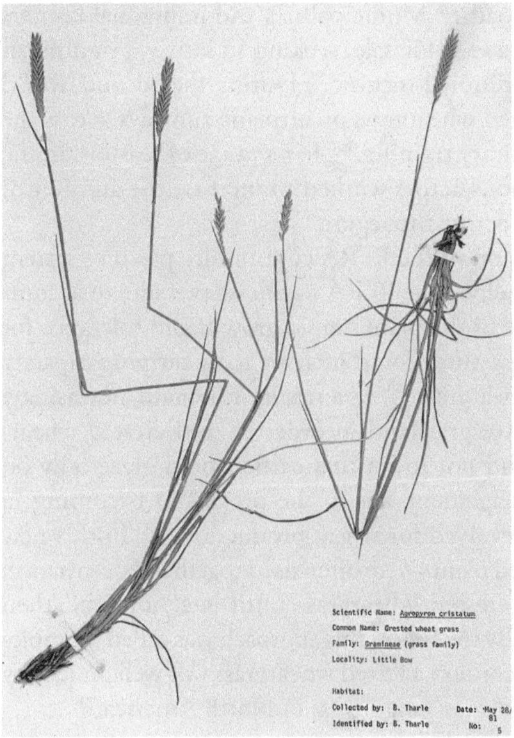

FIGURE 3.7 Crested wheatgrass. The sample was collected in 1981 in Little Bow Provincial Park, Alberta. *University of Lethbridge Library Digitized Collections, Alberta Parks – Southern Region Herbarium, Alberta Environment and Sustainable Resource Development, Parks Division, South Region.*

to establish and particularly successful in outcompeting less-desirable plants, making it an effective tool of weed control.[92]

From the beginning, the PFRA used crested wheatgrass "almost exclusively in seeding community pastures."[93] The grass was resistant to heavy grazing and trampling.[94] It grew rapidly in the early spring when moisture was abundant, providing a source of livestock feed when little else was available. When growth slowed over the summer months, other grasses were coming into their most rapid growth phase.[95] In the view of some twenty-first-century scientists, crested wheatgrass and cattle worked so well together as to constitute allies.[96] *Maclean's Magazine* reporter W.J. Bradley expressed the advantages more specifically in a 1930s article titled "Grass vs. Drought," writing that crested wheatgrass was "nature's answer to soil-drifting, as well as her offering to starving herds of cattle on dried-out western plains."[97]

Crested wheatgrass also seemed like a solution to problems beyond livestock grazing and soil drift on farmed fields. The PFRA provided crested wheatgrass to municipalities, and these bodies then used it to anchor soil on public lands and along roads.[98] Municipalities and individual farmers produced crested wheatgrass seed for sale, seeking to satisfy a significant demand and to generate additional income.[99] During the Second World War, the PFRA seeded crested wheatgrass on airplane runways across the Prairie West to facilitate military training.[100] For a range of reasons, in the mid-twentieth century, various actors worked to increase the amount of crested wheatgrass growing across the region.

As the geographic expansion of the PFRA community pastures system slowed, crested wheatgrass helped the PFRA to finesse pressure to accommodate more cattle. Because of the plant's rapid growth and tolerance for heavy grazing, community pastures could increase their carrying capacity by planting more crested wheatgrass.[101] As a result, it became increasingly common to plough up native grassland in order to seed crested wheatgrass.[102] This intervention did not mean that cattle would graze only on this one plant. Pasture management was in the process of becoming "a science comparable to that evolved for wheat production."[103] In this new science, native and introduced plants were often used together. For instance, cattle might be grazed on crested wheatgrass until late June and then switched to native prairie.[104] By the 1960s, this approach was called "complementary grazing."[105] In this context, crested wheatgrass was well on its way to becoming "the most important range grass in North America."[106]

Yet in the 1970s, criticisms of crested wheatgrass began to accumulate.[107] The plant was increasingly characterized as "a resilient invader that threatens the diversity, quality, and existence of native grasslands."[108] Its negative long-term effects also include lower rates of carbon sequestration than native prairie.[109] In 1996, writing in the *Journal of Soil and Water Conservation,* plant ecologist Peter Lesica and soil scientist Tom DeLuca made a compelling case that the spaces between agricultural crops were so dominated by crested wheatgrass that these in-between spaces were effectively zones of monoculture.[110] Against the critics, others argued that crested wheatgrass was "vital to the economy of the USA and Canada" because of its role in feeding livestock.[111] Some defended the grass for its utility in suppressing weeds and anchoring soils.[112] Crested wheatgrass has made significant contributions to soil conservation and livestock production on the Prairies. Yet as scientists have increasingly recognized, it has also negatively affected regional biodiversity. Researchers continue to explore how crested wheatgrass might be managed so as to capitalize on its advantages while minimizing its negative effects.[113]

PFRA community pastures have been lauded as repositories of biodiversity in a region dominated by large-scale agriculture.[114] They provide habitat for endangered wildlife like the ferruginous hawk, the swift fox, and the burrowing owl. They are landscapes favoured by antelope, sharp-tailed grouse, sage hens, and golden eagles. In these ways, community pastures underwrite prairie biodiversity. But this perspective is a product of something similar to what marine biologist Daniel Pauly calls shifting baselines, which emphasize the consideration of community pastures in relation to the more intensively farmed fields that they abut.[115] Compared instead with prairie landscapes prior to intensive capitalist agriculture, even community pastures are ecologically impoverished, and deliberate seeding of crested wheatgrass has been part of this decline.

Conclusion

Community pastures were transformative, although not always in the ways envisioned or to the extents desired by PFRA officials and other program advocates. Because most community pastures were developed on previously unfarmed land, rather than on failed farms, the program constituted agricultural intensification, not prairie unsettlement. The heavy reliance on crested wheatgrass, now recognized to diminish biodiversity, further underlines the role of the Community Pastures Program in driving forward the transformations associated with capitalist agriculture.

The Community Pastures Program reveals how high modernism and low modernism operated in tandem. The decentralization and cooperation underlying community pastures were characteristic of low modernism. But PFRA officials conceived of community pastures as instruments to promote small-scale stock raising and to improve livestock quality, a thoroughly high-modernist effort. Within the Community Pastures Program, cooperative engagements with prairie farmers helped to position agency leaders to advance expert-conceived changes. Not only did low modernism and high modernism work in tandem, but the former also facilitated the latter.

The Community Pastures Program illustrates the complex context for state action in mid-twentieth-century Canada. The program was complicated by jurisdictional tensions between Ottawa and the prairie provincial governments, as well as by conflicting federal government agricultural policies. Federal government agricultural policies responded to a range of circumstances both within and beyond the prairie region, so agricultural policy bearing on the Prairies was driven in part by considerations that were national and global in scope. The resulting inconsistencies, mostly clearly visible in the operation of the PFAA, bore on the work of the PFRA.

The PFRA's Community Pastures Program has been celebrated as positive and successful.[116] Community pastures provided services and opportunities that many prairie farmers valued. Pastures were often very carefully run by pasture managers and patrons in an effort to balance the needs of the local environment with the imperatives of stock raising. The existence of these pastures may well have protected areas and species from encroachment by more disruptive forms of agriculture. PFRA community pastures were more ecologically diverse than cropped fields. But celebrations of the benefits of these pastures should also recognize their role in processes of agricultural intensification and ecological simplification.

4
Construction and Change
Negotiating the South Saskatchewan Regional Plan, 1940s–50s

In 1967, nearly thirty years after he became director of the Prairie Farm Rehabilitation Administration (PFRA), George Spence published a book. Titled *Survival of a Vision,* Spence's volume commemorated the completion of a large-scale water-development project known as the South Saskatchewan Regional Plan (SSRP). In the book, Spence situated this project in a rendering of regional history that lionized ambitious newcomers and applauded governments for their efforts to advance the agricultural colonization of the Prairie West. As he asserted in the final pages of his book, the SSRP derived from "visions of the prairie region of Western Canada becoming a land where security and social well-being would prevail."[1]

The SSRP involved the construction along the South Saskatchewan River of two dams, now known as the Gardiner Dam and the Qu'Appelle River Dam, and the creation of a large reservoir between them, now known as Lake Diefenbaker. The Gardiner Dam, the more substantial of the dams, remains among the world's largest embankment dams. Measuring 4,800 metres in length and 64 metres in height, it is the third highest dam of that type in Canada, after the Mica Dam and the W.A.C. Bennett Dam, both in British Columbia. Measured by dam volume, Gardiner significantly exceeds both taller structures. Lake Diefenbaker reaches 225 kilometres upstream from the Gardiner Dam, extending through the valley of the South Saskatchewan River and its coulees.[2] The title of Spence's book positions the Gardiner Dam and related infrastructure as the culmination of an enduring dream to undertake a high-modernist redesign of the

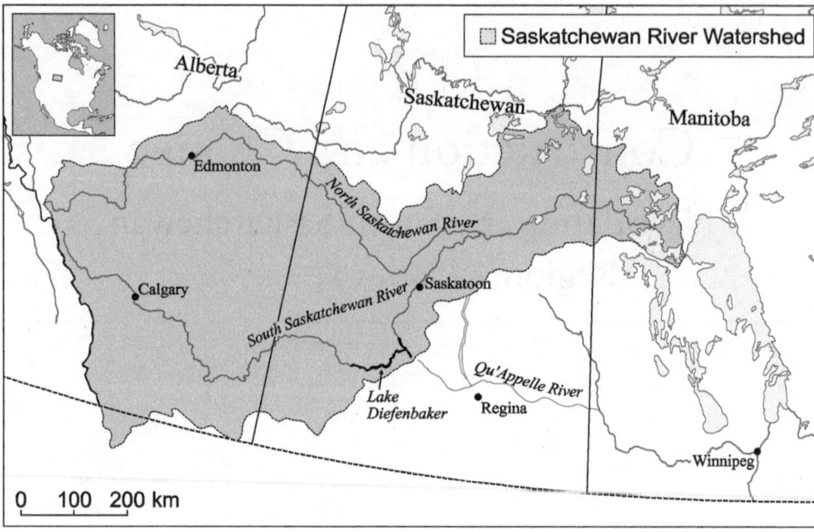

FIGURE 4.1 The location of Lake Diefenbaker within the Saskatchewan River watershed. The Gardiner Dam is located at the northernmost end of the reservoir's tilted "T" shape, and the Qu'Appelle River Dam is at the end of the "T" that is closest to the Qu'Appelle River. *Adapted from Prairie Farm Rehabilitation Administration,* Full Development Possibilities in the Saskatchewan River Basin *(Regina: Hydrology Division, 1952), Figure 1; E. Kuiper, "Sediment Transport and Delta Formation,"* Journal of the Hydraulics Division *86, 2 (1960): 55–68; and* CanVec Series [Admin., Land, Hydro] *(Ottawa: Natural Resources Canada, 2019).*

agricultural prairies, a dream that hinged on the damming of the South Saskatchewan River.

This chapter focuses on the PFRA's work in advancing the SSRP. The first section addresses the PFRA's efforts to plan this regional redesign, an effort that turned both on careful study of the local environment and on the enlisting of American expertise in water-resources management. The second section considers what happened when PFRA plans ran up against political reluctance to move ahead with the SSRP. This reluctance proved difficult to resolve, partly because scientific and engineering experts were divided over the merits of the project. Following James C. Scott's attention to the differences between local and state knowledges in *Seeing Like a State: How Certain Schemes to Improve the Human Condition Have Failed* (1998), studies of high-modernist undertakings often emphasize a gulf between state experts or officials and affected locals, with state representatives typically keen to move ahead with infrastructure projects and locals reluctant to endure the resulting disruption and destruction. In contrast, the first two sections of this chapter focus on debates over the SSRP among scientific experts and political leaders. Paying attention to these debates positions us to understand this high-modernist episode as characterized by ongoing negotiation within the state itself. Rather than a logical outgrowth of state power and expert authority, consensus around the SSRP involved a building process as intensive and protracted as the physical construction of the infrastructure.

This chapter also considers, in its final section, the circumstances that ultimately positioned the project to go ahead. These circumstances derived from change in government and in the prairie region. But what looks like changed circumstances at one analytic scale is revealed as continuity at another. As George Spence suggested by casting the SSRP as an enduring dream in his book's title, the decision to move forward with the project reflected a trajectory that was established on the Prairies with agricultural settlement and that continued throughout the hardships of the 1930s and beyond.

Deciding

The construction of a dam along the South Saskatchewan River was proposed in 1859 by Henry Youle Hind, who worked as a teacher and researcher at Trinity College in Toronto. Hind participated in an expedition to the Prairie West, and his work, if dubious from a scientific perspective, contributed to Canadian officials' belief that significant portions of the region were suitable for agricultural colonization.[3] Hind thought that a dam might facilitate steamboat navigation for some 950 kilometres through the Prairie West, providing key transportation infrastructure to speed the colonization and exploitation of this region.[4] Hind was not the only early colonizer with dam-based dreams for the region. Federal government agent William Pearce, for example, was convinced that various alterations to Alberta rivers and waterbodies might improve regional economic prospects.[5] Envisioning radical changes to the landscape of the south-central Prairies was an early preoccupation for non-Indigenous newcomers who, like Hind and Pearce, believed that the power and resources of the state might make real their dreams.

The PFRA's ambitious plans for regional redesign fitted within this historical trajectory of infrastructure colonialism. The PFRA began investigating the prospect of damming the main stem of the South Saskatchewan

River in the mid-1940s. A major aim of early agency activity was to locate one or more sites with foundation conditions and local topography suitable for dam construction.[6] But this stretch of the river was not ideal in relation to either criteria. The deeply incised channel of the South Saskatchewan River meant that irrigation was thought by some to require pumping to deliver water to farms, with the related expense threatening to tip project costs into unfavourable territory. Another challenge was the character of the ground at the various sites proposed for dam construction.[7] The subsurface prevalence of Bearpaw shale, a notoriously unstable material, meant that there was significant concern about the foundation on which a dam would rest. At this early point and over years to come, there were experts associated with the PFRA who doubted the project's viability and value.[8] For many doubters, the physical challenges of the site and the inflated costs related to overcoming these challenges figured large in their objections.

Despite the project's challenges, the idea of damming the South Saskatchewan gained momentum in the postwar context, as the SSRP became one among many large-scale infrastructure projects across Canada that were under consideration. The St. Lawrence Seaway and the Canso Causeway are examples of other contenders for federal government resources throughout the period of postwar reconstruction and beyond.[9] To some extent, these various projects were in competition with each other for federal dollars. Nevertheless, any proposed project rested on confidence in the state's capacity to bring the undertaking successfully to completion, so each contender served to validate the assumptions that underwrote them all. Also, a project approved for one geographical region could readily be leveraged in efforts to secure the go-ahead for a project in another part of the country. For reasons including the dominance of high-modernist perspectives, interregional competition within Canada's federal system, improvements in engineering capacity, and the imperatives of postwar reconstruction, the mid-twentieth century was defined in part by government involvement in the construction of large-scale infrastructure.

Following several years of intensive fieldwork up and down the South Saskatchewan River, PFRA agents succeeded in establishing the viability of constructing the SSRP near what was termed an elbow in the river, a sharp change in direction from northeast to northwest. The agency proposed to locate a large dam about 200 kilometres northwest of Regina, Saskatchewan's capital, and 100 kilometres south of Saskatoon, the province's other major city. A second dam was required because the anticipated reservoir depth would overflow the height of land separating the South Saskatchewan River from the Qu'Appelle River, which flowed west into the Assiniboine River. This smaller dam would allow for control over the release of water from the South Saskatchewan River toward the Qu'Appelle River. Although there was concern about effects on local land use, PFRA officials worried relatively little at this stage about any destructive consequences of the project, whether with regard to the dams themselves, the substantial reservoir that would stretch between them, or broader changes in regional water-flow patterns.

In identifying a suitable site for the SSRP, PFRA agents depended on careful examination of the local landscape. They also drew on connections with experts far removed from the project site. In establishing the viability of the SSRP, the PFRA relied on guidance and support from prominent American engineers. This was not a new practice. As early as 1939, PFRA agents were engaging with colleagues from the Bureau of Reclamation in the United States, looking to better understand problems that the PFRA was having with water-control infrastructure and to increase their ability to plan successful projects.[10] Notably, work on the St. Mary Dam in the 1940s involved consultation with American engineering experts, even as the dam itself was embroiled in diplomatic tensions between Washington and Ottawa.[11] Throughout the PFRA's early years, its failure to pay salaries sufficient to attract and retain highly skilled engineers and scientists contributed to reliance on outside experts.[12] A further factor was the PFRA's limited access within Canada to specialized research equipment.[13] Over years, for various reasons, the PFRA developed its plans and validated its proposals through engagements with well-established American experts in water-resources engineering.

For the PFRA, a particularly important relationship was with General Harley B. Ferguson of the United States Army Corps of Engineers. As reported by George Spence, Ferguson provided ongoing input over multiple years, an arrangement that the PFRA saw to have "worked out greatly to the advantage of our organization."[14] Elaborating further, Spence explained that PFRA engineers benefited from "day to day consultation with an eminent engineer" as well as with other highly qualified experts within what Spence regarded as "one of the greatest, if not the greatest, engineering organizations in the world."[15] The PFRA's reliance on American experts, well established before work began on the SSRP, only increased as a result of the complexity of environmental circumstances along the South Saskatchewan River. Foundation conditions in particular were persistently problematic, proving a challenge that experts believed surpassed in difficulty those encountered in previous dam-building efforts.[16] Ultimately, the assertion by PFRA agents that they had located a viable dam site along the

South Saskatchewan River took some of its authority from the involvement of prominent American engineers.

With a viable site identified, the PFRA began filling out the argument in favour of the SSRP. The PFRA's case for the SSRP depended on the infrastructure's capacity to serve multiple purposes. By the early twentieth century, spurred by growing demand for hydroelectricity, engineers and government officials in the United States were intentionally designing water-management infrastructure to serve multiple purposes.[17] Irrigation and hydropower were typically emphasized, but multipurpose projects could also take account of other considerations like enhanced domestic water supply and the creation of recreational opportunities. Although debate persisted around its viability and utility, the multipurpose approach to infrastructure planning became associated with an efficient, conservation-minded effort at river basin management.[18] The approach underwrote massive projects of human and environmental change like the reworking of the waterscape along the North China Plain in China and the efforts of the Tennessee Valley Authority in the United States to implement infrastructure-driven solutions to the area's intractable poverty.[19] In the mid-twentieth century, the virtues that proponents associated with multipurpose water management were fundamental to American involvement in overseas infrastructure development.[20]

The multipurpose approach to the design of water-management infrastructure was an odd fit with the original mandate of the PFRA. The agency's early focus on agricultural adjustment did not readily reconcile with the construction of infrastructure designed to serve purposes beyond those such as irrigation and stock watering that directly supported farming. Still, by the 1940s, PFRA officials were interested in multipurpose water-resources management.[21] The PFRA's investigations of the SSRP built on this early interest. This connection is clear in a 1951 summary report that the PFRA generated on the basis of various experts' examinations of the proposed infrastructure, which included attention to municipal water supply, stream control, and recreation as well as irrigation and hydropower.[22] In years to come, the SSRP would be celebrated by PFRA leadership as "the first multiple purpose project that had been proposed in Western Canada."[23] This view is in line with legal scholar and historian Jamie Benidickson's assessment that the PFRA constituted "a comparatively early version of integrated resource planning."[24]

The PFRA's work on the 1951 summary report signals not just the new importance of the multipurpose approach in prairie water-resources management but also a broadening of the PFRA's established concerns. The agency had long argued that its various activities were justified not just by stabilized agricultural production but also by how stabilized production would underwrite an improved quality of life for farm families. In investigating the SSRP as a multipurpose project, the agency involved itself in envisioning an improved quality of life not just for farm families but also for other prairie residents: anyone who might use electricity or swim in a reservoir, even if they did not engage in farming. This agency involvement amounted to a significant expansion of its purview, a broadening that positioned the PFRA at the fore of state-led efforts to, as proponents saw it, engineer improvements in human life through infrastructure construction.

The PFRA's 1951 summary report quantified the various benefits anticipated from the SSRP. Despite the multipurpose orientation of the report, the economic case for the SSRP rested in particular on irrigation and power. Estimates indicated that the project would support the development of 500,000 acres of irrigated land and the production of 475 million kilowatt hours of electricity per year.[25] The report also affixed a price tag: about $103,700,000 for key works.[26] The thrust of the report is captured in a phrase from the shorter outline version, also released in April 1951, which held that the project's central infrastructure could be constructed without encountering "any difficulties that modern engineering skill cannot solve within reasonable cost."[27]

SSRP advocates sought to use the PFRA-authored summary report as the basis to proceed. Minister of Agriculture James Gardiner was among those keen to move forward. In a May 1951 federal government Cabinet meeting, Gardiner actively worked to convert skeptics. He presented the SSRP as a hinge in the history of the prairie region, one that would favourably swing the fortunes of residents. As Gardiner put it, "If nature had placed a ridge of rock across the South Saskatchewan River at the point in question thus creating a lake the whole outlook of those making homes in the area would have been changed."[28] Gardiner went on to note that, although nature had failed in this regard, the Government of Canada could and should undertake this transformation. Gardiner's comments reveal the central place of this project in a long-standing vision of prairie development. The SSRP was the culmination of a dream of regional redesign first expressed by early colonizers who conceived infrastructure-driven transformation as fundamental to the success of a settler society across the Prairie West. Regional redesign as advanced by the PFRA was not only derived from circumstances on the agricultural Prairies but also informed by relationships among technical experts that extended across the

Canadian-American border and by the global influence of the multipurpose approach to water-management infrastructure. As made clear by the agency's preliminary work on the SSRP, the PFRA's scope extended beyond the agricultural Prairies and the region's farming families.

Reconsidering

Although Gardiner was fully convinced that the Government of Canada should move ahead with the SSRP, not all of his colleagues in government were on side. Dams have been termed "brute force" technologies by historian Paul Josephson for their radical effects on landscapes and ecologies.[29] But the SSRP provides an example of how, in a mid-twentieth-century Canadian context at least, manufacturing consensus around a particular large-scale engineering project could be a massive undertaking in itself. The protracted negotiations over the SSRP reflected competing imperatives within the Canadian federal government, as well as disagreements among the provincial governments of the Prairies. Negotiations over the SSRP also demonstrated the fraught intersection between political power and expert knowledge. Ultimately, various sources of complication afflicted the process of deciding whether to proceed with the SSRP. For project advocates like George Spence and James Gardiner, the realization of a grand vision for the prairie region hung in the balance.

In pitching the SSRP, the PFRA was a regionally focused federal agency proposing a Saskatchewan-based project to a federal government with responsibility for the nation at large. Liberal prime minister Louis St. Laurent was not known for his receptiveness to prairie concerns. In fact, Gardiner found reason to worry about Liberal support in the West when St. Laurent came to power, a circumstance not entirely attributable to interpersonal tensions deriving from St. Laurent's 1948 defeat of Gardiner for the party leadership.[30] In the early 1950s, St. Laurent remained unconvinced by Gardiner's argument that the SSRP should rank as a national priority.[31] Additional complexity derived from concern about the SSRP stemming from Saskatchewan's neighbouring provinces. Because the Saskatchewan River watershed extended from the Rocky Mountains to Lake Winnipeg, Alberta and Manitoba were interested in water management along the South Saskatchewan River. Downstream, Manitoba worried that the project would affect its ability to generate hydropower through anticipated infrastructure in the northern portion of that province.[32] Upstream, Alberta favoured an alternative project over the SSRP, one with the potential to bring more direct benefits to that province.[33] Ultimately, disagreements among the prairie provinces further weakened whatever regional claim the Prairies might otherwise have made on Ottawa.

The character of the SSRP as a project designed to serve multiple purposes also came into play. Hydroelectricity generation was positioned alongside irrigation water supply as a key purpose that the project would serve. But the power question proved controversial. One issue was disagreement between Regina and Ottawa over which government should pay for the power-related elements of the project.[34] Saskatchewan was unwilling to bear all related costs, but Ottawa maintained that power was a provincial responsibility. As any deviation from this principle might have implications for power-generating projects nationally, the prospects for compromise were limited. Another issue was ongoing contestation over the power potential of the project. Uncertainty over how much power could actually be generated by the SSRP only served to further intensify intergovernmental disputes.[35]

Considering competing imperatives nationally, disagreements among prairie provinces, and complications related to power, the onus fell on SSRP advocates to make a compelling case for the project. In this context, the various reports produced and arranged by the PFRA were deficient. Generally, these reports were supportive but not brimming with enthusiasm. Assertions of the project's technical and financial viability were not the same as proclamations of the project's promise to drive radical improvements to regional prospects. The sort of high-flown rhetoric characterizing George Spence's rendering of the SSRP in *Survival of a Vision* was simply absent from the reports marshalled by the PFRA, and this absence concerned project advocates. For his part, James Gardiner bemoaned that, on reading the relevant PFRA reports, he found himself with "less confidence in the project than I had before I read them."[36]

What Gardiner saw as the agency's worrying lack of enthusiasm reflected changes within the PFRA. George Spence, the agency's first director, was a political appointee. He spoke the language of politics, often deploying overreaching rhetoric that trumpeted PFRA projects as triumphs. This tendency, evident early on in the cross-Canada speaking tour that he undertook soon after his appointment to head up the PFRA, persisted throughout his years with the agency. When Spence left the PFRA in 1947, he was replaced by L.B. Thomson. Although Thomson had political ambitions of his own, ambitions that included an unsuccessful bid for leadership of the Saskatchewan Liberal Party in 1954, he was by training and profession an agricultural scientist.[37] Thomson was far less inclined to high-flown rhetoric in his work for the PFRA, whether with respect to the SSRP or other agency activities. Under Thomson's direction, the PFRA regularized its operations in keeping with the standards of practice characterizing the fields of expertise that bore most heavily on the agency's work: agricultural science, water-resources engineering, and agricultural economics. Agency recommendations took on a measured tone in keeping with these fields.

The absence of an enthusiastic endorsement from the PFRA complicated Gardiner's efforts to move Cabinet colleagues toward approval of the SSRP.[38] In this context, Prime Minister Louis St. Laurent ultimately determined that a royal commission was necessary to further investigate the project, and the commission was officially appointed in August 1951.[39] Gardiner was frustrated with what he took for the intransigence of his Liberal Party colleagues, but he felt that a royal commission was eminently manageable. As he had previously described it, the need was simply for some respected authority to do what PFRA experts had not done: to assert with confidence that "I am convinced that this thing [the SSRP] is right."[40]

The work of setting up the Royal Commission on the South Saskatchewan River Project fell to Gardiner, and he sought to staff it with international experts sympathetic to ambitious water-engineering projects. For the role of commission chair, Gardiner looked to David Lilienthal, head of the Tennessee Valley Authority.[41] Disappointingly for Gardiner, Lilienthal was unavailable, as were other preferred candidates.[42] Ultimately appointed were Dr. T.H. Hogg, G.A. Gaherty, and Dr. John A. Widstoe. Hogg and Gaherty had backgrounds in hydropower, and Widstoe was, in Gardiner's effusive terms, the "greatest living authority on irrigation."[43] Widstoe also had some prior experience in Canadian water management, having authored a 1925 report that underlined the positive effects of Alberta irrigation developments. With Widstoe aboard, Gardiner was optimistic that the Royal Commission would be an expeditious exercise in producing the enthusiastic endorsement that he believed would move the project ahead.[44]

From Gardiner's perspective, however, the Royal Commission soon went astray. There was substantial disagreement over the commission's terms of reference. It seems that Gardiner and his colleagues had anticipated that the commission might undertake the modest tasks of reviewing existing project assessments and offering an opinion on the importance of the SSRP "as a venture essential to the development of Canada and particularly the Prairie Provinces."[45] But the commission's terms of reference were susceptible to broader interpretation. Commissioners were instructed to adjudicate two matters: whether anticipated social and economic benefits were sufficient to merit project costs and whether the project was the best way to use the involved natural resources. These terms of reference could be taken to require a detailed economic analysis of the intended project and to demand consideration of other ways to use prairie land and water. It was the broader interpretation of the terms of reference that commissioners adopted.[46]

In December 1951, St. Laurent reported in the House of Commons that the work of the Royal Commission was going in a direction that, although not wrong, was different from what had been anticipated by those who had drafted the terms of reference.[47] By that point, it was clear that there was an additional factor complicating the work of the commission: serious illness afflicting two of its members, Hogg and Widstoe.[48] For project advocates, there were also other worrying developments. Although fully expressed only after the Royal Commission concluded its work, there was already concern that Gaherty was, as a result of a career in the private sector, inclined to oppose public investment in hydropower infrastructure.[49] Secretary to the Royal Commission B.T. Richardson was seen by some as hostile and not well matched with the position.[50] For James Gardiner and other project advocates, all of these factors were very concerning.

By early 1952, it was clear that commissioners were undertaking an intensive investigation of the SSRP. In response, and at the request of Gardiner, the PFRA scrambled to make its case for the project. This initiative included an effort to validate for commissioners the project's viability from an engineering perspective, which culminated in an in-person meeting in Washington attended by commissioners Hogg and Gaherty, commission secretary Richardson, PFRA officials, and prominent international engineers, including Harley B. Ferguson.[51] Taking place at a critical moment in relation to the SSRP, this meeting was an excellent illustration of the importance of American expertise in the PFRA's work. PFRA engineer G.L. MacKenzie was satisfied with what the in-person meeting achieved. As he saw it, "there was no uncertainty left as to the feasibility and safety of constructing the dam."[52] But if the matter was settled from an engineering viewpoint, the question of economic viability remained unresolved. Somewhat ominously for those favouring the project, MacKenzie ended his account of the meeting by noting that the members of the Royal Commission might "differ with us as to probable cost."

The Royal Commission returned its report on the SSRP in late December 1952. MacKenzie had been correct in anticipating economic concerns. In their report, commissioners noted that "at present the economic returns to the Canadian people" of the SSRP "are not commensurate with the cost."[53] Commissioners also worried that the existing scientific understanding of the prairie environment, incomplete as they found it to be, indicated that the SSRP "does not represent the most profitable and desirable use which can be made of the physical resources involved."[54] According to the Royal Commission, the SSRP was deficient both in terms of whether the benefits justified the costs and in terms of whether the project reflected the best use of resources. Commissioners recommended against immediately proceeding with the project. Although the report acknowledged that further study or changed economic contexts might make the project more appealing, it included nothing remotely like the enthusiastic endorsement that Gardiner had desired.

Supporters of the SSRP were quick to condemn the commission's report for what they saw as inaccurate economic estimates and an outdated approach to understanding the project's benefits.[55] For his part, PFRA director L.B. Thomson took the opportunity presented by the Royal Commission on Canada's Economic Prospects, launched in 1955, to respond with a brief that presented the SSRP favourably.[56] More broadly, the critical reception received by the report of the Royal Commission on the South Saskatchewan Regional Plan demonstrated the persistence of disagreement among experts and politicians over the value and importance of this large-scale infrastructure project. Expert authority provided no meaningful refuge from the political work of balancing competing interests, making difficult decisions, and taking responsibility for their consequences. Rather, experts and politicians alike remained thoroughly engaged in the ongoing effort of negotiating high modernism.

Reframing

Amid widespread dissatisfaction with the findings of the Royal Commission on the South Saskatchewan Regional Plan, neither Regina nor Ottawa interpreted the report as foreclosing further discussion about the project. Liberal prime minister St. Laurent, one eye on an anticipated federal election, offered comments suggesting that the project might yet go ahead.[57] But in the aftermath of his 1953 election victory, St. Laurent once more backed away from the SSRP. In April 1955, he indicated that there was no immediate prospect that the federal government would proceed, citing heavy defence expenditures in the Cold War context.[58]

In the wake of St. Laurent's continued waffling, two Saskatchewan-based undertakings were significant in changing the context for the SSRP. These two undertakings were quite different in character and mandate, with one consisting of the ongoing efforts of an advocacy organization and one reflecting the operation of a Saskatchewan royal commission. But the work of those involved in each of these initiatives, as well as the provincial scale at which they both operated, allowed for new perspectives on the SSRP. The resulting reframing helped to pave the way for the SSRP to move forward.

The Saskatchewan Rivers Development Association (SRDA) was created in April 1946 with the aim of "promoting the conservation and utilization of the water of the South Saskatchewan River for irrigation, power development and as sources of domestic water supply."[59] The organization understood its mandate to involve both advocacy directed at politicians and education aimed at farmers.[60] Membership in the SRDA was made up primarily of groups and individuals who anticipated benefiting, whether directly or indirectly, from further development of water resources. Chambers of Commerce in potentially irrigated areas and adjacent locales were typically supportive, feeling that their members would benefit from anticipated population growth and economic stimulus. Much of the SRDA's work focused on pushing for the SSRP.

The SRDA was a Saskatchewan variant on the established global pattern of irrigation advocacy groups undertaking significant promotional labour. Historian John Weaver has described irrigation advocacy as a global crusade, one that aimed to build desire for infrastructure expansion.[61] Irrigation advocacy groups were operating in southern Alberta by the early twentieth century.[62] The creation of the SRDA reflected the efforts of Canadian irrigation promoters to mimic the advocacy activity that underwrote irrigation development in the United States.[63] By the mid-1940s, the SRDA and the PFRA were working together to advance what they saw as their common goal: moving ahead with the SSRP.[64] After Spence's 1947 departure from the PFRA, he continued to lobby for the SSRP, at least occasionally enjoying the support of the PFRA in doing so.[65] Spence also worked with the SRDA as a means of amplifying the organization's ability to press for further water development, corresponding with SRDA leaders and delivering speeches at the organization's meetings.[66]

The rhetoric used by the SRDA in its promotional work reflected the influence of George Spence. This influence was evident in the SRDA's written submission to the Royal Commission on the South Saskatchewan Regional Plan.[67] The submission presented the SSRP as an infrastructure project with the potential to radically transform agricultural prospects and human lives. It made the case through an effusive rhetorical style that was similar to the one regularly used by Spence in his time as director of the PFRA and that was also on display in the briefs that Spence himself submitted to the Royal Commission.[68] After Spence's departure from the PFRA, the agency had adopted a more dispassionate tone in communicating about the SSRP and other agency activities. It was this rhetorical shift that had surprised and disappointed James Gardiner in the assessments of the SSRP that were released by the PFRA. Ultimately, the SRDA became a major vehicle through which the sort of promotional work no longer undertaken by the PFRA was continued throughout the late 1940s and into the 1950s. The SRDA even promulgated the framing of the SSRP as a moral responsibility of the federal government stemming from the mistakes of prairie settlement.[69]

The SRDA also helped to advance the SSRP in material ways. Throughout the mid-1950s, when the adverse findings of the Royal Commission persisted as a stumbling block, the agency worked to facilitate intergovernmental negotiations.[70] The SRDA's efforts contributed to a 1954 tentative agreement between Ottawa and Regina, one intended to allow for progress on the SSRP.[71] Although this agreement was not immediately adopted, the agency continued its efforts, which included regular visits to Ottawa by SRDA representatives.[72] The SRDA took on this activity at the urging of James Gardiner, who was positioned to understand the sort of advocacy that might produce results.[73] Some years later, the SRDA's dogged commitment to advancing the SSRP was recognized when former SRDA president William B. Tufts received Saskatchewan's salesperson of the year award.[74]

The second organization involved in reshaping the context for the SSRP was Saskatchewan's Royal Commission on Agriculture and Rural Life (RCARL). Formed in 1952 by that province's Co-operative Commonwealth Federation (CCF) government, the RCARL was conceived to reckon with the effects of agricultural change. With farms increasing in size and rural population declining accordingly, the RCARL was to consider the challenges to maintaining public infrastructure like education, roads, and local government while also wrestling with residents' desires for modern improvements like electricity and water. The RCARL demonstrated the sweeping ambition characterizing the CCF's efforts to reckon with Saskatchewan's various challenges.[75] It also reflected transnational mid-twentieth-century expert discourse on how to drive positive change in human lives. RCARL commissioners understood themselves as engaged in planning for what they called "rural improvement," noting that this phrase was synonymous with the concept of "rural development."[76] Historian Will Langford has explained that development reflected "the idea that rational action can shape socio-economic processes to improve the lives of human beings."[77] Notions of development circulated nationally and transnationally throughout the mid-twentieth century. In Canada, Langford has established that development operated through a patchwork of state-sponsored efforts to drive what advocates saw as positive change.

The RCARL began its work with an intensive process of public consultation reflecting the desire of the commission's leadership to enlist the insights of rural people – in effect, to function as the people's commission, as the RCARL became known.[78] Community forums (ninety-five separate events involving some 8,000 attendees) and public hearings (fifty-seven separate events) were key ways that the commission sought to engage Saskatchewan farming families and communities.[79] These various activities, concentrated over the RCARL's first few years of work, prompted widespread discussion about the problems besetting rural Saskatchewan. RCARL's public consultations helped to cultivate understanding of ongoing transformations in prairie agriculture. By providing a forum for rural residents, the commission validated residents' concerns and underlined the importance of addressing these worries.

Historian Wyatt Mark Skovron has argued that the RCARL's orientation toward public engagement was in tension with commissioners' sympathies for high-modernist, state-sponsored solutions to the problems that the commission brought into focus.[80] A high-modernist orientation is evident in the commission's reliance on input from experts affiliated with universities, governments, and nongovernment organizations, which featured prominently in the fourteen reports that the RCARL released between 1955 and 1957.[81] It is also apparent in the tendency to circumscribe input and to dismiss complaints from rural people, which Skovron sees as a feature of the RCARL's latter years of work. And insofar as the SSRP was an archetypical high-modernist undertaking, the RCARL's bias is clear in the endorsement of the SSRP contained in the commission's thirteenth report. Released in April 1957 and focused on the fundamental question of farm income, this report asserted that "there are great benefits to be secured by the construction" of the SSRP.[82] For SSRP advocates like Gardiner who had been disappointed with the findings of the Royal Commission on the South Saskatchewan Regional Plan, the RCARL offered the unqualified endorsement of the SSRP that they had long sought.

The RCARL's endorsement was particularly significant because it implied that the SSRP made sense not just as a continuation of the process of agricultural colonization but also as a remedy for the particular challenges facing Saskatchewan in the mid-twentieth century. A major concern was electricity, which as of the late 1950s, was produced in Saskatchewan only through thermal generation.[83] The province's geography, as Saskatchewan minister of agriculture Isidore Charles Nollet put it, "provided no cheap power sites on the two great rivers of ours, such as nature provided in Manitoba at Pine Falls or in the Rocky Mountains where all you have to do is dump some cement between two sides of a rocky gorge and you've got all kinds of power potential."[84] As a result of limited access to electricity, rural electrification was slowed and economic diversification was impeded.[85] SSRP-generated hydropower was understood as a potential fix. Another worrying issue was Saskatchewan's declining number of farms, which negatively affected rural communities and complicated efforts to improve rural infrastructure. SSRP-facilitated irrigation was expected to promote more intensive cultivation of smaller farms, serving as a brake on the worrisome trend toward the larger farm unit.[86] The SSRP was also anticipated to provide water for modern domestic purposes and for further industrial development, which might underwrite economic diversification. The Royal Commission on the SSRP had soft-pedalled its negative assessment by indicating that perhaps the SSRP would seem more promising at another moment. The RCARL's documenting of Saskatchewan's various problems amounted to an argument that the moment for the SSRP had arrived.

In reshaping the context in which federal government decision makers considered the SSRP, the persistent enthusiasm of the SRDA was significant. So was the RCARL's call for rural improvement, which the SSRP seemed positioned to answer. Further, the SRDA and the RCARL shared a provincial focus that had consequences for how the SSRP was assessed. Project advocates understood the SSRP as the solution to the problems of lagging development that were particularly significant in Saskatchewan. In the assessment of historian Bill Waiser, by the postwar years, Saskatchewan was "a largely rural, agricultural province out of step with much of the rest of postwar Canada."[87] Some of the earlier opposition to the SSRP stemmed from Alberta and Manitoba, provinces with leaders who believed that the SSRP might not serve their interests. The unfavourable findings of the Royal Commission on the SSRP were based on an assessment of the SSRP's prospective returns to Canada at large. The operation of the RCARL and the SRDA, insofar as each prioritized Saskatchewan over regional or national frameworks, situated the project at the provincial scale. And Saskatchewan seemed particularly in need of the modernization that the SSRP promised. Together, the RCARL and the SRDA contributed to a significant reframing of the SSRP, one that powerfully emphasized the importance of the transformations that the project was anticipated to deliver.

Despite the positioning of the SSRP as a solution to pressing problems in Saskatchewan, right up to the June 1957 federal election, Prime Minister Louis St. Laurent proved unwilling to commit to proceeding. Although St. Laurent did not change his mind, Canadian voters changed theirs. St. Laurent's Liberal Party lost the 1957 federal election to John Diefenbaker's Progressive Conservatives. Diefenbaker was a westerner from Saskatchewan, and he vaulted to power in large measure as a result of protest voting against the perceived lassitude of the long-governing Liberals and, on the Prairies, against the seeming indifference of Ottawa toward the Prairie West. For years, Diefenbaker had pushed for a federal commitment to move ahead with the SSRP.[88] The new government that Diefenbaker came to head was a minority Parliament, and this served only to increase the pressure on him to fulfill commitments to the communities that had voted him into power, including those in Saskatchewan.

Diefenbaker's way forward was facilitated not just by the work of the RCARL and the SRDA but also by an easing of the economic context around the SSRP. Power was no longer a major sticking point between Regina and Ottawa, with the federal government exhibiting a new-found willingness to contribute to projects nationwide that had prospects of generating power.[89] For Regina, improved economic circumstances made the provincial financial contribution less daunting.[90] At the same time, economic diversification still seemed urgent, and provincial leaders hoped that greater availability of water and power would help. In 1958, the involved governments agreed to terms for the construction of the SSRP.[91] Canada would build the main dam on the South Saskatchewan River and the subsidiary dam near the Qu'Appelle River. Costs of construction would be split between Ottawa and Regina, with the provincial share amounting to 25 percent of costs and capped at $25 million. Additionally, the province would bear major responsibility for hydropower and irrigation facilities. The PFRA was put in charge of constructing the largest piece of water-control infrastructure, what would become known as the Gardiner Dam.

As a large-scale water-engineering project, the SSRP had transformative effects on environments and communities both adjacent to the infrastructure and farther afield. Additionally, the negotiation of this high-modernist project itself had transformative effects. The process further integrated

FIGURE 4.2 The South Saskatchewan River early in the construction of the Gardiner Dam, 1959. Although preliminary work has begun, the prior landscape and river are still evident. In the left foreground of the image is the staging area used by the PFRA and contractors in infrastructure construction and project management. *Library and Archives Canada, National Film Board fonds, RG 53, e011177259.*

the PFRA into transnational communities of expertise and cemented the PFRA's participation in projects bearing broadly on the lives of prairie residents, even those not directly involved in agriculture. The decision to move ahead with the SSRP signalled the federal government's willingness to further invest in infrastructure-driven efforts to induce what the government understood as improvements in human lives. This mode of thinking on the part of government leaders would underpin other government initiatives in coming years. As explained before the 1959 annual meeting of the SRDA by Alvin Hamilton, Diefenbaker's recently appointed minister of northern affairs and national resources, the SSRP was viewed as "a good example of the kind of resource development required in Canada."[92] The SSRP, a project developed by the PFRA and advanced to address underdevelopment in Saskatchewan, was being cast as a model for the conservation of natural resources nationwide.

Conclusion

In 2020, Saskatchewan premier Scott Moe announced his government's intention to dramatically expand Lake Diefenbaker's irrigation infrastructure.[93] This effort is meant to address what advocates see as the unfulfilled potential of the SSRP. Although some of the anticipated benefits of the SSRP "have been realized," many have not paid off "to the level originally anticipated."[94] Of the multiple purposes that the SSRP was to serve, most fully realized have been the generation of hydroelectricity and the supply of water for municipal and industrial purposes.[95] Among various unfulfilled promises, irrigation ranks high. Some fifteen years after the SSRP's completion, there were only 37,000 acres under the ditch.[96] By 2008, the amount of agricultural land irrigated with water from the SSRP had risen to about 100,000 acres.[97] Even this coverage fell far short of the 500,000 acres that the PFRA had originally estimated that the project would irrigate. The SSRP brought substantial change to environments and communities in the Prairie West. But irrigation, which along with hydropower was a key justification for the SSRP, proved a significant disappointment.

The first part of the chapter examined the PFRA's ambitious efforts to use mid-twentieth-century engineering expertise to realize early colonizer dreams for the prairie region. It demonstrated the PFRA's orientation to transnational communities of engineering and resource-management expertise. These communities of expertise were as important as local prairie conditions in defining how the PFRA proposed to remake a significant portion of the Saskatchewan River watershed. Despite how the SSRP received approval from authorities outside Canada, the project remained profoundly contested among the experts and politicians associated with federal and provincial governments. Ultimately, this chapter has detailed the protracted negotiations that eventually resulted in a decision to move ahead with the SSRP.

Moving ahead with the SSRP had consequences beyond the directly affected communities and landscapes. Some of the practices and perspectives that underwrote the SSRP would figure in other mid-twentieth-century federal government efforts to conserve natural resources. As agency leadership broadened the PFRA beyond agriculture to tackle multipurpose projects and oriented the agency toward the well-being of all prairie residents, not just farmers, the PFRA came to function as a model and inspiration for federal efforts both to improve the management of natural resources and to improve human lives. From this perspective, the PFRA served as a prototype for development in Canada.

5
Rehabilitation and Colonialism
The PFRA and Prairie Indigenous Peoples, 1930s–60s

Prairie nature writer Trevor Herriot, long an advocate for preserving wildlife and natural spaces in the Prairie West, has described an experience of grappling with the dispossession of prairie Indigenous peoples. Working to protect Prairie Farm Rehabilitation Administration (PFRA) community pastures threatened by administrative change, Herriot became aware that, in the 1930s, the Métis community of Ste. Madeleine had been displaced through the creation of a community pasture along the Saskatchewan-Manitoba border. For Herriot, this event is both a specific historical injustice and an illustration of how settler colonialism operated in the Prairie West. Reflecting on well-known regional histories of agricultural settlement and on the underlying processes of Indigenous dispossession, processes that remain less widely understood, Herriot concludes that colonialism is "an utterly unreliable narrator."[1]

Writing a more robust history of the Prairie Farm Rehabilitation Administration means taking account of the ways that its activities affected prairie Indigenous peoples. It means considering how the agency resonates with existing scholarly literature documenting the harmful effects of state policies and practices on regional Indigenous communities.[2] Understanding the connections between rehabilitation and colonialism on the Canadian Prairies is an essential part of the effort, as Hannah Holleman puts it in her study of the 1930s Dust Bowl in the United States, to move "beyond superficial approaches to historical changes associated with imperialism and capitalist development."[3]

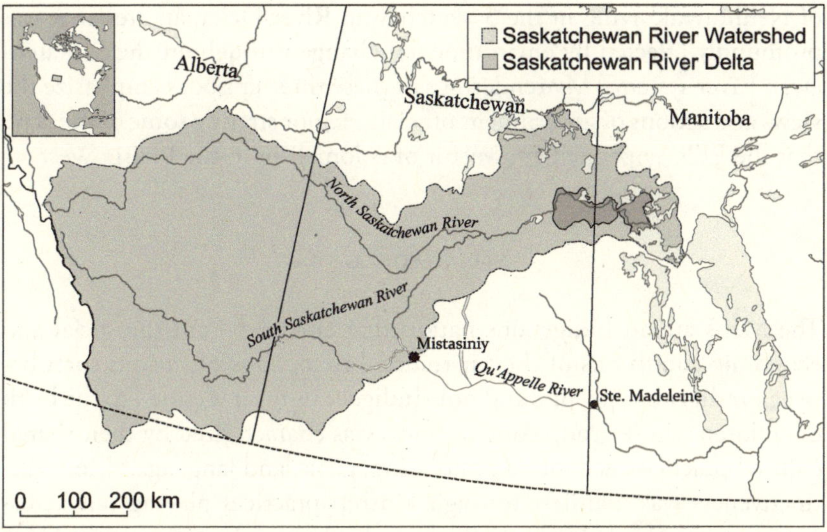

FIGURE 5.1 Ste. Madeleine, Mistasiniy, and the Saskatchewan River Delta in relation to the Saskatchewan River watershed. *Adapted from Prairie Farm Rehabilitation Administration,* Full Development Possibilities in the Saskatchewan River Basin *(Regina: Hydrology Division, 1952), Figure 1; E. Kuiper, "Sediment Transport and Delta Formation,"* Journal of the Hydraulics Division *86, 2 (1960): 55–68; Deanna Christensen,* Ahtahkakoop: The Epic Account of a Plains Cree Head Chief, His People, and Their Struggle for Survival, 1816–1896 *(Altona, MB: Friesens, 2000), inside cover; Ken Zeilig and Victoria Zeilig,* Ste. Madeleine: Community without a Town, Metis Elders in Interview *(Winnipeg: Pemmican, 1987), 13; Razak Abu, Maureen G. Reed, and Timothy D. Jardine, "Using Two-Eyed Seeing to Bridge Western Science and Indigenous Knowledge Systems and Understand Long-Term Change in the Saskatchewan River Delta, Canada,"* International Journal of Water Resources Development *36, 5 (2020): 761; Trevor Herriot,* Towards a Prairie Atonement *(Regina: University of Regina Press, 2016), viii–ix; and* CanVec Series [Admin., Land, Hydro] *(Ottawa: Natural Resources Canada, 2019).*

Historian Brittany Luby has made clear that mid-twentieth-century state development policy, although typically justified by advocates for its role in serving the so-called public good, often drove poverty and created hardship among Indigenous peoples.[4] As Luby puts it, "the benefits of development were inequitably distributed in the past."[5] In an effort to consider the place of the Prairie Farm Rehabilitation Administration within this broader history of inequitable development, this chapter begins with the same episode of Métis displacement considered by Herriot. It then addresses the destruction of Mistasiniy, a Sacred Site of particular importance in nēhiyawak histories and worldviews. Finally, it analyzes the experiences of Nehinuwuk living in the Saskatchewan River Delta, an area that was profoundly affected by environmental change throughout the Saskatchewan River system.[6] My renderings of these three episodes emphasize the views and actions of government officials, demonstrating some of the ways that the PFRA operated as a vector of colonialism in the Prairie West.

Ste. Madeleine

The Métis are an Indigenous nation that emerged from the social and economic conditions of the fur trade.[7] Interactions of various sorts between Indigenous peoples and non-Indigenous fur traders led to the birth of children whose group consciousness was characterized by their shared cultural practices, economic positioning, goals, and language.[8] Métis distinctiveness was manifest through kinship practices playing out across northwestern North America.[9] By the early nineteenth century, some Métis had concentrated at the forks of the Red and Assiniboine Rivers in what was then known as Red River Settlement. Today, the area is known as the City of Winnipeg. Métis people participated in Red River society and practised agriculture in the local area even while continuing to maintain lifestyles characterized by mobility.[10] At the same time, vibrant Métis communities continued to exist at other sites across the Northwest.[11]

As the fur trade declined, more non-Indigenous colonizers came to the Northwest. Many settled at Red River Settlement, and anti-Indigenous racism became a more powerful force within this community. The Métis perceived government-abetted colonization as a threat to their collective well-being. Resistance cohered around the leadership of Louis Riel, culminating in an agreement between the Métis and the Government of Canada to protect Métis rights through the creation of the new province of Manitoba. However, the Government of Canada demonstrated that it had failed to negotiate in good faith by sending an armed force to Red River. Under this threat, Riel and other Métis leaders fled, with some heading across the international border. In years to come, many other Métis people abandoned Red River in an effort to avoid government oppression and anti-Indigenous racism, as well as to preserve key elements of their lifeways. Destinations were generally west and south, with some Métis people heading toward what is now the Canadian province of Alberta and others settling nearer to Red River.

By the late nineteenth century, the human geography of the Prairie West had been dramatically redrawn. The decline of the fur trade, the decimation of bison, and the effects of epidemic illness and starvation had catastrophic effects on the Indigenous nations of the region. The creation of reserves and restrictions on Indigenous peoples' efforts to travel and trade beyond reserve borders created what the Canadian government perceived as space available for settlement by non-Indigenous newcomers, even as these processes devastated Indigenous cultures and economies. The scrip system, used by the Government of Canada to address the land claims of Métis people, proved a means through which many Métis were effectively dispossessed. In this context, Métis people often ended up establishing themselves in areas to which they had uncertain claim in the eyes of the state. These areas included road allowances, which were lands reserved from settlement for the future provision of a system of roads. They also included other lands deemed less desirable by non-Indigenous colonizers and their governments, such as those with obvious agricultural limitations.

In the late nineteenth century, a small group of Métis families established themselves near the contemporary border between Manitoba and Saskatchewan. Known as Ste. Madeleine, the community occupied land that offered only minimal agricultural prospects. The community had originally developed near what had been Fort Ellice, a Hudson's Bay Company trading post built in 1831 and active until 1870. The fort had been a key site within the fur-trading economies in which the Métis participated, and it served as a magnet to some Métis people moving away from Red River.[12] Municipal government came to the area with the early 1880s formation of the rural municipalities of Archie, Ellice, and Russell. These rural municipalities abutted Manitoba's westward border. An important additional attraction drawing Métis people to Ste. Madeleine was the existence of a nearby Catholic mission, established by a French missionary in 1902. Even after the mission was abandoned by the church, Métis families remained in the area.

Over decades, local Métis families practised a form of mixed subsistence, growing food, harvesting wild game, and gathering berries and medicines.[13] Ste. Madeleine's population likely peaked in the 1920s at roughly 400 members. A school was established in 1922. By this point, many local Métis families were working as occasional labourers for surrounding settler families, with their wages used to supplement what they produced and gathered from the land.[14] This economic relationship with settler society played out alongside the racism and prejudice directed toward Métis people.

Joe Venne lived in Ste. Madeleine for years. He has described a caring community where residents worked together to build a church and to support each other. Venne also remembers frequent lively musical celebrations in the Métis tradition, events that helped to create a home community for people who elsewhere faced discrimination.[15] Fellow community member George Fleury recalls that Ste. Madeleine families often struggled to get by but were heartened by prevailing community practices of generosity and mutual assistance.[16] The church served as a major hub in the local area, and generations of Métis families were buried at this site.

After the 1937 amendment to the Prairie Farm Rehabilitation Act that allowed for the creation of community pastures, a different group of people took an interest in the Ste. Madeleine area. Agents of the PFRA saw in the rural municipalities of Archie, Ellice, and Russell something that was relatively rare throughout much of Manitoba: a large landscape suitable for development as a community pasture.[17] The PFRA's director of rehabilitation, George Spence, visited the area in the summer of 1938. In correspondence with the deputy minister of agriculture, he described an area of roughly 70,000 acres that he saw as "definitely non-arable," with soil "too light and sandy for cultivation." As Spence saw it, the "best economic use to which the area could be put is undoubtedly pasture."[18] Spence foresaw that any pasture would be "utilized with just advantage" by "the surrounding farmers who are in need of pasture as the country round about is ideal for mixed farming."[19] Implicit in Spence's comments was the understanding that these surrounding farmers were colonizers, not Indigenous peoples.

This nonarable 70,000 acres included the community of Ste. Madeleine, which Spence described as "forty or fifty squatters."[20] His assessment was that the successful operation of a community pasture necessitated the removal of the community. The PFRA required the Government of Manitoba and the involved rural municipalities to arrange the removal before the agency would develop the community pasture. The provincial government initially planned to move the Ste. Madeleine community to Camperville, a largely Métis community on the western shore of Lake Winnipegosis. Pleased with this arrangement, the federal government agreed to contribute to costs at a rate of up to $150 per family, with estimated costs at $300 per family.[21] Municipal officials John Selby and Benoit Fouillard were to carry out the removal.

With plans in place for the removal of the Ste. Madeleine community, the PFRA began working toward a community pasture.[22] Local non-Indigenous residents were supportive, welcoming an investment in the area amid the difficult decade of the 1930s.[23] The construction of the pasture, including fencing and water supply, offered opportunities for paid work during the Great Depression of the 1930s, when such work was often difficult to secure. The prospect of improved pasture near the local community appealed to those interested in further investment in livestock. And according to Lazare Fouillard, son of one of the municipal councillors involved in the removal, local non-Indigenous peoples may also have welcomed the opportunity to displace a population that they saw as undesirable.[24] Notably, there is evidence of earlier attempts on the Canadian Prairies to promote the creation of publicly administered pastures so as to position colonizers to access lands held by Indigenous peoples.[25]

The plan to move the Ste. Madeleine population to Camperville fell through, but the removal itself went ahead regardless. George Fleury's descriptions of these events make clear that few, if any, Métis families went willingly.[26] Many Ste. Madeleine homes were destroyed by fire, and community dogs were shot.[27] Displaced Ste. Madeleine residents headed in a variety of directions. A significant proportion congregated in nearby road allowance communities south of Binscarth, Manitoba.[28] With grim humour, these two communities were nicknamed Selby Town and Fouillard's Corner after the municipal officials who carried out the expulsion.[29] Afterward, the Ste. Madeleine church was used to house animals, and the graveyard was treated with disrespect. Some former residents of Ste. Madeleine worked on the construction of the community pasture, taking advantage of a rare opportunity to secure some income.[30]

In late 1930s Saskatchewan, even as the PFRA created community pastures as quickly as possible, the agency sought to avoid forced removals of non-Indigenous settlers. Yet the Ste. Madeleine episode played out differently. Why was that? At least in part, it was because the agency determined that, as George Spence put it, "the type of squatter" in the intended pasture was "likely to be a continual Relief problem regardless of where he was moved."[31] Spence's perspective turned on racist views of the abilities and ambitions of the members of this Métis community. A compounding factor was taxation, with many of the Ste. Madeleine residents who held title sitting in arrears.[32] Scholar David Parent has identified taxation as a key technology of dispossession directed at Indigenous peoples in mid-twentieth-century Manitoba.[33] As Parent puts it, the St. Madeleine episode offers "a striking example of how the PFRA program rationalized the land insecurity of Metis for the security and well-being of the white farming population."[34]

In the mid-1980s, Ken Zeilig and Victoria Zeilig interviewed former residents of Ste. Madeleine. Across their informants' various stories, a common perspective emerged: what happened to the residents of Ste. Madeleine was profoundly unfair. When reflecting on their experiences, former residents typically perceived the poverty that they had experienced in the 1930s to be similar to that borne by many other rural prairie dwellers in this difficult decade. But Ste. Madeleine residents saw the removal as a distinctive occurrence and understood that it created circumstances in which poverty persisted for them, even as other prairie residents recovered from 1930s hardships.[35] The PFRA's role in this affair makes clear how enduring poverty for Métis peoples and state-supported rehabilitation for non-Indigenous settlers were fundamentally linked.

In a conversation with Trevor Herriot published in 2016, Métis leader and language teacher Norman Fleury articulated how in losing land, the residents of Ste. Madeleine had lost a community. As Fleury put it, "if your stories are in the land and in your community, and that all gets uprooted and scattered, how do you continue telling your stories?"[36] By late 1940, George Spence was trumpeting the impressive financial showing of a pasture created in the Ste. Madeleine area.[37] The land that had been home to the Ste. Madeleine community became part of a different story, a frequently told tale of the PFRA's role in fixing the mistakes of settlement. It took persistent advocacy by Métis and allies to bring about a summer 2024 agreement to return some lands to the Métis.[38]

Mistasiniy

For many years, on the open plains of what is now central Saskatchewan, a large stone – Mistasiniy, or Mōstos-awāsis asiniy in nēhiyawēwin – marked the horizontal axis.[39] Resembling a seated bison, Mistasiniy was a defining feature in a landscape often used for gatherings and spiritual practices, including fasting and sun dances.[40] Nēhiyaw writer, filmmaker, and scholar Tasha Hubbard has situated Mistasiniy in a study of kinship relations between Indigenous peoples and bison, identifying it as an important site in nēhiyawak cosmology.[41]

Trevor Herriot offers important cautions to colonizers interested in understanding the stories and sanctity of Mistasiniy, variously spelled as Mistaseni or Mistusinne and often known as Buffalo Child Stone. Based on his engagements with Elder Wes Fineday of the Sweetgrass Cree Nation, Herriot recognizes the limitations around when and how the stories of Mistasiniy could be told, limitations that he understands as related to protocol, context, respect, and season.[42] Herriot's discussion of this matter is in tune with the general principles for appropriately managing Traditional Stories laid out by scholar, writer, and editor Gregory Younging.[43] I follow Herriot, Fineday, and Younging in offering only a general comment about the stories surrounding Mistasiniy. Triangulating from a variety of sources, I understand the significance of Mistasiniy to derive from its role in stories about transformations of the physical form that bear on relations between humans and bison.[44]

Early in the agricultural colonization of the Prairie West, Mistasiniy attracted attention from non-Indigenous travellers. On his 1859 trip through the North American interior, Henry Youle Hind noted a large boulder located some 22 kilometres from the South Saskatchewan River. Hind recorded that Indigenous peoples "place on it offerings to Manitou," noting that "at the time of our visit it contained beads, bits of tobacco, fragments of cloth, and other trifles."[45] With the application of the European science of geology, newcomers came to understand Mistasiniy as an erratic, a term delineating a large boulder deposited during glacial retreat.[46] Mistasiniy was made of granite and measured roughly 25 metres in circumference, 8 metres in length and width, and 4 metres in height. It was estimated to weigh more than 400 tons.[47]

Mistasiniy stood amid some distinctive landscape features. It occupied a floodplain near Aiktow Creek, a waterway notable for how it drained toward the Qu'Appelle Valley at low water levels and toward the South Saskatchewan River at high water levels. This positioning led Mistasiniy to sometimes be termed the Aiktow Erratic. It was situated not far from the so-called elbow of the South Saskatchewan, where the river made a pronounced shift in direction of flow from northeasterly to northwesterly. Historian George Colpitts, in his analysis of the pemmican empire on the northern Great Plains, points to the elbow of the South Saskatchewan River as the location for a story of divine retribution targeting deviant young Indigenous men.[48] In her consideration of stories about Mistasiniy, Hubbard emphasizes the importance of place and landscape to those who have told these stories.[49] Mistasiniy was a key feature in a region defined by many notable geographical elements and important Traditional Stories.

Throughout the late nineteenth century, the imposition of a system of reserves and efforts to confine Indigenous peoples to reserve lands limited the ability of nēhiyawak and other Indigenous peoples to visit important sites like Mistasiniy. Restrictions on Ceremony limited long-standing spiritual practices. The operation of the Indian Residential Schools system and the promotion of Christianity challenged efforts by Indigenous peoples to perpetuate cultural traditions of all sorts. As decades passed, many reserve communities were increasingly distinguished from surrounding non-Indigenous communities by higher rates of poverty and by fewer modern conveniences and socio-economic opportunities, as well as other manifestations of colonialism. Indigenous leaders were unrelenting in their efforts to advocate for improvements in the well-being of their peoples, even as they met recalcitrant governments.

In the late 1950s, after years of uncertainty, Regina and Ottawa agreed to move ahead with the South Saskatchewan Regional Plan (SSRP), a multipurpose project involving two dams and a large reservoir that was intended to transform Saskatchewan's prospects. These governments failed to consider the long-standing significance and continuing importance of the affected landscapes to Indigenous peoples. Mistasiniy stood within the area to be flooded by the reservoir, later named Lake Diefenbaker, that was created through the construction of what became known as the Gardiner Dam and the Qu'Appelle River Dam. Engineers felt that Mistasiniy could not just be flooded in place. It had to be removed or destroyed because it might otherwise create a hazard for those boating in the reservoir.[50]

In Saskatchewan at this time, archaeology was developing as a scholarly discipline. Public interest had been aroused by 1930s erosion in agricultural fields, which revealed formerly concealed artifacts.[51] In light of this interest, the Saskatoon Archaeological Society was established, and professional archaeologists increased their work.[52] In 1954, the Saskatoon Archaeological Society's president wrote to the Saskatchewan provincial government to request an archaeological survey of the affected area in advance of SSRP construction.[53] Subsequently, the PFRA was contacted by members of the society. In follow-up internal correspondence, PFRA chief engineer G.L. MacKenzie explained to PFRA director L.B. Thomson that the agency had as of yet given little thought to risks deriving from "the possibility of flooding of archaeological or historical sites by the reservoir of the Saskatchewan River."[54]

Owing to new concern over potentially destructive aspects of the SSRP project, Ottawa and Regina agreed to fund several years of salvage archaeology in the area to be flooded by the reservoir.[55] This effort, underway throughout the final years of the 1950s and the early years of the 1960s, involved William J. Mayer-Oakes, then at the University of Toronto, and Zenon Pohorecky, a prairie-born scholar who received graduate training at the University of California at Berkeley.[56] The available funding was inadequate, so much work was performed by volunteers.[57] Despite this hindrance, the investigations eventually resulted in a 1960 report authored by Pohorecky that included a discussion of Mistasiniy's significance to Indigenous peoples based on the presence of objects like projectile points and iron plates.[58]

Pohorecky and his colleagues with the Saskatoon Archaeological Society also formed a group to advocate for saving Mistasiniy. The so-called Big Rock Committee was interested in preserving Mistasiniy for its archaeological value. Committee members also understood their advocacy as a form of service to local Indigenous communities. As Pohorecky described it, Indigenous peoples "have been made to believe that their various cultural traditions are what has undermined them."[59] From this perspective, an effort to save Mistasiniy was understood by those involved as a potential catalyst to cultural resurgence on the part of Indigenous peoples. The Big Rock Committee included Sidney Fineday of the Sweetgrass Cree Nation.

The focus of the Big Rock Committee was on moving Mistasiniy out of the area to be flooded.[60] In light of growing public concern with Mistasiniy's fate, the PFRA was prompted to investigate the viability of this approach. A major worry was the prospect that Mistasiniy might break apart during a move.[61] Estimates from contractors interested in relocating Mistasiniy ranged from $77,000 at the low end to $206,500 at the high end, with greater care to keep Mistasiniy together increasing the expense.[62]

Faced with a potentially expensive relocation effort, the Big Rock Committee focused on fundraising efforts. The committee solicited donations from the public and undertook a range of activities intended to generate funds.[63] Working in tandem with a local Saskatoon television station, in 1966 the Big Rock Committee hosted benefit performances by Buffy Sainte-Marie and Dick Gregory.[64] In historian Blair Stonechild's assessment, Sainte-Marie's participation helped to establish her as a social activist.[65] Writing in *The Sheaf*, the University of Saskatchewan's student newspaper, Vicki Brook deemed the performances "an overwhelming success."[66] But despite this positive assessment, the problem of paying for relocation was far from solved. All told, the committee raised roughly $3,500, a sum that fell far short of the anticipated cost.[67]

The funds needed to move Mistasiniy were also sought from the Historic Sites and Monuments Board of Canada. As historian Robert Cole explains, despite the board's expressed desire to preserve and protect Indigenous material culture, no contribution to relocation costs was forthcoming.[68] In the spring of 1966, the board decided that Mistasiniy did not merit special efforts at preservation.[69] Despite its significant role in nēhiyawak worldviews and its definitive positioning in a distinctive landscape, Mistasiniy did not, in the view of the board, qualify as "a site of national historic importance."[70]

In the aftermath of the decision by the Historic Sites and Monuments Board of Canada, officials seriously considered the prospect of fracturing Mistasiniy and moving some part of it while allowing the rest to be flooded in place. John Diefenbaker, leader of the opposition Progressive Conservative Party in 1966, argued in the House of Commons that, if it was impossible to save all of Mistasiniy, some portion of it should be preserved.[71] Liberal minister of agriculture J.J. Greene supported an effort to move a fragment.[72] Liberal minister of northern affairs and national resources Arthur Laing concurred, noting that, although Mistasiniy might not be of national historic importance, it was of significance to many people in the area, so salvaging part of it "would certainly create goodwill."[73] The Saskatchewan provincial government was on board, authorizing a grant in the amount of $3,500.[74]

Some members of the Big Rock Committee indicated that they found the fracture and salvage approach to constitute a good way forward. By this stage, the committee had allied itself with the Village of Elbow, located 16 kilometres northwest of Mistasiniy, and some committee members were supporting the village leadership's efforts to have a fragment of Mistasiniy installed locally.[75] In the fall of 1966, rising waters in the soon-to-be-completed reservoir meant that a rapid decision was necessary. By early November, it was clear that Mistasiniy would be fully inundated by the end of December.[76] Within two weeks, the decision was made: Mistasiniy would be fractured, with a portion installed in the Village of Elbow.[77]

Not everyone directly involved in these events was satisfied. Sidney Fineday of the Sweetgrass Cree Nation, originally a member of the Big Rock Committee, was powerfully opposed to the fragmenting of Mistasiniy. By June 1966, Fineday had gone on record with his views, noting that the proposed action, rather than a solution to a problem, would amount to "condoning wilful destruction."[78] In late November 1966, Fineday entreated the PFRA to move Mistasiniy in its intact form. PFRA director Fitzgerald demurred, noting that the majority of the Big Rock Committee had endorsed the approach of fracturing Mistasiniy and moving only part of it.[79] Indeed, members of the Big Rock Committee took pains to indicate to federal government officials that the committee's focus had shifted from moving Mistasiniy in an intact state to establishing a "suitably designed monument incorporating large pieces of the rock in a historic place of honor."[80] The break between Fineday and other members of the Big Rock Committee reflected the fragile character of political alliances between settlers and Indigenous peoples within mid-twentieth-century advocacy efforts.[81]

The waters in the future Lake Diefenbaker continued to rise, submerging the surrounding landscape and approaching Mistasiniy. On 12 December 1966, fourteen holes, each of 15 centimetres in depth, were drilled into Mistasiniy. More than 13 kilograms of explosives were mounted in the holes. As the workers saw it, the resulting blast achieved "excellent fragmentation," with debris concentrated in a 15-metre radius. Some pieces weighed several tons.[82] Historian Bill Waiser has identified the dynamiting of Mistasiniy as an exemplification of the troubled relationship between Indigenous peoples and Canadian governments.[83]

The Mistusinne Cairn, located in the Village of Elbow, was unveiled on 22 July 1967.[84] When Trevor Herriot visited the cairn in the final years of the twentieth century, he found it in disrepair and noted that it had been moved to a less prominent location in order to allow for the expansion of a golf course.[85] During a recent visit to the cairn, Hubbard experienced intense grief over what was done to Mistasiniy while taking comfort in the continued telling of stories about Mistasiniy and in the survival of fragments. For her, the destruction of Mistasiniy represents both loss and endurance.[86]

Saskatchewan River Delta

Given the testimony from affected communities and decades of scientific research, we now recognize a broad range of consequences flowing from large-scale water engineering projects such as those undertaken in the Saskatchewan River watershed. In a global context, dam and reservoir construction has provoked significant changes in water-flow rates and timing, in sedimentation patterns, and in concentrations of nutrients and toxins throughout entire ecosystems, both at sites adjacent to infrastructure as well as downstream. In the case of the Saskatchewan River watershed, the consequences of infrastructure development are particularly evident in the Saskatchewan River Delta.

Deltas are ecologically productive landscapes, offering habitat to fish, birds, animals, insects, and plants of various sorts. Typically, their productivity is linked to their mosaic landscapes of land and water, as well as to their dynamic cycles of high and low water. The Saskatchewan River Delta is a large freshwater inland delta occupying some 10,000 square kilometres and straddling the present-day border between the provinces of Saskatchewan and Manitoba.[87] It is a complex of marshes, meadows, and streams that extends through and around drier wooded expanses.[88] Divided into

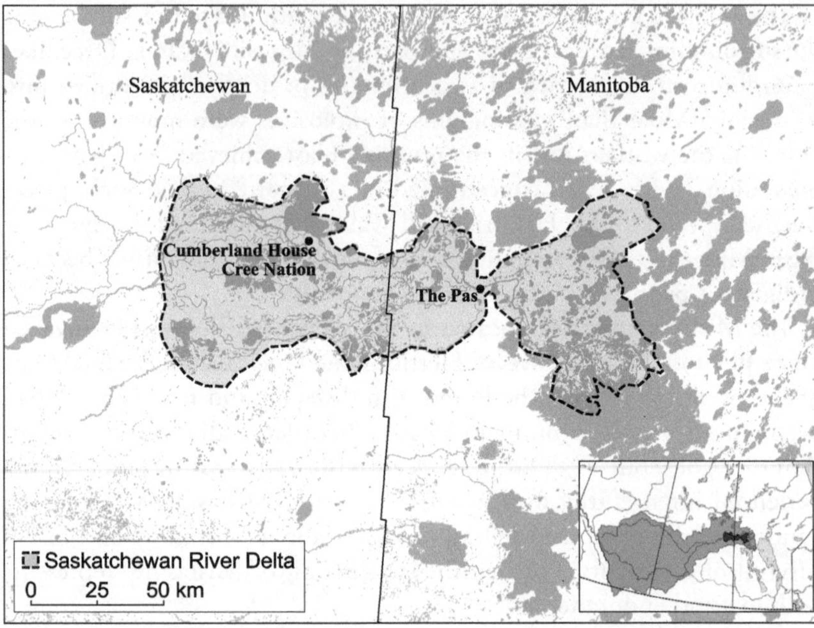

Figure 5.2 The Saskatchewan River Delta, showing the location of The Pas and the main population centre of the Cumberland House Cree Nation. *Adapted from Prairie Farm Rehabilitation Administration,* Full Development Possibilities in the Saskatchewan River Basin *(Regina: Hydrology Division, 1952), Figure 1; Razak Abu, Maureen G. Reed, and Timothy D. Jardine, "Using Two-Eyed Seeing to Bridge Western Science and Indigenous Knowledge Systems and Understand Long-Term Change in the Saskatchewan River Delta, Canada,"* International Journal of Water Resources Development *36, 5 (2020): 761;* CanVec Series [Admin., Land, Hydro] *(Ottawa: Natural Resources Canada, 2019); and* CanMap Content Suite v2021.3 *(Markham, ON: DMTI Spatial, 2021).*

upper (western) and lower (eastern) segments, the delta's upper segment spans the interprovincial border, and its lower segment is situated entirely within Manitoba. The two segments are separated by a strip of drier land, a moraine, which features the Manitoba town of The Pas and the reserve of the Opaskwayak Cree Nation.[89] The Saskatchewan section of the upper segment encompasses the Northern Village of Cumberland House and the Cumberland House Cree Nation, which includes five separate reserves. The Northern Village and the major population centre of the Cumberland House Cree Nation are located on an island near the south end of Cumberland Lake.[90] According to scholar, politician, and community member Keith Napoleon Goulet, the term "Kaminstigominuhigoskak" refers both to the population centre on the island and to the surrounding area accessed by community members.[91]

The Saskatchewan River Delta was valuable to those Nehinuwuk who have long lived in the region.[92] The ecologically productive landscape supported a variety of harvesting practices, including trapping, hunting, gathering, and fishing.[93] Non-Indigenous traders were active in the area from the eighteenth century onward. Established as a key fur trade node, Cumberland House served to facilitate increased exploitation of the region's resources. By the late nineteenth century, the Saskatchewan River Delta was known to fur traders as muskrat country.[94] The eventual decline of the fur trade led to economic shifts in the region, but resource harvesting continued throughout decades of change in the broader political, economic, social, and cultural circumstances bearing on the delta. Historian David Quiring puts the Cumberland House population at about 500 people in these years, with Indigenous peoples forming a substantial majority.[95]

In the mid-twentieth century, the Saskatchewan River Delta was targeted by various efforts to capitalize on what state agents or private parties saw as its potential.[96] An example is the Summerberry Muskrat Rehabilitation Project, in operation from the 1930s in a Manitoba section of the delta. Historical geographer Frank Tough deems the project to have been a success, claiming that it "demonstrated the benefits of economic planning and income redistribution."[97] By the 1930s, both Ducks Unlimited and the Hudson's Bay Company were involved in conservation efforts in the delta, with the former looking to increase waterfowl habitat and the latter seeking to expand muskrat production in its fur leases.[98] After the Second World War, the PFRA became involved in a drainage and flood-prevention project in the delta. The agency developed a reclamation project aimed at supporting agricultural development in a substantial area of the delta (the so-called Sipanok area, mostly in Saskatchewan) and made more detailed plans for work in a smaller area (the Pasquia area in Manitoba).[99] By the 1960s, portions of the delta were being remade according to various imperatives, even as the mixed success of these efforts and the sheer size of the delta meant that the resulting alterations remained relatively modest.

The Saskatchewan River Delta was also changed by developments upstream and downstream. Many of these developments derived from efforts by governments to make what they saw as more productive use of available water. The South Saskatchewan River and its tributaries ran through the area of southern Alberta most profoundly altered by irrigation. Saskatchewan's efforts to develop hydroelectric capacity turned in large measure on the development of the Saskatchewan River system. In 1963, Saskatchewan completed the E.B. Campbell Dam along the Saskatchewan River, creating the Tobin Reservoir.[100] The E.B. Campbell Dam is located about 30 kilometres upstream from the eastern boundary of the Saskatchewan River Delta.[101] In 1967, the Gardiner Dam was completed further upstream along the same river, creating the Diefenbaker Reservoir. The generating stations at the E.B. Campbell and Gardiner Dams were managed in tandem to help meet Saskatchewan's need for power, and together they changed water-flow patterns in ways that affected the delta. In addition to these upstream alterations, downstream infrastructure also affected the delta. Manitoba completed the Grand Rapids Dam in 1968, backing up water into the easternmost reaches of the delta and spelling the end of the Summerberry Muskrat Rehabilitation Project, which Tough deems to have been so successful.[102] There was also significant urbanization, agricultural intensification, and industrial development along both the north and south branches of the Saskatchewan River, with potash mining and chlor-alkali plants in central Saskatchewan being particularly notable for their use of water and release of chemicals.[103]

By the late 1960s, significant change had taken place within the Saskatchewan River Basin. There had been, however, only limited efforts to take account of the effects on water patterns in the Saskatchewan River Delta. These effects were significant, and they took three primary forms. First, there was an overall decline in water levels, largely due to upstream consumptive uses in Saskatchewan and Alberta. This decline resulted in the shrinking of Cumberland Lake, an important waterbody within the delta.[104] Second, there was disruption of established seasonal water-flow patterns. In the assessment of hydrologists John W. Pomeroy, Dirk de Boer, and Lawrence W. Martz, the seasonal variation in water flow was radically reduced due to the operation of the Gardiner Dam.[105] Third, there was a significant increase in the rapid and unpredictable variation of water levels within the Saskatchewan River Delta. This variation occurred because the power infrastructure at the E.B. Campbell Dam was operated as a peaking plant, with water released or held back according to fluctuating demand for electricity.[106]

Changes in the Saskatchewan River Basin also affected environmental processes in the delta related to nutrients and sediment. The suppression of seasonal variation in water flow diminished the delivery of nutrients to the delta, disrupting a process fundamental to the continued ecological productivity of the area. Reservoirs typically have profound effects on sedimentation processes, and the Tobin Reservoir was no exception.[107]

Much of the sediment load that would previously have been deposited in the Saskatchewan River Delta was arrested at the Tobin Reservoir. Further, having dropped its sediment load in the reservoir, the river was poised to undertake significant downstream erosion. In the Saskatchewan River Delta, this erosion led to the enlarging of channels. Despite acknowledging the persistence of uncertainty in the complex landscape of the delta, a 1993 Environment Canada report concluded that "since the construction of the E. B. Campbell Dam," the Saskatchewan River Delta "has changed from a sediment sink to a sediment source."[108]

Change to the physical geography of the Saskatchewan River Delta had significant consequences. Beaver, muskrat, mink, and otter were all directly affected by these alterations. Fish were also impacted, as were moose and waterfowl. Negative effects on animal and fish populations had consequences for hunters, trappers, and fishers, as well as for those who worked as outfitters or guides.[109] Anyone who travelled through the delta was threatened by unpredictable water levels. Equipment could be lost, travel times could be increased, and lives could be endangered when conditions changed dramatically and without warning over a short period. In winter, ice conditions were rendered more hazardous by drops in the water level that created more fragile ice or increases in the water level that created impassable slush on top of ice.[110] River crossings were more challenging even in summer, when low water levels threatened the operation of canoes, power boats, and ferries alike. Health consequences of various sorts resulted, ranging from increased physical risk to diminished access to locally harvested food. With attachments to land understood as an important aspect of well-being for Indigenous peoples, landscape change had health consequences all on its own.[111] As legal scholar Trish Goulet has explained, the changes to the delta environment "impacted the ability" of Nehinuwuk "to exercise meaningfully their Aboriginal and treaty rights."[112] The impacts were profound, despite the efforts of delta residents to adapt to changed circumstances in creative ways.[113]

Not all changes to the delta environment were as readily perceived as changes in water flow or sediment deposition. By the late 1960s, methylmercury was a significant concern in Saskatchewan.[114] Methylmercury is a neurotoxin, teratogen, and possible cardiovascular toxin.[115] Methylmercury accumulates in the bodies of fish and wildlife, and the process of bioaccumulation creates serious risk for people who consume significant quantities of harvested fish or meat. The risks of methylmercury contamination came to global attention through the investigation of harms deriving from industrial processes in Japan and northwestern Ontario.

Concern over methylmercury in Saskatchewan focused on industrial activity using mercury, as well as on the use of mercury in agriculture, dentistry, paint, and other contexts.[116] There was also attention to naturally occurring mercury or methylmercury carried into Saskatchewan from other places. A further factor at play in Saskatchewan's methylmercury problem was the construction of hydroelectric reservoirs. Although the problem varies in severity according to a range of factors, including reservoir characteristics, water management practices, and broader environmental circumstances, it is well established that reservoirs create conditions conducive to the production of methylmercury.[117]

Recent scientific examination of methylmercury in the Tobin Reservoir and the Cumberland House fishery indicates that the creation of the Tobin Reservoir may have contributed to the contamination of fish in the Saskatchewan River Delta. The E.B. Campbell Dam is about 97 kilometres upstream from Cumberland House.[118] Although scientists have noted evidence that the maximum contamination was less extreme than in the Asubpeeschoseewagong First Nation, a community in northwestern Ontario harmed by methylmercury contamination, they assert that the "human population of Cumberland House faced increased [mercury] for decades after implementation of the dam."[119] Scientists recognize the need for additional research to determine the physiological consequences of exposure at these levels.

Within several years of the E.B. Campbell and Gardiner Dams becoming operational, local trappers and hunters were already expressing their dissatisfaction and dismay with changes in the Saskatchewan River Delta.[120] In the early 1970s, the Committee on Saskatchewan River Delta Problems, a government body created in response to complaints from delta residents, undertook a multiyear study of the matter.[121] The committee confirmed that changes in the delta were related to the operation of upstream facilities, including the E.B. Campbell and Gardiner Dams, as well as to other water uses along the North and South Saskatchewan Rivers like irrigation and recreation.[122] The recognition that upstream developments resulted in what the committee called "dis-benefits" downstream was not, to the committee's mind, sufficient reason to consider significant changes to the operation of existing infrastructure.[123] Hydro-related harm and disruption in the delta were consistent with the experiences of other Indigenous peoples in Canadian provincial norths, as was the lack of serious concern by state officials.[124] As Keith Napoleon Goulet puts it in his rendering of the history of the Nehinuwuk of Kaminstigominuhigoskak, the "destruction of the Cumberland Delta was the price to be paid so that the farms, villages, towns and cities to the south could be powered."[125]

Even as matters remained unresolved in the Saskatchewan River Delta, important changes occurred with regard to the evaluation processes typically brought to bear on large-scale infrastructure projects. In Saskatchewan, a hydroelectric dam proposed for the Churchill River Basin was stalled because of concerns for effects on the environment and Indigenous peoples.[126] Farther north, a natural gas pipeline proposed for construction in the Mackenzie Valley was delayed due to the findings of the Mackenzie Valley Pipeline Inquiry. Justice Thomas Berger, head of the inquiry, found that the environmental, social, and economic costs of moving ahead immediately were too high.[127] And in Quebec, faced with substantial pushback from Eeyou, Inuit, Naskapi, and Innu, the provincial government was obliged to negotiate compensation in relation to a substantial hydroelectric development underway in the territories of these Indigenous nations.[128]

In this changed context, and as part of ongoing efforts to seek redress from government, the Cumberland House Cree Nation commissioned anthropologist James Waldram to document the effects of environmental changes on the lives of Nehinuwuk.[129] After spending time in the community, Waldram recorded how the E.B. Campbell Dam had made life in the Saskatchewan River Delta much more precarious.[130] He also noted only modest government efforts at engagement with the Cumberland House Cree Nation prior to construction of the E.B. Campbell Dam and persistent unwillingness to recognize negative effects once the dam was in operation.[131]

Ultimately, prompted in part by a desire to build additional infrastructure on the Saskatchewan River, including what would become the François-Finlay Dam and the Nipawin Hydroelectric Station, the Saskatchewan provincial government participated in mediation aimed at resolving the concerns of the Cumberland House Cree Nation.[132] In 1989, an agreement was reached involving both compensation for harms related to the E.B. Campbell Dam and provisions for community development.[133] In 2004, a minimum-flow requirement was imposed on the operation of the E.B. Campbell Dam.[134]

Efforts to address harms from development remain incomplete. Recent academic research conducted with the Nehinuwuk community in Kaminstigominuhigoskak has identified steps that may lead to a more satisfactory resolution, including rectifying power imbalances.[135] In the spring of 2021,

Rene Chaboyer, chief of the Cumberland House Cree Nation, declared the intention to assert sovereignty over the Saskatchewan River Delta, seeking to safeguard what remains of the delta and to ensure the well-being of community members.[136]

The E.B. Campbell Dam is the infrastructure closest to Kaminstigominuhigoskak. Its operation has had clearly negative effects on people and nonhuman nature in the Saskatchewan River Delta. As Goulet puts it, the dam has caused "the greatest upheaval to the land, resources and culture" of his community.[137] Additionally, the delta catalogues the consequences of multiple processes of environmental change unfolding throughout the entire watershed, including water-engineering projects in Alberta and Manitoba as well as in Saskatchewan and encompassing basin-wide agricultural intensification and industrial modernization. The transformation of the Prairie West has had significant cumulative effects on the Saskatchewan River Delta.[138]

Conclusion

The PFRA, as mandated by the Canadian federal government, pursued regional transformation to the benefit of prairie farmers and communities. George Spence's dismissive view of Ste. Madeleine community members suggests that early PFRA leadership understood Indigenous peoples as unlikely to capitalize on any agricultural supports that they received. The PFRA's transformative vision failed to acknowledge the importance of prior prairie landscapes that were valued by Indigenous communities. This failure is made clear in relation to Mistasiniy, which first went unnoticed by the PFRA and then unappreciated by the National Historic Sites and Monuments Board of Canada. The PFRA's transformative work was broad and multi-faceted, affecting prairie landscapes in multiple ways. The Saskatchewan River Delta, at the downstream end of the Saskatchewan River Basin, served as a barometer of these compounding effects, as well as those driven by other agencies, actors, or historical processes. Although changes in water quantity and quality were most tightly coupled to large-scale water-engineering projects, broader regional transformations related to agricultural intensification and industrial modernization also filtered through the delta landscape. The PFRA was involved in many of them.

In the 1996 report of the federal government's Royal Commission on Aboriginal Peoples, the Ste. Madeleine episode is taken to typify a pattern of relocating Indigenous peoples to accommodate resource development.[139] In this way, the PFRA has been situated within the history of displacements to which Indigenous peoples have been subject. It is important to also appreciate the converse: that harms to Indigenous peoples, including displacement, have been an aspect of state-led efforts at agricultural rehabilitation. To better understand what was happening on the mid-twentieth-century Prairies, it is essential that Ste. Madeleine, Mistasiniy, and the Saskatchewan River Delta are included in the history of the PFRA.

6

The PFRA Overseas

Remaking Water Patterns in Northern Ghana, 1965–70

In February 1946, the director of the Experimental Farms Service, E.S. Archibald, spoke at a meeting of the Prairie Farm Rehabilitation Administration (PFRA) Advisory Committee on Land Utilization. Archibald described what he saw as the importance of the Food and Agriculture Organization (FAO), which had been created under the auspices of the United Nations at the end of the Second World War. He believed that the FAO would play a key role in "improving nutrition, expanding agricultural research and the dissemination of relevant information, and in promoting the development and conservation of the world's food-producing resources." Archibald projected that, as part of the transnational effort that the FAO would lead, the PFRA "could fill an important part on behalf of Canada."[1]

Archibald's transnational vision for the PFRA was shaped by the global recalibrations that followed the Second World War. Postwar reconstruction was a massive undertaking, particularly in the areas of Europe and the Pacific that had served as theatres of war. The emerging Cold War lined up the United States and its allies against the Soviet Union and its sphere of influence, with both sides jockeying for supremacy across decades. It was in this complicated global context that the process of decolonization gained momentum, with peoples in Asia, Africa, and Latin America striving to liberate themselves from the oppressive colonial regimes imposed on them by European powers. Canada's positioning within these processes related to its evolving relations with both the United States and Britain.

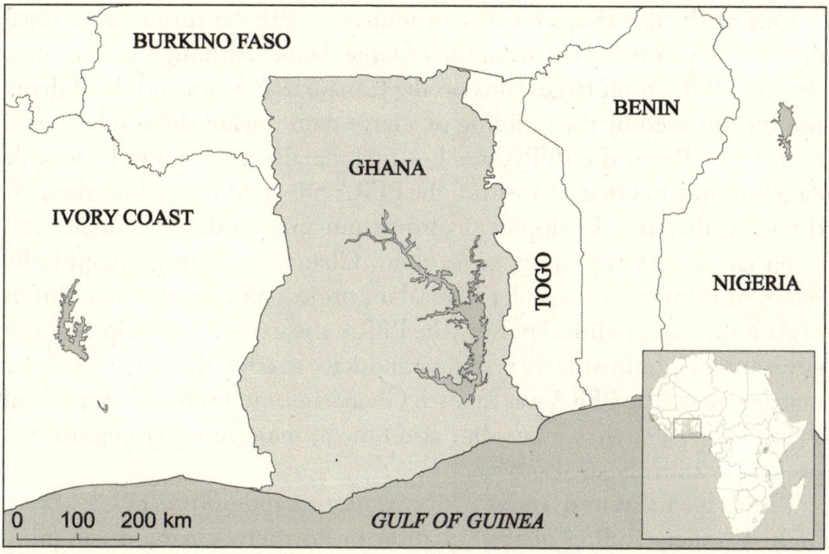

Figure 6.1 Ghana and neighbouring countries along the Gulf of Guinea. *Adapted from "Africa with Countries" and "Ghana," in "Free Vector World and Country Maps," https://freevectormaps.com/.*

Archibald's vision for the PFRA also related to his understanding of the agency's robust capacity to drive human and environmental transformation, both within and beyond the Canadian Prairies. Some two decades later, Archibald's vision was put to the test. Between 1965 and 1970, the PFRA took on a water-development project in the African nation of Ghana. It did so as part of Canada's mid-twentieth-century program of official development assistance, a component of global-scale processes still widely termed international development. As historians David Webster and Greg Donaghy have each made clear, technical expertise played an important role in Canadian official development assistance.[2] The PFRA became involved in Ghana at a time when Canada's development assistance program remained fluid in goals and strategies, and the PFRA's overseas activities help to establish the parameters of Canadian efforts at this juncture. Contemporary analysts have recognized that international development ultimately entrenched and compounded the inequalities characterizing colonialism and capitalism.[3] These inequalities have often taken on racialized dimensions, with racist ideas about nonwhite peoples figuring in the various ways that development efforts are conceived, advanced, and evaluated by historical actors from aid-giving nations.[4]

One of the key characteristics of mid-twentieth-century international development was the construction of large dams.[5] Although it is the case that the PFRA built large dams on the Canadian Prairies and that Ghana was transformed by the building of a large dam toward the southern end of its Volta River, the PFRA was but peripherally involved in large-scale dam building in Ghana.[6] Instead, the PFRA provided the technical expertise to further the development of medium-sized and, later, small-sized water conservation projects in northern Ghana, a region geographically removed from both the Volta River dam project and the nation's centres of economic and political power. The PFRA also expected to help establish government administrative systems conducive to effective water-resources management. The PFRA was to teach Ghanaians not just how to transform their northern environments but also how to manage water-engineering projects within the civil service.

PFRA agents went overseas with enthusiasm and optimism – and very limited understanding of the situation in northern Ghana. Examining Canadian technical experts at work in Ghana makes clear that what historian Michael E. Latham identifies as the technocratic faith animating American mid-twentieth-century overseas efforts was also evident among Canadian experts.[7] Confidence in technical know-how could overwrite uncertainty derived from unfamiliar environments and contexts. Over its years in northern Ghana, the PFRA's actions demonstrate inadequate attention to distinctive aspects of local ecologies and cultures, as well as preoccupation with the experiences and perspectives of overseas Canadians. Ultimately, the agency participated in driving transformation in the region, but the change was not as intended.

The Ghana Context

In 1957, Ghana became the first nation in Sub-Saharan Africa to emerge as independent, uniting the former British colony of the Gold Coast (along the Gulf of Guinea) and the former British Protectorates of Ashanti (farther north) and the Northern Territories (even farther north) under the presidency of Kwame Nkrumah. In contrast with the settler colonialism at play on the Canadian Prairies, Ghana emerged in the aftermath of exploitation colonialism, with the colonizing power exploiting people and resources but not establishing a substantial local settler population.

Some Canadians served in the British administration governing colonial exploitation in Africa, including in the area that would become Ghana.[8]

This practice reflected a shared racialized identity between Britain and the Canadian settler elite, many of whom continued to take pride in affiliation with the British Empire. Although Black people in Canada were not subject to a legally codified regime equivalent to the Jim Crow laws of the United States, they nevertheless endured discriminatory social structures and encountered prejudiced views, even as some Canadian politicians took anti-racist stances in the mid-twentieth-century global arena.[9]

Once he ascended to the presidency, Nkrumah sought to drive forward a process of social, political, and economic change that he described as "jet propelled," striving to bring Ghanaian standards of living more in line with those in the United States and Britain even as he sought to assert African independence amid an international context polarized by Cold War tensions.[10] Although united within a newly independent state, Ghana's north and south were distinguished by multiple factors. In the north, population was lower, cocoa growing was less emphasized, and urbanization and industrialization were little in evidence. Northern Ghana also represented a different political landscape, one characterized by what authorities both beyond and within Ghana saw as comparative isolation and impoverishment.[11] As political scientist Catherine Boone has argued in her study of state building in rural West Africa, some zones were largely left to their own devices even as others were brought under rigorous state control.[12] Northern Ghana was among the former.

The development trajectory for northern Ghana owes much to the final decades of the colonial period, when British authorities became increasingly concerned about what they saw as the worrying state of the environment in the Northern Territories.[13] Input from external experts was solicited, including a 1949 visit to the Northern Territories by American Walter C. Lowdermilk, a conservation expert with extensive transnational experience. Lowdermilk spent two weeks touring what he called "the beautiful country" of the Northern Territories and assured his colonial hosts that the land was "well suited for farming" using "methods of conservation."[14] Despite Lowdermilk's enthusiasm, what colonial officials stationed in the Northern Territories saw as satisfactory progress on land management was slow in coming. In the early 1950s, local land-use planning and soil conservation efforts addressed circumstances on 147 square miles (380 square kilometres), a small fraction of the 7,200 square miles (18,000 square kilometres) perceived to be in need of attention.[15]

Nkrumah's efforts to drive change in the nation that he headed intersected with the efforts of the United States to exert influence in the context of the Cold War. As Michael E. Latham puts it, "the ideal of rapid development provided a framework through which Ghana and the United States found a mutual interest."[16] Ghana desired access to American funds, and the United States sought to influence the new nation's development, to ally itself with emerging African states, and to limit communist influence in postcolonial Africa. Although some aid flowed from the United States to Ghana under the presidency of Dwight Eisenhower, the relationship was strained by Nkrumah's increasing engagement with states on the opposite side of Cold War tensions such as the Soviet Union and China. The situation was exacerbated when Ghana and the United States assumed starkly opposed viewpoints on the civil war underway in Congo, with what Nkrumah saw as "the defense of African unity, nationalism, and non-aligned sovereignty" being seen by the United States as "complicity with Soviet expansionism."[17]

Despite continued tensions, the coming to power of US president John F. Kennedy offered an opportunity to Nkrumah, who desired United States support with a major project: the construction of a massive hydroelectric dam along the Volta River. This project was intended to bring rapid industrialization to southern Ghana and to serve as the centrepiece in the transformation of lifeways across the nation.[18] Kennedy confirmed financial support for the Volta project in mid-1961. That same year, Canada became involved in training the Ghanaian military, due in large measure to the Ghanaian desire to withdraw from direct British influence.[19] Additionally that year, Canadian engineer Frank J. Dobson was appointed as the first chief executive of the Volta River Authority, the entity created to administer dam building along the lower Volta.[20] Canada had also been involved from the late 1950s in aid programs directed at Ghana.[21]

By the end of 1961, the limits of Western influence were clear. Nkrumah adopted a program of state planning and central management of the economy modelled on the techniques of communist and authoritarian states.[22] This program included the creation of state farms using eastern European machinery and the nationalization of key sectors of the economy, and it contributed to increasing distance between Ghana and Western nations such as Canada.[23] By the mid-1960s, relations between Ghana and the United States had completely unravelled, with the Americans becoming actively involved in efforts to overthrow the Nkrumah administration.[24] With opposition to Nkrumah cohering around the Canadian-trained military, Canada was deeply implicated in this process.[25]

Even as high-stakes geopolitics swirled around the issue of the Volta Dam, the United States was also involved in Ghana's north. Between 1957 and 1964, a United States mission to northern Ghana sought to improve water supply across the region, primarily through the "construction of ponds and reservoirs to store excess water from the wet season for later use."[26] Some 192 dams and dugouts were built, with a combined storage capacity of 14,744 acre-feet. A 1964 report on the project by soils expert Charles K. Magee saw this American effort as revolutionary in effect. Enumerating the livestock reliant on stored water constituted a primary means of quantifying the benefits of the program. According to figures from local animal health offices, these livestock included over 56,000 cattle, 31,000 sheep, 30,000 goats, and 2,000 donkeys, as well as horses, swine, and poultry.[27]

The United Nations Food and Agriculture Organization also took on a project in northern Ghana.[28] This effort aimed to "produce an operational plan for the more efficient use of the natural agricultural resources of the Northern and Upper Regions of Ghana with a view to improving the agriculture and the livelihood of the people."[29] The methods were threefold: first, to undertake investigations of various sorts, including hydrological, agronomic, and sociological; second, to produce plans for implementation by government; and third, to train Ghanaian personnel so as to build capacity for future undertakings. The emphasis on information gathering and plan development thrusts into relief the earlier US effort, which had emphasized immediate action in the construction of dams and dugouts.

With international diplomacy hinging on events in the new nation's south, technical experts charted ways forward for the nation's northern reaches. It was this technical momentum that the PFRA picked up. The PFRA became involved through the initiative of PFRA director M.J. Fitzgerald, who in addition to his position with the PFRA maintained an affiliation with the FAO.[30] For fifteen years following the Second World War, Canada contributed to international development in what Greg Donaghy has characterized as a reasonably competent, if somewhat ad hoc, manner.[31] Established in 1960 within the Department of External Affairs, the External Aid Office (EAO), under the oversight of its director general, H.O. Moran, sought to assemble a more coherent program of overseas aid.[32] In this effort, Moran coped with various difficulties related to limited resources, including a lack of personnel. As he put it in 1961, "we do not have people, period."[33]

If Moran worried about limited resources, he also confronted challenges derived from what he perceived as Canada's unsophisticated approach to international development. In a March 1961 letter to the Canadian high commissioner in Ghana, Moran worried about the risks of adopting "a 'buckshot' approach to aid," one based on the fallacious idea that "the needs of Africa are so great that anything which we do is bound to be beneficial."[34] Focused approaches to aid were also likely less costly, which would have appealed to Moran. Fitzgerald expressed an interest in involving the PFRA in overseas activities at a time when Canada was revisiting its approach to international development efforts.[35] Given that a Canadian aid program was still under development and given the desire to deliver aid in an efficient manner, collaboration with the PFRA seemed attractive. As the recently established EAO saw it, the PFRA's involvement in Ghana helped to compensate for "the lack of technical support and direction" that characterized Canada's aid programs at this stage.[36]

The PFRA's involvement in northern Ghana began with a 1963 assessment trip undertaken by Fitzgerald in the company of two other Canadian experts, W.L. Foss (an engineer with the PFRA) and K. Kristjanson (an economist with Manitoba Hydro, a provincial Crown corporation with involvement in hydropower development). The visitors found little current use of irrigation but much potential. Further development of northern Ghana's water resources would, the three Canadians claimed, help to ensure adequate food throughout the year by permitting the growth of a second crop in the dry season.[37] Although irrigation looked promising, the Canadians recommended a gradual approach, one "starting with the smaller, pilot type of project as opposed to the more costly, large scale type of project." This approach was presented as realistic "in relation to the reasonable needs of Ghana and the country's ability to finance."[38]

Notably, Canada's go-slow recommendation was in contrast with the approach promoted by engineer Lewis Smith of the United States Agency for International Development. Working with Ghana's Agricultural Ministry on secondment, Smith advocated the immediate construction of massive irrigation projects. He anticipated the irrigation of 150,000 acres using the Akosombo Dam, currently under construction. Smith's perspective was favoured by Frank J. Dobson, chief executive of the Volta River Authority. The 1963 visitors noted a contrast between the benefits likely from irrigation and the ambitious plans that were being constructed around it. Not only did the Canadians feel that Smith's "rather imaginative plans for water development" were inappropriate given the current situation in northern Ghana, but they also argued that these plans carried significant risks.[39] "In our opinion," the Canadians wrote, such an overambitious move would "set irrigation back 20 years, just as it did in Western Canada 50 years ago."[40] It remains unclear exactly what setbacks in prairie irrigation the Canadians had in mind, but this exchange makes evident that the

PFRA brought to Ghana not just technical expertise but also intellectual frameworks defined by the landscapes and contexts of western Canada.

Although some Canadians worried that Ghanaians would be put off by this caution, Ghana accepted all of the 1963 recommendations.[41] Soon thereafter, the Ghanaian government formally requested that Canada bring the plan to fruition. A two-year agreement between Ghana and Canada governing the project was signed in January 1966.[42] The PFRA's commitments in relation to Ghana were twofold. First, the Canadian agency was "to investigate and design irrigation projects in the Northern and Upper Regions." The PFRA would take a closer look at promising sites for medium-sized undertakings (irrigating 1,000 to 6,000 acres each) that the FAO had identified, and it would develop plans to capitalize on these opportunities.[43] At this stage at least, there was no explicit commitment to Canadian involvement in construction efforts. Second, the PFRA committed "to establish training programs for Ghanaian staff" through a system of counterpart relationships.[44] The idea was that a Canadian would share with a Ghanaian a line position in the Ghanaian civil service with the ultimate aim "of developing the Ghanaian who occupies the position with him to handle the position alone."[45] In a 1967 annual review published by the EAO, the PFRA's activities in Ghana were presented as characteristic of twinning arrangements whereby Canadian efforts promoted the development of greater domestic capacity within aid-receiving countries.[46] Notably, twinning arrangements were consistent with Canadian leaders' desires to mentor decolonizing regions in their transitions to nationhood, desires that turned in part on the paternalistic and racist assumption that Africans were in particular need of such instruction.[47]

Under the arrangement between the PFRA and the EAO, the latter retained responsibility for providing policy direction, as well as administrative advice and assistance.[48] As plans developed, the EAO expressed appreciation to the PFRA for the extent to which the agency "had taken over so effectively in meeting our obligations and commitments" in relation to the Ghana project.[49] Agencies involved in development such as the PFRA often represented what scholar of rural development Doug J. Porter has termed the "nexus of capital, technology and rationality" believed by proponents to be at the core of successful development projects.[50] PFRA involvement was considered a boon by Canadian leadership because avoiding the problematic and expensive buckshot approach to aid was understood to require technical knowledge. The PFRA helped to give substance to Canadian involvement in international development while positioning itself to become further engaged in environmental transformation far from its prairie landscapes of origin.

The PFRA Deploys

Fulfilling the commitments in the 1966 agreement meant deploying Canadians to Ghana. The original complement of staff was to be four engineers and eight technicians.[51] The PFRA was pleasantly surprised with the amount of interest among its staff in going overseas. About ninety applications were received for the dozen available positions.[52] Retrospectively, participating staff identified a variety of motivations driving their interest, including side trips to Europe, professional ambition, a desire for economic gain,

Figure 6.2 A Canadian family prepares to travel to Ghana. Depicting a prosperous family in a well-appointed living room, this photograph helps to establish the lifestyle and material goods available in Canada to families of PFRA employees in this period. *Library and Archives Canada, RG 17, 2015-01238-9, box 3, MIKAN no. 4841913, negative 26196, e011166301. Photograph: Ghana Project [Family and Ghana Book], copyright Government of Canada, reproduced with the permission of Library and Archives Canada (2016), Department of Agriculture fonds, RG 17, file 26196.*

and curiosity about unfamiliar places and cultures.[53] Figure 6.2 shows a PFRA employee and family happily engaged in learning about Ghana. The first staffers were on-scene as of late 1965, even prior to the formal signing of the governing agreement. An early letter back to PFRA staff in Canada rang with optimism: "The meals at the hotel are wonderful"; "the homes seem to be quite nice with beautiful yards"; "the climate is no where near as bad as we had anticipated."[54]

Good food aside, difficulties soon became apparent. As PFRA employees saw it, the major challenge was to effectively deploy technical expertise in a Ghanaian environment that they understood only poorly. The PFRA lacked the basic information through which engineering and technical professionals typically made sense of the landscape, such as hydrometric records documenting key aspects of the local hydrological cycle. This circumstance was not unforeseen. The lack of information was noted even before the 1963 exploratory visit from Fitzgerald and company.[55] Difficulties were compounded when it became clear that what information did exist was problematic. The FAO's reports on the northern region were fundamental to the work of the PFRA, but the information contained within them proved unreliable. By June 1966, for instance, project engineer N.L. Iverson, the senior PFRA official on-scene in Ghana, reported that valley soils labelled "quite good" in FAO reports were known to be of poor quality by employees of the Ghanaian government.[56] PFRA technical staff lacked the data that they considered fundamental for an understanding of the local landscape.

Once the PFRA was on the ground in Ghana, efforts were soon underway to take the sorts of measurements that agency staff felt would help them to better understand the northern Ghana environment. Figure 6.3 features a Ghanaian engaged in work of this nature. But not all the necessary information was readily gathered. A major concern was the need for records of stream flow, which would have outlined the scope of regional environmental variability in terms of minimum and maximum discharges. Few streams in northern Ghana were metered, and even those that were metered had established records of only short duration.[57] There was no technical way to produce in the present moment what amounted to historical information. Additionally, due to difficulties in the collection of stream-flow data, such as the challenges of maintaining gauging stations, there was no guarantee that additional useful information would accumulate even as the years passed. Rapidly, PFRA staff came to understand that they simply could not expect to work with "the same basic investigation data which we would normally obtain."[58]

Figure 6.3 A Ghanaian takes measurements. Depicting the environmental assessments involved in irrigation planning, this photograph captures a Ghanaian working in the field with a PFRA truck in the background. *Library and Archives Canada, RG 17, 2015-01238-9, box 3, MIKAN no. 4841913, negative 85028[-5], e011166300. Photograph: Ghana Project [Rodman and PFRA Truck], copyright Government of Canada, reproduced with the permission of Library and Archives Canada (2016), Department of Agriculture fonds, RG 17, file 85028[-5].*

The absence of data was not, however, considered grounds for lack of progress on the design work that the PFRA was to undertake. Pressure was felt not only by Canadian staff but also by Ghanaians involved with the PFRA. One of the Ghanaian trainees who spent time with the PFRA both in Ghana and overseas in Canada was Robert Ankrah. As he wrote in a draft report that he authored for the PFRA, although "the records are less satisfactory than desired, the forces acting to push development are great!" In this context, as Ankrah put it, "hydrologists cannot become obstructionists."[59] Although Ankrah did not clarify his understanding of the forces at play, pressures were certainly in operation along multiple lines, some linked to local conditions in northern Ghana and others to the tense global Cold War context of the mid-1960s. Pressures also emanated from a global humanitarian crisis related to hunger. Food was understood among Western nations as a hinge on which development turned, with sufficient quantities seen as essential to Western Cold War success.[60] Food was also a key plank in early Canadian foreign aid policy.[61] Iverson expressed the imperative deriving from hunger in his 1967 assertion that the land and water of Ghana represented "such tremendous natural resources that they cannot remain undeveloped forever in a world short of food."[62] But increasing food production was not just about forestalling hunger. Food was also a commodity, and increasing its production to export levels was a technique that might facilitate Ghana's integration into global capitalist networks while weakening its ties to communist nations.

These various pressures meant that international development work in northern Ghana moved ahead even in the absence of basic information about the local environment. Despite concerns about their reliability, the FAO reports were the PFRA's starting place.[63] Working from a list based on FAO investigations, the PFRA identified fourteen promising dam sites, and then narrowed the candidates down even further to focus on Bontango, Pasam, and Kamba.[64] These three sites were selected for their proximity to economic and population centres, as well as on the basis of what hydrologic, agronomic, and climatologic data the agency had.[65] Much of the PFRA's early work in Ghana focused on developing plans for medium-sized water conservation infrastructure suitable to these locations.

In undertaking design work in the absence of basic information about the Ghanaian environment, PFRA staff operated by constructing parallels between the overseas landscape that they sought to understand and the landscape that they knew best: the Canadian Prairies. These parallels were rooted in what were perceived as broad similarities between northern Ghana and the Canadian Prairies: "gently rolling plains, slowly winding river valleys, with rainfalls, although heavy at times, limited to 30 to 45 inches a year."[66] On the basis of such perceived similarities, a PFRA guidebook for use in land evaluation, titled *Handbook for the Classification of Irrigated Land in the Prairie Provinces* (1964), was shipped to Ghana.[67] The construction of parallels also operated at smaller scales. With respect to investigations underway at the Pasam site, a particular environmental feature ("swelling shale") was understood through comparison to similar circumstances at the site of the Morden Dam, a PFRA project in southwestern Manitoba.[68]

PFRA staff understood that they were in the process of comparing environments that were, in many ways, dissimilar. For instance, they recognized that wood could not be used in the construction of Ghanaian infrastructure because of the risk of destruction by termites or theft by locals, for whom wood was a scarce resource.[69] Staff also sought to fill in the blanks in their environmental data through other geographic comparisons, such as assessing Ghanaian watersheds in relation to better-documented watersheds in adjacent African regions.[70] And it was recognized that constructing environmental parallels represented a way forward that merited caution. As put by Iverson, the senior PFRA official in Ghana at the time, in such circumstances, "the general procedure is to guess and use a large factor of safety."[71] Still, through the practice of compensating for what technical staff saw as inadequate information, a projected future for the lands of northern Ghana was extrapolated in part from the history of irrigation on the Canadian Prairies.

The PFRA's experience was far from unique. As geographer William M. Adams sees it, many development efforts involved "bringing ideas drawn from the experience of industrialized countries and using them as a blueprint for African development."[72] But if the PFRA's strategy was common, not all people from aid-giving countries agreed, even at the time, that it was wise. C.F. Bentley, a Canadian academic consulted by the PFRA, recognized in 1968 that very few Canadians possessed training in tropical agriculture, noting that it was both "wasteful" and "embarrassing" for them to nevertheless be attempting to work in such environments overseas.[73] Bentley worried not only about the basic data that the PFRA lacked but also about the absence among agency staff of the local environmental expertise that would enable them to make good use of what data did exist. The problem was too significant for even Iverson's large factor of safety to adequately mitigate.

Beyond Technical Matters

PFRA staff worried about their incomplete understanding of the environment of northern Ghana. They were similarly ignorant of the region's human context, which looked little like that of the mid-twentieth-century Canadian Prairies. A great number of linguistic and cultural groups existed within or maintained ties to areas of northern Ghana.[74] Throughout the period under consideration, all land in northern Ghana remained officially vested in the government.[75] However, the apparent simplicity of government authority belied a complex set of land claims, with layers of land rights held by multiple parties.[76] Insofar as irrigation infrastructure amounted to a public investment that increased the value of affected lands, it could, as scholar of international development Christian Lund puts it, occasion a "renegotiation of land rights."[77] Irrigation works conceptualized by the PFRA as promoting agricultural stability within the region could in fact contribute to destabilizing property relations.[78]

In addition to property relations, agricultural practices further distinguished northern Ghana from the Canadian Prairies. Anthropologist Alexis B. Tengan has examined the significance of the hoe-farming work of the Dagara people of northwestern Ghana. As Tengan presents it, hoe-farming signified "an inter-personal relationship between humans and different aspects of the universe personified as beings."[79] For the Dagara, hoe-farming represented not just a means of subsistence but also a practice that involved maintaining appropriate relationships with other people and the nonhuman world. Casual comments in less formal correspondence contained within PFRA archival materials make clear that PFRA staff maintained a general interest in what they perceived as the exotic cultural practices characterizing northern Ghana.[80] But there is a telling silence in the agency's professional records related to cultural practices bearing directly on the viability of irrigated agriculture. Engaged in the design of infrastructure that was to anchor the development of capitalist agriculture in northern Ghana, PFRA agents saw little professional reason to attend to local farming practices that they expected to help render extinct.

PFRA agents also had little understanding of the socio-economic circumstances bearing on the lives of the Ghanaians with whom they were twinned. They regularly expressed concerns about the work ethic of their Ghanaian counterparts, with erratic attendance a particular problem. There is no evidence that the PFRA considered whether absenteeism may have amounted to protest against a foreign agency advancing work begun in the colonial period. Further, it is unclear whether the PFRA recognized that, for Ghanaians, regular attendance could actually detract from their capacity to provide for a family. Scarcity in essential goods prevailed in mid-1960s Ghana, with many items available only through the time-consuming process of accessing black markets. Economically necessary second jobs further shrank the amount of time that any Ghanaian could invest in a primary occupation. As explained by Jack Goody, an anthropologist who spent time in Ghana during the period in question, locally "it was understood that everyone had to make a living," but outsiders found these practices inimical to proper procedure.[81] PFRA staff seem not to have perceived or understood the contexts in which their Ghanaian counterparts made decisions about how to prioritize their commitments to the PFRA project. Racialized conceptions about the work ethic of

Figure 6.4 A Canadian (left) and two Ghanaians at work over a desk. The composition of this photograph, with the Canadian seated behind the desk and the two Ghanaians in front of it, underlines a power dynamic that positioned Canadians as the experts and Ghanaians as the learners. *Library and Archives Canada, RG 17, 2015-01238-9, box 3, MIKAN no. 4841913, negative 85031[-6], e011166299. Photograph: Ghana Project [Canadian and Ghanaian Engineers], copyright Government of Canada, reproduced with the permission of Library and Archives Canada (2016), Department of Agriculture fonds, RG 17, file 85031[-6].*

Africans were a factor here, with the racist ideas that prevailed in mid-twentieth-century Canada making it more likely that Canadians would perceive Ghanaians as insufficiently committed to their jobs.[82]

The inattentiveness of PFRA staff toward northern Ghana's human landscape derived not just from the presumption of Western superiority that characterized mid-twentieth-century international development but also from a preoccupation with what were, for PFRA agents and their families, difficult personal circumstances. Many PFRA staff took wives and children with them to Ghana. In choosing team members, the agency had made selections "not only on the basis of technical qualifications and personal suitability, but also on the basis of the individual applicant's family situation." Men with "large families" or partners "apprehensive about living in an under-developed country" were left off the team.[83] But even such an approach failed to forestall the development of circumstances that, although not directly related to the PFRA agents' professional activities or technical expertise, affected the operation of the project.

Housing became an immediate point of contention. Canada originally understood that Ghana would provide newly constructed houses for the Canadian personnel, to be ready on their arrival in the country. Even prior to the arrival of the majority of the team, concerns were raised about this commitment. Shortages of needed materials barred the construction of new dwellings, although Ghana continued to offer assurances that all staff would be appropriately housed.[84] Ultimately, new staff members arriving in Ghana were obliged to spend up to six months in hotels.[85] The absence of the cultural and social buffer of familiar housing was seen as a significant hardship. Particularly for staff with families, there were also logistical problems, like how to offer young children food and play space in keeping with Canadian middle-class norms.

If new housing had been intended to offer one buffer for Canadians, another was an arrangement by which PFRA staff would be permitted, even encouraged, to import substantial quantities of familiar foodstuffs and goods not readily available in Ghana. Although Canadian staff would pay for the materials, the Canadian federal government would foot the bill for shipping them to Ghana.[86] Ghana granted such import privileges in the memorandum of agreement governing the project, signalling the extent to which this arrangement was fundamental to the entire endeavour.[87] This arrangement both provided access to familiar staples and helped to compensate for the generalized shortages affecting Ghana at this time.[88] Imported products included many brand-name goods, such as Campbell's Beef Soup and Sunkist Lemon Juice.

Even with assured access to familiar food, Canadians in Ghana coped with disruptions to their normal state of health. Preparing for travel to Ghana meant vaccinations against illnesses not of concern in Canada and ongoing precautions against malaria. It also meant coping with digestive disruption. The latter was evident from the earliest stages of the project. Kris Kristjanson, in a letter sent to Fitzgerald about a week after his fall 1963 return to Canada, reported having had that morning his first "good solid ________."[89] The comment clearly followed up on an earlier dialogue that the two had been having on their bowel function. The experience for

Canadians overseas was not that of their bodies deployed in an unfamiliar environment but that of their formerly familiar bodies transformed by their new location. However, minor health upsets such as digestive problems were ultimately dwarfed by worries about access to appropriate medical care.[90] There were no Canadian doctors serving in Ghana, and the "shortage of Canadian medical services is of great concern to the families of the PFRA team."[91] Even the presence of Canadian military medical personnel was not, in the view of PFRA team members, sufficient to safeguard the well-being of Canadians overseas.

Both Canadian and Ghanaian project leaders took a keen interest in how the experiences of Canadian staff and their families might affect their work. The relation between the experiences of Canadians and the work underway was conceptualized primarily through the notion of morale, which could be invoked to suggest how circumstances not directly related to conditions of work could nevertheless have a significant bearing on the success of the project. Inadequate housing was problematic because of how "the morale of the team greatly suffered as a result."[92] Canadian project leaders made the case for adjustments to the team (through the addition of "a small medical service," for instance) based on the argument that it would boost morale.[93] Proposed restrictions on imports by Canadians were opposed on the grounds that morale would be hindered, even potentially creating "difficulty in maintaining a staff in Ghana."[94]

Project leaders were of two minds about the issue of morale. Some felt that inappropriate expectations were at issue, with a prominent Ghanaian administrator reportedly noting that some aid personnel "seemed to forget that they were in an underdeveloped country when making demands related to housing conditions."[95] Canadian officials concurred that the "over-optimistic impression" that team members had received in Canada was at least partly to blame for discontent.[96] Still, it was understood among those planning the project that the personal experiences of foreign staff affected their professional contribution and thus needed to be taken into account. Decisions about where to locate PFRA staff, for instance, were based on the expectation that the Canadians would be "happier and therefore give more to the country if put in a place where living conditions are easier."[97]

The experiences and needs of PFRA staff and their families became important factors affecting the agency's undertakings in Ghana. PFRA efforts became self-referential, as the project was calibrated not just to the aim of promoting development in northern Ghana but also to the imperative of safeguarding the morale of a small number of foreign technical experts. Focus by overseas Canadians on their own experiences may well have rendered them less likely to respond to, or even perceive, local considerations like distinctive landholding arrangements and agricultural practices.

Evaluating the PFRA

Despite the PFRA's limited understanding of the northern Ghana environment and the personal challenges faced by PFRA agents and their families, work in northern Ghana moved ahead, with Canadian officials marking progress in part through regular project evaluations. Reports issued in 1967 and 1968 reflect efforts to adjust the project in order to better position it for success.

The first formal evaluation of the project was undertaken by N.L. Iverson. His report identified the PFRA's contributions to research and planning for dam projects such as those anticipated for the Pasam and Bontanga sites. Based on experiences during the first year, Iverson also suggested some changes to the project. Ghanaians had voiced a desire for assistance with small-sized undertakings (irrigating 10 to 100 acres each), and Iverson saw potential in this approach.[98] Based in part on Iverson's recommendation, the PFRA effort was expanded to include small-sized projects, and put in charge of these was PFRA field engineer W.K. Dobson (no apparent relation to Frank J. Dobson).

W.K. Dobson began his assignment with the onerous task of inventorying small dams or dugouts throughout northern Ghana to assess how existing infrastructure was being used.[99] Dobson's findings were not encouraging. As he saw it, "no effort is being made to make full beneficial use of the irrigation potential of the water."[100] His view was that only 17 of the 267 small dams that he had located were being used for purposes of irrigation, only 5 of which were working to capacity.[101] Notably, Dobson's assessment echoed those of others who had voiced concerns about water-control infrastructure that was falling apart in the absence of the expertise, workforce, machinery, and funds necessary to ensure appropriate upkeep.[102] Despite his worrying assessment of the physical infrastructure, Dobson's view was that the more serious deficits were related to the administrative structures needed to support water development. Focusing on the Ghanaian bureaucracy, Dobson found insufficient institutional commitment to practical training in irrigation, few meaningful opportunities to apply what knowledge was gained through training, a lack of appropriate supervision for involved staff, and the absence of fundamental supplies such as petrol. As a result of what he saw as an inadequate commitment to promoting water conservation on the part of Ghanaian leaders, Dobson felt that it was "almost impossible for an advisor from a foreign country to achieve anything."[103]

Dobson's personal frustration reflects something of the PFRA's broader experience. The PFRA, successful in a Canadian context partly for the effective ways that it built on the capacities of other Canadian federal and provincial government agencies, found itself flailing in the absence of Ghanaian entities positioned to take on the many aspects of regional water development that did not fall under the purview of the PFRA project. The agency was operating in the northern reaches of a country undergoing significant political turmoil. The overthrow of the Nkrumah government in 1966 heralded a period of political instability but brought no change to the mandate of the PFRA: the agency was to accomplish the same goals in what had become a far more volatile situation.[104] Given Canada's alignment with the Western powers that supported the coup, especially Canada's role in training the Ghanaian military that drove Nkrumah's overthrow, the bureaucratic black hole that frustrated Canadian PFRA staff was partly their own country's creation.[105] But the perversity of the situation remained unapparent to PFRA staff worried about what they took for a lack of support and cooperation in service both to the immediate task of improving local water conservation and to the broader goal of establishing capitalist agriculture across Ghana's north.

A second significant evaluation of PFRA efforts in Ghana began in the fall of 1968, when PFRA official J.E. Beamish weighed in. After an investigation, Beamish determined that "regardless of the good intentions of this project," it exhibited some basic problems. In fact, he went so far as to express significant doubt that the project as currently conceived "warrants the cost in resources and manpower."[106] As Beamish saw it, the project had failed dramatically in one of the key goals established in the project's original memorandum of understanding: to develop something like the PFRA within the Ghanaian civil service in the form of a professional staff capable of continuing irrigation after the withdrawal of the Canadians. In response, other officials laid out what they saw as the reasons for the failure of the twinning effort. They had trouble finding sufficient qualified men to train, especially for the most advanced engineering positions.[107] They perceived their agency's experience as part of broader circumstances affecting Ghana as a whole, where a shortage of qualified Ghanaian staff meant that technical expertise was often supplied by foreign personnel.[108] Additional challenges were seen to ensue from the fact that opportunities with the PFRA were field positions in remote locations. As a PFRA staff member put it, for Ghanaians, "prestige is gained by sitting behind a desk, not in getting their hands dirty."[109] The agency's replies to critiques of its efforts to mentor Ghanaians were presented in ways that resonated with racist ideas about the ambitions and capacities of African peoples, with a purported disinclination for fieldwork taken for laziness.

Beamish was not entirely pessimistic about the PFRA effort in Ghana. Rather, he argued that a "reorientation of Canada's aid program" could "provide a lasting benefit to Ghana."[110] Beamish's thought was that the PFRA should take on particular projects on what he called a "package" basis. Canada would undertake all aspects of promising projects, providing design components, agronomic and water-management support, construction expertise, and operational capability. Notably, the changes proposed by Beamish were linked not only to the perceived needs of northern Ghana but also to those of Canadian project staff. Growing discontent among the Canadians was attributed in part to their inability to drive projects through to completion, including the construction phase.[111] Degradation of existing infrastructure was also recognized as potentially disheartening. As put by PFRA official C.A. L'Ami, there was reason for concern about "the effect on the Ghanaian public, Canada, and the Division staff of further failure or disuse of constructed projects."[112] In the ultimate expression of the significance of PFRA staff morale, the issue figured in the decision to revisit the fundamental principles on which the northern Ghana project was based.

Beamish's recommendations were accepted, and the administrative adjustments to bring them about were undertaken. By this point, Canada's External Aid Office had been remade into the Canadian International Development Agency (CIDA).[113] Created in 1968, CIDA was, in the view of researcher Molly Kane, an effort to establish "greater autonomy and clarity of mandate" than had been available through the External Aid Office.[114] To better operate on a "package" basis, the Ghana project was to be moved from its initial location in CIDA's "advisers" program to its "capital assistance" division. The new vision was for the PFRA to act as "a consulting engineering firm engaged by the Ghana Government" instead of as "an aid organization."[115]

Although Beamish ended his evaluation of the PFRA project in an optimistic vein, W.K. Dobson's report on water conservation in northern

Ghana served as a springboard to an even broader critical appraisal. In a letter that ended up in the hands of CIDA president Maurice Strong, Dobson offered a far-reaching critique of PFRA efforts. Armed with previous experience in Africa, knowledge gained through his tour of Ghana's north, and a personality that his superiors recognized as inclined to be critical, Dobson made clear his view that the PFRA operated not out of concern for the well-being of the local population but out of a desire on the part of both involved nations – Canada and Ghana – to demonstrate technical prowess and capital resources. Dobson thought that the PFRA's continued efforts would only "add to the wasted aid" being "given so liberally to Ghana by many countries."[116] Although Dobson's critique stands out from the recorded perspectives of other Canadian PFRA employees, it resonates with the viewpoint of Robert Ankrah, a Ghanaian trained by the PFRA. In a frank memorandum from C.A. L'Ami to N.L. Iverson, L'Ami described Ankrah as wondering "if aiding countries were more interested in developments which would reflect to their glory than in those which might provide the best approaches to the country's orderly development."[117]

Dobson's critique, combined with the administrative adjustments required to shift the focus of the PFRA program from advising to capital assistance, prompted CIDA to determine that a further program evaluation was necessary. This third examination of the PFRA project, dated March 1969 and authored by T.M. Pallas with the Capital Assistance Division, amounted to little more than a list of project shortcomings. As Pallas summed it up, "when one attempts to relate the total cost of this project with the physical achievements and the training of Ghanaians the price appears to be very high."[118] In the aftermath of Pallas's critical report, while continuing to blame project shortcomings on purportedly insufficiently committed Ghanaians, the PFRA began to threaten withdrawal. Eventually, what had first seemed even to Canadians an idle threat evolved into a reality, with both CIDA and the PFRA agreeing to undertake what they termed "a 'gracious withdrawal.'"[119] By the early 1970s, the PFRA was sending home its project team. Although PFRA officials and their CIDA correspondents discussed the withdrawal as the logical outcome of an unsuccessful project, other factors – including the administrative and conceptual changes that took place as the EAO was remade into CIDA – may have rendered it particularly convenient to back away at this point. The PFRA's withdrawal from northern Ghana occurred even as parliamentary appropriations for international development continued to rise in Canada throughout the early 1970s, although Canadian expenditures remained low relative to those of other aid-giving nations.[120]

By the time PFRA agents were on their way home, fifteen years of international development had significantly changed the landscape of northern Ghana. The dams and dugouts that resulted from water conservation efforts had important positive impacts in the realm of health, with the potential of increased food production for locals being a major reason for this outcome. But the infrastructure that allowed for a second annual crop came with significant risks. In a landmark study published in 1970, Charles C. Hughes and John M. Hunter documented the association between development projects in Africa and the exacerbation of public health problems.[121] Irrigation development was associated with increased risk of schistosomiasis (both *Schistosoma haematobium* and *Schistosoma mansoni*) because dams and dugouts created habitat for the snails that spread the disease and because this infrastructure promoted concentration of human populations. Irrigation was also associated with increased prevalence of a number of additional health concerns, including malaria, onchocerciasis, and lymphatic filariasis. In one important study of the northeastern region of Ghana, Hunter determined that lymphatic filariasis was perceived as a problem only in those areas where small dams had been constructed in the late 1950s and early 1960s and that it was particularly severe in areas with more extensive irrigation infrastructure. He went so far as to call lymphatic filariasis a "disease of development."[122] Dealing with schistosomiasis, Hunter argued that high rates of infection in northern Ghana were at least partially "an artefact of agricultural interventions, specifically the building of dams in the immediate post-colonial years."[123] The negative health effects of water development in northern Ghana are attributable not to the actions of one nation or agency but to the cumulative effects of multiple engagements by foreign agents, with all involved parties being complicit in the outcome – including Canada's PFRA.

The health hazards related to irrigation in Africa were established well before the PFRA went to work in Ghana. A 1949 study of Egypt's Aswan Dam project, for instance, highlighted a rapid increase of schistosomiasis.[124] The World Health Organization held a conference in Ghana in 1954 at which experts discussed measures to be used in treating onchocerciasis.[125] There is some evidence that PFRA officials recognized the health implications of their activities. In 1968, as the PFRA was considering expanding its mandate to include work on small projects, Iverson argued that Canada's investment in irrigation development in Ghana entailed an obligation to attend to health concerns "so that we merely do not replace one hardship with another."[126] But like other aspects of Ghana's human history, the matter of public health failed to receive significant attention from Canadians involved in international development in northern Ghana.

Conclusion

In deploying to Ghana, the PFRA went to work in the northern reaches of a recently decolonized nation, one where Cold War tensions hinged on political and economic dynamics in its south. The PFRA was to contribute to agricultural transformation in northern Ghana through the planning of water-control infrastructure and the training of Ghanaians. Agency staff worried about their limited knowledge of the local environment, even as they found ways to press ahead regardless. Staff seemed unconcerned with their equally limited understanding of the local cultures that were to be displaced by northern Ghana's anticipated incorporation into a global system of capitalist agriculture. Racist ideas figured in Canadians' assessments of project shortcomings, and the morale of Canadians serving overseas became a factor in decisions about how to recalibrate PFRA efforts. Ultimately, the project was deemed unsuccessful, and the Canadians were shipped home.

As an agency with technical expertise in water conservation, the PFRA provided options to Canada's EAO at a time when it did not have sufficient resources at its disposal. In this way, the PFRA helped to establish the parameters of early federal government involvement in international development. The agency provides a concrete demonstration of what historian Will Langford has called "the domestic and foreign entanglement of development ideas, practices, and expertise."[127] The PFRA's activities in Ghana also highlight the plurality of the development imperative. The PFRA effort was dominated by technical expertise rather than by the antipoverty focus that Langford sees in international development efforts undertaken at about the same time in Tanzania by the Canadian University Service Overseas.[128]

The most striking aspect of PFRA activities in northern Ghana is the agency's complicity in the tragic exacerbation of local health risks. In a 1970 article, published the year that the PFRA withdrew, Hughes and Hunter asserted the need for development to be considered within "a comprehensive ecological framework" if the result was to be "an overall betterment of social and economic conditions of life."[129] In the absence of a comprehensive understanding of northern Ghana's environmental and human contexts, the PFRA contributed to exacerbating disease risk in the region.

7

Hope and Disappointment

The PFRA in the 1960s and 1970s

In September 1968, the University of Reading in Berkshire, England, convened a seminar on the broad topic of "Change in Agriculture." Organizers aimed to explore possibilities for "putting agricultural science and technology to work to fill bellies and help to diminish poverty."[1] Spanning some eleven days, the seminar was well attended. It featured 235 senior representatives from agricultural agencies across thirty-five countries. Among the Canadian participants was H.J. Hargrave in his role as director of the Prairie Farm Rehabilitation Administration (PFRA). At the seminar, Hargrave presented a case study focused on the PFRA. The material that he prepared was included in the seminar's published proceedings, where it was featured alongside contributions from agricultural experts in Kenya and Germany in a section titled "Rehabilitation Schemes." The three case studies were presented as examples from nations that had made globally significant efforts toward rectifying agricultural problems.

Hargrave's presence at this international gathering is an important reminder that, throughout the postwar period and into the late 1960s, the PFRA was a prairie agency of broad significance. In its mission and its mode of operation, the agency was understood as worthy of attention at national and global scales. This chapter begins by examining the agency's influence on Canadian federal government policy, explaining how the PFRA drove change in prevailing approaches to the twin problems of conserving natural resources and remediating inequality within human society. As an agency focused on the rural Prairies, the PFRA was particularly concerned with rural disadvantage relative to urban quality of life, disadvantage that the agency thought could be addressed through improved management of agricultural resources like land and water. Scholars like Tina Loo and Will Langford have examined the global problem of poverty, which mid-twentieth-century activists, experts, and politicians saw as requiring concerted action.[2] In its efforts to promote conservation and to improve rural quality of life, the PFRA laid groundwork for and continued to operate alongside state-sponsored poverty-reduction efforts.

Amid the anti-racist and anti-colonial global movements brewing in the 1960s, and as part of ongoing efforts to improve resources management, some federal government administrators reflected anew on how the PFRA should engage prairie Indigenous peoples.[3] Over many years, the PFRA's water-development work on reserves played out in an ad hoc manner, and an eventual attempt to regularize it was unsuccessful. The creation of community pastures on reserve lands prioritized colonizer needs and failed to substantially benefit Indigenous peoples. As a branch of the federal government, the PFRA reflected the haphazard and ineffective character of many mid-twentieth-century state-led efforts to improve the circumstances of Indigenous peoples.

The 1968 election of Pierre Trudeau's Liberal federal government had significant consequences for the PFRA. Trudeau's efforts at driving social change focused on urban transformation and industrial actors. For the PFRA, an agency that remained oriented to farmers and agricultural landscapes, this shift was disconcerting. Further, under Trudeau, new fiscal approaches took root. A greater emphasis on cost recovery and on user-pay schemes in federal government programs disadvantaged the PFRA, an agency rooted in the notion that public investment in agriculture paid society-wide dividends. As a result of both shifts, the PFRA's influence and ambition waned in the 1970s.

Incubating Hope

The mid-twentieth century has been characterized by historian Tina Loo as a time of hope on the part of Canadian politicians, government administrators, and technical experts. These influential actors were united by their belief that they could harness state power to, as they saw it, improve the lives of the disadvantaged.[4] The PFRA incubated this hope by offering what many leaders and policy makers took as an example of effective state action addressing the linked challenges of improving resources management and enhancing human well-being. The significance of the PFRA example is evident in the work that the Senate conducted through its Special Committee on Land Use between 1957 and 1963. It is also evident in the 1961 passage of the federal government's Agricultural Rehabilitation and Development Act (ARDA), as well as in intersections between the ARDA and the PFRA.

If "the story of Canada is the story of federalism," as historians Dimitry Anastakis and P.E. Bryden have asserted, the PFRA reflected the start of a new chapter.[5] Created only a few short years after the 1930 transfer of natural resources to the prairie provinces, the agency represented a different form of federal involvement in the prairie region. The director of the Experimental Farms Service, E.S. Archibald, claimed in 1944 that the PFRA delineated "a marked new phase of Federal-Provincial relationship."[6] Unlike many other elements of the Canadian New Deal, the PFRA persisted throughout a postwar period characterized by careful examination of Canada's federal system, including by the Royal Commission on Dominion-Provincial Relations (1937–40), also known as the Rowell-Sirois Commission after the lead commissioners, and by the Royal Commission on Canada's Economic Prospects (1955–57), also known as the Gordon Commission. Throughout these tumultuous years in Canadian federalism, the PFRA served as a beacon marking the prospect of Ottawa and the provinces working together in productive ways.

In the postwar years, the PFRA focused on water-resources engineering and on community pastures as key means to improve the lives of farm families and to address rural disadvantage. These two sets of activities were important not only for the specific regional problems that they addressed (namely insufficient access to water and pasture) but also because they served the ultimate goal of driving what the PFRA saw as positive change in the prairie region. George Spence, the first director of the PFRA, helped to set the agency on this postwar trajectory by arguing for greater federal government involvement in managing social change based on what he saw as the success of the PFRA in doing exactly that.[7] The agency's accomplishments in this vein were widely recognized within the federal government. For instance, discussions in the early 1950s about moving the PFRA from the federal Department of Agriculture to the newly created Department of Resources and Development reflected a broad appreciation for the agency's contributions to driving positive change on the rural Prairies.[8]

The postwar PFRA operated amid big shifts in prairie farming. At a global scale, agriculture was being remade by a range of forces often described in sum as agricultural industrialization.[9] Although the process had begun decades earlier, depression and war had caused delay in Canada, and so many areas of the Prairies felt the full force of industrialization only after the Second World War. Horses were replaced by tractors, which could pull larger machinery.[10] Combines replaced threshers, which streamlined harvesting.[11] The application of pesticides and herbicides became thoroughly established among agricultural practices. The PFRA was knitted into agricultural industrialization in various ways. For instance, the agency-funded dugouts that forestalled fears of drought also served as sources of the water necessary for herbicide spraying.[12]

Amid the various changes associated with agricultural industrialization, farmers found themselves vulnerable to a potent cost-price squeeze, one characterized by higher machinery and equipment costs even as returns remained variable due to the environmental uncertainties characteristic of farming and to the vagaries of global markets for farm products.[13] Farms became larger as farmers sought to maximize their incomes. In the short-grass prairie, what had once been a landscape of 320-acre farms rapidly came to feature farms of 960 acres.[14] Expanding farm sizes were matched by declining rural populations, which bore not just on residents' experiences of the rural Prairies but also on governments' abilities to provide infrastructure of various sorts, including roads and schools. Rural disadvantage took on new implications as it came to be defined not just in comparison with urban industrial norms but also by what seemed like a downward trajectory in rural quality of life.

In the mid-1950s, Canadian governments at various levels recognized the need to reckon with change in farming and rural communities. In Saskatchewan, the Royal Commission on Agriculture and Rural Life (RCARL) was a key part of the provincial response. On a national basis, concerns about agriculture led to the formation of the Special Committee on Land Use. Formed in 1957 and operational through 1963, this Senate committee both reflected and spurred change in agriculture and resources management in Canada. Although the Special Committee emerged out of concern over the national problem of inappropriate land use across Canada, its work included significant attention to the prairie region.

In a manner consistent with the investigatory approach typical of the 1950s Senate, the Special Committee on Land Use undertook to gather evidence and to interview witnesses.[15] By 1963, the committee had met fifty-six times and heard from 109 witnesses.[16] The contributions of key witnesses are a window on the proceedings. Both the Canadian Federation of Agriculture (formed in the mid-1930s as a unified voice for Canadian farmers) and the Agricultural Institute of Canada (formed in the mid-1940s out of the earlier Canadian Society for Technical Agriculturalists to advance scientific farming) appeared before the committee. In their presentations, the two organizations underlined problems with farmer income, or as the representative of the latter put it, they expressed "the growing feeling that agriculture has not shared sufficiently in recent years in the general prosperity that has been enjoyed by other segments of our economy."[17] The problem of rural disadvantage, which had long worried PFRA leadership, had become a matter of national concern. In their presentations before the Special Committee, both the Canadian Federation of Agriculture and the Agricultural Institute of Canada called for federal government action on soil and water conservation, believing that such work would address income disparity across the rural-urban divide.

Before the Special Committee, the Canadian Federation of Agriculture argued that government action on conservation should be based on the PFRA precedent.[18] Many other witnesses also mentioned the PFRA in positive terms, making clear that the agency was viewed as a model for federal government efforts to improve land and water management. For instance, Professor Harold Spence-Sales, involved in establishing Canada's first planning program at McGill University, used his testimony to celebrate the PFRA as "a most distinguished planning organization."[19] As Spence-Sales saw it, the PFRA's work in conserving prairie lands and resources for the future provided an example of the sort of action that was needed nationally.[20]

The work of the Special Committee on Land Use was amplified in importance by a major federal political upheaval that transpired only months after the committee was created. After twenty-two years of Liberal rule in Ottawa, Progressive Conservative John Diefenbaker became the head of a minority government. The Diefenbaker campaign had been buoyed by ambitious visions for national development inspired by John A. Macdonald's national policy and by the work of economists June Menzies and Merril Menzies, who saw in Diefenbaker a politician willing to explore a more activist role for the federal state.[21] They advised Diefenbaker to look to large-scale infrastructural projects (including the South Saskatchewan Regional Plan) and to northern development as the twin anchors for his national vision.[22]

Although Diefenbaker's campaign was fuelled by a national vision, its success was due in part to prairie discontent with what seemed the staid and patronage-riddled federal Liberal Party. Born in Saskatchewan, Diefenbaker was well positioned to capitalize on dissatisfaction in the Prairie West with a rhetoric of change. Prairie dissatisfaction may have been rooted in long-standing grievances, but it was exacerbated by grain surpluses on the global market that hurt Canadian farmers.[23] Diefenbaker pledged to use the prime minister's office to address persistent inequalities in Canada's federal system. Given this promise, it is unsurprising that many of Diefenbaker's signature policies took on a regional dimension.[24] The year of Diefenbaker's election in 1957 has been called a "watershed ... insofar as it marked a decisive redirection of interest at the federal level towards the understanding and alleviation of regional deficiencies."[25]

Within the suite of legislation passed during the Diefenbaker administration, the two imperatives of regional development and resource conservation were perhaps nowhere so profoundly linked as in the Agricultural Rehabilitation and Development Act of 1961.[26] This federal government legislation introduced tools to support government-driven efforts to address rural disadvantage and resource degradation in tandem. Parallel pieces of legislation passed provincially provided for projects intended to address perceived problems in agriculturally oriented areas of the nation. The ARDA operated primarily by putting federal money in the hands of the provinces, which were then responsible for implementation. The ARDA also involved federally funded research efforts such as the Canada Land Inventory and technological innovations such as the Canada Geographic Information System.[27]

The ARDA has been evocatively described as a social movement in reverse.[28] A typical social movement might stem from public dissatisfaction leading to citizen-driven, bottom-up efforts to drive change of some sort. In contrast, the ARDA was a top-down effort to create conditions conducive to social and economic change, one oriented to problems and challenges as perceived by government politicians and bureaucrats. The relation between the ARDA and the PFRA was complicated. The ARDA was to drive forward a process of rural development intended to reckon with ongoing change in agriculture. It was about adapting to bigger farms, new technologies, and lower rural populations. The PFRA operated in a dual and inconsistent manner. Some programs, like community pastures, operated to support a model of farming involving small-scale stock raising that seemed increasingly outdated. Some programs, like water-resources engineering in service to irrigation development, were consistent with the aim of maximizing agricultural production. Any potential tension between the ARDA and the PFRA was defused by the federal government's decision to rely on the PFRA as something like the ARDA's operating arm, with PFRA staff taking on the federal government's new responsibilities on the Prairies as defined by the ARDA.[29]

PFRA staff perceived the arrangement between the PFRA and the ARDA in a variety of ways. For his part, PFRA director M.J. Fitzgerald was optimistic. With regard specifically to water management in southern Alberta, Fitzgerald wrote in 1963 that it would take "a combination of the ARDA and PFRA programs" to make meaningful improvements.[30] But there was at least one significant downside for the PFRA. As the prairie agency became enmeshed in a larger federal government bureaucracy focused on development, its centre of gravity moved away from Regina and toward Ottawa. The ARDA was in some ways the realization of ambitions to go national that had long been held by PFRA insiders and supporters. In other ways, the ARDA established a larger federal bureaucracy around inequality and conservation that diminished the distinctiveness of the PFRA and so moderated the prairie agency's power and influence.

Among the politicians and administrators involved in considering new roles for the state in the mid-twentieth century – those who dealt in hope – the PFRA was an important influence and a key touchstone. The agency was seen to indicate what Ottawa might do to advance the conservation of natural resources, to address concerning inequalities, and even to remake federalism.

Water Development, Community Pastures, and Prairie Indigenous Peoples

The PFRA inspired mid-twentieth-century politicians, administrators, and experts to hope that state action could effectively address problems of resources management and rural inequality. But as Tina Loo has emphasized in her attention to state-sponsored community relocations, acting on this hope did not always produce the desired results and even caused harm. On the Prairies in the 1960s and 1970s, PFRA leadership engaged in new ways with the federal government's Department of Indian Affairs and Northern Development (DIAND), as well as with Indigenous peoples directly. The outcomes of these efforts were mixed at best.

Initially, prairie Indigenous peoples seem to have encountered barriers to accessing PFRA supports. In the late 1930s, PFRA director George Spence declined to consider a request for financial assistance in relation to two projects, presumably for water development, that were to benefit Indigenous peoples living on the Cowessess Reserve. In conveying his decision, Spence explained, "It has never been the policy of PFRA to include such projects in its program."[31] Notwithstanding Spence's early declaration, by the 1950s, the PFRA was providing engineering expertise to the federal government's Indian Affairs Branch.[32] In the mid-1960s, J.E. Beamish, chief of the PFRA's Water Development Service, specified that he and his staff sought to treat residents of reserves or reserve leadership on terms equivalent to those available to non-Indigenous farmers or municipalities.[33]

In line with Ottawa's concern with rural development, the DIAND was by the mid-1960s planning to undertake what it termed the "physical improvement of Indian Reservations."[34] This work included efforts to enhance water supply on reserves. In light of the PFRA's experience with water development, F.A. Clark, regional director of the Indian Affairs Branch, reached out to PFRA leadership to explore formalizing the PFRA's involvement in water development on reserves.[35] PFRA director M.J. Fitzgerald thought that this undertaking "might have deep policy implications."[36] Ultimately, it was determined that the PFRA would participate in on-reserve water-development activity as a technical agency, supporting the work of the DIAND by conducting project investigations, issuing recommendations, and designing larger undertakings.[37] The DIAND would pay most of the costs.[38]

The new arrangement did not last long. Constraints in the DIAND budget led the PFRA to draw on its own resources in order to fund projects that it saw as necessary to maintain the principle of treating Indigenous peoples on terms equivalent to non-Indigenous people.[39] The size of intended projects affected how they would be undertaken and funded, and this contingency undermined efforts to define clear roles for the two federal agencies.[40] Ultimately, in the late 1960s and early 1970s, funding limitations and administrative complications constrained the water-development services that the PFRA made available to Indigenous peoples. Circumstances were similarly challenging for Métis communities seeking PFRA assistance given the need to negotiate a satisfactory arrangement with provincial authorities because Métis people fell under provincial jurisdiction.[41]

The PFRA's Community Pastures Program was, by the late 1950s, desperate to identify additional large blocks of land where new pastures could be developed. This effort was part of the reason why the Community Pastures Program expanded northward, establishing pastures in the Aspen Parkland ecoregion.[42] In this context, the PFRA was keen to capitalize on what its director, H.J. Hargrave, described as the "idle" lands on reserves.[43] This phrasing suggests that the considerations guiding Indigenous communities in tending these lands were not legible or significant to agency leaders. The PFRA started developing community pastures on reserves in

FIGURE 7.1 Placing fence posts. This image captures the fence building that was required for the creation of a PFRA community pasture spanning the Cowessess and Sakimay Reserves, mid-1960s. *Courtesy of Glenbow Archives, Glenbow Western Research Centre, PA 1599-341-6, file 336S-354B, Calgary Herald fonds (F0358), file FL0370 – Irrigation. Image appeared alongside an article addressing the creation of the community pasture. See "Reserve Pastures Proving Boom to Western Bands,"* Indian Record, *March 1968, 15.*

the mid-1960s. The effort began with the creation of two pastures, each of which spanned two reserves: Ochapowace No. 71 and Kahkewistahaw No. 72, on the one hand, and Cowessess No. 73 and Sakimay No. 74, on the other, all of which were located along the Qu'Appelle Valley in southwestern Saskatchewan.[44]

Over the next eight years, the PFRA developed eleven on-reserve pastures through an investment of about $2 million.[45] Each had to be large enough to accommodate at least 1,000 head of cattle. As on other PFRA community pastures, cattle owners would be charged grazing fees roughly equivalent to the costs of pasture operation and maintenance. The PFRA committed to transferring a third of these revenues to host communities.[46] Employment opportunities would be made available to local Indigenous peoples, with work primarily available in pasture construction or cattle

FIGURE 7.2 Cattle arriving for summer grazing. The image captures the arrival of cattle at a PFRA community pasture spanning the Cowessess and Sakimay Reserves, mid-1960s. It also depicts some of the infrastructure used to manage cattle. *Courtesy of Glenbow Archives, Glenbow Western Research Centre, PA 1599-341-5, file 336S-354B, Calgary Herald fonds (F0358), file FL0370 – Irrigation. Image appeared alongside an article addressing the creation of the community pasture. See "Reserve Pastures Proving Boom to Western Bands,"* Indian Record, *March 1968, 15.*

roundup.[47] By 1970, on-reserve pastures served 343 patrons by accommodating 7,309 head of cattle.[48] A 1968 article in *The Indian Record,* a publication of the Missionary Oblates of Mary Immaculate that addressed matters related to Indigenous peoples, emphasized the revenue to Indigenous peoples anticipated from these pastures. Paralleling the disregard toward prior Indigenous land-management practices exhibited by PFRA leaders, the article celebrated so-called improvements to land that was taken to have previously "yielded no agricultural products and was infrequently utilized for hunting and wood cutting."[49]

On-reserve pastures boosted the grazing land available to nearby non-Indigenous farmers. From this perspective, the program was a success. But considered in relation to the benefits made available to Indigenous peoples, the outcomes of the program look quite different. Of the $2 million invested in pasture construction, only $196,000 was paid in wages to Indigenous people. Fewer than fifteen Indigenous people were employed in pasture operations, mostly on a seasonal basis, and none of them were in the position of pasture manager. For this more prestigious and remunerative role, the PFRA hired non-Indigenous people, citing an absence of sufficiently qualified Indigenous candidates.[50] Of the 343 stock raisers served and the 7,309 head of cattle accommodated on these pastures, only fifteen patrons were Indigenous, and together they pastured only 411 head of cattle.[51]

Retrospectively, the PFRA recognized that there were barriers keeping Indigenous peoples from becoming sufficiently involved in stock raising so as to derive more benefit from these pastures. Buying into the cattle business involved a substantial up-front investment, and Indigenous peoples lacked access to the financing that might have helped them to overcome this hurdle.[52] An effort by an Indigenous person to enter the cattle industry despite these barriers could, as the PFRA noted, lower their "short term living standard to a level below that which would be experienced in the absence of the cattle enterprise."[53] In the early 1970s, the federal government acknowledged that pastures on reserve land were "a costly and far from effective method of promoting income and employment opportunities for native people."[54] Further, the on-reserve pasture program fitted within a long-standing pattern of co-opting Indigenous peoples' lands to benefit non-Indigenous people.[55] With regard to both water development and community pastures, the PFRA formed part of a colonial state apparatus that hindered Indigenous peoples in their efforts to improve their circumstances.

Changed Contexts

The PFRA spent decades seeking to transform the landscapes of the Prairie West. But in the final years of the 1960s and throughout the 1970s, changes in the practices, approaches, and priorities of the federal government resulted in a significant recalibration for the PFRA.

The Liberal Party returned to power in Ottawa in 1963. After two minority governments under Lester B. Pearson, the Liberals took a more convincing hold on power with Pierre Trudeau's 1968 election victory. Trudeau's ambitious agenda, which he branded as the pursuit of a so-called just society, bore on the work of development. The year after Trudeau came to power, the new government created the Department of Regional Economic Expansion (DREE).[56] This new department offered greater coherence to the diffuse regional development programs operating across Canada.[57] It also introduced a new way of conceiving regional development: through the concept of the growth pole, which held that the most effective way for government to support development was by assisting and incentivizing the establishment and expansion of industrial development in urban settings.[58] Urban growth poles would pull wealth into a region, the thinking ran, with wealth then diffusing outward to rural areas. As scholar Anthony G.S. Careless puts it, DREE maintained the emphasis in the ARDA on promoting "jobs, parity of income, social adjustment, and labour mobility" but differed in its prioritization of urban industrialization as the most effective way to achieve these goals.[59]

Trudeau's forays into regional development reflect his preoccupation with countering the centrifugal forces that affected Canada, such as Quebec separatism and discontent in impoverished Atlantic Canada. His government's approach to regional development differed from the precedent set by the PFRA, whose focus on the rural agricultural Prairies in earlier efforts had helped to inspire the ARDA. Under DREE, 70 percent of regional development funds would be expended on areas east of Ottawa – so decidedly not in the prairie region.[60] Nevertheless, the PFRA was brought into DREE on its creation.[61] After this transfer, the PFRA was a West-oriented, rural-focused agency in a department that was East-oriented and that embraced urban-focused policies. The fit was awkward.

By the early 1970s, the PFRA had recalibrated its operations to better align with those of DREE by expanding its capacity to serve urban needs.[62] These changes particularly affected the PFRA's water-development undertakings. As early as the 1940s, experts and officials concerned with prairie cities and towns were calling on the PFRA to participate in improving services for residents of urban areas.[63] In the mid-1950s, PFRA director L.B. Thomson noted that the agency was involved in improving urban water supply only when projects oriented to agricultural needs could also serve urban purposes, citing as examples the St. Mary Reservoir in Alberta, the Duncairn Reservoir in Saskatchewan, and various projects along the Souris River in Manitoba.[64] After the PFRA was incorporated into DREE, the prairie agency was positioned to undertake a wider array of water-development projects, including those primarily intended to meet urban demand for water.[65] This specific change to the water-development program reflected a broader shift within the PFRA: the agency was being reoriented away from the specific task of supporting prairie agriculture and toward the broader goal of regional economic adjustment, which involved facilitating population movement from rural contexts to urban centres.[66]

If Trudeau's administration brought a different philosophy to regional development, so too did it bring a different style. According to Careless, in the mid to late 1960s, federal government bureaucrats grew increasingly uncomfortable with the degree of power extended to the provinces under prevailing regional development programs.[67] This discomfort found purchase in the political sphere under Trudeau. Through DREE, the federal government remade regional development programs, many of which had previously turned on cooperation between Ottawa and the provinces, by altering them in ways that re-enforced federal power. This process resulted in more careful federal scrutiny over the goals of development and the methods used to pursue them, effectively curtailing efforts emanating from places other than Ottawa. If the PFRA's incorporation into the ARDA had shifted some power from Regina to Ottawa, the shift became more pronounced and more significant under Trudeau.

The centralization of authority over regional development was accompanied by the adoption within the federal civil service of new models of fiscal accountability.[68] Greater onus was put on departments to explain and justify their expenditures. This need for justification had implications for the evaluation of long-standing PFRA offerings like community pastures. By the mid-1970s, PFRA leadership had come to feel that an intensive program of pasture improvement was necessary. Most pastures were at capacity, and an anticipated rise in beef consumption suggested that farmer demand for pasture was likely to increase.[69] The pasture program had already pushed northward and had experimented with creating pastures on reserves. PFRA officials believed that a further opportunity to expand capacity lay in efforts to fine-tune the mix of plants growing on existing pastures. This proposal drew on new scientific understandings of grazing and built on the long-standing PFRA practice of replacing native grasses with introduced species, often crested wheatgrass. The PFRA sought funds from the federal government's Treasury Board to undertake a five-year, $12-million pasture-improvement program aimed at increasing carrying capacity by 45 percent.[70]

The Treasury Board responded to the PFRA's request by asserting that the necessary funds would be made available only if the PFRA revised its fees so as to recover from pasture users all costs related to the Community Pastures Program. Under the user-pay, cost-recovery approach being promoted by the Treasury Board, pasture patrons would be charged fees to cover the total costs related to yearly pasture operation and maintenance, to future programs of improvement and construction, and to administration and overhead, like expenditures on postage or staff training.[71] At the inception of the Community Pastures Program, fees charged to patrons had covered only operation and maintenance. Later adjustments brought some increases in pasture fees, but these did not involve any substantial deviations from the original arrangement.[72] So the Treasury Board's proposal amounted to a significant departure from long-established patterns.

The PFRA was not pleased at the prospect of adopting a cost-recovery, user-pay approach to community pastures. Agency officials worried that the resulting hike in pasture fees would discourage farmers, particularly small operators, from beginning or continuing to raise cattle. In this way, the change might be seen as "working at cross purposes to continuing federal and provincial efforts to encourage the diversification of Prairie agriculture."[73] Agency officials were also concerned that the change might disadvantage PFRA pastures relative to the provincially run pastures operating on the Prairies.

Underlying these immediate reactions by PFRA leadership was a deeper issue related to how the PFRA was conceptualized and understood. The PFRA drew power from the willingness of federal government officials to see the agency as a necessary remedy to mistakes made in settling the Prairies, mistakes that had contributed to the 1930s crisis that underpinned the PFRA's creation. The continued influence of this idea prompted PFRA leaders to argue that a cost-recovery, user-pay model for community pastures would "run directly counter to the concept and intent of PFRA."[74] PFRA leadership also maintained that public investment in agriculture paid broad societal dividends. Jean Chrétien, president of the Treasury Board, was unmoved by either of these arguments.[75]

In responding to the Treasury Board, the PFRA questioned exactly which costs could appropriately be charged to pasture users. The agency argued that the Community Pastures Program had, over decades, served two key objectives: preventing the cultivation of unsuitable land and increasing pasture availability for individual farmers. The first of these was a public good, the agency asserted, and should be paid out of the public purse. And so only costs attributable to the second objective could rightly be charged to pasture patrons. The PFRA then went on to document a range of side benefits conferred to the public at large by community pastures. These outcomes included increased local recreational opportunities, improvement in the quality of livestock, and invigoration of rural farm communities. The agency argued that the costs of these side benefits should not be passed onto pasture patrons, which amounted to an argument for further public involvement in pasture funding.[76] Ultimately, the PFRA's approach was somewhat successful. The Treasury Board accepted the need to moderate the user-pay, cost-recovery approach in recognition that pastures should be publicly funded to the extent that they conferred public benefits.[77] But the principle that public investment in the PFRA paid society-wide benefits had been shaken.

At least some within the PFRA mourned the loss of the agency's operating model that they remembered and continued to believe in. In December 1979, F.G. Wagner, a PFRA staff member, bemoaned how political leaders and powerful bureaucrats within the federal government appeared narrowly "oriented toward meeting the need of technocrats for efficiency and effectiveness."[78] As Wagner put it to PFRA director Harry M. Hill, community pastures were being assessed "from the vantage of a government agency looking down rather than clients (patrons) looking up."[79] To Wagner's mind, the PFRA had changed – and not for the better.

Conclusion

The mid-twentieth-century Prairies were a laboratory for experiments in federalism. This was the case because challenges in the regional agricultural economy, in the 1930s but also beyond, reflected broader national difficulties with maintaining prosperity and with ensuring that it was shared widely. It was also the case because the PFRA was taken to represent a potential model for federal government involvement in economic adjustment in needy areas across Canada. The example of the PFRA positioned officials to think in new ways about government's role in addressing perceived challenges, making the agency relevant even to those who had no particular interest in the Prairies. The PFRA helped to inspire the ARDA and then became part of the administrative infrastructure that facilitated the ARDA's functioning. The prairie agency's decades of operation inspired federal government administrators who hoped to use their power and positioning in order to drive what they saw as improvement in the lives of people in Canada.

Throughout the 1960s and 1970s, the PFRA engaged with prairie Indigenous peoples and with the federal government bureaucracy directly responsible for matters related to Indigenous communities. With respect to water-development work, PFRA assistance to Indigenous peoples remained haphazard. Community pastures on reserves offered only very modest benefits to Indigenous peoples and helped non-Indigenous farmers by giving them access to reserve lands. Ultimately, the PFRA's programs did not successfully account for the particular needs and circumstances of Indigenous communities.

In the early years covered by this chapter, the PFRA provided a model for federal government action. In later years, the PFRA demonstrated a limited ability to even defend its programs in response to political pressure for spending cuts. By the 1970s, the PFRA operated largely as a technical agency, one positioned to deploy specialized expertise as required, rather than as a broad-minded, ambitious agency keen to articulate a vision for the rural Prairies and positioned to bring this vision to fruition. The PFRA, long an instrument of transformation on the Canadian Prairies, had itself been transformed.

Conclusion

The Prairie Farm *Transformation* Administration

In the early 1980s, senior PFRA officials began planning a party. The agency was approaching the fiftieth anniversary of its 1935 creation, and the occasion demanded commemoration. Although officials agreed that something was necessary, it seemed unclear what exactly was appropriate. A 50th Anniversary Committee was struck, and the committee solicited suggestions on the best way to mark the moment.[1]

A range of responses was forthcoming from agency employees, some of which were deemed of a "special nature" and earmarked for publication in an upcoming internal PFRA newsletter, presumably for humour value. These responses included the suggestions that all employees should be given an extra month's vacation, that a blowout party should be hosted in the PFRA's original Regina headquarters, and that a senior PFRA leader should "roller skate across Canada pulling a Charolais Bull in a coaster wagon painted robin's egg blue."[2] Although understood by those in charge in a lighthearted spirit, these comments suggest some of the internal complexity of the PFRA, with employees relishing the opportunity to poke fun at their superiors. Other responses captured a fear likely shared across the agency's ranks. One respondent advised to "cancel the party" given doubt over whether "this outfit will last until 1985."[3]

The longevity of the PFRA was no idle worry. The agency's finances had recently come under scrutiny, with proposed changes in the management of community pastures being among the tangible results of this examination. There were questions about the PFRA's administrative home. With significant shifts in the organization of federal government bureaucracy in the early 1980s, including the effective elimination of the Department of Regional Economic Expansion, there was uncertainty about whether the PFRA should be accommodated within the Department of the Environment or returned to the Department of Agriculture.[4] And most revealingly, as officials, farmers, and a broader public increasingly recognized in the late 1970s and early 1980s that a crisis in soil conservation was emerging anew on the Canadian Prairies, the PFRA was surprisingly poorly positioned to help address it.

The PFRA, an agency born of a 1930s agricultural crisis, was caught flat-footed by a similar circumstance in the early 1980s. Considering how that happened usefully casts into relief the PFRA's activities analyzed in previous chapters by making clear what the agency was *not* doing throughout the decades under consideration: focusing on soil degradation. How the agency was caught out in the early 1980s becomes clearer if we track the agricultural practice of summerfallow.

The Long History of Summerfallow

In the late nineteenth century, the practice of leaving a portion of a farm uncropped for an entire growing season was adopted by many prairie farmers as an important way of maximizing moisture availability in a dry landscape. Summerfallow also helped with weed control and soil nitrogen supply through the mineralization of organic matter, although the latter was not recognized until the mid-twentieth century.[5] Over years, black summerfallow – where repeated cultivation during fallow forestalled unwanted plant growth, leaving bare soils exposed – came to operate as a visual signifier of diligent farming.[6]

By the early 1900s, however, agricultural experts recognized that moisture availability and weed control came at a steep price.[7] Summerfallow served to break down soil structures, increasing the likelihood of soil drift. Still, despite serious drawbacks, summerfallow remained a key means through which many farmers sought to bolster the odds of decent crops. At the start of the 1930s, on an annual basis, about 30 percent of total cropland in the prairie provinces was in fallow throughout the growing season.[8]

Amid the difficult years of the 1930s, the connection between black summerfallow and blowing soil received significant attention. A number of agricultural techniques promoted by the PFRA like strip farming and trash cover were intended to anchor blowing soils. PFRA efforts to address soil degradation associated with black summerfallow, alongside efforts to facilitate withdrawal of agriculture from inappropriate areas, are at the centre of many accounts of the agency's attempts to fix the mistakes of settlement. For instance, in a chapter in *Men against the Desert* titled "From Strip Farming to Trash Farming," James H. Gray asserts that 1930s farmers were involved in the expert-facilitated "unlearning" of many formerly "common-sense notions" about successful agriculture.[9]

But the practice of summerfallow persisted long beyond the crisis of the 1930s. In Alberta and Saskatchewan, annual rates of summerfallow ranged between 30 and 40 percent from the early 1940s to the early 1970s.[10] Some of the drawbacks of black summerfallow had become clear, and farmers across the North American Great Plains were increasingly interested in the use of a trash cover on fallowed lands.[11] But even in modified form, summerfallow contributed to the deterioration of prairie soils. If summerfallow constituted a mistake of settlement, it was not one that the PFRA managed to fix definitively in the 1930s.

Summerfallow persisted for a range of reasons. For some farmers, what they perceived as its agricultural benefits outweighed its increasingly understood harms to soils. Economic circumstances and policy frameworks also perpetuated summerfallow. The Canadian Wheat Board, the sole buyer of wheat produced by prairie farmers, set farmers' delivery quotas not in relation to farm production but in relation to total cropland, which included fallow.[12] In an era of increasing farm yields, fallow helped farmers to ensure that they could sell what they produced. The federal government's Lower Inventories for Tomorrow (LIFT) program was also implicated. In light of a global wheat glut in the late 1960s, Ottawa established the program, paying farmers to reduce acreage sown with wheat. This resulted in a sharp but short-lived increase in fallow – from 12 million to 15 million acres – between 1969 and 1970.[13] These examples help to explain why fallow remained entrenched throughout the mid-twentieth century. Farmers who fallowed were operating in ways that made sense in relation to the prevailing economic and policy contexts.

In figuring out how to work their fields, farmers also took account of new techniques and technologies. Throughout the mid-twentieth century, during which the PFRA was focused on community pastures and water-resources engineering, change in agricultural practice swept across the agricultural Prairies. In the years following the Second World War, large machinery, agricultural chemicals, and expanding farm sizes became increasingly common. These changes proved sufficient to drive up rates of agricultural production even as ongoing processes of soil degradation hampered the prairie region's fertility. The consequences for regional soil fertility of agricultural practices like summerfallow were not immediately apparent because of the heightened farm productivity driven by agricultural industrialization.

It was in the early 1970s that the critique of summerfallow increased in volume on the Canadian Prairies, notwithstanding the temporary boost given to the practice by the short-lived LIFT program. Although experts had long recognized the negative effects of summerfallow on prairie soils, these effects began registering in new ways with a broader public, including practising farmers. Facing a crowd of resistant farmers at an early 1970s event, agricultural scientist D.A. Rennie, employed for years at the University of Saskatchewan, laid out the case against summerfallow.[14] This meeting took place during a pivotal period when farmers were beginning to consider other perspectives on summerfallow. Encouraged at the incipient shift, Rennie did what he could to generate momentum. He teamed up with fellow agricultural scientist J.G. Ellis to further raise awareness of what they saw as a worrying constellation of agricultural problems, co-authoring a 1978 volume titled *The Shape of Saskatchewan.* The volume's final section, "Man and Soil," documented worrying outcomes of common agricultural practices, including summerfallow. Erosion, loss of organic matter, acidification, compaction, and salinization were all presented as resulting from decades of capitalist agriculture on the Canadian Prairies. Rennie and Ellis concluded that "there is no doubt that farming systems must change" in order to protect against continued soil degradation.[15]

New agricultural technologies presented options to farmers concerned about soils. In the early 1960s, paraquat, a broad-spectrum herbicide, became available in Canada.[16] On the Prairies, some farmers increased their reliance on herbicides, rather than soil disturbing tillage, for weed control. The development of new equipment like no-till drill seeders and air seeders further increased the choices available to farmers interested in techniques that protected soils.[17] However, the cost of paraquat and new equipment, as well as the mixed results achieved by both, limited farmers' immediate uptake of alternative methods.[18] In the mid-1970s, glyphosate became available, a new and highly effective broad-spectrum herbicide marketed by chemical company Monsanto under the trade name Roundup.[19] Improved no-till drill seeders were available by the late 1970s.[20] In the 1970s and 1980s, new varieties of oilseeds and pulses were introduced to the Prairies.[21] Using them in rotation with wheat diminished problems with agricultural pests and diseases. Armed with new chemicals, new machines, and new crops, prairie farmers gradually began experimenting in greater numbers with farming practices that avoided or minimized summerfallow.[22]

From the mid-1940s, the PFRA focused on water-resources engineering and community pastures management, neither of which involved the agency in advocating for the widespread adoption of more soil-friendly farming practices. In these years, the agency did not have a substantial role in critiquing the practice of summerfallow. In the late 1960s and the 1970s, the PFRA operated in a manner largely subservient to the federal government's development agenda. Under Pierre Trudeau, economic development focused on population centres and supports for industry, both of which amounted to new realms of activity for the PFRA. Throughout these decades, soil conservation, although not entirely expunged from the PFRA's purview, was not among the agency's key undertakings.[23] Rates of summerfallow on the Canadian Prairies entered a period of decline not in the 1930s but in the 1970s, occurring at a point when the PFRA was not meaningfully involved in substantive engagements around field-level agricultural practices.[24]

In definitive illustration of a major claim of this book – that the PFRA should not be understood as primarily or solely engaged in fixing the so-called mistakes of settlement – the practice of summerfallow began diminishing in significance while the PFRA was busy with other matters.

Renewed Focus on Prairie Soils

The eventual decline of summerfallow formed part of a broader process of agricultural reckoning on the Canadian Prairies. A particularly dry year in 1977 renewed concern about the vulnerability of the prairie region to lower-than-expected precipitation. Bert Hargrave, Progressive Conservative member of Parliament for Medicine Hat, felt that conditions in 1977 made it seem like the hard years of the 1930s really could return.[25] Worse, some feared that the regional and agricultural changes of recent decades would exacerbate the consequences of any drought. There was increased domestic and urban water use on the Prairies, as well as greater reliance on hydropower for electricity. These changes expanded the populations and industries immediately affected by lower-than-expected precipitation. There were higher capital and operating costs for farmers, with significant farm indebtedness raising the stakes in relation to any year's crop. There was concern that regional environmental changes related to sustained agricultural activity had decreased the soil's moisture-holding capacity and increased its vulnerability to erosion. Although the troubles of 1977 proved short-lived, Elmer Mackay, minister of regional economic expansion, worried that a drought of any longer duration "would probably be more devastating than the one of the 1930's" because of mid-twentieth-century regional change.[26]

This concerning prospect moved governments to action. Within a few years, Ottawa and the provinces undertook further study of drought's likely effects on the Prairies and began to work on mitigation strategies.[27] Renewed concern with drought meant renewed interest in the PFRA. Although the agency was oriented in other directions, under the circumstances, a history with drought remediation was seen as a useful proxy for present activity. Under the direction of Harry Hill, the PFRA was soon considering the creation of a new branch focused on soil and water conservation, as well as considering greater investment in analytical and promotional capacity related to conservation. These efforts reflected the conclusion on the part of PFRA leaders that, as stated in an internal document in March 1980, they had been "neglecting our responsibilities" in this regard.[28]

In worrying anew about soil conservation, the PFRA was in good company. In the late 1960s and early 1970s, what was widely understood as catastrophic drought in Africa's Sahel region focused expert and public attention on the question of desertification in particular and soil degradation more broadly.[29] International focus on soils and agriculture is reflected in the 1982 adoption of a World Soil Charter by the United Nations Food and Agriculture Organization.[30] Soil degradation was a significant concern for the Worldwatch Institute, an early environmental think tank based in the United States.[31] In a Worldwatch publication focused on global soil erosion, Lester R. Brown and Edward C. Wolf asserted that current agricultural techniques were diminishing the available soil resource by 0.7 percent per year. As the authors put it, "the world is mining much of its cropland, treating it as a depletable resource."[32] As Brown and Wolf explained, the global-scale problem raised questions of intergenerational equity, with present land use threatening the well-being of future populations.[33]

By the 1980s, catalyzed by dry years in 1977 and again in 1980, and building on increasingly widespread concern about the degradation of agricultural lands, the PFRA was engaging directly with the problem of prairie soils. The PFRA formed a new Soil and Water Conservation Branch, creating the sort of specialized capacity that had been lacking in the agency since the mid-1940s.[34] By 1982, the PFRA was sharing in draft form a document titled "Land Degradation and Soil Conservation Issues on the Canadian Prairies: An Overview."[35] A product of the new Soil and Water

Conservation Branch, the document was shared widely with farm organizations, provincial agencies, research institutions (including universities), and other interested parties.[36] Circulating this document amounted to an effort to build consensus on the point that Rennie and Ellis had put forward some years earlier in *The Shape of Saskatchewan* (1978) – namely that farming systems must change.

The following year, the PFRA document was published in modestly revised form. The 1983 version reflected widespread expert concern about three key issues affecting prairie agriculture. The first was soil salinization, the process through which salts accumulate in agricultural soils, inhibiting plant growth. By the early 1980s, salinity afflicted some 10 percent of the cultivated lands of the agricultural Prairies, with an additional 1 percent potentially affected every year.[37] The second was soil erosion, a process that had continued throughout the mid-twentieth century despite the attention that it had received in the 1930s.[38] And the third was declining rates of organic matter in soils, which resulted in deteriorated soil structures and diminished availability of soil nutrients.[39] Although all three processes of soil degradation were particularly associated with summerfallow, they could also derive from other practices characterizing prairie agriculture at this time, including the use of large agricultural machinery and the expansion in size of agricultural fields, which eliminated field breaks that might have interrupted erosion processes. The 1983 document asserted that, if agriculture was to continue on the Canadian Prairies, soil degradation would need to be addressed.[40]

The 1983 document culminated in what the authors termed their thesis. They argued that the PFRA was "the logical vehicle for the development of a federal initiative and contribution to the enhancement and unification of soil conservation programs across the Prairies."[41] Also in 1983, the federal government transferred the PFRA to the Department of Agriculture, a move that expanded this department's capacity to undertake work on soils. Within a few years, the department published an overview of agricultural land degradation in western Canada. This document confirmed that high rates of agricultural productivity and serious processes of soil degradation were in coexistence on the Canadian Prairies, with worrying future economic, social, and environmental consequences.[42] Seeking inspiration on how to tackle the problem of soil degradation, the Department of Agriculture also undertook a study of American efforts in this regard. S.C. Lok, the author of this piece, explained that "soil and water conservation activities have received in the past, and continue to receive in the present, a much higher priority in the U.S. Great Plains than they have traditionally received in the Prairies."[43]

By the mid-1980s, the PFRA was far from the only Canadian organization concerned about soil degradation. In 1984, the Standing Senate Committee on Agriculture, Fisheries and Forestry published *Soil at Risk: Canada's Eroding Future.* The committee chair, H.O. Sparrow, explained that the report's goals were to "help make soil conservation a national issue" and to establish that action was necessary to address soil degradation.[44] That same year, journalist Garry Lawrence Fairbairn published *Will the Bounty End?* Fairbairn had been hired to take on this work by the Agricultural Institute of Canada, a national organization representing professionals involved in all facets of scientific agriculture. The book was an effort to build the general public's understanding of the ongoing agricultural emergency.[45] In 1985, the Canadian Environmental Advisory Council charged two agricultural scientists with considering land and soils issues in relation to current agricultural practices. L.A. Leskiw and C.F. Bentley argued that "massive, sustained, long-term soil conservation programs and policies" were required to "ensure the sustainability of productivity of Canada's farmed lands."[46] In 1986, the Science Council of Canada released a statement titled *A Growing Concern: Soil Degradation in Canada.* The document opened by proclaiming that although soil degradation remained associated in the public mind with the 1930s, circumstances in the 1980s were more alarming than those of the so-called Dirty Thirties. As the Science Council of Canada put it, "soil degradation poses a much greater threat to Canadian agriculture today than it ever has in the past."[47] A further effort to prompt action on soil conservation was a conference convened in Saskatoon in 1986. Organized by a range of actors in the agricultural sector, including the Canadian Society of Soil Science, the Agricultural Institute of Canada, and the Canadian Federation of Agriculture, the conference sought to "develop and recommend strategies for a Soil Conservation Policy in Canada."[48]

It was in the context of a reoriented PFRA and a renewed public appetite for action on soil conservation that the PFRA celebrated its fiftieth anniversary. The agency used the occasion to confirm its pivot back toward activities that had been at the centre of the agency's undertakings at its inception. A national and transnational context newly attuned to soil and water issues facilitated this about-face, and a history with soil conservation allowed the PFRA to follow broad trends while nevertheless positioning itself as a leader. The slogan chosen to unite the various aspects of the

PFRA's fiftieth anniversary celebrations – "soil and water for the future" – reflects the agency's efforts to capitalize on its history while positioning itself for the years ahead.[49] If the agency's anniversary activities had a strategic element, they also contained a dose of humility. The production of a celebratory film focused on the PFRA was nearly derailed by PFRA officials' discomfort with the boasting, flowery tone of the filmmakers.[50] The film was ultimately called *A Link in the Chain,* a title that reflects the understanding on the part of PFRA leadership that the agency was by no means to be accorded sole credit for whatever useful changes to prairie agriculture the preceding years had seen.

The PFRA's anniversary celebrations included a seminar intended to, as the published proceedings put it, "recognize the many accomplishments of this important prairie institution over the past half century."[51] At the same time, the event was intended to prompt the more than 150 attendees to "give some thought to what the future may hold for PFRA."[52] This dual mandate set the stage for an event that, even as participants proclaimed it enjoyable, held a fair number of discordant notes. In his presentation before the seminar, PFRA director Harry Hill acknowledged the harms resulting from the PFRA's failure to engage in a sustained manner with soil conservation.[53] At the same time, Hill took inspiration from what he saw as the PFRA's tradition as "a do it, change it, fix it organization." He attributed this tradition to those who had proceeded him in leadership, including politicians such as Jimmy Gardiner and previous PFRA directors like George Spence and L.B. Thomson.[54] If "a review of history," as Hill put it, indicated that the PFRA had failed to persist in needed soil conservation work, it also showed that the agency had helped people to "develop dreams into realities."[55] In what he saw as a year when the future of the PFRA would be decided, this aspect of the agency's history buoyed Hill's spirits.[56]

Economically, the 1980s were a very difficult period for prairie farmers. Europe had long been an important market for Canadian wheat, but government subsidies propelled European wheat farmers to new levels of production. The United States responded with subsidies of its own, global wheat prices dropped, and fierce competition for agricultural markets ensued.[57] Particularly due to the low prices for key commodities like wheat, and despite supports from Ottawa, high interest rates meant that farmers who borrowed to acquire machinery or land had difficulty servicing their debts.[58] The political and economic philosophy of neoliberalism was increasingly coming to bear on government management of the agricultural sector.[59] Even amid challenging economic circumstances, faced with a crisis in soils, prairie farmers in the late 1980s and the 1990s experimented with conservation tillage, a set of agricultural practices involving retaining crop residues on fields, controlling weeds by herbicides with minimal or no cultivation, seeding and fertilizing without tillage, and using crop rotation to control pests, diseases, and weeds.[60] Beyond widespread concern over prairie soils, the shift toward conservation tillage hinged on factors including a glyphosate price drop, improvements in no-till machinery, an eventual moderation in interest rates (which made new machinery more affordable), and increased fuel costs (which made conventional tillage more expensive).[61] The PFRA had a role in promoting farmer adoption of conservation tillage in this period, with the agency providing various supports to farmers coping with soil degradation and seeking to foster what it called a "conservation ethic" among prairie farmers and society at large.[62] Greater concern with soil conservation led farmers to plant more trees in shelterbelts, an activity that was by this time again under PFRA purview.[63] Scholar Murray Fulton has argued that, even in the absence of a sustained effort at soil conservation, the PFRA's 1930s activities laid the groundwork for these later efforts.[64]

Conservation tillage transformed prairie agriculture. Scholar Lana Awada has estimated that adopting zero tillage, a form of conservation tillage, decreased farm fuel needs by 39 percent, machinery operating hours by 48 percent, and labour requirements by 31 percent. It also increased herbicide use by 48 percent.[65] Zero tillage in particular and conservation tillage more broadly both protected and improved soils.[66] Conservation tillage led to a significant decline in the greenhouse gases emitted by crop growers on the Canadian Prairies.[67] At its best, conservation tillage involves farmers in intimate and careful relations with their lands, requiring that farmers make considered judgments about how to maximize production while safeguarding soils. By 2011, western Canada was a global leader in zero tillage, with 68 percent of the region's farms practising this form of agriculture.[68]

Conservation tillage has been subject to critique. A system of agriculture heavily reliant on chemical weed control can seem intuitively at odds with sustainability, particularly in the context of a North American environmental movement defined in part by concern with the harms of herbicides and pesticides. Significant uncertainty remains about the effects of glyphosate on human health.[69] Increased fertilizer application contributes to the eutrophication of prairie lakes, with excess nutrients in agricultural runoff driving algae blooms and oxygen depletion.[70] Even as conservation tillage addressed regional problems with soil conservation, it more thoroughly enmeshed the agricultural Prairies in the global market for agricultural chemicals.[71] Sociologists Michael Gertler and JoAnn Jaffe and interdisciplinary scholar Mary A. Beckie propose the alternative label "neo-conventional farming" to emphasize the continuities between conservation tillage and earlier unsustainable agricultural practices. They point to problems like herbicide resistance and soil compaction in questioning whether conservation tillage represents a satisfactory solution to long-standing agricultural problems. The term "neo-conventional farming" highlights neoliberal elements within conservation tillage, including the central role of profit-driven corporations in supplying agricultural inputs and farming guidance.[72] Farmers who once coproduced agricultural knowledge with government scientists may now largely be consumers of information disseminated by representatives of private corporations.[73] Some farmers may end up with an impoverished understanding of the techniques and technologies that they use in producing their crops, a circumstance that sociologists Harry P. Diaz and Robert Stirling understand as part of the degradation of agricultural labour.[74]

Some critics of conservation tillage have concerns over the use of genetic modification to produce herbicide-resistant crops. Genetically engineered Roundup Ready canola, developed by Monsanto and now produced by Bayer, allows farmers to chemically control unwanted plants without fear of harming the desired crop, even once the crop has emerged from the soil. Although growing Roundup Ready canola simplifies some aspects of farm work, it is expensive and imposes significant constraints on farmers. Scholar Wilhelm Peekhaus argues that the production of genetically engineered seed for sale amounts to the privatization of the biological commons, a process that generates private profit while introducing risks to public well-being that may not yet be fully understood.[75] The operations of multinational agrichemical companies may reflect an overreaching faith in scientific and technical progress characteristic of the worst of high modernism.[76] The situation is particularly concerning because multinational corporations operate to maximize value for shareholders rather than to pursue some idea of the public interest. Environmental historian Bartow Elmore's study of Monsanto confirms that the company's genetic engineering work has been "more about selling chemicals than investing in real solutions to our food problems, which has resulted in wasted opportunities and wasted resources."[77] Even amid this complex and changing agricultural landscape, prairie farmers are actively engaged in determining how best to farm prairie lands.[78]

In the final years before the PFRA's elimination in 2009, its leadership made clear the agency's position that conservation tillage should be critiqued and improved. The agency's 1980s return to soil conservation was followed by a shift some years later toward a broader environmental orientation. In 2000, the agency released a document titled *Prairie Agricultural Landscapes: A Land Resource Review.* The document updated earlier PFRA publications on prairie soils in relation to concerns over erosion, salinity, and organic matter. The document also brought wider environmental circumstances into consideration, particularly the quality of the region's water and the state of its riparian areas.[79] The PFRA warned that further increases to agricultural production might exacerbate environmental harms. Although the shift to considering the broader prairie environment mirrored growing society-wide concern with sustainability, the PFRA was distinguished by how it raised such issues in relation to prairie farming. As journalist Laura Rance puts it, within agricultural circles, the PFRA was "a lone voice speaking for the environment."[80] In the years immediately prior to its elimination, the PFRA was working to figure out how best to foster regional agriculture while conserving the wider prairie environment.

Prairie Pasts, Prairie Futures

The Prairie Farm Rehabilitation Administration has at times played an important role in soil conservation and environmental stewardship on the agricultural prairies. But the agency's history is defined by a sustained and multipronged effort at regional transformation, not by its intermittent attention to soils or by its late-emerging environmental orientation. Particularly given that the PFRA is often understood as an important historical actor and a model for future action, it is important to reckon thoroughly with the agency's history.

The PFRA was a state-led effort to drive transformation on the mid-twentieth-century agricultural Prairies. In reckoning with the crisis of the 1930s and then in creating community pastures and undertaking water-engineering projects, the agency worked to advance the stability and prosperity of prairie farmers. Further, the PFRA helped to establish the state as a vehicle through which to address key problems in mid-twentieth-century society. The agency served as a prototype for other efforts in Canada at state-led social and environmental change.

In considering the environmental history of the PFRA, the starting point matters. If the starting point falls relatively late in the agricultural colonization of the Prairie West – after the radical ecological transformations that settlement entailed – the PFRA may appear to have improved the situation by prompting farmers to reassess some of their most harmful practices, with the result that many farmers, for instance, switched from black summerfallow to fallowing with a soil-protecting trash cover. But if an environmental history of the PFRA is calibrated to the prior ecologies of the Prairie West in all their diversity, the agency falls in line with the larger trajectory of agricultural colonization, one defined by ongoing efforts to harness ecological processes so as to facilitate farm production. Even with a trash cover, fallow can degrade the soil, as the PFRA had recognized by the early 1980s. And even a community pasture, a reservoir of ecological diversity in comparison to fields farmed more intensively, is an impoverished version of the prior prairie landscape.

Although the PFRA's involvement in large-scale water-engineering projects offers perhaps the clearest illustration of the agency's transformative effects on the landscape, the PFRA transformed prairie environments in multiple ways. Rural water supply was improved, and community pastures safeguarded vulnerable lands from more intensive forms of agriculture. As made clear by the examples of the wheat stem sawfly and crested wheatgrass, the agency's changes could have unanticipated outcomes. Intentionally or otherwise, PFRA-driven transformations consolidated and extended the environmental consequences of agricultural colonization. Contextualizing the PFRA in the longer history of prairie agriculture and tracing the agency's history past the 1930s offers a new perspective on the PFRA, one that also enriches understanding of mid-twentieth-century prairie agriculture.

The agricultural colonization of the Prairie West in the late nineteenth and early twentieth centuries turned on ideas of race. Alberta irrigation in the early twentieth century illustrates this circumstance and also makes clear how the creation and operation of the PFRA spurred processes that were defined in racialized terms. Sugar beet farming depended on abundant water and cheap labour, and amid prevailing white supremacy, Indigenous peoples, Asian peoples, and migrants from southern, central, and eastern Europe were particularly vulnerable to exploitation. In irrigation farming as in prairie farming more broadly, with respect to white supremacy as well as environmental change, although the PFRA did not necessarily put key processes in motion, the agency contributed to furthering them. Understanding this dynamic is essential to understanding the PFRA.

Settler colonialism structured the agricultural Prairies beyond the 1930s and was manifest in the actions of the PFRA. This colonial orientation was palpably evident in the experiences of the Métis at Ste. Madeleine, in the fate of the Sacred Site known as Mistasiniy, and in the degradation of the Saskatchewan River Delta, a landscape that was home to Nehinuwuk. It was also evident in the halting efforts to extend PFRA water-resources services to Indigenous peoples and in the creation of on-reserve community pastures, which largely benefitted non-Indigenous peoples. The actions of the PFRA illustrate how modern state agencies, even those not explicitly conceived to engage with Indigenous peoples, functioned as vectors of colonialism.

The PFRA's efforts at transformation are also instructive in other ways. The agency's operations frequently reflected tensions between and among experts and politicians. In some instances, engineers and scientists pulled one way, and political leaders pulled the other. In other instances, experts and politicians themselves held divergent views. And so this study reveals the negotiated character of high modernism in mid-twentieth-century Canada. At the same time, the operation of the PFRA situated the Prairies in relation to transnational communities of expertise. Just as the chapter about the agency's work in Ghana offers a robust example of the PFRA's transnational work, other chapters illustrate how the PFRA connected the Prairies to ideas, techniques, and approaches in circulation globally. This history of the rural Prairies is a thoroughly transnational tale.

In the early 1970s, the Department of Regional Economic Expansion undertook an assessment of the PFRA's community pastures and small water-development programs. Assessors found that the small water-development programs "contributed significantly to the development of stable water supplies in the Prairies."[81] With respect to community pastures, assessors found that these lands demonstrated appropriate management, helped to improve the quality of livestock, and provided nearby farmers with summer grazing.[82] But if assessors lauded aspects of the Community Pastures Program, they also questioned its significance, noting that only 7 percent of Saskatchewan cattle and 2.6 percent of Manitoba cattle were accommodated on PFRA community pastures.[83] By this time, the prairie cattle population was increasing but becoming concentrated on a smaller number of farms.[84] Feedlots in Alberta were growing in importance.[85] Assessors found that, in the early 1970s, the PFRA's Community Pastures Program "does not play a significant role in the total livestock picture in the West."[86] This view of the Community Pastures Program points to an important perspective on the PFRA at large. Across decades and various areas of activity, the agency aimed at transformation. Change often resulted, sometimes in unexpected ways. Sometimes change did not occur or fell short of the desired outcome. Many of the key drivers of agricultural transformation on the mid-twentieth-century Canadian

Prairies, including technological innovation and the vagaries of international markets, were simply beyond the scope of the PFRA. Global-scale processes proved intractable to a regionally focused federal government agency.

In the 1970s, the PFRA's Community Pastures Program was deemed to be of only modest importance in relation to the prairie livestock industry; in the early 1980s, the agency found itself wanting in its attention to soil conservation. Historian Will Langford has recognized that failure amounts to a recurring theme in studies of past efforts at development, whether led by governments or by other entities.[87] At least insofar as it might be considered a development agency, the PFRA's failure to fully realize its own ambitions is not unusual. But the PFRA's mixed record becomes remarkable in the context of public discourse that lauds the agency for its success. Politicians, analysts, and advocacy groups have all, in the years since the PFRA's 2009 elimination, referenced the agency within calls for government investment in environmental management and social change. For some, the admirable aspect of the agency was its ability to collaborate with farmers in the public interest. Given the worrisome effects of privatization and multinational capitalism on the agricultural Prairies and beyond, this aspect is a crucial consideration. But it is important to recognize that, over decades, notwithstanding its public-interest mandate, the PFRA engaged in activities that sometimes had negative outcomes, whether for the regional environment or for disadvantaged social groups. Those of us who believe in the ideal of public administration must critique its historical reality when it falls short or produces mixed results, particularly when a historical example is proposed as a model or inspiration for future action.

Recent arguments for the resuscitation of the PFRA were anticipated by a document that the agency itself released in the early 1980s. Part of the agency's pivot back to soil conservation, the document argued that ameliorating current soil degradation would require "an approach akin to that originally given by PFRA to the soil erosion of the 1930's."[88] At the PFRA's 1985 fiftieth anniversary celebrations, Harry Hill asserted his pride in directing an organization that helped people to "develop dreams into realities."[89] By documenting the mixed environmental and social legacies of this agency, this book demonstrates why we should be cautious in casting an aspirational eye on the PFRA. Dreams for a future that is more just and more sustainable may well need other inspiration.

Notes

Foreword: "The best-laid schemes …/ go oft awry"

1 Bruno Latour, "Visualisation and Cognition: Drawing Things Together," in *Knowledge and Society: Studies in the Sociology of Culture Past and Present,* vol. 6, ed. Henrika Kuklick and Elizabeth Long, 1–40 (Greenwich, CT: Jai, 1986), 7.

2 Shannon Stunden Bower, *Wet Prairie: People, Land, and Water in Agricultural Manitoba* (Vancouver: UBC Press, 2011).

3 Michiel Horne, *The Great Depression of the 1930s in Canada* (Ottawa: Canadian Historical Association, 1984).

4 W.L. Morton, "Seeing an Unliterary Landscape," in *Contexts of Canada's Past: Selected Essays of W.L. Morton,* ed. A.B. McKillop (Montreal/Kingston: McGill-Queen's University Press, 1980), 17. Originally published in *Mosaic: A Journal for the Comparative Study of Literature and Ideas* 3, 3 (1970): 1–10.

5 Ian McKay, "The Liberal Order Framework: A Prospectus for a Reconnaissance of Canadian History," *Canadian Historical Review* 81, 4 (2000): 616–45.

6 John Warkentin, "Water and Adaptive Strategies in Settling the Canadian West," *Manitoba Historical Society Transactions,* series 3, no. 28 (1971–72), http://www.mhs.mb.ca/docs/transactions/3/waterstrategies.shtml.

7 Trevor Herriot, *Towards a Prairie Atonement* (Regina: University of Regina Press, 2016), 13.

8 Paul G. McHugh, *Aboriginal Societies and the Common Law: A History of Sovereignty, Status and Self-Determination* (Oxford: Oxford University Press, 2005), 20; for a discussion of this question, see also 1–58.

9 Alain Beaulieu, "Une histoire instrumentalisée: réflexions sur l'usage du passé dans les revendications autochtones," in *Vert, le droit? Conférence des juristes de l'État 2009,* 349–71 (Cowansville, QC: Éditions Yvon Blais, 2009), translated as "An Instrumentalized History: Reflections on the Use of the Past in Aboriginal Claims," quote at 7, https://www.academia.edu/5129408/An_Instrumentalized_History_Reflections_on_the_Use_of_the_Past_in

_Aboriginal_Claims. Beaulieu also observes that the legal system's use of history (and historians) to identify a "usable" past on which to base decisions about Indigenous claims under the 1982 Canadian Charter of Rights and Freedoms has often worked in similar ways to categorize rather than to understand the past.

10 Patrick Wolfe, *Settler Colonialism and the Transformation of Anthropology: The Politics and Poetics of an Ethnographic Event* (London/New York: Cassell, 1999).

11 Quoted in Ben Silverstein, "Patrick Wolfe (1949–2016)," *History Workshop Journal* 82, 1 (2016): 318.

12 Beaulieu, "Instrumentalized History," 10.

13 Andrew Woolford and Jeff Benvenuto, "Canada and Colonial Genocide," *Journal of Genocide Research* 17, 4 (2015): 381.

14 Silverstein, "Patrick Wolfe," 318. See also Woolford and Benvenuto, "Canada and Colonial Genocide," 380.

15 Béatrice Craig, *Backwoods Consumers and Homespun Capitalists: The Rise of a Market Culture in Eastern Canada* (Toronto: University of Toronto Press, 2009), 4, 13.

16 E.P. Thompson, *The Making of the English Working Class* (London: Victor Gollancz, 1963). Worth reading in this context is Harold Perkin, "'The Condescension of Posterity': The Recent Historiography of the English Working Class," *Social Science History* 3, 1 (1978): 87–101, not least for his acerbic critique of labour history devoid of "imagination and empathy precisely because it uses the working class as an object." This form of history, he avers, "offends and misrepresents the working class" by treating it "not as individual people to be understood for their own sake, and categorized, where this is necessary, into discriminate groups which they themselves would recognize and understand but treats it as a monolithic block to be set against the opposing monolithic block of the capitalist bourgeoisie, the nether millstone to be ground against the upper in the theoretical mill of historical inevitability" (90).

17 I am thinking here of Brian Friel's stage play *Faith Healer* (London/Boston: Faber and Faber, 1980), reprinted in Brian Friel, *Collected Plays: Volume Two,* 361–410 (Oldcastle, Ireland/London: Gallery Press/Faber and Faber, 2016); and Ben Brantley's review of a New York production of the play, "Review/Theater: Faith Healer; From 3 Versions of a Shared Past, a Vision of Memory's Power," *New York Times,* 26 April 1994.

18 James C. Scott, *Seeing Like a State: How Certain Schemes to Improve the Human Condition Have Failed* (New Haven, CT: Yale University Press, 1998). For an effective summary of both Scott and critiques of his work, see Tina Loo, "High Modernism, Conflict, and the Nature of Change in Canada," *Canadian Historical Review* 97, 1 (2016): 34–58.

19 Jess Gilbert, *Planning Democracy: Agrarian Intellectuals and the Intended New Deal* (New Haven, CT: Yale University Press, 2015).

20 Dean Bavington, *Managed Annihilation: An Unnatural History of the Newfoundland Cod Collapse* (Vancouver: UBC Press, 2010); Christopher D. Stone, *Should Trees Have Standing? Law, Morality, and the Environment,* 3rd ed. (Oxford: Oxford University Press, 2010).

21 Shannon Stunden Bower, "Strip Farming and the Wheat Stem Sawfly on the Canadian Prairies, 1930s–1940s," *Folklore* 41, 3 (2020): 4–8. https://niche-canada.org/2020/04/09/strip-farming-and-the-wheat-stem-sawfly-on-the-canadian-prairies-1930s-1940s/.

22 Robert Burns, "To a Mouse, on Turning Her Up in Her Nest with the Plough, November, 1785," in *Poems, Chiefly in the Scottish Dialect* (Kilmarnock: John Wilson, 1786), 138. A modern-English translation by American poet Michael R. Burch reads, "But mouse-friend, you are not alone/ in proving foresight may be vain:/ The best laid schemes of Mice and

Men/ go oft awry,/ and leave us only grief and pain,/ for promised joy!" See https://www.rcsdk12.org/cms/lib/NY01001156/Centricity/Domain/3732/to-a-mouse-translation.pdf.

23 On this general point, see Joan Sangster, "Presidential Address: Confronting Our Colonial Past: Reassessing Political Alliances over Canada's Twentieth Century," *Journal of the Canadian Historical Association* 28, 1 (2017): 1–43.

24 Burns, "To a Mouse," 140.

Introduction

1 Green Party of Canada, *Platform 2021: Green Future, Life with Dignity, Just Society* (Ottawa: Green Party of Canada, 2021), 23, https://www.greenparty.ca/sites/default/files/gpc_platform_en_v-02.pdf. Notably, the 2019 election platform included the same commitment. See Green Party of Canada, *Honest. Ethical. Caring. Leadership: Election Platform 2019* (Ottawa: Green Party of Canada, 2019), 39, https://fipa.bc.ca/wp-content/uploads/2019/10/platform_2019_en_web_update_09-16.pdf.

2 Liberal Party of Canada, *Forward. For Everyone* (Ottawa: Liberal Party of Canada, 2021), 48, https://liberal.ca/wp-content/uploads/sites/292/2021/09/Platform-Forward-For-Everyone.pdf; Liberal Party of Canada, *Forward: A Real Plan for the Middle Class* (Ottawa: Liberal Party of Canada, 2019), 36, https://2019.liberal.ca/wp-content/uploads/sites/292/2019/09/Forward-A-real-plan-for-the-middle-class.pdf; Ralph Goodale, "Goodale: How to Make Progress on Prairie Priorities?" *Regina Leader-Post*, 16 November 2019, https://leaderpost.com/opinion/columnists/how-to-make-progress-on-prairie-priorities; Karen Briere, "Goodale Brand Expected to Prevail in Sask," *Western Producer*, 17 October 2019, https://www.producer.com/news/goodale-brand-expected-to-prevail-in-sask/; Colin Slark, "Politicians Pitch Platforms at Regenerative Ag Conference," *Brandon Sun*, 15 November 2023, https://www.brandonsun.com/local/2023/11/15/politicians-pitch-platforms-at-regenerative-ag-conference. In 2023, the Liberals announced the creation of the Canada Water Agency, which will be headquartered on the Canadian Prairies. See Ed White, "Canada Water Agency to Be Located in Winnipeg," *Western Producer*, 3 April 2023, https://www.producer.com/news/canada-water-agency-to-be-located-in-winnipeg/.

3 Darrin Qualman, with the National Farmers Union, *Tackling the Farm Crisis and the Climate Crisis: Transformative Strategy for Canadian Farms and Food Systems* (Saskatoon: National Farmers Union, 2019), 6–7. See also Darrin Qualman, "Canada Needs Climate Change Agency," *Western Producer*, 17 November 2022, https://www.producer.com/opinion/canada-needs-climate-change-agency/.

4 Richard Florizone, "Help Canada's Workers Now – but Don't Lock Us into a High-Carbon Future," *Hill Times*, 25 March 2020, https://www.hilltimes.com/story/2020/03/25/help-canadas-workers-now-but-dont-lock-us-into-a-high-carbon-future/266952/. See also Julia M.L. Laforge, Vanessa Corkal, and Aaron Cosbey, *Farming the Future: Agriculture and Climate Change on the Canadian Prairies* (Winnipeg: International Institute for Sustainable Development, 2021), https://www.iisd.org/publications/report/farming-future-agriculture-and-climate-change-canadian-prairies.

5 See, for instance, John Morris, "Comment: Bring Back the PFRA," *Manitoba Co-operator*, 26 May 2019, https://www.manitobacooperator.ca/news-opinion/opinion/comment-bring-back-the-prairie-farm-rehabilitation-administration/; and Marc Fawcett-Atkinson, "A 1930s-Era Federal Agency Helped Farms Recover from an Ecological Crisis. It's Time for a Replacement, Advocates Say," *National Observer*, 5 October 2020, https://www.national

observer.com/2020/10/05/news/1930s-era-federal-agency-helped-farms-recover-ecological-crisis-its-time-replacement.

6 Agriculture and Agri-Food Canada, Agri-Environment Services Branch, *PFRA 1935 – AESB 2010: 75 Years* (Ottawa: Departmental Publications Service, 2010), 6, https://publications.gc.ca/site/eng/9.901970/publication.html.

7 John Dupuis, "The Canadian War on Science: A Long, Unexaggerated, Devastating Chronological Indictment," *Georgia Straight*, 28 May 2013, https://www.straight.com/news/385761/canadian-war-science-long-unexaggerated-devastating-chronological-indictment; Chris Turner, *The War on Science: Muzzled Scientists and Wilful Blindness in Stephen Harper's Canada* (Vancouver: Greystone Books, 2013). The elimination of the former PFRA's remaining functions was achieved through the 2012 passage of Bill C-38, an omnibus budget bill. The wrap-up of PFRA activities extended into 2013.

8 Chester Martin, *"The Natural Resources Question": The Historical Basis of Provincial Claims* (Winnipeg: King's Printer, 1920); Lewis H. Thomas, "Introduction to the Carleton Library Edition," in Chester Martin, *"Dominion Lands" Policy*, ed. Lewis H. Thomas (Toronto: McClelland and Stewart, 1973), xi.

9 Arthur S. Morton and Chester Martin, *History of Prairie Settlement and "Dominion Lands" Policy* (Toronto: Macmillan, 1938), 524–34.

10 Ibid., 544.

11 Ibid., 543–44; Thomas, "Introduction," xvii.

12 W.J. Patterson, Premier of Saskatchewan, to James G. Gardiner, Federal Minister of Agriculture, 3 August 1937, Provincial Archives of Saskatchewan (PAS), GR 80, VI, file 13r; James G. Gardiner, Federal Minister of Agriculture, to W.J. Patterson, Premier of Saskatchewan, 22 September 1937, Glenbow Western Research Centre (GWRC), C0048, file M-3761-364. Although William John Patterson and James G. Gardiner differed slightly in their understanding of what constituted the mistakes of settlement, they agreed that mistakes had occurred and that a government response was required.

13 L.B. Thomson, Director, PFRA, "Place of P.F.R.A. in Land Use Plan," address to Agricultural Representatives Conference, 10 January 1949, 13, PAS, GR 6-2, R-324, file 7.16.

14 W.M. Drummond and W. Mackenzie, *Progress and Prospects of Canadian Agriculture*, ed. Royal Commission on Canada's Economic Prospects (Ottawa: Queen's Printer, 1957), 356–57; Saskatchewan, Royal Commission on Agriculture and Rural Life, *Farm Income* (Regina: Government of Saskatchewan, 1957), 171.

15 George Spence, Director of Prairie Farm Rehabilitation, "Submission to the Saskatchewan Reconstruction Council," 16 December 1943, PAS, GR 80, VI, file 50h; George Spence and John Vallance, "Organization of the P.F.R.A. for Water Conservation and Resettlement," *C.S.T.A. Review* 23 (December 1939): 30. Historian Bill Waiser has recognized the prevalence of the "mistakes of settlement" narrative within official discourse. In his 2005 history of Saskatchewan, Waiser argued that some federal officials saw the PFRA as "the only realistic solution to the mistake of opening the area to farming." Bill Waiser, *Saskatchewan: A New History* (Calgary: Fifth House, 2005), 321.

16 George Edwin Britnell, *The Wheat Economy* (Toronto: University of Toronto Press, 1939), 216. See also George Edwin Britnell, "The Rehabilitation of the Prairie Wheat Economy," *Canadian Journal of Economics and Political Science* 3, 4 (1937): 508–29.

17 Director of Rehabilitation George Spence to Professor of Political Science G.E. Britnell, 21 November 1939, PAS, GR 80, VI, file 37.

18 Vernon Fowke, *Canadian Agricultural Policy: The Historical Pattern* (Toronto: University of Toronto Press, 1946), 240.

19 Vernon Fowke, *The National Policy and the Wheat Economy* (Toronto: University of Toronto Press, 1957), 285–86.

20 George Edwin Britnell and Vernon Fowke, *Canadian Agriculture in War and Peace, 1935–1950* (Stanford, CA: Stanford University Press, 1962), 75–79.

21 James H. Gray, *Men against the Desert* (Saskatoon: Western Producer Prairie Books, 1967).

22 Charles Mandel, "(James H.) Gray in Name Only: Alberta Loses a Pioneering and Brilliant Social Historian," *Alberta Report,* 30 November 1998, 38; Bill Brennan, *How the West Was Written: The Life and Times of James H. Gray* (Calgary: Fifth House, 2006), 24–36.

23 Gray, *Men against the Desert,* viii.

24 James H. Gray, *The Winter Years: The Depression on the Prairies* (Toronto: Macmillan of Canada, 1966), 166.

25 Untitled speaking notes starting "I think that first of all ... " 10, University of Calgary Archives and Special Collections (U of C Archives), F0060, 67/73.17, 7.15.8.

26 R.E. McKenzie, *Saskatchewan Institute of Agrologists, 1946–1970: An Account of the First 25 Years* (Saskatoon: Saskatchewan Institute of Agrologists, 1970), 5–6.

27 Brennan, *How the West Was Written,* 105; John Herd Thompson and Ian MacPherson, "'How You Gonna Get 'Em Back to the Farm': Writing the Rural/Agricultural History of the Prairie West," paper presented at the Western Canadian Studies Conference, Saskatoon, 23 October 1987, 8, quoted in Daniel M. Balkwill, "The Prairie Farm Rehabilitation Administration and the Community Pasture Program, 1937–1947" (MA thesis, History, University of Saskatchewan, 2002), 18n65.

28 Admin – Public Relations, "Men against the Desert," Library and Archives Canada (LAC), RG 17, 2015-01238-9, negative 34626, e011166295. The PFRA's enthusiasm for Gray's work is also indicated by the inclusion of an epigraph from *Men against the Desert* in the agency's 1979–80 annual report. Prairie Farm Rehabilitation Administration, *Prairie Farm Rehabilitation Administration Annual Report, 1979–1980* (Ottawa: Department of Regional Economic Expansion, 1981).

29 Amy von Heyking, "Teaching Prairie Pasts in 20th-Century Alberta and Saskatchewan Schools," *Prairie History* 12 (2023): 14.

30 Gerald Friesen, *The Canadian Prairies: A History* (Toronto: University of Toronto Press, 1984), 392.

31 David C. Jones, *Empire of Dust: Settling and Abandoning the Prairie Dry Belt* (Edmonton: University of Alberta Press, 1987), 222. See also David C. Jones, ed., *"We'll all be buried down here": The Prairie Dryland Disaster, 1917–1926* (Calgary: Historical Society of Alberta, 1986).

32 Barry Potyondi, *In Palliser's Triangle: Living in the Grasslands, 1850–1930* (Saskatoon: Purich, 1995). Potyondi also collaborated on an earlier project that focused on the Grasslands National Park area. In this earlier work, he noted that the hardships of the 1930s meant that the "fallacy of 'effective settlement' under the Dominion Lands Policy had become self-evident." D.M. Loveridge and Barry Potyondi, *From Wood Mountain to the Whitemud: A Historical Survey of the Grasslands National Park Area* (Ottawa: National Historic Parks and Sites Branch, Parks Canada, 1983), 229.

33 David Wood, *Places of Last Resort: The Expansion of the Farm Frontier into the Boreal Forest in Canada, c. 1910–1940* (Montreal/Kingston: McGill-Queen's University Press, 2006), 164.

34 Curtis R. McManus, *Happyland: A History of the "Dirty Thirties" in Saskatchewan, 1914–1937* (Calgary: University of Calgary Press, 2011), 214–21.

35 Gregory P. Marchildon, "The Prairie Farm Rehabilitation Administration: Climate Crisis and Federal-Provincial Relations during the Great Depression," *Canadian Historical Review* 90, 2 (2009): 277.

36 Murray Knuttila, *Eroding a Way of Life: Neoliberalism and the Family Farm* (Regina: University of Regina Press, 2023).

37 James C. Scott, *Seeing Like a State: How Certain Schemes to Improve the Human Condition Have Failed* (New Haven, CT: Yale University Press, 1998); James C. Scott, "High Modernist Social Engineering: The Case of the Tennessee Valley Authority," in *Experiencing the State,* ed. Lloyd I. Rudolph and John Kurt Jacobsen (New Delhi: Oxford University Press, 2006), 7–8. Note that Scott has acknowledged that, as a student, he worked with the United States Central Intelligence Agency (CIA). James C. Scott, "James C. Scott: Agrarian Studies and Over 50 Years of Pioneering Work in the Social Sciences," interview by Todd Holmes, Berkeley, California, 2020, 8-9, Bancroft Library, Oral History Centre, https://digicoll.lib.berkeley.edu/record/219393?ln=en&v=pdf. On links between scholars and the CIA, see: David H. Price, *Cold War Anthropology: the CIA, the Pentagon, and the growth of dual use anthropology* (Durham: Duke University Press, 2016); David H. Price, *Cold War Deceptions: The Asia Foundation and the CIA* (Seattle: University of Washington Press, 2024).

38 Tina Loo, "People in the Way: Modernity, Environment, and Society on the Arrow Lakes," *BC Studies,* 142–43 (2004): 161–96; Philip Van Huizen, "Building a Green Dam: Environmental Modernism and the Canadian-American Libby Dam Project," *Pacific Historical Review* 79, 3 (2010): 418–53; James L. Kenny and Andrew Secord, "Engineering Modernity: Hydroelectric Development in New Brunswick, 1945–1970," *Acadiensis* 39, 1 (2010): 3–26; Danielle Robinson, "Modernism at a Crossroad: The Spadina Expressway Controversy in Toronto, Ontario, ca. 1960–1971," *Canadian Historical Review* 92, 2 (2011): 295–322; Will Langford, "Gerald Sutton Brown and the Discourse of City Planning Expertise in Vancouver, 1953–1959," *Urban Studies Review* 41, 2 (2013): 30–41; Valérie Poirier, "'L'autoroute est-ouest, c'est pas le progrès!': environnement et mobilisation citoyenne en opposition au projet d'autoroute est-ouest à Montréal en 1971," *Bulletin d'histoire politique* 23, 2 (2015): 66–91; Tina Loo, "High Modernism, Conflict, and the Nature of Change in Canada," *Canadian Historical Review* 97, 1 (2016): 34–58; Daniel Macfarlane, "Negotiating High Modernism: The St. Lawrence Seaway and Power Project," in *Made Modern: Science and Technology in Canadian History,* ed. Edward Jones-Imhotep and Tina Adcock, 326–47 (Vancouver: UBC Press, 2018); Daniel Macfarlane, *Negotiating a River: Canada, the US, and the Creation of the St. Lawrence Seaway* (Vancouver: UBC Press, 2014); Tina Loo and Meg Stanley, "An Environmental History of Progress: Damming the Peace and Columbia Rivers," *Canadian Historical Review* 92, 3 (2011): 399–427; Daniel Sims, "Dam Bennett: The Impacts of the W.A.C. Bennett Dam and Williston Lake Reservoir on the Tsek'ehne of Northern British Columbia" (PhD diss., History, University of Alberta, 2017); Frank Leonard, "'Eighth Wonder of the World': The Cariboo Wagon Road as British Columbia's First Megaproject," *Journal of the Canadian Historical Association* 27, 1 (2016): 169–200; Daniel Macfarlane, "'A Completely Man-Made and Artificial Cataract': The Transnational Manipulation of Niagara Falls," *Environmental History* 18, 4 (2013): 759–84; Daniel Macfarlane, "Creating the St. Lawrence Seaway: Mobility and a Modern Megaproject," in *Moving Natures: Environments and Mobility in Canadian History,* ed. Ben Bradley, Jay

Young, and Colin M. Coates, 127–49 (Calgary: NiCHE–University of Calgary Press Environmental History Series, 2016).

39 Matthew Farish and P. Whitney Lackenbauer, "High Modernism in the Arctic: Planning Frobisher Bay and Inuvik," *Journal of Historical Geography* 35, 3 (2009): 517–44; Peter C. Dawson, "Seeing Like an Inuit Family: The Relationship between House Form and Culture in Northern Canada," *Inuit Studies* 30, 2 (2006): 113–35; David M. Quiring, "From the Bush to the Village in Northern Saskatchewan: Contrasting CCF Community Development Projects," *Journal of the Canadian Historical Association* 17, 1 (2006): 151–78; David Meren, "'Commend me the Yak': The Colombo Plan, the Inuit of Ungava, and 'Developing' Canada's North," *Histoire sociale/Social History* 50, 102 (2017): 343–70; Jill Campbell-Miller, "Encounter and Apprenticeship: The Colombo Plan and Canadian Aid in India, 1950–1960," in *A Samaritan State Revisited: Historical Perspectives on Canadian Foreign Aid,* ed. Greg Donaghy and David Webster, 27–52 (Calgary: University of Calgary Press, 2019); Jennifer Anderson, "The Pro-Soviet Message in Words and Images: Dyson Carter and Canadian 'Friends' of the USSR," *Journal of the Canadian Historical Association* 18, 1 (2007): 179–206; Christopher Dummitt, *The Manly Modern: Masculinity in Postwar Canada* (Vancouver: UBC Press, 2007), 9, 14; Sean Kheraj, "A History of Oil Spills on Long-Distance Pipelines in Canada," *Canadian Historical Review* 101, 2 (2020): 161–91; Tina Loo, *Moved by the State: Forced Relocation and Making a Good Life in Postwar Canada* (Vancouver: UBC Press, 2019); Ronald Rudin, *Kouchibouguac: Removal, Resistance, and Remembrance at a Canadian National Park* (Toronto: University of Toronto Press, 2016); Wyatt Mark Skovron, "A People's Commission? High Modernism, Direct Democracy and Rural Life, 1952–57" (MA thesis, History, Simon Fraser University, 2011); Mariana Valverde, "Seeing Like a City: The Dialectic of Modern and Premodern Ways of Seeing in Urban Governance," *Law and Society Review* 45, 2 (2011): 277–312; Richard White, "Urban Renewal Revisited: Toronto, 1950 to 1970," *Canadian Historical Review* 97, 1 (2016): 1–33; Shannon Stunden Bower, "Tools for Rational Development: The Canada Land Inventory and the Canada Geographic Information System in Mid-Twentieth Century Canada," *Scientia Canadensis* 40, 1 (2018): 44–75.

40 This new perspective on the PFRA was anticipated by Tina Loo's brief attention to the agency in a recent article. Loo, "High Modernism," 49–50.

41 This use of the concept of negotiation derives from the work of Daniel Macfarlane. See Macfarlane, "Negotiating High Modernism"; and Macfarlane, *Negotiating a River.*

42 Sarah Carter, *Imperial Plots: Women, Land, and the Spadework of British Colonialism on the Canadian Prairies* (Winnipeg: University of Manitoba Press, 2016); Molly Rozum, *Grasslands Grown: Creating Place on the U.S. Northern Plains and Canadian Prairies* (Lincoln: University of Nebraska Press, 2021); Gerald Friesen, "2005 Presidential Address of the CHA: Space and Region in Canadian History," *Journal of the Canadian Historical Association* 16, 1 (2005): 1–22.

43 Erika Dyck and Alex Deighton, *Managing Madness: Weyburn Mental Hospital and the Transformation of Psychiatric Care in Canada* (Winnipeg: University of Manitoba Press, 2017); Valerie J. Korinek, *Prairie Fairies: A History of Queer Communities and People in Western Canada, 1930–1985* (Toronto: University of Toronto Press, 2018); Esyllt Jones, *Radical Medicine: The International Origins of Socialized Health Care in Canada* (Winnipeg: ARP Books, 2019).

44 This approach amounts to a regional variant on the "Canada in the world" interpretive framework articulated by Asa McKercher and Philip Van Huizen, "Introduction," in *Undiplomatic History: The New Study of Canada and the World,* ed. Asa McKercher and

Philip Van Huizen, 3–29 (Montreal/Kingston: McGill-Queen's University Press, 2019). See also the various volumes in the Rethinking Canada in the World series, edited by Ian McKay and Sean Mills and published by McGill-Queen's University Press.

45 Diana K. Davis, *The Arid Lands: History, Knowledge, Power* (Cambridge: MIT Press, 2016); Hannah Holleman, *Dust Bowls of Empire: Imperialism, Environmental Politics, and the Injustice of "Green" Capitalism* (New Haven, CT: Yale University Press, 2018); Eve E. Buckley, *Technocrats and the Politics of Drought and Development in Twentieth-Century Brazil* (Chapel Hill: University of North Carolina Press, 2017); Kate Barger Showers, *Imperial Gullies: Soil Erosion and Conservation in Lesotho* (Athens: Ohio University Press, 2005); Diana K. Davis, *Resurrecting the Granary of Rome: Environmental History and French Colonial Expansion in North Africa* (Athens: Ohio University Press, 2007).

46 Deborah Fitzgerald, *Every Farm a Factory: The Industrial Ideal in American Agriculture* (New Haven, CT: Yale University Press, 2003).

47 Ian MacPherson and John Herd Thompson, "An Orderly Reconstruction: Prairie Agriculture in World War Two," *Canadian Papers in Rural History* 4 (1984): 23–24; Britnell and Fowke, *Canadian Agriculture,* 409–10.

48 T.S. Vreeman and A.A. Fantino, *The Economics of Agricultural Chemical Use in Prairie Agriculture: Productivity and Environmental Impacts* (Edmonton: Alberta Agricultural Research Institute 1994).

49 Grant MacEwan, *Between the Red and the Rockies* (Toronto: University of Toronto Press, 1952), 294.

50 Meredith McKittrick, "Industrial Agriculture," in *A Companion to Global Environmental History,* ed. J.R. McNeill and Erin Stewart Mauldin (Chichester, UK: Wiley-Blackwell, 2012), 411.

51 William J. Carlyle, "Rural Population Change on the Canadian Prairies," *Great Plains Research* 4, 1 (1994): 65–87; Waiser, *Saskatchewan,* esp. chs. 17 and 19.

52 Royden Loewen, *Diaspora in the Countryside: Two Mennonite Communities and Mid-Twentieth-Century Rural Disjuncture* (Toronto: University of Toronto Press, 2006), 228. See also Royden Loewen, "Rurality, Ethnicity, and Gender Patterns of Cultural Continuity during the 'Great Disjuncture' in the R.M. of Hanover, 1945–1961," *Journal of the Canadian Historical Association* 4, 1 (1993): 161–82; Friesen, *Canadian Prairies,* 418–60; John Herd Thompson, *Forging the Prairie West* (Toronto: Oxford University Press, 1998), 137–68; Alan Hall, "Canadian Agricultural Policy: Liberal, Global, Sustainable," in *Fighting for the Farm: Rural America Transformed,* ed. Jane Adams, 209–28 (Philadelphia: University of Pennsylvania Press, 2003); Canada, Federal Task Force on Agriculture, *Canadian Agriculture in the Seventies: Report of the Federal Task Force on Agriculture* (Ottawa: Queen's Printer, 1969).

53 I follow the Standard Roman Orthography for the Cree language in spelling nēhiyawak without capitalization. See Jean Okimāsis and Arok Wolvengrey, *How to Spell It in Cree: The Standard Roman Orthography* (oskana kā-asastēki: miywāsin ink, 2008), 5.

54 In including the Nehinuwuk, I follow Keith Napoleon Goulet, "Land and Colonization: A Nehinuw (Cree) Perspective" (PhD diss., History, University of Regina, 2021), 2–4.

55 Robert Alexander Innes, *Elder Brother and the Law of the People: Contemporary Kinship and Cowessess First Nation* (Winnipeg: University of Manitoba Press, 2013); Robert Alexander Innes, "Multicultural Bands on the Northern Plains and the Notion of 'Tribal' Histories," in *Finding a Way to the Heart: Feminist Writings on Aboriginal and Women's History in Canada,* ed. Robin Brownlie and Valerie J. Korinek, 122–45 (Winnipeg: University of Manitoba Press, 2012).

56 J.R. McNeill and Verena Winiwarter, "Soils, Soils Knowledge, and Environmental History," in *Soils and Societies: Perspectives from Environmental History,* ed. J.R. McNeill and Verena Winiwarter (Isle of Harris, UK: White Horse, 2006), 3. See also Markus Dotterweich, "The History of Human-Induced Soil Erosion: Geomorphic Legacies, Early Descriptions and Research, and the Development of Soil Conservation – A Global Synopsis," *Geomorphology* 201 (2013): 1–34; Eva-Maria Swidler, "The Social Production of Soil," *Soil Science* 174, 1 (2009): 2–8.

57 Les Fuller, "Chernozemic Soils of the Prairie Region of Western Canada," *Prairie Soils and Crops Journal* 3 (2010): 37–45; Janis E. Dale, "Focus Study 5.2: Soils of Saskatchewan," in *Saskatchewan: Geographical Perspectives,* ed. Bernard D. Thraves, M.L. Lewry, Janis E. Dale, and Hansgeorg Schlichtmann, 94–98 (Regina: Canadian Plains Research Centre, University of Regina, 2007). Whereas in the 1960s soil taxonomists in the United States switched to another system of classification, this nomenclature persists in Canada. See Bret Wallach, "Physical Environment," in *Encyclopedia of the Great Plains,* ed. David J. Wishart (Lincoln: University of Nebraska Press, 2004), 617.

58 Statistics Canada, *Ecological Land Classification, 2017* (Ottawa: Minister of Industry, 2018), https://www.statcan.gc.ca/en/subjects/standard/environment/elc/elc2017.

59 James Daschuk, "A Dry Oasis: The Canadian Plains in Late Prehistory," *Prairie Forum* 34, 1 (2009): 1–29.

60 John C. Weaver, *The Great Land Rush and the Making of the Modern World, 1650–1900* (Montreal/Kingston: McGill-Queen's University Press, 2003).

61 Arthur J. Ray, J.R. Miller, and Frank J. Tough, *Bounty and Benevolence: A History of Saskatchewan Treaties* (Montreal/Kingston: McGill-Queen's University Press, 2000); Harold Cardinal and Walter Hildebrandt, *Treaty Elders of Saskatchewan: Our Dream Is That Our Peoples Will One Day Be Clearly Recognized as Nations* (Calgary: University of Calgary Press, 2000).

62 James Daschuk, *Clearing the Plains: Disease, Politics of Starvation, and the Loss of Indigenous Life* (Regina: University of Regina Press, 2013).

63 Morton and Martin, *History of Prairie Settlement.*

64 Carter, *Imperial Plots.*

65 David Sauchyn, "Prairie Climate Trends and Variability," in *The New Normal: The Canadian Prairies in a Changing Climate,* ed. David Sauchyn, Harry P. Diaz, and Suren Kulshreshtha (Regina: Canadian Plains Research Centre Press, 2021), 32–33.

66 Morton and Martin, *History of Prairie Settlement,* 538. On the unusual quantity of rain, see Dave Sauchyn and Samantha Kerr, "Canadian Prairies Drought from a Paleoclimate Perspective," in *Vulnerability and Adaptation to Drought: The Canadian Prairies and South America,* ed. Harry P. Diaz, Margot Hurlbert, and Jim Warren (Calgary: University of Calgary Press, 2016), 53–54.

67 Morton and Martin, *History of Prairie Settlement,* 525.

68 Shannon Stunden Bower, *Wet Prairie: People, Land, and Water in Agricultural Manitoba* (Vancouver: UBC Press, 2011).

69 Johanna Wandel, Harry P. Diaz, Jim Warren, Monica Hadarits, Margot Hurlbert, and Jeremy Pittman, "Drought and Vulnerability: A Conceptual Approach," in *Vulnerability and Adaptation to Drought: The Canadian Prairies and South America,* ed. Harry P. Diaz, Margot Hurlbert, and Jim Warren, 16–21 (Calgary: University of Calgary Press, 2016).

70 Gregory P. Marchildon, Jeremy Pittman, and David J. Sauchyn, "The Dry Belt and Changing Aridity in the Palliser Triangle, 1895–2000," *Prairie Forum* 34, 1 (2009): 31–44;

Donald Lemmen and Lisa Dale-Burnett, "The Palliser Triangle," in *Atlas of Saskatchewan,* 2nd ed., ed. Ka-iu Fung, 41 (Saskatoon: University of Saskatchewan, 1999).

71 Sauchyn and Kerr, "Canadian Prairies Drought," 53. See also Gerald T. Davidson, "An Interdisciplinary Approach to the Role of Climate in the History of the Prairies," in *Toward Defining the Prairies: Region, Culture, and History,* ed. Robert A. Wardhaugh, 101–19 (Winnipeg: University of Manitoba Press, 2001). For an early and influential articulation of a similar perspective offered in relation to the entire Great Plains region, see Walter P. Webb, *The Great Plains* (Lincoln: University of Nebraska Press, 1931), 17–33.

72 Jess Gilbert, *Planning Democracy: Agrarian Intellectuals and the Intended New Deal* (New Haven, CT: Yale University Press, 2015); Jess Gilbert, "Low Modernism and the Agrarian New Deal: A Different Kind of State," in *Fighting for the Farm: Rural America Transformed,* ed. Jane Adams, 129–46 (Philadelphia: University of Pennsylvania Press, 2003).

73 Gregory P. Marchildon, "Drought and Public Policy in the Palliser Triangle," in *Vulnerability and Adaptation to Drought: The Canadian Prairies and South America,* ed. Harry P. Diaz, Margot Hurlbert, and Jim Warren, 181–97 (Calgary: University of Calgary Press, 2016); Gregory P. Marchildon, Suren Kulshreshtha, Elaine Wheaton, and Dave Sauchyn, "Drought and Institutional Adaptation in the Great Plains of Alberta and Saskatchewan, 1914–1939," *Natural Hazards* 45 (2008): 391–411; Robert McLeman, *Climate and Human Migration: Past Experiences, Present Challenges* (Cambridge, UK: Cambridge University Press, 2013), 168–77; Robert A. McLeman, Juliette Dupre, Lea Berrang Ford, James Ford, Konrad Gajewski, and Gregory P. Marchildon, "What We Learned from the Dust Bowl: Lessons in Science, Policy, and Adaptation," *Population and Environment* 35 (2013): 417–40.

74 Jim Warren and Harry P. Diaz, *Defying Palliser: Stories of Resilience from the Driest Region of the Canadian Prairies* (Regina: Canadian Plains Research Centre Press, 2012).

Chapter 1: Contexts and Mistakes

1 George Spence to Mrs. P.A. Wheeler, Central Secretary, Canadian Clubs, 21 April 1939, Provincial Archives of Saskatchewan (PAS), GR 80, VI, file 11x.

2 George Spence to Professor J.H. Ellis, University of Manitoba, 10 December 1938, and attached document titled "Prairie Farm Rehabilitation or The Fight against the Ravages of Drouth," PAS, GR 80, VIII, file 28.

3 George Spence to Mrs. P.A. Wheeler, Central Secretary, Canadian Clubs, 21 April 1939, PAS, GR 80, VI, file 11x.

4 George Spence, *Survival of a Vision* (Ottawa: Department of Agriculture, 1967), 83; Grant MacEwan, *Fifty Mighty Men* (Saskatoon: Western Producer Prairie Books, 1970), 241–46.

5 Quoted in Robert A. Wardhaugh, *Mackenzie King and the Prairie West* (Toronto: University of Toronto Press, 2000), 205–6.

6 Jess Gilbert, *Planning Democracy: Agrarian Intellectuals and the Intended New Deal* (New Haven, CT: Yale University Press, 2015), 8. On the American New Deal more broadly, see Kiran Klaus Patel, *The New Deal: A Global History* (Princeton, NJ: Princeton University Press, 2016).

7 This assertion is consistent with the findings of historian Ronald Rudin, whose examination of the Maritime Marshland Reclamation Act led him to some consideration of the PFRA because of how the former agency was derived from and related to the latter. See Ronald Rudin, *Against the Tides: Reshaping Landscape and Community in Canada's Maritime Marshlands* (Vancouver: UBC Press, 2021), 16–17.

8 Diana K. Davis, *The Arid Lands: History, Power, Knowledge* (Cambridge, MA: MIT Press, 2015), 30.
9 Ibid., 32.
10 Ibid., 36.
11 James M. Richtik, "Mapping Land for Agriculture in Western Canada," *Great Plains Quarterly* 5, 4 (1985): 236–48.
12 John Bracken, *Dry Farming in Western Canada* (Winnipeg: Grain Growers' Guide, 1921). Relevant scholarly works on dry farming include Peter A. Russell, "The Far-from-Dry Debates: Dry Farming on the Canadian Prairies and the American Great Plain," *Agricultural History* 81, 4 (2007): 493–521; Mary W.M. Hargreaves, *Dry Farming in the Northern Great Plains: Years of Readjustment* (Lawrence: University Press of Kansas, 1993).
13 Bracken, *Dry Land Farming,* 167. See also Peter A. Russell, *How Agriculture Made Canada: Farming in the Nineteenth Century* (Montreal/Kingston: McGill-Queen's University Press, 2012), 233.
14 William J. Carlyle, "The Decline of Summerfallow on the Canadian Prairies," *Canadian Geographer* 41, 3 (1997): 268. See also Saskatchewan, *Report of the Royal Commission of Inquiry into Farming Conditions* (Regina: J.W. Reid, King's Printer, 1921), 35.
15 Clinton L. Evans, *The War on Weeds in the Prairie West: An Environmental History* (Calgary: University of Calgary Press, 2002).
16 Carlyle, "Decline of Summerfallow," 268.
17 Peter Grant Anderson, "Field Experiments: Critical Historical Geographies of Canada's Central Experimental Farm, 1886–1938" (PhD diss., Geography, Queen's University, 2017); T.H. Anstey, *One Hundred Harvests: Research Branch, Agriculture Canada, 1886–1986* (Ottawa: Supply and Services Canada, 1986), 13; Vittorio G.M. de Vecchi, "Science and Scientists in Government, 1878–1896 – Part II," *Scientia Canadensis* 9, 2 (1985): 107.
18 John F. Gilpin, *Quenching the Prairie Thirst: A History of the Magrath Irrigation District, Raymond Irrigation District, Taber Irrigation District, St. Mary Irrigation District* (Altona, MB: Friesens, 2000), 10–12; A.A. den Otter, "Adapting the Environment: Ranching, Irrigation, and Dry Land Farming in Southern Alberta, 1880–1914," *Great Plains Quarterly* 6, 3 (1986): 177.
19 Gilpin, *Quenching the Prairie Thirst,* 6; N.F. Dreisziger, "The Canadian-American Irrigation Frontier Revisited: The International Origins of Irrigation in Southern Alberta, 1885–1909," *Historical Papers/Communications historiques* 10, 1 (1975): 211–29; A.A. den Otter, *The Philosophy of Railways: The Transcontinental Railway Idea in British North America* (Toronto: University of Toronto Press, 1997), 189–91.
20 den Otter, "Adapting the Environment," 185.
21 Samuel P. Hays, *Conservation and the Gospel of Efficiency* (1959; reprint, Pittsburgh: University of Pittsburgh Press, 1999), 265. Hays's book was originally published in 1959 by Harvard University Press. On the character and influence of conservationist thinking in Canada, see D.J. Hall, *Clifford Sifton: A Lonely Eminence, 1901–1929* (Vancouver: UBC Press, 1985), esp. ch. 11.
22 George Colpitts, *Game in the Garden: A Human History of Wildlife in Western Canada to 1940* (Vancouver: UBC Press, 2003); Janet Foster, *Working for Wildlife: The Beginning of Preservation in Canada,* 2nd ed. (Toronto: University of Toronto Press, 1998); Darcy Ingram, *Wildlife, Conservation, and Conflict in Quebec, 1840–1914* (Vancouver: UBC Press, 2013); Tina Loo, *States of Nature: Conserving Canada's Wildlife in the Twentieth Century* (Vancouver: UBC Press, 2006); John Sandlos, *Hunters at the Margin: Native People and Wildlife*

Conservation in the Northwest Territories (Vancouver: UBC Press, 2007); H.V. Nelles, *The Politics of Development: Forests, Mines, and Hydro-Electric Power in Ontario, 1849–1941,* 2nd ed. (Montreal/Kingston: McGill-Queen's University Press, 2005); Darcy Ingram, "Governments, Governance, and the 'Lunatic Fringe': The Resources for Tomorrow Conference and the Evolution of Environmentalism in Canada," *International Journal of Canadian Studies* 51 (2015): 69–96; Stephen Bocking, "The Politics of Endangered Species: A Historical Perspective," in *Politics of the Wild: Canada and Endangered Species,* ed. Karen Beazley and Robert Boardman, 119–36 (Don Mills, ON: Oxford University Press, 2001); J. Alexander Burnett, *A Passion for Wildlife: The History of the Canadian Wildlife Service* (Vancouver: UBC Press, 2003); George Colpitts, "Fish and Game Associations in Southern Alberta, 1907–1928," *Alberta History* 42, 4 (1994): 16–26; Arn Keeling, "A Dynamic, Not a Static Conception: The Conservation Thought of Roderick Haig-Brown," *Pacific Historical Review* 71, 2 (2002): 239–68; Arn Keeling and Robert McDonald, "The Profligate Province: Roderick Haig-Brown and the Modernizing of British Columbia," *Journal of Canadian Studies* 36, 3 (2001): 7–23; Gerald Killan, *Protected Places: A History of Ontario's Provincial Parks System* (Toronto: Dundurn, 1993); Gerald Killan and George Warecki. "The Algonquin Wildlands League and the Emergence of Environmental Politics in Ontario, 1965–1974," *Environmental History Review* 16, 4 (1992): 1–27; Paul Kopas, *Taking the Air: Ideas and Change in Canada's National Parks* (Vancouver: UBC Press, 2007); Tina Loo, "Making a Modern Wilderness: Conserving Wildlife in Twentieth-Century Canada," *Canadian Historical Review* 82, 1 (2001): 91–121; George Warecki, *Protecting Ontario's Wilderness: A History of Changing Concepts and Preservation Politics, 1927–1973* (New York: Peter Lang, 2000); Jeremy Wilson, "For the Birds? Neoliberalism and the Protection of Biodiversity in British Columbia," *BC Studies,* 142–43 (2004): 241–77; Frank Zelko, *Make It a Green Peace! The Rise of Countercultural Activism* (Oxford: Oxford University Press, 2013); John Sandlos, "From the Outside Looking In: Aesthetics, Politics, and Wildlife Conservation in the Canadian North," *Environmental History* 6, 1 (2001): 6–31; John Sandlos, "Nature's Nations: The Shared Conservation History of Canada and the USA," *International Journal of Environmental Studies* 70, 3 (2013): 358–71; Theodore (Ted) Binnema and Melanie Niemi, "'Let the line be drawn now': Wilderness, Conservation, and the Exclusion of Aboriginal People from Banff National Park in Canada," *Environmental History* 11, 4 (2006): 724–50; John Sandlos, "Not Wanted in the Boundary: The Expulsion of the Keeseekoowenin Ojibway Band from Riding Mountain National Park," *Canadian Historical Review* 89, 2 (2008): 189–221.

23 Canada, Commission of Conservation, *Report of the First Annual Meeting* (Ottawa: Commission of Conservation, 1910), 3; Michel Girard, *L'écologisme retrouvé: essor et déclin de la Commission de la conservation du Canada* (Ottawa: University of Ottawa Press, 1988).

24 Hall, *Clifford Sifton,* 254.

25 Canada, Commission of Conservation, *Report of the Third Annual Meeting* (Ottawa: Commission of Conservation, 1912), 62.

26 J.R. McNeill and Verena Winiwarter, "Breaking the Sod: Humankind, History, and Soil," *Science,* 11 June 2004, 1627–29.

27 Hannah Holleman, *Dust Bowls of Empire: Imperialism, Environmental Politics, and the Injustice of 'Green' Capitalism* (New Haven, CT: Yale University Press, 2018), 53. Holleman's interpretation is informed by earlier works, including Richard H. Grove, *Green Imperialism: Colonial Expansion, Tropical Island Edens, and the Origins of Environmentalism* (Cambridge, UK: Cambridge University Press, 1995); Kate Barger Showers, *Imperial Gullies: Soil Erosion and Conservation in Lesotho* (Athens: Ohio University Press, 2005); Alfred W. Crosby,

Ecological Imperialism: The Biological Expansion of Europe, 900–1900, 2nd ed. (Cambridge, UK: Cambridge University Press, 2004); Thomas Dunlap, *Nature and the English Diaspora: Environment and History in the United States, Canada, Australia, and New Zealand* (Cambridge, UK: Cambridge University Press, 1999); Libby Robin, "Ecology: A Science of Empire?" in *Ecology and Empire: Environmental History of Settler Societies,* ed. Libby Robin and Tom Griffiths, 63–75 (Edinburgh: Keele University Press, 1997); Corey Ross, *Ecology and Power in the Age of Empire: Europe and the Transformation of the Tropical World* (Oxford: Oxford University Press, 2017); Sarah T. Phillips, "Lessons from the Dust Bowl: Dryland Agriculture and Soil Erosion in the United States and South Africa, 1900–1950," *Environmental History* 4, 2 (1999): 245–66; Sarah T. Phillips, "Drylands, Dust Bowl, and Agro-technical Internationalism in Southern Africa," in *Transatlantic Rebels: Agrarian Radicalism in Comparative Context,* ed. Thomas Summerhill and James C. Scott, 265–97 (East Lansing: Michigan State University Press).

28 David C. Jones, *Empire of Dust: Settling and Abandoning the Prairie Dry Belt* (Edmonton: University of Alberta Press, 1987); David C. Jones, *"We'll all be buried down here": The Prairie Dryland Disaster, 1917–1926* (Calgary: Historical Society of Alberta, 1986); Curtis McManus, *Happyland: A History of the "Dirty Thirties" in Saskatchewan, 1914–1937* (Calgary: University of Calgary Press, 2011). The 1920s were also difficult on the northern Great Plains in the United States, as described in Rolland Dewing, *Regions in Transition: The Northern Great Plains and the Pacific Northwest in the Great Depression* (Lanham, MD: University Press of America, 2006).

29 McManus, *Happyland,* 13–110.

30 Jones, *Empire of Dust;* Jones, *"We'll all be buried."*

31 Canada, Commission of Conservation, *Conservation of Soil Fertility and Soil Fibre,* report of a conference held at Winnipeg, Manitoba, 14–16 July 1920 (Ottawa: Thomas Mulvey, 1920), 30.

32 Ibid., 30.

33 Saskatchewan, *Report of the Royal Commission,* 10–11.

34 Hays, *Conservation and the Gospel of Efficiency,* 265; Canada, Commission of Conservation, *Conservation of Soil Fertility,* 31, 79–82.

35 Arthur S. Morton and Chester Martin, *History of Prairie Settlement and "Dominion Lands" Policy* (Toronto: Macmillan, 1938), 173.

36 Saskatchewan, *Report of the Royal Commission,* 36.

37 Alberta, *Report of the Survey Board for Southern Alberta* (1922), 16.

38 Jones, *Empire of Dust,* 221; A. Stewart, "The Prairie Farm Rehabilitation Programme," *Canadian Journal of Economics and Political Science* 5, 3 (1939): 315. For further information on Special Areas, see Alberta, *A Report on the Rehabilitation of the Dry Areas of Alberta and Crop Insurance, 1935–1936* (Edmonton: King's Printer, 1936), 44–45; David C. Jones, "Schools and Social Disintegration in the Alberta Dry Belt of the Twenties," *Prairie Forum* 3, 2 (1978): 1–20; Gregory P. Marchildon, "Institutional Adaptation to Drought and the Special Areas of Alberta, 1909–1939," *Prairie Forum* 32, 2 (2007): 251–71; Gregory P. Marchildon, Suren Kulshreshtha, Elaine Wheaton, and Dave Sauchyn, "Drought and Institutional Adaptation in the Great Plains of Alberta and Saskatchewan, 1914–1939," *Natural Hazards* 45 (2008): 391–411; Johanna Wandel and Gregory P. Marchildon, "Institutional Fit and Interplay in a Dryland Agricultural Social-Ecological System in Alberta, Canada," in *Adaptive Capacity and Environmental Governance,* ed. Derek Armitage and Ryan Plummer, 179–95 (Berlin: Springer, 2010).

39 Robert A. McLeman, Sam Herold, Zoran Reljic, Mike Sawada, and Daniel McKenney, "GIS-Based Modeling of Drought and Historical Population Change on the Canadian Prairies," *Journal of Historical Geography* 36, 1 (2010): 43–56; Julia M.L. Laforge and Robert McLeman, "Social Capital and Drought-Migrant Integration in 1930s Saskatchewan," *Canadian Geographer* 57, 4 (2013): 488–505; McManus, *Happyland*, 165–83.

40 Michiel Horn, *The Great Depression of the 1930s in Canada* (Ottawa: Canadian Historical Association, 1984), 3–4; Patel, *New Deal*, 1–3; Dietmar Rothermund, *The Global Impact of the Great Depression, 1929–1939* (London: Routledge, 1996), 48–58.

41 John Herd Thompson, with Allen Seager, *Canada 1922–1939: Decades of Discord* (Toronto: McLelland and Steward, 1985), 195.

42 Horn, *Great Depression*, 9–10; A.E. Safarian, *The Canadian Economy in the Great Depression*, 3rd ed. (Montreal/Kingston: McGill-Queen's University Press, 2009), 1.

43 Rothermund, *Global Impact*, 38–40.

44 E.W. Stapleford, *Report on Rural Relief in the Prairie Provinces Due to Drought Conditions and Crop Failures in Western Canada* (Ottawa: Minister of Agriculture, 1939), 25.

45 Ibid., 24.

46 Ibid., 24–25; George Edwin Britnell, *The Wheat Economy* (Toronto: University of Toronto Press, 1939), 62–64; Paul W. Riegert, *Outbreaks of Grasshoppers and Control Campaigns in Alberta, 1939–1980* (Regina: Rampeck, 1999), 1–4.

47 Stapleford, *Report on Rural Relief*, 25.

48 Safarian, *Canadian Economy*, 156.

49 Hilda Neatby, *The Politics of Chaos: Canada in the Thirties* (Toronto: Macmillan of Canada, 1972), 66–67; Gregory P. Marchildon, "The Prairie Farm Rehabilitation Administration: Climate Crisis and Federal-Provincial Relations during the Great Depression," *Canadian Historical Review* 90, 2 (2009): 285.

50 Prairie Farm Rehabilitation Administration, *Report of the Work Conducted under the Prairie Farm Rehabilitation Act for the Fiscal Year 1935–36* (Ottawa: Department of Agriculture, 1936), 1; Canada, *Bill 55: An Act to Provide for the Rehabilitation of Drought and Soil Drifting Areas in the Provinces of Manitoba, Saskatchewan and Alberta*, 17th Parliament, 6th Session, 11 April 1935, https://parl.canadiana.ca/view/oop.bills_HOC_1706_1/709.

51 Prairie Farm Rehabilitation Administration, "Report of Activities under the Prairie Farm Rehabilitation Act," 15 November 1935, 15, PAS, GR 6, R-261, file 22.23; Canada, *Bill 63: An Act to Create Employment by Public Works and Undertakings throughout Canada and to Authorize the Guarantee of Certain Railway Equipment Securities*, 17th Parliament, 6th Session, 27 May 1935, https://parl.canadiana.ca/view/oop.bills_HOC_1706_2/27.

52 C.H. Anderson, *A History of Soil Erosion by Wind in the Palliser Triangle of Western Canada* (Ottawa: Research Branch, Department of Agriculture, 1975), 11; James H. Gray, *Men against the Desert* (Saskatoon: Western Producer Prairie Books, 1967), 18–19.

53 Norman M. Ross, *Tree-Planting on the Prairies of Manitoba, Saskatchewan and Alberta* (Ottawa: Dominion Experimental Farms, Department of Agriculture, 1933), 3–4.

54 Prairie Farm Rehabilitation Administration, *Shelterbelt Centre: History of the Tree Nursery, 1901–1993* (Ottawa: Agriculture Canada, 1993), 1.

55 Prairie Farm Rehabilitation Administration, *Report of the Work Conducted ... 1935–36*, 13–14.

56 Prairie Farm Rehabilitation Administration, *Report of Proceedings under the Prairie Farm Rehabilitation Act for the Fiscal Year Ending March 31, 1937* (Ottawa: Department of Agriculture, 1937), 22.

57 David C. Jones, "The Canadian Prairie Dryland Disaster and the Reshaping of 'Expert' Farm Wisdom," *Journal of Rural Studies* 1, 2 (1985): 135–46.

58 John Bracken, *The Rehabilitation of the Drought Area: An Address Delivered by the Honourable John Bracken before the Canadian Club of Winnipeg, October 25th, 1934* (Winnipeg: Manitoba Department of Agriculture, 1934). On Bracken's role in events leading to the creation of the PFRA, see Carl J. Anderson, "'This Land Must Be Good for Some Kind of Farming ... ': Dominion Lands Policy, Drought and Agricultural Rehabilitation in Southwestern Saskatchewan, 1908–1935" (MA thesis, History, University of Regina, 2008), esp. ch. 4.

59 Ian Macpherson and John Herd Thompson, "The Business of Agriculture: Prairie Farmers and the Adoption of 'Business Methods,' 1880–1950," in *The Prairie West: Historical Readings*, 2nd ed., ed. R. Douglas Francis and Howard Palmer (Edmonton: Pica Pica, 1995), 481.

60 Norman Ward and David Smith, *Jimmy Gardiner: Relentless Liberal* (Toronto: University of Toronto Press, 1990); Robert A. Wardhaugh, "James G. Gardiner, Land Policy, and Dominion-Provincial Relations" (MA thesis, History, University of Saskatchewan, 1990).

61 Prairie Farm Rehabilitation Administration, *Report on Proceedings under the Prairie Farm Rehabilitation Act for the Fiscal Year Ending March 31, 1938* (Ottawa: Department of Agriculture, 1938), 1; H.J. Hargrave, "The Prairie Farm Rehabilitation Administration, Canada," in *Change in Agriculture*, ed. A.H. Bunting (London: Gerald Duckworth, 1970), 472; Canada, *Bill 18: An Act to Amend the Prairie Farm Rehabilitation Act*, 1st Reading, 18th Parliament, 2nd Session, 9 February 1937, https://parl.canadiana.ca/view/oop.bills_HOC_1802_1/123. See also "Minutes of Water Development Committee Meeting, Held in Confederation Building, Ottawa, February 10th to 12th, 1936, Session 5," 10–12, Glenbow Western Research Centre (GWRC), Irrigation Research Project (W.L. Jacobson) Collection (C0048), file M-3761-362; "The Chairman Asked the Minister to Speak," GWRC, C0048, file M-3761-363.

62 Prairie Farm Rehabilitation Administration, "Report on the Prairie Farm Rehabilitation Program, Regina, Saskatchewan," March 1938, GWRC, C0048, file M-3761-367; Stapleford, *Report on Rural Relief*, 94.

63 Prairie Farm Rehabilitation Administration, "Executive Committee – Afternoon Session: Land Utilization and Rehabilitation, PFRA, 31 May 1937," GWRC, C0048, file M-3761-367. The boundary, after being modified a number of times, was eliminated altogether in the early 1960s. See Prairie Farm Rehabilitation Administration, *Annual Report on Prairie Farm Rehabilitation and Related Activities, 1961–1962* (Ottawa: Department of Agriculture, 1962).

64 Prairie Farm Rehabilitation Administration, *Report on Progress under the Prairie Farm Rehabilitation Act for the Fiscal Year Ending March 31, 1939* (Ottawa: Department of Agriculture, 1939), 1; Canada, *Bill 36: An Act to Amend the Prairie Farm Rehabilitation Act*, 1st Reading, 18th Parliament, 4th Session, 9 March 1939, https://parl.canadiana.ca/view/oop.bills_HOC_1804_1/243.

65 George Spence, "Review of P.F.R.A. Policies," 29 May 1939, PAS, GR 6, R-261, file 22.36.

66 Anstey, *One Hundred Harvests*, 79.

67 W. Leland Clark, "The Location of Experimental Farms and Illustration Stations: An Agricultural or Political Consideration?" in *The Developing West: Essays on Canadian History in Honor of Lewis H. Thomas*, ed. John E. Foster, 203–18 (Edmonton: University of Alberta Press, 1983).

68 Prairie Farm Rehabilitation Administration, *Report on Activities under the Prairie Farm Rehabilitation Act for the Fiscal Year Ending March 31, 1940* (Ottawa: Department of Agriculture, 1940), 57.

69 Anstey, *One Hundred Harvests*, 79.
70 Alberta, *Report on the Rehabilitation*, 57.
71 Prairie Farm Rehabilitation Administration, *Report on Proceedings ... 1938*, 6.
72 "Transcript of interview with A.E. Palmer, 10 June 1966," 34, University of Calgary Archives and Special Collections (U of C Archives), F0060, 67/73/17, 11.2.1-11.2.8.
73 Ibid., 9.
74 Ibid., 13.
75 Prairie Farm Rehabilitation Administration, *Report on Proceedings ... 1938*, 6.
76 Prairie Farm Rehabilitation Administration, *Report of Proceedings ... 1937*, 10.
77 Prairie Farm Rehabilitation Administration, *Report on Proceedings ... 1938*, 12.
78 Ibid.
79 Gray, *Men against the Desert*, 111–12.
80 Prairie Farm Rehabilitation Administration, *Report of the Work Conducted ... 1935–36*, 9; Grant MacEwan, *Between the Red and the Rockies* (Toronto: University of Toronto Press, 1952), 271–72.
81 Prairie Farm Rehabilitation Administration, *Report of the Work Conducted ... 1935–36*, 9.
82 Prairie Farm Rehabilitation Administration, *Report on Proceedings under the Prairie Farm Rehabilitation Act for the Fiscal Year Ending March 31, 1941* (Ottawa: Department of Agriculture, 1941), 37.
83 Prairie Farm Rehabilitation Administration, *Prairie Farm Rehabilitation Act: Annual Report of Activities, Year Ended March 31st, 1943* (Ottawa: Department of Agriculture, 1943), 5.
84 Prairie Farm Rehabilitation Administration, *Report on Proceedings ... 1938*, 12.
85 Prairie Farm Rehabilitation Administration, *Report on Proceedings ... 1941*, 37.
86 Prairie Farm Rehabilitation Administration, *Report of Proceedings ... 1937*, 39.
87 Ibid., 36.
88 Canada, *Annual Report of the Minister of Agriculture for the Dominion of Canada for the Year Ended March 31, 1941* (Ottawa: Department of Agriculture, 1941), 161.
89 Letter included in "Further Services Rendered to Water Development and Land Utilization of PFRA," November 1940, PAS, GR 80, VI, file 57b.
90 Water Development Committee, Session No. 1, "Minutes of Water Development Committee Meeting, Held at Hotel Saskatchewan, Regina, May 1st and 2nd, 1935," 8, GWRC, C0048, file M-3761-362.
91 "Meeting of the Advisory Committee on Land Utilization, Prairie Farm Rehabilitation Act, Regina, Sask., Hotel Saskatchewan, May 29th, 1939," 104–10, GWRC, C0048, file M-3761-369.
92 "A meeting of farmers was held at Retlaw Wednesday Jan. 26th 1938 for the purpose of organizing an Agricultural Improvement Ass.," GWRC, Alfred Rawlins fonds (F1527), M-1024-11.
93 "In presenting this Brief before this Commission, it is my intention ... " 4, GWRC, F1527, M-1024-9.
94 Prairie Farm Rehabilitation Administration, *Report on Proceedings ... 1938*, 17.
95 This view is in line with the assessment of early PFRA activities put forward in Julia M.L. Laforge and Stéphane M. McLachlan, "Environmentality on the Canadian Prairies: Settler-Farmer Subjectivities and Agri-environmental Objects," *Antipode* 50, 2 (2017): 369.
96 A. Leahey, "Soil Surveys and Soil Research," *C.S.T.A. Review* 23 (December 1939): 10; Prairie Farm Rehabilitation Administration, *Report on Proceedings ... 1938*, 17.
97 Leahey, "Soil Surveys and Soil Research," 10.

98 Ibid., 12.

99 Prairie Farm Rehabilitation Administration, *Report on Proceedings … 1938,* 22; Don W. Thomson, *Skyview Canada: A Story of Aerial Photography in Canada* (Ottawa: Department of Energy, Mines and Resources, 1975), esp. ch. 16.

100 "Aerial Survey," 10–11, GWRC, C0048, file M-3761-363.

101 Water Development Committee, Session No. 1, "Minutes of Water Development Committee Meeting, Held at Hotel Saskatchewan, Regina, May 1st and 2nd, 1935," 17–18, GWRC, C0048, file M-3761-362.

102 Ibid.

103 "Recommendations to the Advisory Committee from the Water Development Committee Concerning the Water Development Projects Planned in Connection with the Rehabilitation of Drought and Soil Drifting Areas in the Provinces of Manitoba, Saskatchewan, and Alberta," 4, GWRC, C0048, file M-3761-362.

104 Water Development Committee, Session No. 3, "Minutes of Water Development Committee Meeting, Held at Swift Current, Saskatchewan, August 30th and 31st, 1935," 15, GWRC, C0048, file M-3761-362.

105 G.A.D. Will, "Soil and Economic Survey," PAS, GR 80, VI, file 49a.

106 On the concept of marginality as deployed in the United States context, see Sarah T. Phillips, *This Land, This Nation: Conservation, Rural America, and the New Deal* (New York: Cambridge University Press, 2007), 39–40.

107 G.A.D. Will, "Soil and Economic Survey," PAS, GR 80, VI, file 49a.

108 Phillips, *This Land, This Nation,* 46.

109 James C. Scott, *Seeing Like a State: How Certain Schemes to Improve the Human Condition Have Failed* (New Haven: Yale University Press, 1998).

110 Venus Bivar, "Agricultural High Modernism and Land Reform in Postwar France," *Agricultural History* 93, 4 (2019): 636–55. See also Sigrid Schmalzer, *Red Revolution, Green Revolution: Scientific Farming in Socialist China* (Chicago: University of Chicago Press, 2016), esp. ch. 5, which attends to experts who sought to navigate between high-modernist imperatives and local circumstances.

111 Horn, *Great Depression,* 22–23.

112 Prairie Farm Rehabilitation Administration, *Report on Activities … 1940,* 8.

113 Gilbert, *Planning Democracy;* Jess Gilbert, "Low Modernism and the Agrarian New Deal: A Different Kind of State," in *Fighting for the Farm: Rural America Transformed,* ed. Jane Adams, 129–46 (Philadelphia: University of Pennsylvania Press, 2003).

114 Calculated on the basis of figures included in Prairie Farm Rehabilitation Administration, *Report of Proceedings … 1937,* 49.

115 Rudin, *Against the Tides,* 57.

116 Wardhaugh, *Mackenzie King,* 191. For his part, political scientist Reginald Whitaker terms Gardiner the "prairie lieutenant." Reginald Whitaker, *The Government Party: Organizing and Financing the Liberal Party of Canada, 1930–58* (Toronto: University of Toronto Press, 1977), 88.

117 Dale Eisler, *Rumours of Glory: Saskatchewan and the Thatcher Years* (Edmonton: Hurtig, 1987), 34–35; David E. Smith, *Prairie Liberalism: The Liberal Party in Saskatchewan, 1905–1971* (Toronto: University of Toronto Press, 1975), 6, 169; Whitaker, *Government Party,* 355–56. On the Liberal political machine in Saskatchewan in a slightly earlier period, see Escott Reid, "The Saskatchewan Liberal Machine before 1929," *Canadian Journal of Economics and Political Science* 2, 1 (1936): 27–40.

118 Marchildon, "Prairie Farm Rehabilitation Administration," 292; Wardhaugh, *Mackenzie King,* 212; Ward and Smith, *Jimmy Gardiner,* 216; David E. Smith, "James G. Gardiner: Political Leadership in the Agrarian Community," in *Swords and Ploughshares: War and Agriculture In Western Canada,* ed. R.C. Macleod (Edmonton: University of Alberta Press, 1993), 207–8.

119 Luc Juillet and Ken Rasmussen, *Defending a Contested Ideal: Merit and the PSC of Canada, 1908–2008* (Ottawa: University of Ottawa Press, 2008), 48–71; J.E. Hodgetts, William McCloskey, Reginald Whitaker, and V. Seymour Wilson, *The Biography of an Institution: The Civil Service Commission of Canada, 1908–1967* (Montreal/Kingston: McGill-Queen's University Press, 1972), 8.

120 Ward and Smith, *Jimmy Gardiner,* 176.

121 Ibid., 218.

122 "Federal Record of Activities, Prairie Farm Rehabilitation Act by Electoral Districts, Province of Saskatchewan," PAS, F 65, VII 2b, PFRA 1935–1957, 25865-25910. It has been suggested that the 1957 federal election, which the Liberal Party lost, was the end of this particularly blunt approach to patronage. See Joseph Wearing, *The L-Shaped Party: The Liberal Party of Canada, 1958–1980* (Toronto: McGraw-Hill Ryerson, 1981), 52–57.

123 A.W. Platt, "Breeding Wheat for Sawfly Resistance," *Canadian Geographical Journal* 33, 3 (1946): 138.

124 J. Gavloski and S. Meers, "Arthropods of Cereal Crops in Canadian Grasslands," in *Arthropods of Canadian Grasslands,* vol. 2, *Inhabitants of a Changing Landscape,* ed. K.D. Floate, 217–37 (Ottawa: Biological Survey of Canada, 2011).

125 Vincent Lesieur, Jean-François Martin, David K. Weaver, Kim A. Hoelmer, David R. Smith, Wendell L. Morrill, Nassera Kadiri, Frank B. Peairs, Darren M. Cockrell, Terri L. Randolph, Debra K. Waters, and Marie-Claude Bon, "Phylogeography of the Wheat Stem Sawfly, *Cephus cinctus* Norton (Hymenoptera: Cephidae): Implications for Pest Management," *PLOS ONE* 11, 12 (2016): e0168370, https://doi.org/10.1371/journal.pone.0168370.

126 Norman Criddle, "The Western Wheat-Stem Sawfly in Canada," *Report of the Entomological Society of Ontario* 36 (1922): 18. See also N.J. Holliday, "Norman Criddle: Pioneer Entomologist of the Prairies," *Manitoba History* 51 (2006): 8–15.

127 Criddle, "Western Wheat-Stem Sawfly," 18.

128 Kenneth Hoeppner, *The Ordinary Genius: A Life of Arnold Platt* (Edmonton: University of Alberta Press, 2007), 48.

129 Paul W. Riegert, *From Arsenic to DDT: A History of Entomology in Western Canada* (Toronto: University of Toronto Press, 1980), 216–17.

130 "Minutes and Report, PFRA Conference, 29–31 May 1939," GWRC, C0048, file M-3761-369; G.D. Matthews, "Review of District Experiment Sub-Stations," 30 May 1939, 53, GWRC, C0048, file M-3761-369; Riegert, *From Arsenic to DDT,* 219–20.

131 Canada, Division of Entomology, Science Service, *The Wheat Stem Sawfly Situation in Manitoba, Saskatchewan, and Alberta for 1942* (Ottawa: Department of Agriculture, 1942); Riegert, *From Arsenic to DDT,* 219–20; John Bracken, *Crop Production in Western Canada* (Winnipeg: Grain Growers' Guide, 1920), 375.

132 H.L. Seamans, "Insect Surveys in the Rehabilitation Program," *C.S.T.A. Review* 23 (December 1939): 99.

133 Alberta, *Report on the Rehabilitation,* 30–31.

134 H.L. Seamans, C.W. Farstad, and C.L. Neilson, "Wheat Stem Sawfly Research and Control with Special Reference to Tillage and Temperature," GWRC, C0048, file M-3761-371.

135 Ibid.
136 C. Shirrif, Agricultural Adviser, Dominion Experimental Station, "The Prairie Farm Rehabilitation Program: Radio Address," 21 December 1937, GWRC, C0048, file M-3761-352.
137 Experimental Farms Service, "Report on Cultural Activities under the Prairie Farm Rehabilitation Act for the Fiscal Year Ending March 31 1940," GWRC, C0048, file M-3761-354.
138 "Report on Cultural Activities under the Prairie Farm Rehabilitation Act for the Fiscal Year Ending March 31 1941," PAS, GR 6, R-261, 22.39; Prairie Farm Rehabilitation Administration, *Report on Progress ... 1939,* 14.
139 Experimental Farms Service, "Report on Cultural Activities under the Prairie Farm Rehabilitation Act for the Fiscal Year Ending March 31 1940," GWRC, C0048, file M-3761-354.
140 "Sawfly Control Experiments on Substations," PAS, GS 44, file 130.
141 Ibid.
142 Prairie Farm Rehabilitation Administration, *Report on Proceedings ... 1941,* 14.
143 Experimental Farms Service, "Report on Cultural Activities under the Prairie Farm Rehabilitation Act for the Fiscal Year Ending March 31 1941," GWRC, C0048, file M-3761-354; H.L. Seamans, C.W. Farstad, and C.L. Neilson, "Wheat Stem Sawfly Research and Control with Special Reference to Tillage and Temperature," GWRC, C0048, file M-3761-371; Prairie Farm Rehabilitation Administration, *Report on Proceedings ... 1941,* 37.
144 A.E. Palmer, "Soil Drifting Control," in "Report of Meeting of Experimental Farms Superintendents and Regina Rehabilitation Staff re: PFRA Cultural Work, 18–19 November 1940," GWRC, C0048, file M-3761-370.
145 H.L. Seamans, C.W. Farstad, and C.L. Neilson, "Wheat Stem Sawfly Research and Control with Special Reference to Tillage and Temperature," GWRC, C0048, file M-3761-371.
146 F.H. Auld, Saskatchewan Deputy Minister of Agriculture, to Dr. H. Barton, Ottawa Deputy Minister of Agriculture, 11 February 1941, PAS, GS 44, file 130.
147 L. Ogilvie, "Section 7D: Statement of Sawfly Control Campaign to Advisory Committee on Land Utilization, PFRA," in "Report of Meeting of the Advisory Committee on Land Utilization, 26–28 February 1945," GWRC, C0048, file M-3761-375.
148 C.W. Farstad, "The Wheat Stem Sawfly," in "Minutes and Report of Meeting of P.F.R.A. Advisory Committee on Land Utilization, February 17th and 18th 1943," GWRC, C0048, file M-3761-372.
149 "Statement on Sawfly Control Campaign to Advisory Committee on Land Utilization P.F.R.A.," PAS, GS 44, file 130.
150 Ibid.
151 Edmund P. Russell, "'Speaking of Annihilation': Mobilizing for War against Human and Insect Enemies, 1914–1945," *Journal of American History* 82, 4 (1996): 1505–29.
152 K.M. King, Canada Department of Agriculture Entomological Branch, to G.D. Matthews, Superintendent, Scott Dominion Experimental Station, 3 November 1944, PAS, GS 44, file 130.
153 "Paper No. 18, Sawfly Control Campaigns by Mr. L.M. Ogilvie," in "Proceedings of a Meeting of the P.F.R.A. Advisory Committee on Land Utilization and P.F.R.A. Conference, February 25th, 26th, and 27th, 1946," 29, PAS, GR 6, R-259, III, file 20; "How Can P.F.R.A. More Actively Support Provincial Programs in Agriculture in Relation to Sawfly Control Campaigns?" PAS, GS 44, file 130.

154 "Minutes and Report, Meeting of P.F.R.A. Advisory Committee on Land Utilization, 17–18 February 1943," x, 54, GWRC, C0048, file M-3761-372; Hargreaves, *Dry Farming*, 193.

155 Platt, "Breeding Wheat." See also Hoeppner, *Ordinary Genius*, 56–67; and Anstey, *One Hundred Harvests*, 269–71.

156 Lew E. Wallace, "Field-Plot Tests of Chemicals for Wheat Stem Sawfly Control," *Journal of Economic Entomology* 55, 1 (1962): 910. For more recent discussion of the limitations of chemical controls, see Brian L. Beres, L.M. Dosdall, David K. Weaver, Hector A. Cárcamo, and D.M. Spaner, "Biology and Integrated Management of Wheat Stem Sawfly and the Need for Continuing Research," *Canadian Entomologist* 143, 2 (2011): 105–25.

157 "Labour Requirements, Sawfly Control Blocks 1944: Preliminary Report to the Saskatchewan Department of Agriculture, Oct. 7, 1944," 8, PAS, GS 44, file 130; "Sawfly Control Experiments on Substations," PAS, GS 44, file 130.

158 Gavloski and Meers, "Arthropods of Cereal Crops," 226.

159 Loo, *States of Nature*, 31.

160 Thompson and Seager, *Canada 1922–1939*, 263; Ian McKay, "The Canadian Passive Revolution, 1840–1950," *Capital and Class* 34, 3 (2010): 361–81.

161 Prairie Farm Rehabilitation Administration, *Eleventh Annual Report on Activities under the Prairie Farm Rehabilitation Act for the Fiscal Year Ended March 31, 1946* (Ottawa: Department of Agriculture, 1946), 2.

162 G.D. Matthews, "Increased Activities of A.I.A.'s to Meet Community Problems," GWRC, C0048, file M-3761-377.

163 Prairie Farm Rehabilitation Administration, *Eleventh Annual Report*, 2; John Elmer Glenn, "The Role of Government Legislation, Policy and Agency Activity in Irrigation Development: The Cypress Hills Area, 1888–c. 1968" (MA thesis, Geography, University of Calgary, 1969), 158–59.

Chapter 2: Delimiting the Public Good

1 "Record of Interview with Asael E. Palmer by W.L. Jacobson in Lethbridge, Alberta, September 18, 1958," 3, Glenbow Western Research Centre (GWRC), Irrigation Research Project (W.L. Jacobson) Collection (C0048), file M-3761-169; "How Irrigation Has Developed in Southern Alberta: An Address by A.E. Palmer, June 15, 1951," 4, GWRC, C0048, file M-3761-169. Palmer's experience of beet labour as an adolescent is not unusual. Children frequently worked in beet fields in the industry's early years. See Belinda Crowson, *Southern Alberta's Sugar-Coated History: The Sugar Beet Industry* (Lethbridge, AB: Lethbridge Historical Society, 2013), 20–21.

2 James H. Gray, *Men against the Desert* (Saskatoon: Western Producer Prairie Books, 1967), 222–23.

3 C.C. Spence, B.H. Kristjanson, and J.L. Anderson, *Farming in the Irrigation Districts of Alberta* (Ottawa: Minister of Agriculture, 1947), 19. This area of the province was seen by some as "one of the world's natural sugar bowls." See A.E. Palmer, "Irrigation in Western Canada: Its Possible Effect on Industry and Population," *The Engineering Journal* 31, 9 (1948): 498.

4 A.S. Archibald, "Exhibit 'A': Report of Dr. A.S. Archibald on the Alberta Sugar Beet Situation Dated October 28, 1937," in Alberta Co-operative Sugar Beet Growers Association, *Submission to the Royal Commission on Dominion-Provincial Relations* (Lethbridge, AB: Alberta Co-operative Sugar Beet Growers Association, 1938), 2.

5 W.D. Porter, "Some Interesting Aspects of Irrigated Farming," transcript of radio talk, CKUA, 9 January 1942, 5, GWRC, C0048, file M-3761-134; J. Sutton, "The Vital Importance of the Beet Sugar Industry to the Irrigation Projects of Alberta," GWRC, C0048, file M-3761-273.

6 Howard Palmer, *Patterns of Prejudice: A History of Nativism in Alberta* (Toronto: McClelland and Stewart, 1982); Sarah Carter, *Imperial Plots: Women, Land, and the Spadework of British Colonialism on the Canadian Prairies* (Winnipeg: University of Manitoba Press, 2016); Adele Perry, *Aqueduct: Colonialism, Resources, and the Histories We Remember* (Winnipeg: ARP Books, 2016); Mary Jane MacCallum and Adele Perry, *Structures of Indifference: An Indigenous Life and Death in a Canadian City* (Winnipeg: University of Manitoba Press, 2018); Kenichi Matsui, *Native Peoples and Water Rights: Irrigation, Dams, and the Law in Western Canada* (Montreal/Kingston: McGill-Queen's University Press, 2009); Evelyn Peters, Matthew Stock, and Adrian Werner, *Rooster Town: The History of an Urban Métis Community, 1901–1961* (Winnipeg: University of Manitoba Press, 2018); Owen Toews, *Stolen City: Racial Capitalism and the Making of Winnipeg* (Winnipeg: ARP Books, 2018); Karina Vernon, *The Black Prairie Archive: An Anthology* (Waterloo, ON: Wilfrid Laurier University Press, 2020); James M. Pitsula, *Keeping Canada British: The Klu Klux Klan in 1920s Saskatchewan* (Vancouver: UBC Press, 2013); Ryan Eyford, *White Settler Reserve: New Iceland and the Colonization of the Canadian West* (Vancouver: UBC Press, 2016); Constance Backhouse, *Colour-Coded: A Legal History of Racism in Canada, 1900–1950* (Toronto: University of Toronto Press, 1999).

7 Kate A. Berry and Sue Jackson, "The Making of White Water Citizens in Australia and the Western United States: Racialization as a Transnational Project of Irrigation Governance," *Annals of the American Association of Geographers* 108, 5 (2018): 1354–69; James Beattie and Ruth Morgan, "Engineering Edens on This 'Rivered Earth'? A Review Article on Water Management and Hydro-Resilience in the British Empire, 1860s–1940s," *Environment and History* 23, 1 (2017): 39–63.

8 R.F. Smith, "History and Current Status of Irrigation in Alberta," *Canadian Water Resources Journal* 3, 1 (1978): 6–18.

9 Stan Klassen and John Gilpin, "Alberta Irrigation in the Old and New Millenium," *Canadian Water Resources Journal* 24, 1 (1999): 61–69; Matthew Evenden, "Precarious Foundations: Irrigation, Environment, and Social Change in the Canadian Pacific Railway's Eastern Section, 1900–1930," *Journal of Historical Geography* 32, 1 (2006): 74–95; Christopher Armstrong, Matthew Evenden, and H.V. Nelles, *The River Returns: An Environmental History of the Bow* (Montreal/Kingston: McGill-Queen's University Press, 2009), 167–76.

10 Rob C. de Loë, "Stability and Change in Southern Alberta Water Management" (PhD diss., Geography, University of Waterloo, 1994).

11 William G. Hartley, "Mormon Sugar in Alberta: E.P. Ellison and the Knight Sugar Factory," *Journal of Mormon History* 23, 2 (1997): 1–29; Crowson, *Southern Alberta's Sugar-Coated History*, 5; John A. Eagle, *The Canadian Pacific Railway and the Development of Western Canada, 1896–1914* (Montreal/Kingston: McGill-Queen's University Press, 1989), 209; Brooke Brassard, "Thirsty Land into Springs of Water: Negotiating a Place in Canada as Latter-Day Saints, 1887–1947" (PhD diss., Religious Studies, University of Waterloo, 2018), 117–18.

12 P.M. Sauder, *Irrigation in Southern Alberta* (Edmonton: Department of the Environment, Government of Alberta, n.d.), 43–44.

13 "Record of Interview with Asael E. Palmer by W.L. Jacobson in Lethbridge, Alberta, September 18, 1958," 32, GWRC, C0048, file M-3761-169. See also A.E. Palmer, "Sugar Beets in Relation to Irrigation Development in Western Canada," 135–39, in "Minutes and Report of Meeting of P.F.R.A. Advisory Committee on Land Utilization, February 17th and 18th, 1943," GWRC, C0048, file M-3761-372; "Biographical Sketch of Asael E. Palmer," 3, GWRC, C0048, file M-3761-169.

14 "Record of Interview with Asael E. Palmer by W.L. Jacobson in Lethbridge, Alberta, September 18, 1958," 33, GWRC, C0048, file M-3761-169.

15 M.A. Clarke and M.F.G. Cleary, "Sugarbeet," in *Encyclopedia of Food Sciences and Nutrition*, 2nd ed., ed. Benjamin Caballero, Luiz C. Trugo, and Paul M. Finglas (Cambridge, MA: Academic, 2003), 5652.

16 John Schreiner, *The Refiners: A Century of BC Sugar* (Vancouver: Douglas and McIntyre, 1989), 188–92; John Herd Thompson and Allen Seager, "Workers, Growers and Monopolists: The 'Labour Problem' in the Alberta Beet Sugar Industry during the 1930s," *Labour/Le Travail* 3 (1978): 154; Crowson, *Southern Alberta's Sugar-Coated History*, 8–9.

17 Thompson and Seager, "Workers, Growers and Monopolists," 154; C.A. Dawson, *Group Settlement: Ethnic Communities in Western Canada* (Toronto: Macmillan, 1936), 234.

18 Crowson, *Southern Alberta's Sugar-Coated History*, 21–27; Dawson, *Group Settlement*, 236.

19 Keith W. Regular, *Neighbours and Networks: The Blood Tribe in the Southern Alberta Economy, 1884–1939* (Calgary: University of Calgary Press, 2009), 105–11. See also D.J. Hall, *From Treaties to Reserves: The Federal Government and Native Peoples in Territorial Alberta, 1870–1905* (Montreal/Kingston: McGill-Queen's University Press, 2015), 183; Aya Fujiwara, "Japanese-Canadian Internally Displaced Persons: Labour Relations and Ethno-religious Identity in Southern Alberta, 1942–1953," *Labour/Le Travail* 69 (2012): 70; John F. Gilpin, *Quenching the Prairie Thirst: A History of the Magrath Irrigation District, Raymond Irrigation District, Taber Irrigation District, St. Mary Irrigation District* (Altona, MB: Friesens, 2000), 49; Ian MacLachlan, "Industrial Development of Lethbridge: A Geographer's Interpretation" (Unpublished ms, 2004), 5; Crowson, *Southern Alberta's Sugar-Coated History*, 24–27; David B. Iwaasa, "The Mormons and Their Japanese Neighbours," *Alberta History* 53, 1 (2005): 7–11.

20 Regular, *Neighbours and Networks*, 106–9; Hall, *From Treaties to Reserves*, 159–62.

21 Regular, *Neighbours and Networks*, 110. See also Thompson and Seager, "Workers, Growers and Monopolists," 156; and Hall, *From Treaties to Reserves*, 183.

22 Palmer, *Patterns of Prejudice*.

23 Thompson and Seager, "Workers, Growers and Monopolists," 156.

24 Ibid.; Palmer, *Patterns of Prejudice*, 34.

25 A.A. den Otter, "Adapting the Environment: Ranching, Irrigation, and Dry Land Farming in Southern Alberta, 1880–1914," *Great Plains Quarterly* 6, 3 (1986): 180.

26 *An Act Respecting Irrigation Districts*, SA 1915, c. 13, https://canlii.ca/t/54204.

27 Evenden, "Precarious Foundations"; Armstrong, Evenden, and Nelles, *River Returns*, 167–76.

28 Thompson and Seager, "Workers, Growers and Monopolists," 154; Gilpin, *Quenching the Prairie Thirst*, 72–74.

29 Smith, "History and Current Status"; de Loë, "Stability and Change," 119.

30 Smith, "History and Current Status"; Eric J. Hanson, *Financial History of Alberta, 1905–1950* (Calgary: University of Calgary Press, 2003), 101–10, 316.

31 Smith, "History and Current Status."

32 John A. Widstoe, *An Examination into the Conditions on the Lethbridge Northern Irrigation District* (Edmonton: J.W. Jeffery, King's Printer, 1925), 6.

33 Ibid., 6.

34 Ibid., 5.

35 Committee on St. Mary and Milk River Water Development, "Calgary and Lethbridge," 293–303, GWRC, C0048, file M-3761-280.

36 "Record of Interview with Asael E. Palmer by W.L. Jacobson in Lethbridge, Alberta, September 18, 1958," 34, GWRC, C0048, file M-3761-169.

37 "How Irrigation Has Developed in Southern Alberta: An Address by A.E. Palmer, June 15, 1951," 4, GWRC, C0048, file M-3761-169; Gilpin, *Quenching the Prairie Thirst,* 169; Charles L. Schmalz, "The Second Raymond Sugar Factory: U&I Sugar's Canadian Venture, 1925–1931," *Alberta History* 64, 2 (2014): 2–9.

38 Sauder, *Irrigation in Southern Alberta,* 239–50.

39 James B. Hedges, *Building the Canadian West: The Land and Colonization Policies of the Canadian Pacific Railway* (New York: Russell and Russell, 1971), 360–62; Howard Palmer, "Nativism in Alberta, 1925–1930," *Historical Papers/Communications historiques* 9, 1 (1974): 188; Palmer, *Patterns of Prejudice,* 94–122.

40 Thompson and Seager, "Workers, Growers and Monopolists," 157–58.

41 Ibid., 173; "Record of Interview with Asael E. Palmer by W.L. Jacobson in Lethbridge, Alberta, September 18, 1958," 41, GWRC, C0048, file M-3761-169. When first formed, the group was dubbed the Sugar Beet Growers Cooperative Association, but the term "cooperative" was dropped. See Thompson and Seager, "Workers, Growers and Monopolists," 157n7.

42 Palmer, "Nativism in Alberta," 200.

43 Cecilia Danysk, "'Showing These Slaves Their Class Position': Barriers to Organizing Prairie Farm Workers," in *Building beyond the Homestead: Rural History on the Prairies,* ed. David C. Jones and Ian MacPherson (Calgary: University of Calgary Press, 1985), 169.

44 Palmer, "Nativism in Alberta," 190–91; Pitsula, *Keeping Canada British,* 124–33.

45 Cecilia Danysk, *Hired Hands: Labour and the Development of Prairie Agriculture, 1880–1930* (Toronto: McClelland and Stewart, 1995), 122–41.

46 Palmer, "Nativism in Alberta," 190–91; Pitsula, *Keeping Canada British,* 124–33; Danysk, *Hired Hands,* 122–41.

47 On M.L. Wilson, see Deborah Fitzgerald, *Every Farm a Factory: The Industrial Ideal in American Agriculture* (New Haven, CT: Yale University Press, 2003); Jess Gilbert, *Planning Democracy: Agrarian Intellectuals and the Intended New Deal* (New Haven, CT: Yale University Press, 2016); Mary W.M. Hargreaves, *Dry Farming in the Northern Great Plains: Years of Readjustment, 1920–1990* (Lawrence: University Press of Kansas, 1993); Sarah T. Phillips, *This Land, This Nation: Conservation, Rural America, and the New Deal* (New York: Cambridge University Press, 2007).

48 M.L. Wilson, W.H. Fairfield, and L.C. Charlesworth, *Report of Commission Appointed to Report on the Lethbridge Northern and Other Irrigation Districts in Alberta* (Edmonton: Government of Alberta, 1930), 14, https://open.alberta.ca/publications/1551414.

49 Ibid.

50 Lawrence B. Lee, "Dominion Ditches and British Columbia Canals: A History of the Western Canada Irrigation Association," *Journal of the West* 7 (1968): 38.

51 P.M. Sauder, Lethbridge Northern Irrigation District Project Manager, to L.C. Charlesworth, Alberta Director of Water Resources, 5 October 1937, GWRC, C0048, file M-3761-158.

52 "Recommendations to the Advisory Committee from the Water Development Committee Concerning the Water Development Projects Planned in Connection with the Rehabilitation of Drought and Soil Drifting Areas in the Provinces of Manitoba, Saskatchewan and Alberta," 1 May 1935, Library and Archives Canada (LAC), RG 17, acc. 1991-92/086, box 011, file 616.3W6-4, vol. 1.

53 Ibid.

54 "Advisory Committee Meeting re Prairie Farm Rehabilitation Act, Regina, 3–4 May 1935," LAC, RG 17, vol. 3283, file 559-12-1-(1). The Advisory Committee included Augustus Griffin, L.B. Thomson, Victor Meek, and W.L. Jacobson.

55 Christian Jensen, Chair, Board of Trustees, Magrath Irrigation District, to L.B. Thomson, Chair, Water Development Committee, PFRA, 17 September 1935, GWRC, C0048, file M-3761-85.

56 "Magrath Irrigation District," GWRC, C0048, file M-3761-85.

57 Gilpin, *Quenching the Prairie Thirst,* 133.

58 A. Griffin, "The Relation of Irrigation to Community Development," in Water Development Committee, Session No. 4, "Minutes of Meeting Held at Regina, December 4th and 5th, 1935," LAC, RG 17, acc. 1991-92/086, file 112.25, vol. 2.

59 "Biographical Sketch of Augustus Griffin," GWRC, C0048, file M-3761-173.

60 A. Griffin, "The Relation of Irrigation to Community Development," in Water Development Committee. Session No. 4, "Minutes of Meeting Held at Regina, December 4th and 5th, 1935," LAC, RG 17, acc. 1991-92/086, file 112.25, vol. 2. For further evidence that Packard's work was influential in a Canadian context, see D.W. Hays, "Economic Development for Irrigable Lands," *The Engineering Journal* 24, 5 (1941): 232–35.

61 Walter E. Packard, "Land and Power Development in California, Greece, and Latin America," vol. 2, interview by Willa Klug Baum, Berkeley, California, 1970, 275, Bancroft Library, Oral History Centre, https://digitalassets.lib.berkeley.edu/rohoia/ucb/text/packardlandpower02waltrich.pdf.

62 Edward T. O'Donnell, *Henry George and the Crisis of Inequality: Progress and Poverty in the Gilded Age* (New York: Columbia University Press, 2015).

63 Ramsay Cook, *The Regenerators: Social Criticism in Late Victorian English Canada,* 2nd ed. (Toronto: University of Toronto Press, 2016), 107–9. For more on George's influence in Canada, see Shirley Tillotson, *Contributing Citizens: Modern Charitable Fundraising and the Making of the Welfare State, 1920–1966* (Vancouver: UBC Press, 2008), 32; Elsbeth Heaman, *Tax, Order, and Good Government: A New Political History of Canada, 1867–1917* (Montreal/Kingston: McGill-Queen's University Press, 2017), 289–92.

64 *Report of Commission Appointed in 1936 to Inquire into the Various Phases of Irrigation Development in Alberta* (Lethbridge, AB: Lethbridge Herald, 1937), 12, https://archive.org/details/P006001. For a summary of the Ewing commission authored by a PFRA employee, see D.W. Kirk, *The Bow River Irrigation Project Part 1* (Ottawa: Department of Agriculture, 1955), 22–23.

65 Thompson and Seager, "Workers, Growers and Monopolists," 159; Schreiner, *Refiners,* 95; Leonard J. Arrington, *Beet Sugar in the West: A History of the Utah-Idaho Sugar Company, 1891–1966* (Seattle: University of Washington Press, 1966), 198, Appendix B.

66 Thompson and Seager, "Workers, Growers and Monopolists," 160.

67 Ibid.

68 Ibid., 159–71; Crowson, *Southern Alberta's Sugar-Coated History,* 41–55.

69 Edward Dunsworth, "Green Gold, Red Threats: Organization and Resistance in Depression-Era Ontario Tobacco," *Labour/Le Travail* 79 (2017): 123–24.
70 Schreiner, *Refiners*, 99–100.
71 Thompson and Seager, "Workers, Growers and Monopolists," 173–74.
72 Schreiner, *Refiners*, 113–16.
73 Carmela Patrias, "Race, Employment Discrimination, and State Complicity in Wartime Canada, 1939–1945," *Labour/Le Travail* 59 (2007): 32–33.
74 Thompson and Seager, "Workers, Growers and Monopolists," 172.
75 Historian Aya Fujiwara argues that Japanese people in the sugar beet landscape should be understood as informally interned because of the significant strictures and difficult conditions that characterized their lives. Aya Fujiwara, "Informal Internment: Japanese Canadian Farmers in Southern Alberta, 1941–1945," in *Civilian Internment in Canada: Histories and Legacies*, ed. Rhonda L. Hinther and Jim Mochoruk, 167–79 (Winnipeg: University of Manitoba Press, 2020).
76 Ann Gomer Sunahara, *The Politics of Racism: The Uprooting of Japanese Canadians during the Second World War* (Toronto: James Lorimer, 1981); Barry Broadfoot, *Years of Sorrow, Years of Shame: The Story of the Japanese Canadians in World War II* (Toronto: Doubleday, 1977); Patricia Roy, J.L. Granatstein, Masako Lino, and Hiroko Takamura, *Mutual Hostages: Canadians and Japanese during the Second World War* (Toronto: University of Toronto Press, 1990); Jordan Stanger-Ross, ed., *Landscapes of Injustice: A New Perspective on the Internment and Dispossession of Japanese Canadians* (Montreal/Kingston: McGill-Queen's University Press, 2020); Patricia Roy, *The Triumph of Citizenship: The Japanese and Chinese in Canada, 1941–1967* (Vancouver: UBC Press, 2007).
77 Jordan Stanger-Ross with Kaitlin Findlay, Eiji Okawa, Yasmin Railton, Josh van Es, and Trevor Wideman, "Introduction," in *Landscapes of Injustice: A New Perspective on the Internment and Dispossession of Japanese Canadians*, ed. Jordan Stanger-Ross (Montreal/Kingston: McGill-Queen's University Press, 2020), 29.
78 Patrias, "Race, Employment Discrimination," 34; Fujiwara, "Japanese-Canadian," 65.
79 Patrias, "Race, Employment Discrimination," 34; David B. Iwaasa, "The Japanese in Southern Alberta, 1941–45," *Alberta History* 24, 3 (1976): 5–19.
80 Fujiwara, "Japanese-Canadian," 68–71; Shelly Ikebuchi Ketchell, "Carceral Ambivalence: Japanese Canadian 'Internment' and the Sugar Beet Programme during WWII," *Surveillance and Society* 7, 1 (2009): 22–23; Alvin Finkel, *Working People in Alberta: A History* (Edmonton: Athabasca University Press, 2021), 113, 275–76.
81 Sunahara, *Politics of Racism*, 81–82.
82 Palmer, *Patterns of Prejudice*, 166–67.
83 Michael O'Hagan, "Beyond the Barbed Wire Fence: POW Labour Projects in Canada during the Second World War" (PhD diss., History, University of Western Ontario, 2020), 1–2; Vic Satzewich, *Racism and the Incorporation of Foreign Labour: Farm Labour Migration to Canada since 1945* (London: Routledge, 1991), 73.
84 Georgia Green Fooks, *Prairie Prisoners: POWs in Lethbridge during Two World Wars* (Lethbridge, AB: Lethbridge Historical Society, 2002), 39–45, 83–85; O'Hagan, "Beyond the Barbed Wire Fence," 47.
85 O'Hagan, "Beyond the Barbed Wire Fence," 332.
86 Ibid., 331; John Joseph Kelly, "The Prisoner of War Camps in Canada, 1939–1947" (MA thesis, History, University of Windsor, 1976), 151–53.

87 O'Hagan, "Beyond the Barbed Wire Fence," 334. For more on labour by prisoners of war, see Crowson, *Southern Alberta's Sugar-Coated History,* 68–70.
88 O'Hagan, "Beyond the Barbed Wire Fence," 355–56. On conscientious objectors, see Satzewich, *Racism,* 76–77.
89 J.N. Pollock, Vice-President, Alberta Co-operative Sugar Beet Growers, to Prime Minister W.L. Mackenzie King, 29 May 1940, GWRC, C0048, File M-3761-99.
90 Ibid.
91 Committee on Western Water Problems, "Report of the Committee on Western Water Problems," *The Engineering Journal* 24, 5 (1941): 222–23.
92 Emma S. Norman, *Governing Transboundary Waters: Canada, the United States, and Indigenous Communities* (London: Routledge, 2015), 45–46.
93 Nigel Bankes and Elizabeth Bourget, "Apportionment of the St. Mary and Milk Rivers," in *Water without Borders? Canada, the United States, and Shared Waters,* ed. Emma S. Norman, Alice Cohen, and Karen Bakker (Toronto: University of Toronto Press, 2013), 165; B. Timothy Heinmiller, "The Boundary Waters Treaty and the International Joint Commission in the St. Mary–Milk Basin," in *The First Century of the International Joint Commission,* ed. Daniel Macfarlane and Murray Clamen, 143–64 (Calgary: University of Calgary Press, 2020).
94 Bankes and Bourget, "Apportionment of the St. Mary," 167.
95 "Meeting of the P.F.R.A. Advisory Committee on Land Utilization and P.F.R.A. Conference, February 24–26 1947," GWRC, C0048, file M-3761-99.
96 Rob C. de Loë, "Return of the Feds, Part I: The St. Mary Dam," *Canadian Water Resources Journal* 22, 1 (1997): 25–34; Committee on Western Water Problems, "Report of Committee on Western Water Problems," *The Engineering Journal* 23, 3 (1940): 127.
97 St. Mary and Milk Rivers Water Development Committee, *Report on Further Storage and Irrigation Works Required to Utilize Fully Canada's Share of International Streams in Southern Alberta* (Ottawa: Department of Mines and Resources, 1942), iii.
98 Gilpin, *Quenching the Prairie Thirst,* 181–83.
99 G.L. MacKenzie, "The St. Mary-Milk River Irrigation Project," *The Engineering Journal* 31, 9 (1948): 488.
100 George Spence, Director of Rehabilitation, to V. Meek, Controller, Dominion Water and Power Bureau, 21 January 1947, PAS, GR 80, VI, file 11m.
101 M.J. Fitzgerald to E.C. Aquilina, 16 December 1968, LAC, RG 17, acc. 1991-92/086, file 170.603, vol. 1; P.C. 2298, PAS, GR 212, VI, file 6.
102 "Minutes of Ad Hoc Committee on Irrigation Economics," 9 June 1964, University of Alberta Archives, UAA-1983-123, box 6, file 94; South Saskatchewan River Project Negotiations, "Interim Report of the Irrigation Committee," 2, PAS, F 117, V, file 89.
103 Schreiner, *Refiners,* 190; Finkel, *Working People in Alberta,* 118.
104 Ronald F. Laliberte and Vic Satzewich, "Native Migrant Labour in the Southern Alberta Sugar-Beet Industry: Coercion and Paternalism in the Recruitment of Labour," *Canadian Review of Sociology and Anthropology* 36, 1 (1999): 66, 73–74; Ronald F. Laliberte, "The 'Grab-a-Hoe' Indians: The Canadian State and the Procurement of Aboriginal Labour for the Southern Alberta Sugar Beet Industry," *Prairie Forum* 31, 2 (2006): 305–23; Joan Sangster, *Transforming Labour: Women and Work in Postwar Canada* (Toronto: University of Toronto Press, 2010), 213–18; Finkel, *Working People in Alberta,* 118.; Crowson, *Southern Alberta's Sugar-Coated History,* 77–79; Jane Komori, "The Canadian 'War of the Two Sugars': Home-

grown Sugar Beets and the Racial Stratification of Labour," *Historical Materialism: Research in Critical Marxist Theory* 31, 3 (2023): 252–75.

105 George Edwin Britnell and Vernon Fowke, *Canadian Agriculture in War and Peace, 1935–1950* (Stanford, CA: Stanford University Press, 1962), 354.

106 Laliberte and Satzewich, "Native Migrant Labour," 66; Ronald F. Laliberte, "Why Move Aboriginal Labour In and Then Out? The Transition of Migrant Labour from Aboriginal to Mexican Workers in Southern Alberta's Sugar Beet Industry" (PhD diss., Sociology, University of Calgary, 2007); Komori, "Canadian 'War of the Two Sugars.'"

107 Independent Committee of Inquiry, *Report of an Independent Committee of Inquiry Established to Examine the Conditions of Migrant Workers in the Sugar Beet Industry in Alberta* (Edmonton: Department of Lands and Mines, 1970). For more on racialized labour in the postwar period, see Satzewich, *Racism*; Bob Barnetson, "The Regulatory Exclusion of Agricultural Workers in Alberta," *Just Labour: A Canadian Journal of Work and Society* 14 (2009): 50–74; and Laliberte, "'Grab-a-Hoe' Indians."

108 George Spence, "Contribution of the P.F.R.A. Programme to Prairie Agriculture during Wartime," 12, in "Minutes and Report of Meeting of P.F.R.A. Advisory Committee on Land Utilization, February 17th and 18th, 1943," GWRC, C0048, file M-3761-372.

109 William Dickson, "Agricultural Reconstruction in Canada: A Summary of Recommendation Made to the Dominion and Provincial Governments by Various Reconstruction Committees," 8 August 1945, 28, LAC, RG 17, acc. 1991-92/086, file 142.5, vol. 2.

110 Ibid.; "Agriculture Workshop B," in Canada, Department of Northern Affairs and National Resources, *Resources for Tomorrow: Proceedings of the Resources for Tomorrow Conference Held in Montreal, Oct. 23–28, 1961,* vol. 3 (Ottawa: Queen's Printer, 1962), 67.

111 Sub-committee on Agriculture and Combined Resources, "Summary for Meeting No. 3, Held on July 10th, 1945, at 10:30 am," LAC, RG 17, acc. 1991-2/086, file 142.5, vol. 2; George Spence, "Post-war Projects for the Prairies," *The Engineering Journal,* February 1945, 76–78, PAS, GR 80, VIII, file 21.

112 Director of Rehabilitation to Paul L. Farnalls, 23 February 1943, PAS, GR 80, VI, file 11f.

113 Ronald Rudin, *Against the Tides: Reshaping Landscape and Community in Canada's Maritime Marshlands* (Vancouver: UBC Press, 2021).

114 Jenny Kerber, "Pulling up Roots: Border-Crossing and Migrancy on Southern Alberta's Irrigation Frontier," *Dalhousie Review* 90, 1 (2010), 55.

Chapter 3: Intensification and Simplification

1 "Municipal Taxation – Community Pastures," stapled document, 3 August 1937 (starts on page 7), 25, University of Calgary Archives and Special Collections (U of C Archives), F0060, acc. 67/73/17, 12.4.

2 Derek Wall, *The Commons in History: Culture, Conflict, and Ecology* (Cambridge, MA: MIT Press, 2014), 20. For an analysis of PFRA community pastures that considers how they operated as commons, see Katherine Arbuthnott and Josef K. Schmutz, "PFRA Community Pastures: History and Drama of a Prairie Commons," *Saskatchewan Notes* (Canadian Centre for Policy Alternatives), April 2013, 1–8, https://policyalternatives.ca/sites/default/files/uploads/publications/Saskatchewan%20Office/2013/04/SKnotes_PFRA_0.pdf.

3 Simon Evans, *The Bar U: Canadian Ranching History* (Calgary: University of Calgary Press, 2004); David Breen, *The Canadian Prairie West and the Ranching Frontier, 1874–1924* (Toronto: University of Toronto Press, 1983); Edward Brado, *Cattle Kingdom: Early Ranching in Alberta* (Surrey, BC: Heritage House, 2004); L.V. Kelly, *The Range Men: Pioneer Ranchers of Alberta* (Toronto: W. Briggs, 1913); Warren Elofson, *So Far and Yet So Close: Frontier Cattle Ranching in Western Canada and the Northern Territory of Australia* (Calgary: University of Calgary Press, 2015); Warren Elofson, *Somebody Else's Money: The Walrond Ranch Story, 1883–1907* (Calgary: University of Calgary Press, 2009); Warren Elofson, *Cowboys, Gentlemen and Cattle Thieves: Ranching on the Western Frontier* (Montreal/Kingston: McGill-Queen's University Press, 2000); Warren Elofson, *Frontier Cattle Ranching in the Land and Times of Charlie Russell* (Montreal/Kingston: McGill-Queen's University Press, 2004). According to the PFRA annual report for 1939–40, only three early community pastures were located in the area of southwest Saskatchewan focused on ranching. These were the Battle Creek, Nashlyn, and Govenlock pastures. The rest were established in areas primarily dedicated to grain farming. Prairie Farm Rehabilitation Administration, *Report on Activities under the Prairie Farm Rehabilitation Act for the Fiscal Year Ending March 31, 1940* (Ottawa: Department of Agriculture, 1940), 18.

4 Max Foran, *Trails and Trials: Markets and Land Use in Alberta Beef Cattle Industry, 1881–1948* (Calgary: University of Calgary Press, 2003), 78–79, 132–35; Nic W. Monte, Administrator, Montana Grazing Commission, to Paul L. Farnalls, 10 July 1937, Glenbow Western Research Centre (GWRC), Paul L. Farnalls fonds (F0748), file M-6281-19; "General Discussion – Community Pastures," 19–21, U of C Archives, F0060, 67/73/17, 12.4.

5 Arthur S. Morton and Chester Martin, *History of Prairie Settlement and "Dominion Lands" Policy* (Toronto: Macmillan, 1938), 495.

6 Prairie Farm Rehabilitation Administration, *Report on Proceedings under the Prairie Farm Rehabilitation Act for the Fiscal Year Ending March 31, 1938* (Ottawa: Department of Agriculture, 1938), 23.

7 Chester Martin, *"Dominion Lands" Policy*, ed. Lewis H. Thompson (Toronto: McClelland and Stewart, 1973), 9–10.

8 Gregory P. Marchildon, "The Prairie Farm Rehabilitation Administration: Climate Crisis and Federal-Provincial Relations during the Great Depression," *Canadian Historical Review* 90, 2 (2009): 275–301; Daniel Balkwill, "The Prairie Farm Rehabilitation Administration and the Community Pasture Program, 1937–1947" (MA thesis, History, University of Saskatchewan, 2002).

9 "Development of Community Pastures," Provincial Archives of Saskatchewan (PAS), GR 6, R-261, file 22.26; F.H. Auld, "Problems of Land Control in Connection with Community Pastures," in "Minutes and Report, PFRA Conference, Regina, Saskatchewan, 29–31 May 1939," 39, PAS, GR 6, R-261, file 22.36.

10 "Land Utilization Legislation and the Land Utilization Board," 1–6, PAS, GR 80, VI, file 25c; Curtis R. McManus, *Happyland: A History of the "Dirty Thirties" in Saskatchewan, 1914–1937* (Calgary: University of Calgary Press, 2011), 179.

11 "Land Utilization Legislation and the Land Utilization Board," 1–6, PAS, GR 80, VI, file 25c.

12 Balkwill, "Prairie Farm Rehabilitation Administration," 48–57.

13 Ibid., 57–62.

14 O. Freer, "Development of Community Pastures in Saskatchewan under PFRA," *Canadian Cattlemen*, September 1938, 89.

15 Prairie Farm Rehabilitation Administration, *Report on Activities ... 1940,* 23.

16 O. Freer, Superintendent of Land Utilization, "Community Pastures & Re-settlement Policies," PAS, GR 6, R-261, file 22.23.

17 Prairie Farm Rehabilitation Administration, *Report on Activities Conducted under the Prairie Farm Rehabilitation Act for the Fiscal Year Ending March 31, 1942* (Ottawa: Department of Agriculture, 1942), 8. Later annual reports would moderate this figure, arguing that 10,000 acres was sufficient for economical operation. See Prairie Farm Rehabilitation Administration, *Report on Activities under the Prairie Farm Rehabilitation Act for the Year Ending March 31, 1945* (Ottawa: Department of Agriculture, 1945), 19; and Prairie Farm Rehabilitation Administration, *Eleventh Annual Report on Activities under the Prairie Farm Rehabilitation Act for the Fiscal Year Ended March 31, 1946* (Ottawa: Department of Agriculture, 1946), 24.

18 Prairie Farm Rehabilitation Administration, *Prairie Farm Rehabilitation Act: Annual Report of Activities, Year Ended March 31st, 1943* (Ottawa: Department of Agriculture, 1943), 16; "Appendix J: Financial Analysis of PFRA Community Pasture Program," in "PFRA Pasture Program Growth," Library and Archives Canada (LAC), RG 17, acc. 1991-92/86, box 5, file 520.8, vol. 01(S); Department of Regional Economic Expansion, "PFRA Small Water Development and Community Pasture Programs: A Consolidated Report," 30 March 1972, LAC, RG 17, acc. 1991-92/86, box 5, file 520.8, vol. 01(S). Please note that the values in the latter retrospective report are not entirely consistent with those listed in year-to-year annual reports, although the general trends are similar.

19 O. Freer, Superintendent of Land Utilization, "Bottlenecks in PFRA Community Pasture Work," report of a meeting of the PFRA's Advisory Committee on Land Utilization, 5–6 November 1943, PAS, GR 6, R-261, file 22.43.

20 Ibid.

21 "Appendix D: Memorandum from the Saskatchewan Land Utilization Board to the Director of Prairie Farm Rehabilitation Regarding Pasture Development and Land Settlement," 29 December 1942, PAS, GR 6, R-261, 22.43. See also Department of Regional Economic Expansion, "PFRA Small Water Development and Community Pasture Programs: A Consolidated Report," 30 March 1972, 47, LAC, RG 17, acc. 1991-92/86, box 5, file 520.8, vol. 01(S).

22 Paul Voisey, *Vulcan: The Making of a Prairie Community* (Toronto: University of Toronto Press, 1988), 85. See also Paul Voisey, "A Mix-Up over Mixed Farming: The Curious History of the Agricultural Diversification Movement in a Single Crop Area of Southern Alberta," in *Building beyond the Homestead: Rural History on the Prairies,* ed. David C. Jones and Ian MacPherson, 179–205 (Calgary: University of Calgary Press, 1985).

23 Ian MacLachlan, *Kill and Chill: Restructuring Canada's Beef Commodity Chain* (Toronto: University of Toronto Press, 2002), 76; G.A. MacEachern, *Retention of the Crow Rate and the Alberta Livestock Economy* (Ottawa: Agricultural Economics Research Council of Canada/Alberta Cattle Commission, 1978). On the mid-twentieth-century history of the Crow Rate, see Laura Larsen, "The Public Good and Private Business of the Crow Rate: Prairie Grain Handling and Transportation Policy" (PhD diss., History, University of Saskatchewan, 2020).

24 Grant MacEwan, *Between the Red and the Rockies* (Toronto: University of Toronto Press, 1952), 225.

25 Paula Fay Rein, "These Changing Conditions: A Study of the Saskatchewan Royal Commission on Agriculture and Rural Life" (MA thesis, History, University of Regina, 1994),

11; Vernon Fowke, "Economic Effects of the War on the Prairie Economy," *Canadian Journal of Economics and Political Science* 11, 3 (1945): 375–76; John H. Archer, *Saskatchewan: A History* (Saskatoon: Western Producer Prairie Books, 1980), 250.

26 L.B. Thomson, PFRA Director, "Conservation in Action," address, Annual Field Day, Lethbridge, Alberta, 28 July 1948, LAC, RG 17, vol. 3283, file 559-13-(8).

27 Prairie Farm Rehabilitation Administration, *Report on Activities ... 1940,* 22.

28 O. Freer, Superintendent of Land Utilization, "Community Pastures & Re-settlement Policies," PAS, GR 6, R-261, file 22.23.

29 G.A.D. Will, Senior Organization Officer, Prairie Farm Rehabilitation, "Community Pastures – Their Development, Construction and Possibilities," broadcast, CJRM Radio, Regina, 7 March 1939, PAS, GR 6, R-261, file 22.25.

30 Ibid.

31 T.L. Shepherd to Mr. Freer, 1 December 1939, PAS, GR 80, VI, file 37.

32 O. Freer, "Reconstruction Conference, Dec. 16, 1943," LAC, RG 17, acc. 1991-92/086, file 142.5, vol. 1.

33 O. Freer, Superintendent of Land Utilization, "Bottlenecks in PFRA Community Pasture Work," report of a meeting of the PFRA's Advisory Committee on Land Utilization, 5–6 November 1943, PAS, GR 6, R-261, file 22.43.

34 "PFRA (Land Utilization Branch) Fieldmen's Conference Held at Regina, December 29 and 30, 1942," 10, PAS, GR 6, R-261, file 22.40.

35 Ibid.

36 Prairie Farm Rehabilitation Administration, *Report of Proceedings ... 1938,* 23.

37 Prairie Farm Rehabilitation Administration, *Report on Activities ... 1940,* 18.

38 Prairie Farm Rehabilitation Administration, *Report on Prairie Farm Rehabilitation and Related Activities, 1952–53* (Ottawa: Department of Agriculture, 1953), 8.

39 Prairie Farm Rehabilitation Administration, *Report on Progress under the Prairie Farm Rehabilitation Act for the Fiscal Year Ending March 31, 1939* (Ottawa, Department of Agriculture, 1939), 25.

40 Prairie Farm Rehabilitation Administration, *Annual Report on Prairie Farm Rehabilitation and Related Activities, 1956–57* (Ottawa: Department of Agriculture, 1957), 3–4; Prairie Farm Rehabilitation Administration, *Report of Proceedings ... 1938,* 23; Saskatchewan, *Thirty-Second Annual Report of the Department of Agriculture of the Province of Saskatchewan for the Twelve Months Ended April 30, 1937* (Regina: King's Printer, 1938), 196.

41 Prairie Farm Rehabilitation Administration, *Report on Prairie Farm Rehabilitation and Related Activities, 1954–55* (Ottawa: Department of Agriculture, 1955), 4.

42 Prairie Farm Rehabilitation Administration, *Report on Activities ... 1939,* 25–26; "Summary of a Letter from Dr. F.H. Auld (LUB) to Mr. George Spence (PFRA), Development of Community Pastures," 1 January 1940, PAS, GR 6, R-261, file 22.26.

43 MacLachlan, *Kill and Chill,* 50.

44 For references to women working on community pastures, see Myrna L. Lamontagne, *D'Amour: An Era of Change* (Altona, MB: Friesens, 1983), esp. ch. 6. See also Lorrie Bergson, comp., *Somebody Had To Do It! A Collection of Stories and Poetry from PFRA Community Pastures* (Winnipeg: n.p., 1995), 1.

45 MacLachlan, *Kill and Chill,* 70; Grant MacEwan, *The Feeding of Farm Animals* (Toronto: Thomas Nelson and Sons, 1945), 194.

46 MacLachlan, *Kill and Chill,* 58–59, 72–75.

47 Foran, *Trails and Trials*, 159–60.
48 O. Freer to George Spence, 15 August 1938, PAS, GR 80, VI, file 121.
49 C.M. (Red) Williams, "Always the Bridesmaid: The Development of the Saskatchewan Beef Production System," part 2, "Historical Highlights and Integral Factors," *Saskatchewan History* 44, 2 (1992): 69; S.W. Garland and S.C. Hudson, *Government Involvement in Agriculture: A Report Prepared for the Federal Task Force on Agriculture* (Ottawa: Queen's Printer, 1968), 4–5.
50 Ian McLaughlin, "The Historical Development of Cattle Production in Canada" (Unpublished ms, 2006), 26; MacLachlan, *Kill and Chill*, 37; MacEwan, *Between the Red*, 220–21.
51 Prairie Farm Rehabilitation Administration, *Report on Activities ... 1940*, 19.
52 Grant MacEwan, *The Breeds of Farm Live-Stock in Canada* (Toronto: Thomas Nelson and Sons, 1941).
53 Ibid., 336.
54 W.L. Jacobson, "Prairie Relief and Rehabilitation," April 1938, 6, PAS, GR 80, VI, file 49a; "Report of Prairie Farm Rehabilitation Conference, Regina, 6 May 1937," LAC, RG 17, vol. 3283, file 559-13-1-(3).
55 "Report of Prairie Farm Rehabilitation Conference, Regina, 6 May 1937," LAC, RG 17, vol. 3283, File 559-13-1-(3).
56 Director of Rehabilitation to F.E. Cursons, 15 June 1938, PAS, GR 80, VI, file 120.
57 On evolutionary history and biotechnology, see Susan Schrepfer and Philip Scranton, *Industrializing Organisms: Introducing Evolutionary History* (New York: Routledge, 2003); and Edmund P. Russell, *Evolutionary History: Uniting History and Biology to Understand Life on Earth* (New York: Cambridge University Press, 2011).
58 MacLachlan, *Kill and Chill*, 42–43; A.M. Shaw and Grant MacEwan, "An Experiment in Beef Production in Western Canada," *Scientific Agriculture* 19, 4 (1938): 177–98.
59 MacLachlan, *Kill and Chill*, 45, 328.
60 Saskatchewan, *Forty-Third Annual Report of the Department of Agriculture of the Province of Saskatchewan for the Twelve Months Ended April 30, 1948* (Regina: King's Printer, 1948), 90–95.
61 MacLachlan, *Kill and Chill*, 37.
62 O. Freer, Superintendent of Land Utilization, "Bottlenecks in PFRA Community Pasture Work," report of a meeting of the PFRA's Advisory Committee on Land Utilization, 5–6 November 1943, PAS, GR 6, R-261, file 22.43.
63 Saskatchewan, Royal Commission on Agriculture and Rural Life, *Crop Insurance* (Regina: Government of Saskatchewan, 1956), 18; Canada, *Bill 83: An Act to Assist Agriculture in the Prairie Provinces*, 1st Reading, 18th Parliament, 4th Session, 6 April 1939, https://parl.canadiana.ca/view/oop.bills_HOC_1804_1/739.
64 "Prairie Farm Assistance," PAS, F 65, R-1022, VII, file: Articles and Speeches on the South Sask. River Project, item 27416.
65 Saskatchewan, Royal Commission on Agriculture and Rural Life, *Crop Insurance*, 19; "Appendix D: Memorandum from the Saskatchewan Land Utilization Board to the Director of Prairie Farm Rehabilitation Regarding Pasture Development and Land Settlement," 29 December 1942, PAS, GR 6, R-261, file 22.43.
66 L.B. Thomson, *Brief to the Royal Commission on Canada's Economic Prospects* (Ottawa: Department of Agriculture, 1955), Appendix 2.

67 Canada, Standing Committee on Agriculture and Colonization, *Minutes of Proceedings and Evidence,* 21st Parliament, 2nd Session, 30 May 1950, 10–11, https://parl.canadiana.ca/view/oop.com_HOC_2102_1_1/19.

68 Grace Skogstad, *Internationalization and Canadian Agriculture: Policy and Governing Paradigms* (Toronto: University of Toronto Press, 2008), 43.

69 E.C. Hope, "Coordination of Activities and Policies of the Various Agencies Assisting Agriculture in the Prairie Provinces," PAS, GR 6, R-261, file 22.41. For a useful discussion, see Garland and Hudson, *Government Involvement.*

70 "Figure 1.3: PFRA and Related Agencies (Sask.), Marv Anderson & Associates," in "Economic Evaluation of the PFRA Community Pasture Program," 11, LAC, RG 17, acc. 1991-92/086, box 6, file 520.802, vol. 01(S).

71 E.C. Hope, "Coordination of Activities and Policies of the Various Agencies Assisting Agriculture in the Prairie Provinces," PAS, GR 6, R-261, file 22.41; G.R. Fanset, "The Work of Ducks Unlimited," PAS, GR 6, R-261, file 22.41.

72 Balkwill, "Prairie Farm Rehabilitation Administration," 63–65.

73 L.B. Thomson, PFRA Director, "Conservation in Action," address, Annual Field Day, Lethbridge, Alberta, 28 July 1948, LAC, RG 17, vol. 3283, file 559-13-(8).

74 W.M. Drummond and W. Mackenzie, *Progress and Prospects of Canadian Agriculture,* ed. Royal Commission on Canada's Economic Prospects (Ottawa: Queen's Printer, 1957), 368; Canada, Federal Task Force on Agriculture, *Canadian Agriculture in the Seventies: Report of the Federal Task Force on Agriculture* (Ottawa: Queen's Printer, 1969), 393.

75 Charles Schwartz, *The Search for Stability* (Toronto: McClelland and Stewart, 1959), 197–99.

76 "Memorandum from the Saskatchewan Land Utilization Board to the Director of PFRA Regarding Pasture Development and Land Settlement," 28 December 1942, PAS, GR 6, R-261, file 22.26; "Appendix D: Memorandum from the Saskatchewan Land Utilization Board to the Director of Prairie Farm Rehabilitation Regarding Pasture Development and Land Settlement," 29 December 1942, PAS, GR 6, R-261, file 22.43.

77 E.C. Hope, "Coordination of Activities and Policies of the Various Agencies Assisting Agriculture in the Prairie Provinces," PAS, GR 6, R-261, file 22.41.

78 Canada, Royal Commission on Canada's Economic Prospects, *Final Report* (Ottawa: Queen's Printer, 1957), 173.

79 Canada, Federal Task Force on Agriculture, *Canadian Agriculture in the Seventies,* 393. Also relevant is the assessment of Vernon Fowke, who called the PFAA "a primitive and poorly rationalized form of state-subsidized income assurance to western Canadian wheat growers." Vernon Fowke, *The National Policy and the Wheat Economy* (Toronto: University of Toronto Press, 1957), 293.

80 On the global context for these policies and supports, see Kym Anderson, ed., *The Political Economy of Agricultural Price Distortions* (Cambridge, UK: Cambridge University Press, 2010). On the American context, see R. Douglas Hurt, *Problems of Plenty: The American Farmer in the Twentieth Century* (Chicago: Ivan R. Dee, 2002). On the Canadian context, see Grace Skogstad, *The Politics of Agricultural Policy-Making in Canada* (Toronto: University of Toronto Press, 1987); W.M. Drummond, W.J. Anderson, and T.C. Kerr, *A Review of Agricultural Policy in Canada* (Ottawa: Agricultural Economics Research Council of Canada, 1966); Canada, Federal Task Force on Agriculture, *Canadian Agriculture in the Seventies,* 274–78, 390; Garland and Hudson, *Government Involvement.*

81 "Memorandum from the Saskatchewan Land Utilization Board to the Director of PFRA Regarding Pasture Development and Land Settlement," 29 December 1942, PAS, GR 6, R-261, file 22.26.
82 Ibid.
83 Williams, "Always the Bridesmaid," 110.
84 L.E. Kirk, T.M. Stevenson, and S.E. Clarke, *Crested Wheat Grass* (Ottawa: Department of Agriculture, 1934), 6. See also H.J. Taylor, *To Plant the Prairies and the Plains: The Life and Work of Niels Ebbesen Hansen* (Mount Vernon, VA: Bios, 1941), 19–26.
85 H.L. Westover and George A. Rogler, *Crested Wheatgrass* (Washington, DC: United States Department of Agriculture, 1941), 2, https://digital.library.unt.edu/ark:/67531/metadc1567/m1/2/. This rendering fits within the pattern identified in David Moon, *The American Steppes: The Unexpected Russian Roots of Great Plains Agriculture, 1870s–1930s* (Cambridge, UK: Cambridge University Press, 2020), 16, 96–97.
86 Russell J. Lorenz, "Introduction and Early Use of Crested Wheatgrass in the Northern Great Plains," in *Crested Wheatgrass: Its Values, Problems, and Myths: A Symposium,* ed. Kendall L. Johnson (Logan: Utah State University, 1986), 16.
87 Kay H. Asay, "Breeding Strategies in Crested Wheatgrass," in *Crested Wheatgrass: Its Values, Problems, and Myths: A Symposium,* ed. Kendall L. Johnson, 53–57 (Logan: Utah State University, 1986).
88 Kirk, Stevenson, and Clarke, *Crested Wheat Grass,* 17.
89 Ibid., 5.
90 Ibid., 11; "Comments from Hon. Mr. Taggart," 6, U of C Archives, F0060, 67/73/17, 2.5.10.
91 W.L. Jacobson, "Prairie Relief and Rehabilitation," April 1938, 10, PAS, GR 80, VI, file 49a. See also George Edwin Britnell, *The Wheat Economy* (Toronto: University of Toronto Press, 1939), 55.
92 Moon, *American Steppes,* 375.
93 W.L. Jacobson, "Prairie Relief and Rehabilitation," April 1938, 10, PAS, GR 80, VI, file 49a; Prairie Farm Rehabilitation Administration, *Report on Activities ... 1940,* 21.
94 Kirk, Stevenson, and Clarke, *Crested Wheat Grass,* 7.
95 D.H. Heinrichs, "Pastures in Saskatchewan – Their Management and Improvement," January 1950, PAS, GR 6, R-259, III, file 20.
96 Kenneth P. Vogel and John Hendrickson, "History of Grass Breeding for Grazing Lands in the Northern Great Plains of the USA and Canada," *Rangelands* 41, 1 (2019): 14; Kenneth P. Vogel, "Humans, Climate, and Plants: The Migration of Crested Wheatgrass and Smooth Bromegrass to the Great Plains of North America," in *Biological Resources and Migration,* ed. Dietrich Werner, 35–45 (Berlin: Springer, 2004).
97 W.J. Bradley, "Grass vs. Drought," *Maclean's Magazine,* 15 June 1938, 24.
98 "Working Toward Permanent Agriculture through the PFRA," 1942, 7, PAS, GR 80, VIII, file 20; "Regulations Governing the Free Distribution of Crested Wheat Grass Seed to Rural Municipalities," April 1941, PAS, GR 6, R-259, III, file 20.
99 "Sowing the Forage Seed Plot," PAS, GS 44, file 109.
100 E.S. Archibald to W.H. Gibson, 25 April 1938, LAC, RG 17, acc. 1987-88/005, file 135; S.E. Clarke to W.H. Gibson, 8 March 1938, LAC, RG 17, acc.1987-88/005, file 139.
101 Raymond Youngman, "Government of Canada Community Pastures," *Journal of Range Management* 4, 6 (1951): 384.

102 D.H. Heinrichs, "Pastures in Saskatchewan – Their Management and Improvement," January 1950, PAS, GR 6, R-259, III, file 20; R.P. Knowles, *Crested Wheat Grass* (Ottawa: Department of Agriculture, 1956), 8–9.
103 D.H. Heinrichs, "Pastures in Saskatchewan – Their Management and Improvement," January 1950, PAS, GR 6, R-259, III, file 20.
104 Knowles, *Crested Wheat Grass,* 8–9.
105 Robert W. Lodge, "Complementary Grazing Systems for Sandhills of the Northern Great Plains," *Journal of Range Management* 16, 5 (1963): 240–44.
106 Kendall L. Johnson, "Foreword," in *Crested Wheatgrass: Its Values, Problems and Myths: Symposium Proceedings,* ed. Kendall L. Johnson (Logan: Utah State University, 1986), vii.
107 Don D. Dwyer, "Setting the Stage for the Crested Wheatgrass Symposium," in *Crested Wheatgrass: Its Values, Problems and Myths: Symposium Proceedings,* ed. Kendall L. Johnson (Logan: Utah State University, 1986), 1.
108 Brenda M. Vaness and Scott D. Wilson, "Impact and Management of Crested Wheatgrass (*Agropyron cristatum*) in the Northern Great Plains," *Canada Journal of Plant Science* 87, 5 (2007): 1026.
109 Janice M. Christian and Scott D. Wilson, "Long-Term Ecosystem Impacts of an Introduced Grass in the Northern Great Plains," *Ecology* 80, 7 (1999): 2397–407; Darcy C. Henderson and M. Anne Naeth, "Multi-scale Impacts of Crested Wheatgrass Invasion in Mixed-Grass Prairie," *Biological Invasions* 7, 4 (2005): 639–50.
110 Peter Lesica and Thomas H. DeLuca, "Long-Term Harmful Effects of Crested Wheatgrass on Great Plains Grassland Ecosystems," *Journal of Soil and Water Conservation* 51, 5 (1996): 408–9.
111 Vogel, "Humans, Climate, and Plants," 35.
112 Mike Pellant and Cindy R. Lysne, "Strategies to Enhance Plant Structure and Diversity in Crested Wheatgrass Seedings," in *Sage-Grouse Habitat Restoration Symposium Proceedings,* comp. Nancy L. Shaw, Mike Pellant, Stephen B. Monsen (Fort Collins, CO: Forest Service, Rocky Mountain Research Station, US Department of Agriculture, 2005), 89.
113 Joseph G. Robins and Kevin B. Jensen, "Breeding of the Crested Wheatgrass Complex (*Agropyron* spp.) for North American Temperate Rangeland Agriculture and Conservation," *Agronomy* 10, 8 (2020): 1134, https://doi.org/10.3390/agronomy10081134.
114 E.S. Forsyth, "Value of Community Pastures as Game Preserves," paper presented to the PFRA Land Utilization Branch, Community Pasture Managers' Conference, 26–27 January 1944, PAS, GR 6, R-261, File 22.43.
115 Daniel Pauly, "Anecdotes and the Shifting Baseline Syndrome of Fisheries," *Trends in Ecology and Evolution* 10, 10 (1995): 430. See also Jeremy B.C. Jackson, Michael Xavier Kirby, Wolfgang H. Berger, Karen A. Bjorndal, Louis W. Botsford, Bruce J. Bourque, Roger H. Bradbury, Richard G. Cooke, Jon Erlandson, James A. Estes, Terence P. Hughes, Susan M. Kidwell, Carina B. Lange, Hunter S. Lenihan, John M. Pandolfi, Charles H. Peterson, Robert S. Steneck, Mia J. Tegner, and Robert R. Warner, "Historical Overfishing and the Recent Collapse of Coastal Ecosystems," *Science,* 27 July 2001, 629–38; Jeremy B.C. Jackson, Karen E. Alexander, and Enric Sala, eds., *Shifting Baselines: The Past and Future of Ocean Fisheries* (Washington, DC: Island, 2011).
116 Forrest Hisey, Melissa Heppner, and Andrea Olive, "Supporting Native Grasslands in Canada: Lessons Learned and Future Management of the Prairie Pastures Conservation

Area (PPCA) in Saskatchewan," *Canadian Geographer* 66, 4 (2022): 683–95; Arbuthnott and Schmutz, "PFRA Community Pastures."

Chapter 4: Construction and Change

1 George Spence, *Survival of a Vision* (Ottawa: Department of Agriculture, 1967), 165.

2 Canadian Dam Association, *Dams in Canada – 2019* (Ottawa: Canadian Dam Association, 2019), 25, https://cda.ca/publications/dams-in-canada-2019.

3 Richard A. Jarrell, "Hind, Henry Youle," in *Dictionary of Canadian Biography,* vol. 13, http://www.biographi.ca/en/bio/hind_henry_youle_13E.html.

4 Henry Youle Hind, *Reports of Progress Together with a Preliminary and General Report, on the Assiniboine and Saskatchewan Exploring Expedition: Made under Instructions from the Provincial Secretary, Canada* (Toronto: J. Lovell, 1859), 24.

5 B. Russell, "Pertinent Data: North Saskatchewan Project," 15 June 1943, Glenbow Western Research Centre (GWRC), Irrigation Research Project (W.L. Jacobson) Collection (C0048), file M-3761-237. This document includes a description of the William Pearce Stockwatering Project, named after the federal government agent who conceived it.

6 G.L. Mackenzie, "Engineering Features and Estimated Costs in Water Development," in "Report of Meeting of the Advisory Committee on Land Utilization, 26–28 February 1945," 48–51, GWRC, C0048, file M-3761-375.

7 Director of Rehabilitation to John R. MacNicol, Member of Parliament, 10 October 1945, Provincial Archives of Saskatchewan (PAS), GR 80, VI, file 13K.

8 "Report of Interview with Benjamin Russell by W.L. Jacobson, 13 April 1959," GWRC, C0048, file M-3761-236; Benjamin Russell, "Study of Merits of Alternative Plans for the Use of Waters of the Saskatchewan River Drainage Basin in Alberta and Saskatchewan," Library and Archives Canada (LAC), RG 89, acc. 1983-84/146, vol. 120; L.B. Thomson to W.L. Jacobson, 26 February 1954, GWRC, C0048, file M-3761-175.

9 J.W. Pickersgill, *My Years with Louis St. Laurent: A Political Memoir* (Toronto: University of Toronto Press, 1975), 192.

10 Robert Peterson, "Soil Mechanics as Related to the PFRA Water Development Program," in *Proceedings of 1949 Civilian Soil Mechanics Conference,* 52–53 (Ottawa: National Research Council of Canada, 1950), https://nrc-publications.canada.ca/eng/view/accepted/?id=3fb69faa-504b-413b-8d1f-3848c84da924.

11 Director of Rehabilitation to Dr. H.H. Bennett, Director, United States Soil Conservation Service, 9 February 1945, PAS, GR 80, VI, file 11b.

12 "Low Pay for Agricultural Scientists," *Saskatoon StarPhoenix,* 10 July 1947, 11; John R. MacNicol, Member of Parliament, to Director of Rehabilitation, 18 February 1944, PAS, GR 80, VI, file 13K; "Enlarged Organization Required for Expanded P.F.R.A. Program," 1946, PAS, GR 80, VI, file 50r.

13 George Spence, "Appendix: Report on Proceedings of a Meeting of the PFRA Land Utilization Committee, 24–26 February 1947," in "PFRA Progress Report for 1946," 20, PAS, GR 6-2, R-324, file 7.16.

14 Ibid.

15 Ibid.

16 Ibid.

17 David P. Billington and Donald C. Jackson, *Big Dams of the New Deal Era: A Confluence of Engineering and Politics* (Norman: University of Oklahoma Press, 2006), 71.

18 Samuel P. Hays, *Conservation and the Gospel of Efficiency: The Progressive Conservation Movement* (1959; reprint, Pittsburgh: University of Pittsburgh Press, 1999), 5, 100–5. See also Donald Pisani, *To Reclaim a Divided West: Water, Law, and Public Policy, 1848–1902* (Albuquerque: University of New Mexica Press, 1992), 327–36.

19 David Pietz, *The Yellow River: The Problem of Water in Modern China* (Cambridge, MA: Harvard University Press, 2015), 5–9; James C. Scott, "High Modernist Social Engineering: The Case of the Tennessee Valley Authority," in *Experiencing the State,* ed. Lloyd I. Rudolph and John Kurt Jacobsen, 3–52 (New Delhi: Oxford University Press, 2006); Paul R. Josephson, *Industrialized Nature: Brute Force Technology and the Transformation of the Natural World* (Washington, DC: Island, 2002); David Ekbladh, *The Great American Mission: Modernization and the Construction of an American World Order* (Princeton, NJ: Princeton University Press, 2009).

20 Christopher Sneddon, *Concrete Revolution: Large Dams, Cold War Geopolitics, and the US Bureau of Reclamation* (Chicago: University of Chicago Press, 2015), esp. ch. 3.

21 Director of Rehabilitation to Dr. E.S. Archibald, Director Experimental Farms Service, 19 January 1945, PAS, GR 80, VI, file 11a.

22 Prairie Farm Rehabilitation Administration, "South Saskatchewan River Project: Summary Report of Investigations (Revised)," April 1951, LAC, RG 17, box 33, file 1001-S-10 04 (S).

23 G.L. MacKenzie, "The South Saskatchewan River Dam," Engineering Institute of Canada, Western Technical Conference pre-print, 17 August 1959, 3, GWRC, C0048, file M-3761-432; "Address by George Spence on the Proposed South Saskatchewan River Development, 20 June 1952," PAS, GR 212, R-160, II, file 2.

24 Jamie Benidickson, "The Evolution of Canadian Water Law and Policy: Securing Safe and Sustainable Abundance," *McGill Journal of Sustainable Development Law* 13, 1 (2017): 70.

25 Prairie Farm Rehabilitation Administration, "South Saskatchewan River Project: Summary Report of Investigations (Revised)," April 1951, 11, LAC, RG 17, box 33, file 1001-S-10 04 (S).

26 Ibid., 13.

27 Prairie Farm Rehabilitation Administration, "An Outline of the Proposed South Saskatchewan River Project," April 1951, 1, LAC, RG 17, box 33, file 1001-S-10 04 (S).

28 "Particulars re South Saskatchewan Project," 28 May 1951, PAS, F 65, R-1022, VII, 26393-26396.

29 Josephson, *Industrialized Nature.*

30 Robert A. Wardhaugh, *Mackenzie King and the Prairie West* (Toronto: University of Toronto Press, 2000), 261.

31 David E. Smith, "James G. Gardiner: Political Leadership in the Agrarian Community," in *Swords and Ploughshares: War and Agriculture in Western Canada,* ed. R.C. Macleod (Edmonton: University of Alberta Press, 1993), 216.

32 D.M. Stephens, "The Saskatchewan River and Manitoba's Problem," in Canada, *Report of the Royal Commission on the South Saskatchewan River Project,* 343–48 (Ottawa: Queen's Printer, 1952), https://publications.gc.ca/site/eng/9.827922/publication.html.

33 Benjamin Russell, *Report on Surface Water Supplies and Water Power of Alberta: Their Present and Ultimate Uses* (Alberta: n.p., 1948), 36–37.

34 "The South Saskatchewan River Project Construction Delayed in 1951," PAS, F 65, R-1022, VII, 27420.

35 "General Engineering Report on Dam and Reservoir, South Saskatchewan River Project," March 1952, 83–84, LAC, RG 17, box 33, file 1001-S-13 01(S).
36 James G. Gardiner to Walter Tucker, Member of the Saskatchewan Legislative Assembly, 11 June 1951, PAS, F 65, R-1022, VII, 26399-26401.
37 "I wish to announce my name as a candidate for the leadership ... " 17 November 1954, GWRC, C0048, file M-3761-203; F.J. Greaney, "L.B. Thomson, Director, P.F.R.A.," *Seedtime and Harvest,* 22 July 1948, GWRC, C0048, file M-3761-201.
38 "South Saskatchewan River Project," Cabinet conclusions, 31 May 1951, 2–3, LAC, RG 2, series A-5-a, vol. 2648, microfilm reel T-2367.
39 Canada, *Report of the Royal Commission on the South Saskatchewan River Project* (Ottawa: Queen's Printer, 1952), xi, https://publications.gc.ca/site/eng/9.827922/publication.html.
40 James G. Gardiner to Walter Tucker, Member of the Saskatchewan Legislative Assembly, 11 June 1951, PAS, F 65, R-1022, VII, 26399-26401.
41 Hand-written notes regarding potential commission members, PAS, F 65, R-1022, VII, 26402. On Lilienthal's tenure as head of the Tennessee Valley Authority, see David Ekbladh, "'Mr. TVA': Grass-Roots Development, David Lilienthal, and the Rise and Fall of the Tennessee Valley Authority as a Symbol for U.S. Overseas Development, 1933–1973," *Diplomatic History* 26, 3 (2002): 335–74.
42 James G. Gardiner to T.C. Douglas, Premier of Saskatchewan, 15 August 1951, PAS, F 65, R-1022, VII, 26415-26416.
43 Hand-written notes regarding potential commission members, PAS, F 65, R-1022, VII, 26402.
44 James G. Gardiner to Fred Larson, Member of Parliament, 25 August 1951, PAS, F 65, R-1022, VII, 26422-24424.
45 Hand-written notes regarding potential commission members, PAS, F 65, R-1022, VII, 26402.
46 G.A. Gaherty to Prime Minister Louis St. Laurent, 3 March 1952, PAS, GR 80, VI, file 48h; John A. Widstoe to James G. Gardiner, 28 November 1951, PAS, F 65, R-1022, VII 26431.
47 Canada, *House of Commons Debates,* 21st Parliament, 5th Session, December 1951, https://parl.canadiana.ca/view/oop.debates_HOC2105_02/285. See also "Secret: The South Saskatchewan River Project," 22–23, PAS, F 65, R-1022, VII, 26504-39–26504-72.
48 "Memorandum for Dr. J.G. Taggart, Deputy Minister, Department of Agriculture, re: South Saskatchewan Commission," 13 December 1951, PAS, F 65, R-1022, VII, 26434; G.A. Gaherty to Prime Minister Louis St. Laurent, 3 March 1952, PAS, GR 80, VI, file 48h.
49 James C. Gardiner to J.M. Dechene, Member of Parliament, 8 March 1956, PAS, F 65, R-1022, VII, 27169-27172; Hu Harries to L.B. Thomson, 17 March 1953, PAS, F 65, R-1022, VII, 26683-26687.
50 Hu Harries to L.B. Thomson, 17 March 1953, PAS, F 65, R-1022, VII, 26683-26687.
51 G.L. Mackenzie, Chief Engineer, to Dr. L.B. Thomson, 12 April 1952, PAS, F 65, R-1022, VII, 26464-26467.
52 Ibid.
53 Canada, *Report of the Royal Commission,* 6.
54 Ibid., 7.
55 David L. MacFarlane, "Book Review: Report of the Royal Commission on the South Saskatchewan River Project, Ottawa, Queen's Printer and Controller of Stationery, 1952,

pp. 423, xix," *Canadian Journal of Agricultural Economics* 1, 2 (1953): 31–34; Prairie Farm Rehabilitation Administration, "Review of Royal Commission Report on South Saskatchewan River Project," 22 February 1953, PAS, F 65, R-1022, VII, 27617-27656; Prairie Farm Rehabilitation Administration, "South Saskatchewan River Project, Economic and Financial Considerations," 13 April 1953, PAS, F 65, R-1022, VII, 27657-27672.

56 L.B. Thomson, *Brief to the Royal Commission on Canada's Economic Prospects* (Ottawa: Department of Agriculture, 1955), 11–14. It is not clear, however, that members of the Royal Commission found Thomson's arguments entirely convincing. See Canada, Royal Commission on Canada's Economic Prospects, *Final Report* (Ottawa: Queen's Printer, 1957), 172.

57 "Address by Prime Minister St. Laurent in Regina, 14 July 1953," partial transcript, PAS, F 65, R-1022, VII, 6, 47238-47383.

58 Premier T.C. Douglas, "Press Release," 29 April 1955, PAS, F 65, R-1022, VII, 27612-27613.

59 "Brief of the South Saskatchewan River Development Association," 10 November 1947, 1, PAS, GR 212, R-160, IV, file 2. Known upon its creation as the South Saskatchewan River Development Association, the organization would alter its name in the late 1940s. On the organization's change of name, see "Report of the Secretary Treasurer to the Annual Meeting SSRDA," 9 September 1949, PAS, GR 212, R-160, III, file 4.

60 South Saskatchewan River Development Association, "Bulletin No. 4: Report to Members," 18 February 1947, PAS, GR 80, VII, 1a.

61 John C. Weaver, *The Great Land Rush and the Making of the Modern World, 1650–1900* (Montreal/Kingston: McGill-Queen's University Press, 2003), 347. On promotional work in prairie irrigation, see Christopher Armstrong, Matthew Evenden, and H.V. Nelles, *The River Returns: An Environmental History of the Bow* (Montreal/Kingston: McGill-Queen's University Press, 2009), 152–86. In the American context, irrigation advocates form one side of the so-called iron triangles (which also include politicians and government agencies) that have been critiqued by scholars of American water policy. See Richard Berkman and W. Kip Viscusi, *Damming the West* (New York: Penguin, 1973); Donald Worster, *Rivers of Empire: Water, Aridity and the Growth of the American West* (New York: Pantheon Books, 1985); Marc Reisner, *Cadillac Desert: The American West and Its Disappearing Water* (New York: Viking Penguin, 1986).

62 Lawrence B. Lee, "Dominion Ditches and British Columbia Canals: A History of the Western Canada Irrigation Association," *Journal of the West* 7 (1968): 33.

63 Harold N. Pope, interview by Pamela Taylor, Moose Jaw, Saskatchewan, 19 September 1977, PAS, Saskatchewan Rivers Development Association Oral History Project, Tapes R-A1269 and R-A1269.2; George Spence to Dr. H. Barton, Deputy Minister of Agriculture, 17 November 1943, PAS, GR 80, VI, file 28.

64 Harold W. Pope to George Spence, 16 August 1946, PAS, GR 80, VII, file 2; "Report of the Secretary at the Annual Meeting of the SSRDA," 25 June 1947, PAS, GR 212, R-160, VI, file 1.

65 George Spence to B.T. Richardson, Editor, Saskatoon Star-Phoenix, 24 April 1948, PAS, GR 80, I, file 39c; George Spence to L.B. Thomson, PFRA Director, 23 April 1952, PAS, GR 80, VI, file 48h.

66 "Address by Dr. George Spence on the Proposed South Saskatchewan River Development Project at the Annual Meeting of the Saskatchewan Rivers Development Association, 20 June 1952," PAS, GR 80, VIII, file 25.

67 G. O'Shaughnessy, Secretary-Treasurer, Saskatchewan Rivers Development Association, to George Spence, 5 May 1952, PAS, GR 80, VI, file 48h.

68 George Spence, "Submission by Dr. George Spence," in Canada, *Report of the Royal Commission,* 318–29.

69 "Talk to the Rosetown Board of Trade Meeting, 23 February 1955," PAS, GR 212, R-160, II, file 47.

70 William Tufts, President, Saskatchewan Rivers Development Association, "The South Saskatchewan River Project," 15 November 1957, PAS, GR 212, R-160, VII, file 10.

71 Prime Minister Louis S. St.-Laurent, Secretary-Treasurer of the South Saskatchewan Rivers Development Association, to G. O'Shaughnessy, 31 March 1955, PAS, F 65, R-1022, VII, file: South Sask. River Project.

72 G. O'Shaughnessy, Secretary-Treasurer of the Saskatchewan Rivers Development Association, to I.C. Nollet, Saskatchewan Minister of Agriculture, 11 February 1957, PAS, GR 212, R-160, II, file 10; Dr. William D. Tufts, President, SRDA, "The South Saskatchewan River Project," 15 November 1957, PAS, GR 212, R-160, II, file 26.

73 G. O'Shaughnessy, Secretary-Treasurer of the Saskatchewan Rivers Development Association, to James G. Gardiner, 4 February 1957, PAS, GR 212, R-160, VI, file 10.

74 William C. Tufts, Director, Saskatchewan Rivers Development Association, "What Is the Future Role of the Saskatchewan Rivers Development Association?" PAS, GR 80, VII, file 4.

75 David M. Quiring, *CCF Colonialism in Northern Saskatchewan: Battling Parish Priests, Bootleggers, and Fur Sharks* (Vancouver: UBC Press, 2004).

76 Saskatchewan, Royal Commission on Agriculture and Rural Life, *The Scope and Character of the Investigation* (Regina: Government of Saskatchewan, 1955), 9; Paula Fay Rein, "These Changing Conditions: A Study of the Saskatchewan Royal Commission on Agriculture and Rural Life" (MA thesis, History, University of Regina, 1994), 169–70.

77 Will Langford, *The Global Politics of Poverty in Canada: Development Programs and Democracy, 1964–1979* (Montreal/Kingston: McGill-Queen's University Press, 2020), 6.

78 Kathleen Carlisle, *Fiery Joe: The Maverick Who Lit Up the West* (Regina: University of Regina Press, 2017), 255; William M. Harding, "The Royal Commission on Agriculture and Rural Life," in *Dignity and Growth: Citizen Participation in Social Change: Essays in Honor of W.B. "Bill" Baker,* ed. Harold R. Baker, James A. Draper, and Brett T. Fairbairn, 49–62 (Calgary: Detselig Enterprises, 1991).

79 Rein, "These Changing Conditions," 67, 73–74.

80 Wyatt Mark Skovron, "A People's Commission? High Modernism, Direct Democracy, and the Royal Commission on Agriculture and Rural Life, 1952–1957" (MA thesis, History, Simon Fraser University, 2011), 18. See also Jim Lotz, "The Beginning of Community Development in English-Speaking Canada," in *Community Organizing: Canadian Experiences,* ed. Brian Wharf and Michael Clague (Toronto: Oxford University Press, 1997), 22.

81 Skovron, "People's Commission?" 46–50.

82 Saskatchewan, Royal Commission on Agriculture and Rural Life, *Farm Income* (Regina: Government of Saskatchewan, 1957), 169–77.

83 G.L. MacKenzie, "The South Saskatchewan River Dam," Engineering Institute of Canada, Western Technical Conference pre-print, 17 August 1959, 5, GWRC, C0048, file M-3761-432.

84 "Speech by I.C. Nollet at the Annual Meeting of the Saskatchewan Rivers Development Association, 17 August 1955," PAS, GR 212, R-160, II, file 39.
85 Clinton O. White, *Power for a Province: A History of Saskatchewan Power* (Regina: University of Regina, 1976), 266.
86 "Submission of Saskatchewan Rivers Development Association to the Royal Commission on Canada's Economy," 17 November 1955, PAS, GR 6-2, R-1138, file 11.7j(vi)f.
87 Bill Waiser, *Saskatchewan: A New History* (Calgary: Fifth House, 2005), 351.
88 "Diefenbaker Dam Blocks Mr. Pearson," *Ottawa Journal*, 4 February 1953, PAS, GR 80, VI, file 48i.
89 "New Policy on Power," PAS, F 65, R-1022, VII, 27422; Saskatchewan Premier T.C. Douglas to Prime Minister L.S. St. Laurent, 29 March 1957, PAS, F 65, R-1022, VII, 27320-27324.
90 "Discussions proceeded for one year ... " PAS, F 65, R-1022, VII, South Sask. River Dam Project, 27295-27296.
91 G.L. MacKenzie, "The South Saskatchewan River Dam," Engineering Institute of Canada, Western Technical Conference pre-print, 17 August 1959, 3, GWRC, C0048, file M-3761-432.
92 "An Address Given by the Honourable Alvin Hamilton at the Annual Meeting of the Saskatchewan Rivers Development Association, 3 November 1959," 4, GWRC, C0048, file M-3761-311.
93 Saskatchewan, "Saskatchewan Announces $4 Billion Irrigation Project at Lake Diefenbaker," 2 July 2020, https://www.saskatchewan.ca/government/news-and-media/2020/july/02/irrigation-project.
94 Adrian A. Seaborne and R.L. Blackwell, "Patterns of Irrigation Development in the South Saskatchewan River Basin," *Prairie Forum* 18, 1 (1993): 98.
95 Ibid.
96 Saskatchewan Water Corporation, *History of South Sask. River Irrigation Project* (Moose Jaw: Operations Division, Irrigation Services, Saskatchewan Water Corporation, 1987), 9.
97 Saskatchewan Irrigation Projects Association, *Time to Irrigate*, vol. 2, *The Economic, Social and Environmental Benefits of Expanding Irrigation in Saskatchewan* (Regina: Clifton Associates, 2008), 28.

Chapter 5: Rehabilitation and Colonialism

1 Trevor Herriot, *Towards a Prairie Atonement* (Regina: University of Regina Press, 2016), 13.
2 This literature is broad. Examples include Sarah Carter, *Lost Harvests: Prairie Indian Reserve Farmers and Government Policy* (Montreal/Kingston: McGill-Queen's University Press, 1993); Kenichi Matsui, *Native Peoples and Water Rights: Irrigation, Dams, and the Law in Western Canada* (Montreal/Kingston: McGill-Queen's University Press, 2009); Adele Perry, *Aqueduct: Colonialism, Resources, and the Histories We Remember* (Winnipeg: ARP Books, 2016); Mary Jane MacCallum and Adele Perry, *Structures of Indifference: An Indigenous Life and Death in a Canadian City* (Winnipeg: University of Manitoba Press, 2018); James Daschuk, *Clearing the Plains: Disease, Politics of Starvation, and the Loss of Indigenous Life* (Regina: University of Regina Press, 2013); Evelyn Peters, Matthew Stock, and Adrian Werner, *Rooster Town: The History of an Urban Métis Community, 1901–1961* (Winnipeg: University of Manitoba Press, 2018); and Keith D. Smith, *Liberalism, Surveillance, and Resistance: Indigenous Communities in Western Canada, 1877–1927* (Edmonton: Athabasca University Press, 2009).

3 Hannah Holleman, *Dust Bowls of Empire: Imperialism, Environmental Politics, and the Injustice of "Green" Capitalism* (New Haven, CT: Yale University Press, 2018), 72.

4 Brittany Luby, *Dammed: The Politics of Loss and Survival in Anishinaabe Territory* (Winnipeg: University of Manitoba Press, 2020), 167.

5 Ibid., 72.

6 In using the term "Nehinuwuk," I follow Keith Napoleon Goulet, a member of the community that is here under consideration. This community is also known as the Cumberland House Cree Nation. Goulet explains that the term Nehinuwuk is used for both First Nations and Metis peoples. Goulet notes that he prefers the spelling "Metis" (without the accent) because he sees it as more reflective of understandings prevailing in his own community. Keith Napoleon Goulet, "Land and Colonization: A Nehinuw (Cree) Perspective" (PhD diss., History, University of Regina, 2021), 2–4. See also Linda M. Goulet and Keith Napoleon Goulet, *Teaching Each Other: Nehinuw Concepts and Indigenous Pedagogies* (Vancouver: UBC Press, 2014); Réal Carrière, "Kikicîtowek Insiniwuk: Nehinuw Governance in Nehinuw Terms" (PhD diss., Policy Studies, Ryerson University, 2018).

7 On the contemporary political question of Métis nationhood, see Chris Andersen, *"Métis": Race, Recognition, and the Struggle for Indigenous Peoplehood* (Vancouver: UBC Press, 2014); and Jennifer Adese and Chris Andersen, eds., *A People and A Nation: New Directions in Contemporary Métis Studies* (Vancouver: UBC Press, 2021).

8 Brenda Macdougall, "The Myth of Metis Cultural Ambivalence," in *Contours of a People: Metis Family, Mobility, and History,* ed. Nicole St-Onge, Carolyn Podruchny, and Brenda Macdougall, 422–64 (Norman: University of Oklahoma Press, 2012); Gerhard Ens and Joe Sawchuk, *From New Peoples to New Nations: Aspects of Métis History and Identity from the Eighteenth to the Twenty-First Centuries* (Toronto: University of Toronto Press, 2015), 65–66.

9 Brenda Macdougall, "Wahkootowin: Family and Cultural Identity in Northwestern Saskatchewan Metis communities," *Canadian Historical Review* 87, 3 (2006): 431–62; Brenda Macdougall, *One of the Family: Metis Culture in Nineteenth-Century Saskatchewan* (Vancouver: UBC Press, 2010).

10 Michel Hogue, *Metis and the Medicine Line: Creating a Border and Dividing a People* (Chapel Hill: University of North Carolina Press, 2015); Brenda Macdougall, Carolyn Podruchny, and Nicole St-Onge, "Introduction: Cultural Mobility and the Contours of Difference," in *Contours of a People: Metis Family, Mobility, and History,* ed. Nicole St-Onge, Carolyn Podruchny, and Brenda Macdougall, 3–21 (Norman: University of Oklahoma Press, 2012); Nicole St-Onge and Carolyn Podruchny, "Scuttling along a Spider's Web: Mobility and Kinship in Metis Ethnogenesis," in *Contours of a People: Metis Family, Mobility, and History,* ed. Nicole St-Onge, Carolyn Podruchny, and Brenda Macdougall, 59–92 (Norman: University of Oklahoma Press, 2012).

11 Macdougall, *One of the Family.*

12 Fleury, *Kanawayihtamaahk li taan paassii,* 8–9. In speaking to these historical events, George Fleury relied on Marcel Giraud, *The Métis in the Canadian West,* vol. 2, trans. Michel Woodcock (Edmonton: University of Alberta Press, 1986), 457, 497, 510.

13 Ken Zeilig and Victoria Zeilig, *Ste. Madeleine: Community without a Town, Metis Elders in Interview* (Winnipeg: Pemmican, 1987), 55–57, 97–98, 120, 146–47, 157–58, 168; Fleury, *Kanawayihtamaahk li taan paassii,* 14–21.

14 Zeilig and Zeilig, *Ste. Madeleine,* xi.

15 Cited in ibid., 41–43. For more on Joe Venne, see Lynn Whidden and Lawrence J. Barkwell, "Venne, Joe (1906–1990)," Gabriel Dumont Institute of Native Studies and Applied Research, Virtual Museum of Métis History and Culture, https://www.metismuseum.ca/resource.php/149413.

16 Fleury, *Kanawayihtamaahk li taan paassii,* 10–11. For more on George Fleury, see Lawrence J. Barkwell, "Fleury, George (b. 1935)," Gabriel Dumont Institute of Native Studies and Applied Research, Virtual Museum of Métis History and Culture, https://www.metismuseum.ca/resource.php/14741.

17 O. Freer, Superintendent, Land Utilization, PFRA, to John Bracken, Premier of Manitoba, 1 February 1939, Provincial Archives of Saskatchewan (PAS), GR 80, VI, file 12m.

18 George Spence to H. Barton, Deputy Minister of Agriculture, 22 August 1938, PAS, GR 80, VI, file 13a. See also Manitoba Agriculture and Prairie Farm Rehabilitation, "Memorandum from the Manitoba Department of Agriculture to the Director of Prairie Farm Rehabilitation," July 1943, 22, 29, PAS, GR 80, VI, file 26a.

19 George Spence to H. Barton, Deputy Minister of Agriculture, 22 August 1938, PAS, GR 80, VI, file 13a.

20 George Spence to J. Allison Glen, Speaker of the House of Commons, 13 December 1940, PAS, GR 80, VI, file 12n.

21 George Spence to Dr. H. Barton, Deputy Minister of Agriculture, 4 November 1938, PAS, GR 80, VI, file 13a.

22 George Spence to J. Allison Glen, Speaker of the House of Commons, 13 December 1940, PAS, GR 80, VI, file 12n.

23 Zeilig and Zeilig, *Ste. Madeleine,* 191.

24 Ibid., 191–92.

25 Alberta, *Report of the Survey Board for Southern Alberta* (1922), 33, 39.

26 Fleury, *Kanawayihtamaahk li taan paassii,* 11–12.

27 Olivia N. Sammons, "Leaving Ste. Madeleine: A Michif Account," *Canadian Journal of Native Studies* 33, 2 (2013): 157–58; Lawrence J. Barkwell, *20th Century Métis Displacement and Road Allowance Communities in Manitoba* (Winnipeg: Louis Riel Institute, 2016), 7–8, https://www.metismuseum.ca/media/document.php/149555.

28 Lawrence J. Barkwell, *The Metis Homeland: Its Settlements and Communities* (Winnipeg: Louis Riel Institute, 2016) 181–82, 198.

29 Zeilig and Zeilig, *Ste. Madeleine,* 190.

30 Ibid., 72.

31 George Spence to J. Allison Glen, Speaker of the House of Commons, 13 December 1940, PAS, GR 80, VI, file 12n.

32 Zeilig and Zeilig, *Ste. Madeleine,* xii.

33 David Parent, "Governing Metis Indigeneity: The Settler-Colonial Dispossession and Regulation of Metis in Mid-Twentieth Century Manitoba" (PhD diss., Native Studies, University of Alberta, 2021), 178.

34 Ibid., 172.

35 Zeilig and Zeilig, *Ste. Madeleine,* 70–72.

36 Herriot, *Towards a Prairie Atonement,* 72.

37 George Spence to J. Allison Glen, Speaker of the House of Commons, 13 December 1940, PAS, GR 80, VI, file 12n.

38 Nicole Buffie, "Manitoba Returns 100 Acres to Métis," *Winnipeg Free Press,* 19 July 2024, https://www.winnipegfreepress.com/breakingnews/2024/07/19/manitoba-returns-100-acres-to-metis.

39 Barry Ahenakew, âtayôhkewina: Mōstos-awāsis asiniy Buffalo Child Stone (Regina: All Nations Hope Network, 2019).

40 Deanna Christensen, *Ahtahkakoop: The Epic Account of a Plains Cree Head Chief, His People, and Their Struggle for Survival, 1816–1896* (Altona, MB: Friesens, 2000), 4, 34–35; Barry Ahenakew, "The Story of Buffalo Child Stone, Part I," *Saskatchewan Archaeological Society Newsletter* 30, 3 (2009): 119; Barry Ahenakew, "The Story of Buffalo Child Stone, Part II," *Saskatchewan Archaeological Society Newsletter* 31, 1 (2010): 22–23.

41 Tasha Hubbard, "The Call of the Buffalo: Exploring Kinship with the Buffalo in Indigenous Creative Expression" (PhD diss., English, University of Calgary, 2016).

42 Trevor Herriot, *River in a Dry Land: A Prairie Passage* (Toronto: Stoddart, 2000), 70–72.

43 Gregory Younging, *Elements of Indigenous Style: A Guide for Writing by and about Indigenous Peoples* (Edmonton: Brush Education, 2018), 11–13, 38, 57, 79.

44 I have heard Dwayne Donald tell the story of Mistasiniy. Other places where the story is discussed or recorded include Christensen, *Ahtahkakoop,* 34–46; Beth Ahenakew and Stan Hardlotte, *Cree Legends,* vol. 2 (Saskatoon: Saskatchewan Indian Cultural College, 1973), 61–74; Lynne Seavy, "Mistaseni Project Under Way," *The Sheaf,* 14 January 1966; Bradley David Himour, "An Archaeological Reconnaissance of the Lake Diefenbaker Region in South Central Saskatchewan" (MA thesis, Archaeology, University of Saskatchewan, 1997), Appendix 7, 274–75; Neal McLeod, *Cree Narrative Memory: From Treaties to Contemporary Times* (Saskatoon: Purich, 2007), 19–24; Ahenakew, "Story of Buffalo Child Stone, Part I"; Ahenakew, "Story of Buffalo Child Stone, Part II"; Hubbard, "Call of the Buffalo," 19; and Ahenakew, âtayôhkewina.

45 Henry Youle Hind, *Reports of Progress Together with a Preliminary and General Report, on the Assiniboine and Saskatchewan Exploring Expedition: Made under Instructions from the Provincial Secretary, Canada* (Toronto: J. Lovell, 1859), 57.

46 W.O. Kupsch, "Latest Erratic in Saskatchewan? *Blue Jay* 21, 1 (1963), Library and Archives Canada (LAC), RG 17, acc. 1994-95/225, file 1001-D-85A, vol. 1; Tim Jones and Lorne Lepp, "Glacial Erratics Enduring Reminder of Ice Age," *Saskatchewan Archaeological Society Newsletter* 23, 1 (2002): 16.

47 W.O. Kupsch, "Latest Erratic in Saskatchewan? *Blue Jay* 21, 1 (1963), LAC, RG 17, acc. 1994-95/225, file 1001-D-85A, vol. 1; Himour, "Archaeological Reconnaissance," 38–39.

48 George Colpitts, *Pemmican Empire: Food, Trade, and the Last Bison Hunts in the North American Plains, 1780–1882* (Cambridge, UK: Cambridge University Press, 2015), 219–20.

49 Hubbard, "Call of the Buffalo," 40.

50 Himour, "Archaeological Reconnaissance," 42.

51 Eldon Johnson, "The Saskatchewan Archaeological Society: A History," *Saskatchewan Archaeology* 8 (1987): 3.

52 Zenon Stephen Pohorecky, "Archaeology and Prehistory: The Saskatchewan Case," in *A Region of the Mind: Interpreting the Western Canadian Plains,* ed. Richard Allen, 47–72 (Regina: Canadian Plains Studies Centre, University of Saskatchewan, 1973). It should be noted, however, that there was at least some minor archaeological attention to Mistasiniy before the mid-1950s. On this history, see Ian G. Dyck, "Eighty-One Years of Archaeology in the Saskatchewan Museum of Natural History," *Saskatchewan Archaeology* 8 (1987): 19.

53 Dyck, "Eighty-One Years," 22.

54 G.L. MacKenzie to L.B. Thomson, 3 December 1955, LAC, RG 17, acc. 1998-00888-6 (a), box 014, file 1001-D-20, vol. 1.

55 Tim E.H. Jones, *Archaeological Resource Management in Saskatchewan: An Overview* (Regina: Government of Saskatchewan, Department of Culture and Youth, 1978), 22.

56 Himour, "Archaeological Reconnaissance," 20–21; Dyck, "Eighty-One Years," 24.

57 Tim E.H. Jones, Muriel Carlson, and T.R. Smith, "People, Potsherds and Projectile Points: Pondering the Saskatoon Archaeological Society's Past," in *Out of the Past: Sites, Digs and Artifacts in the Saskatoon Area,* ed. Urve Linnamae and Tim E.H. Jones (Saskatoon: Saskatoon Archaeological Society, 1988), 17.

58 Zenon Stephen Pohorecky, *Report on the South Saskatchewan Reservoir Archaeological Survey, June–September, 1960* (Ottawa: National Museum of Canada, 1960), 12.

59 Lynne Seavy, "Mistaseni Project Under Way," *The Sheaf,* 14 January 1966, 6.

60 Zenon Stephen Pohorecky, *Field Status Report on the South Saskatchewan Reservoir Archaeological Survey Covering the Period between July 8 and August 10, 1960* (Ottawa: National Museum of Canada, 1960), 2.

61 J.G. Watson to M.J. Fitzgerald, Operation Mistaseni, 1 April 1966, LAC, RG 17, acc. 1994-95/225, box 001, file 1001-D-85A, vol. 1.

62 "South Saskatchewan River Development Board Meeting 47," 660, LAC, RG 17, acc. 1998-00888-6(a), box 011, file 1001-B, vol. 6.

63 Daniel Coleman, *White Civility: The Literary Project of English Canada* (Toronto: University of Toronto Press, 2006), 32–33.

64 Jones, Carlson, and Smith, "People, Potsherds," 22.

65 Blair Stonechild, *Buffy Sainte-Marie: It's My Way* (Markham, ON: Fifth House, 2012), 144–45.

66 Vicki Brook, "Mistaseni Night," *The Sheaf,* 1 April 1966, 10.

67 "The Cost of Moving Mistaseni," *Indian Record,* June 1966, 6.

68 Robert Cole, "The Historic Sites and Monuments Board of Canada's Representation of Indigenous History from 1945 to 1982" (MA thesis, History, University of Ottawa, 2017), 73–75.

69 "Memorandum by PFRA Associate Director D.J. Thiessen to PFRA Director M.J. Fitzgerald," 16 May 1966, LAC, RG 17, acc. 1994-95/225, box 001, file 1001-D-85A, vol. 1; "Memorandum by PFRA Associate Director D.J. Thiessen to PFRA Director M.J. Fitzgerald," 6 June 1966, LAC, RG 17, acc. 1994-95/225, box 001, file 1001-D-85A, vol. 1.

70 Minister of Agriculture J.J. Greene to Minister of Northern Affairs and National Resources Arthur Laing, 25 July 1966, LAC, RG 17, acc. 1994-95/225, box 001, file 1001-D-85A, vol. 1.

71 Canada, *House of Commons Debates,* 27th Parliament, 1st Session, 17 June 1966, https://parl.canadiana.ca/view/oop.debates_HOC2701_06/1057.

72 Minister of Agriculture J.J. Greene to Minister of Northern Affairs and National Resources Arthur Laing, 25 July 1966, LAC, RG 17, acc. 1994-95/225, box 001, file 1001-D-85A, vol. 1.

73 Arthur Laing to J.J. Greene, 9 August 1966, LAC, RG 17, acc. 1994-95/225, box 001, file 1001-D-85A, vol. 1.

74 W.R. Parks, Deputy Minister, to J.J. Greene, 2 September 1966, LAC, RG 17, acc. 1994-95/225, box 001, file 1001-D-85A, vol. 1.

75 E.M. Muriel Miller, Secretary-Treasurer of the Village of Elbow, to PFRA Director M.J. Fitzgerald, 26 October 1966, LAC, RG 17, acc. 1994-95/225, box 001, file 1001-D-85A, vol. 1; Tim Jones, Big Rock Committee member, to PFRA Director M.J. Fitzgerald, 25 October 1966, LAC, RG 17, acc. 1994-95/225, box 001, file 1001-D-85A, vol. 1.

76 "Memorandum: Mistaseni, by PFRA Chief Engineer J.G. Watson to PFRA Director M.J. Fitzgerald," 2 November 1966, LAC, RG 17, acc. 1994-95/225, box 001, file 1001-D-85A, vol. 1.

77 PFRA Director M.J. Fitzgerald to G. Joel, Village of Outlook Overseer, 14 November 1966, LAC, RG 17, acc. 1994-95/225, box 001, file 1001-D-85A, vol. 1.

78 "The Cost of Moving Mistaseni," *Indian Record,* June 1966, 6.

79 "Memorandum to File, Re: Mistaseni Rock, PFRA Director M.J. Fitzgerald," 29 November 1966, LAC, RG 17, acc. 1994-95/225, box 001, file 1001-D-85A, vol. 1.

80 Dennis Fisher and Professor Zenon Pohorecky on behalf of the Big Rock Committee to Hon. J. J. Green, Federal Minister of Agriculture, 9 December 1966, LAC, RG 17, acc. 1994-95/225, box 001, file 1001-D-85A, vol. 1.

81 Joan Sangster, "Presidential Address: Confronting Our Colonial Past: Reassessing Political Alliances over Canada's Twentieth Century," *Journal of the Canadian Historical Association* 28, 1 (2017): 1–43.

82 E.G. Davis, "Mistaseni," report by resident engineer, 12 December 1966, LAC, RG 17, acc. 1994-95/225, box 001, file 1001-D-85A, vol. 1.

83 Bill Waiser, *Saskatchewan: A New History* (Calgary: Fifth House, 2005), 401.

84 "Mistusinne Dedication Program," 22 July 1967, LAC, MG 31-D 173, vol. 18, file e011167423.

85 Herriot, *River in a Dry Land,* 96.

86 Hubbard, "Call of the Buffalo," 45–46.

87 Alli Morrison and Iain Davidson-Hunt, *Opaskwayak Cree Nation Guide to the Wetlands of the Saskatchewan River Delta* (Winnipeg: Aboriginal Issues, 2012), 3.

88 H.J. Dirschl, A.S. Goodman and M.C. Dennington, *Land Capability for Wildlife Production and Utilization in the Western Saskatchewan River Delta* (Regina: Saskatchewan River Delta Development Committee, 1967), vii.

89 According to the Cree Literacy Network, the Cree language (Swampy dialect) name for the Opaskwayak Cree Nation is opâskwêyâhk. "Cree Names of Cree-Speaking Communities," Creeliteracy.org, 6 November 2017, http://creeliteracy.org/2017/11/06/indigenous-mapping-workshop-2017-supporting-cree-as-a-21st-century-language/.

90 Merle Massie and Maureen G. Reed, "Cumberland House in the Saskatchewan River Delta: Flood Memory and the Municipal Response, 2005 and 2011," in *Climate Change and Flood Risk Management: Adaptation and Extreme Events at the Local Level,* ed. E. Carina H. Keskitalo (Cheltenham, UK: Edward Elgar, 2013), 162.

91 Goulet, "Land and Colonization," 6–7. According to the Cree Literacy Network, the Cree language (Swampy dialect) name for the Cumberland House Cree Nation is kâministikominahikoskâk. "Cree Names of Cree-Speaking Communities," Creeliteracy.org, 6 November 2017, http://creeliteracy.org/2017/11/06/indigenous-mapping-workshop-2017-supporting-cree-as-a-21st-century-language/.

92 Goulet, "Land and Colonization," 8–9; David Meyer and Paul C. Thistle, "Saskatchewan River Rendezvous Centers and Trading Posts: Continuity in a Cree Social Geography," *Ethnohistory* 42, 3 (1995): 403–44; Victor P. Lytwyn, *Muskekowuck Athinuwick: Original People of the Great Swampy Land* (Winnipeg: University of Manitoba Press, 2002), 201–4.

93 Morrison and Davidson-Hunt, *Opaskwayak Cree Nation Guide,* 40; Loriena Pearl Melnick, "Fish, Food and the Fur Trade: The Use of Hudson's Bay Company's Post Journals for Moose Factory, Cumberland House, Edmonton House, Fort Athabasca, and Ile a la Crosse

to Reconstruct the Provisioning of Fish, Fowl and Game, ca. 1777–1827" (MA thesis, Native Studies, University of Alberta, 2018).

94 Arthur J. Ray, *The Canadian Fur Trade in the Industrial Age* (Toronto: University of Toronto Press, 1990), 20–24. For more on the fur trade history of Cumberland House, see George Colpitts, "'Victuals to Put into Our Mouths': Environmental Perspectives on Fur Trade Provisioning Activities at Cumberland House, 1775–1782," *Prairie Forum* 22, 1 (1997): 1–19; Dale R. Russell, *Eighteenth-Century Western Cree and Their Neighbours* (Ottawa: Canadian Museum of Civilization, 1991); Frank J. Tough, *"As Their Natural Resources Fail": Native Peoples and the Economic History of Northern Manitoba, 1870–1930* (Vancouver: UBC Press, 1996); Colpitts, *Pemmican Empire.*

95 David M. Quiring, *CCF Colonialism in Northern Saskatchewan: Battling Parish Priests, Bootleggers, and Fur Sharks* (Vancouver: UBC Press, 2004), 53.

96 Ibid. For more on provincial government efforts targeting the Saskatchewan north, see F. Laurie Barron, *Walking in Indian Moccasins: The Native Policies of Tommy Douglas and the CCF* (Vancouver: UBC Press, 1997).

97 Frank J. Tough, "'The World's Largest Muskrat Ranch': The Summerberry Muskrat Rehabilitation Project, 1935–1965," *Meridian*, Spring–Summer 2008, 24, https://publications.gc.ca/collections/collection_2008/cpc-ccap/R102-4-2008-1E.pdf.

98 Dirschl, Goodman, and Dennington, *Land Capability*, 15–16; J.H. Ellis, *The Pasquia Land Settlement Project Interim Report No. 1* (Winnipeg: Department of Mines and Natural Resources, 1956), 14; Massie and Reed, "Cumberland House," 159.

99 Ellis, *Pasquia Land Settlement Project*, 23–24; H.G. Riesen and E. Kuiper, *Report: Saskatchewan River Reclamation Project* (Ottawa: Prairie Farm Rehabilitation Administration, Department of Agriculture, 1956), Synopsis, n.p.; Quiring, *CCF Colonialism*, 75; E. Kuiper, "Sediment Transport and Delta Formation," *Journal of the Hydraulics Division* 86, 2 (1960): 64–65.

100 The E.B. Campbell Dam's original name included a derogatory term. Today, the dam and related infrastructure are officially known as the E.B. Campbell Hydroelectric Station.

101 James B. Waldram, *Cumberland House and the E.B. Campbell Dam: An Economic Impact Study* (Thunder Bay, ON: Centre for Northern Studies, Lakehead University, 1989), 2.

102 Tough, "'World's Largest Muskrat Ranch,'" 24; Helen Buckley, *From Wooden Ploughs to Welfare: Why Indian Policy Failed in the Prairie Provinces* (Montreal/Kingston: McGill-Queen's University Press, 1992), 116–20.

103 E.G. Bligh, "Mercury Contamination in Fish," in *A Summary of Material Presented at the Twentieth Annual Institute for Public Health Inspectors* (Winnipeg: Department of Health and Social Development, 1970), 19. The term "chlor-alkali plants" refers to plants using mercury to produce chlorine and sodium hydroxide.

104 M.A. Carson and Associates, *Sediment Issues in the Cumberland Lake Area, Saskatchewan River Delta Complex* (Regina: Water Resources Branch, Western and Northern Region, Inland Waters Directorate, Environment Canada, 1993), 22; Norman Smith, "Evolution of Upper SRD Following the 1870's Evulsion and Subsequent Geomorphic Effects of E.B. Campbell Dam," in *Saskatchewan River Delta Symposium: Past, Present and Future, April 1–3, 2008, Saskatoon, Saskatchewan: Proceedings*, 29 (Saskatoon: Partners for the Saskatchewan River Basin, 2008); Alec Ross, "Cumberland House, Saskatchewan: Rising Waters, Rising Hope," *Equinox* 8, 47 (1989): 111–28.

105 John W. Pomeroy, Dirk de Boer, and Lawrence W. Martz, *Hydrology and Water Resources of Saskatchewan* (Saskatoon: Centre for Hydrology, University of Saskatchewan, 2005), 8.

106 Massie and Reed, "Cumberland House," 161; Clinton O. White, *Power for a Province: A History of Saskatchewan Power* (Regina: University of Regina, 1976), 158, 168–69; Calibre Consultants Inc., *Environmental Effects of Major Hydro-Electric Projects* (Saskatoon: Saskatchewan Energy Conservation and Development Authority, 1994), 102.

107 Norman Smith, Galina S. Morozova, Marta Pérez-Arlucea, and Martin R. Gibling, "Dam-Induced and Natural Channel Changes in the Saskatchewan River below the E.B. Campbell Dam, Canada," *Geomorphology* 269 (2016): 186–202; G.M. Kondolf, "Hungry Water: Effects of Dams and Gravel Mining on River Channels," *Environmental Management* 21, 4 (1997): 533–51; Lin Li, Pouya Sabokruhie, and Karl-Erich Lindenschmidt, "Dam-Induced Riverbed Degradation in the Saskatchewan River Delta," *Land Degradation and Development* 35, 2 (2024): 772–83.

108 M.A. Carson and Associates, *Sediment Issues,* 23. See also Partners for the Saskatchewan River Basin, *From the Mountains to the Sea: The State of the Saskatchewan River Basin* (Saskatoon: Partners for the Saskatchewan River Basin, 2009), 133.

109 Goulet, "Land and Colonization," 313–16; Razak Abu and Maureen G. Reed, "Adaptation through Bricolage: Indigenous Responses to Long-Term Social-Ecological Change in the Saskatchewan River Delta, Canada," *Canadian Geographer* 62, 4 (2018): 444; Evan J. Andrews, "Environmental Justice and Dam Management: A Case Study in the Saskatchewan River Delta" (MA thesis, Environment and Sustainability, University of Saskatchewan, 2015).

110 Quiring, *CCF Colonialism,* 76, 85–86; Evan J. Andrews, Maureen G. Reed, Timothy D. Jardine, and Toddi A. Steelman, "Damming Knowledge Flows: POWER as a Constraint on Knowledge Pluralism in River Flow Decision-Making in the Saskatchewan River Delta," *Society and Natural Resources* 31, 8 (2018): 901–2.

111 Andrews et al., "Damming Knowledge Flows," 903.

112 Trish Goulet, "Revitalizing Cree Legal Traditions: Cumberland House and Pelican Narrows" (LLM thesis, University of Manitoba, 2013), 8; Andrews, "Environmental Justice," 124.

113 Abu and Reed, "Adaptation through Bricolage."

114 Bligh, "Mercury Contamination in Fish," 11; Arthur K. Sumner, Jadu G. Saha, and Young W. Lee, "Mercury Residues in Fish from Saskatchewan Waters with and without Known Sources of Pollution – 1970," *Pesticides Monitoring Journal* 6, 2 (1972): 122–25; Bicentennial Committee of Cumberland House, *A History of Cumberland House ... as Told by Its Own Citizens, 1774 to 1974* (Cumberland House, SK: Bicentennial Committee of Cumberland House, 1974), 25–26; Florence Fehr and C.A.R. Dennis, *Investigations into the Use and Health Hazard of Mercury in Saskatchewan* (Regina: Prairie Institute of Environmental Health, 1975), 8.

115 Derek J. Green, Mark Duffy, David M. Janz, Keven McCullum, Gary Carrière, and Timothy D. Jardine, "Historical and Contemporary Patterns of Mercury in a Hydroelectric Reservoir and Downstream Fishery: Concentration Decline in Water and Fishes," *Archives of Environmental Contamination and Toxicology* 71, 2 (2016): 157–70; R.E. Hecky, D.J. Ramsey, R.A. Bodaly, and N.E. Strange, "Increased Methylmercury Contamination in Fish in Newly Formed Freshwater Reservoirs," in *Advances in Mercury Toxicology,* ed. Tsuguyoshi Suzuki, Nobumasa Imura, and Thomas W. Clarkson, 33–53 (New York: Springer, 1991).

116 Bligh, "Mercury Contamination in Fish," 12; Fehr and Dennis, *Investigations into the Use;* J.T. Harrison and D.T. Waite, *Mercury Survey of the Saskatchewan River System in Saskatchewan* (Ottawa: Environment Canada, 1988); A.R. Murray, *An Analysis of Mercury*

Contamination in Fish from Northern Saskatchewan Lakes, 1969–1976 (La Ronge: Department of Northern Saskatchewan, 1978).

117 James J. Willpacker, Collin A. Eagles-Smith, Michelle A. Lutz, Michael T. Tate, Jesse M. Lepak, and Joshu T. Ackerman, "Reservoirs and Water Management Influence Fish Mercury Concentrations in the Western United States and Canada," *Science of the Total Environment* 568 (2016): 739–48.

118 Waldram, *Cumberland House,* 2.

119 Green et al., "Historical and Contemporary Patterns," 167.

120 Richard H. Bartlett, "Hydroelectric Power and Indian Water Rights," *Prairie Forum* 14, 2 (1989): 191.

121 Committee on Saskatchewan River Delta Problems, *Resources, Development and Problems of the Saskatchewan River Delta* (Regina: Saskatchewan Water Resources Commission, 1972), 5.

122 Ibid., 53.

123 Ibid., 53–54.

124 Thibault Martin and Steven Hoffman, eds., *Power Struggles: Hydro Development and First Nations in Manitoba and Quebec* (Winnipeg: University of Manitoba Press, 2008); Caroline Desbiens, *Power from the North: Territory, Identity, and the Culture of Hydroelectricity in Quebec* (Vancouver: UBC Press, 2013); Daniel Sims, "Dam Bennett: The Impacts of the W.A.C. Bennett Dam and Williston Lake Reservoir on the Tsek'ehne of Northern British Columbia" (PhD diss., History, University of Alberta, 2017); James Waldram, *As Long as the Rivers Run: Hydroelectric Development and Native Communities in Western Canada* (Winnipeg: University of Manitoba Press, 1993).

125 Goulet, "Land and Colonization," 316.

126 Daniel Macfarlane and Andrea Olive, "Whither Wintego: Environmental Impact Assessment and Indigenous Opposition in Saskatchewan's Churchill River Hydropower Project in the 1970s," *Canadian Historical Review* 102, 4 (2021): 620–46.

127 Thomas R. Berger, *Northern Frontier, Northern Homeland: The Report of the Mackenzie Valley Pipeline Inquiry* (Ottawa: Minister of Supply and Services Canada, 1977).

128 Thibault Martin, "Hydro Development in Quebec and Manitoba: Old Relationships or New Social Contract?" in *Power Struggles: Hydro Development and First Nations in Manitoba and Quebec,* ed. Thibault Martin and Steven Hoffman, 19–37 (Winnipeg: University of Manitoba Press, 2008).

129 Waldram, *Cumberland House,* 3.

130 Ibid., 12.

131 Waldram, *As Long as the Rivers Run,* 61–70.

132 Bartlett, "Hydroelectric Power," 190.

133 Ibid., 191; Claudia Notzke, *Aboriginal Peoples and Natural Resources in Canada* (Concord, ON: Captus University Publications, 1994), 20–22; Goulet, "Land and Colonialism," 318–19.

134 Andrews et al., "Damming Knowledge Flows," 898.

135 Ibid.; Razak Abu, Maureen Reed, and Tim Jardine, "Using Two-Eyed Seeing to Bridge Western Science and Indigenous Knowledge Systems and Understand Long-Term Change in the Saskatchewan River Delta, Canada," *International Journal of Water Resources Development* 36, 5 (2020): 757–76.

136 Nick Pearce, "First Nation Declares Sovereignty over Saskatchewan River Delta," *Saskatoon StarPhoenix,* 11 June 2021; Michael Bramadat-Willcock, "Cumberland House Cree Nation Calls on Premier to Meet over Water Supply," *Prince Albert Daily Herald,* 10 October 2021.

137 Goulet, "Land and Colonization," 313.

138 Andrews et al., "Damming Knowledge Flows," 901; Abu and Reed, "Adaptation through Bricolage," 442–43.

139 Canada, *Report of the Royal Commission on Aboriginal Peoples,* vol. 1, *Looking Forward, Looking Back* (Ottawa: Queen's Printer, 1996), 450–53. https://publications.gc.ca/site/eng/9.819007/publication.html.

Chapter 6: The PFRA Overseas

1 "Chairman's Opening Remarks," in "Proceedings of a Meeting of the P.F.R.A. Advisory Committee on Land Utilization and P.F.R.A. Conference, 25–27 February 1946," 4, Provincial Archives of Saskatchewan (PAS), GR 6, R-259, III, file 20.

2 David Webster, "Developing the World in Canada's Image: Hugh Keenleyside and Technical Assistance," in *A Samaritan State Revisited: Historical Perspectives on Canadian Foreign Aid,* ed. Greg Donaghy and David Webster, 73–99 (Calgary: University of Calgary Press, 2019); Greg Donaghy, "'Reasonably Well-Organized': A History of Early Aid Administration," in *A Samaritan State Revisited: Historical Perspectives on Canadian Foreign Aid,* ed. Greg Donaghy and David Webster, 53–72 (Calgary: University of Calgary Press, 2019). On the role of technical assistance more broadly, see Gisela Mateos and Edna Suárez-Díaz, "Development Interventions: Science, Technology and Technical Assistance," *History and Technology* 36, 3–4 (2020): 293–309.

3 Arturo Escobar, *Encountering Development: The Making and Unmaking of the Third World* (Princeton, NJ: Princeton University Press, 1995), 4; Joseph Morgan Hodge, "Writing the History of Development (Part 2: Longer, Deeper, Wider)," *Humanity: An International Journal of Human Rights, Humanitarianism, and Development* 7, 1 (2016): 148–49.

4 Sarah C. White, "Thinking Race, Thinking Development," *Third World Quarterly* 23, 3 (2002): 407–19; Robtel Neajai Pailey, "De-centering the 'White Gaze' of Development," *Development and Change* 51, 3 (2020): 729–45; Barbara Heron, *Desire for Development: Whiteness, Gender, and the Helping Imperative* (Waterloo, ON: Wilfrid Laurier University Press, 2007). On the Canadian context in particular, see David Webster, "Foreign Policy, Diplomacy, and Decolonization," in *Canada and the Third World: Overlapping Histories,* ed. Karen Dubinsky, Sean Mills, and Scott Rutherford (Toronto: University of Toronto Press, 2016), 182–84.

5 Richard P. Tucker, "Containing Communism by Impounding Rivers: American Strategic Interests and the Global Spread of High Dams in the Early Cold War," in *Environmental Histories of the Cold War,* ed. J.R. McNeill and Corinna R. Unger (Washington, DC: Cambridge University Press, 2010), 139.

6 On the Volta River project, see Stephan F. Miescher, "'Nkrumah's Baby': The Akosombo Dam and the Dream of Development in Ghana, 1952–1966," *Water History* 6, 4 (2014): 341–66; Stephan F. Miescher, "'No One Should Be Worse Off': The Akosombo Dam, Modernization, and the Experience of Resettlement in Ghana, in *Modernization as Spectacle in Africa,* ed. Peter J. Bloom, Stephan F. Miescher, and Takyiwaa Manuh, 184–204 (Bloomington: Indiana University Press, 2014); Stephan F. Miescher, "Building the City of the Future: Visions and Experiences of Modernity in Ghana's Akosombo Township," *Journal of African History* 53, 3 (2012): 367–90; Stephan F. Miescher and Dzodzi Tsikata, "Hydro-Power and the Promise of Modernity and Development in Ghana: Comparing the Akosombo and Bui Dam Projects," *Ghana Studies* 12–13 (2009–10): 15–53; Dzodzi

Tsikata, *Living in the Shadow of the Large Dams: Long-Term Responses of Downstream and Lakeside Communities of Ghana's Volta River Project* (Leiden: Brill, 2006); Lawrence Agbemabiese and John Byrne, "Commodification of Ghana's Volta River: An Example of Ellul's Autonomy of Technique," *Bulletin of Science, Technology and Society* 25, 1 (2005): 17–25; David Hart, *The Volta River Project: A Case Study in Politics and Technology* (Edinburgh: Edinburgh University Press, 1980); Kwaku Obosu-Mensah, *Ghana's Volta Resettlement Scheme: The Long-Term Consequences of Post-colonial State Planning* (San Francisco: International Scholars, 1996); Jon Olav Hove, "The Volta River Project and Decolonization, 1945–1957: The Rise and Fall of an Integrated Aluminum Project," in *Aluminum Ore: The Political Economy of the Global Bauxite Industry*, ed. Robin S. Gendron, Mats Ingulstad, and Espen Storli, 185–210 (Vancouver: UBC Press, 2013).

7 Latham, *The Right Kind of Revolution: Modernization, Development, and U.S. Foreign Policy from the Cold War to the Present* (Ithaca, NY: Cornell University Press, 2011), 109–20.

8 Anthony H.M. Kirk-Greene, Suzann Buckley, and John E. Flint, "Taking Canada into Partnership in 'The White Man's Burden': The British Colonial Service and the Dominion Selection Scheme of 1923," *Revue canadienne des études africaines/Canadian Journal of African Studies* 15, 1 (1981): 33–54; Anthony H.M. Kirk-Greene, "Canada in Africa: Sir Percy Girouard, Neglected Colonial Governor," *African Affairs* 83, 331 (1984): 207–39.

9 Barrington Walker, "Immigration Policy, Colonization, and the Development of a White Canada," in *Canada and the Third World: Overlapping Histories,* ed. Karen Dubinsky, Sean Mills, and Scott Rutherford, 37–59 (Toronto: University of Toronto Press, 2016); Barrington Walker, "Finding Jim Crow in Canada, 1789–1967," in *A History of Human Rights in Canada: Essential Issues,* ed. Janet Miron, 81–98 (Toronto: Canadian Scholars' Press, 2009); Saje Mathieu, "North of the Color Line: Sleeping Car Porters and the Battle against Jim Crow on Canadian Rails, 1880–1920," *Labour/Le Travail* 47 (2001): 9–42; James W. St. G. Walker, *"Race," Rights and the Law in the Supreme Court of Canada* (Toronto/Waterloo, ON: Osgoode Society for Canadian Legal History/Wilfrid Laurier University Press, 1997); Linda Freeman, *The Ambiguous Champion: Canada and South Africa in the Trudeau and Mulroney Years* (Toronto: University of Toronto Press, 1997), 24–26.

10 Latham, *Right Kind of Revolution,* 83–84; Kwame Nkrumah, *Ghana: The Autobiography of Kwame Nkrumah* (1957; reprint, New York: International, 1971), x.

11 Catherine Boone, *Political Topographies of the African State: Territorial Authority and Institutional Choice* (Cambridge, UK: Cambridge University Press, 2003), 162.

12 Ibid., 3–8.

13 On the role of technical experts in the late colonial period, see Joseph Morgan Hodge, *Triumph of the Expert: Agrarian Doctrines of Development and the Legacies of British Colonialism* (Athens: Ohio University Press, 2007).

14 Walter C. Lowdermilk, "Full Use with Conservation of Lands in the Northern Territories, an Objective and Report of Field Study," n.d., in *Lan[d] Planning and Utilisation Policy [1947–1958],* British Library (BL), EAP541/1/1/118, https://eap.bl.uk/archive-file/EAP541-1-1-118.

15 "Memorandum: C.D. & W Scheme for Land Planning and Soil Conservation in the Northern Territories," n.d., *Land Planning and Utilisation Policy [1952–53],* BL, EAP541/1/1/83, https://eap.bl.uk/archive-file/EAP541-1-1-83.

16 Latham, *Right Kind of Revolution,* 85–86.

17 Ibid.

18 Miescher, "'Nkrumah's Baby'"; Miescher, "Building the City"; Miescher and Tsikata, "Modernity and Development."

19 Christopher R. Kilford, *The Other Cold War: Canada's Military Assistance to the Developing World, 1945–1975* (Kingston, ON: Canadian Defence Academy Press, 2010), 140–42; John P. Schlegel, *The Deceptive Ash: Bilingualism and Canadian Policy in Africa, 1957–1971* (Washington, DC: University Press of America, 1978), 53–59.

20 Miescher, "'No One Should Be,'" 186.

21 Robert O. Matthews, "Canada and Anglophone Africa," in *Canada and the Third World*, ed. Peyton V. Lyon and Tareq Y. Ismael (Toronto: Macmillan of Canada/Maclean-Hunter, 1976), 103–5.

22 Odd Arne Westad, *The Global Cold War: Third World Interventions and the Making of Our Times* (Cambridge, UK: Cambridge University Press, 2005), 91–92.

23 "Ghana's Foreign Policy and Relations with CDA," Library and Archives Canada (LAC), RG 74, box 772, file 36-18-1-1, vol. 4.

24 Latham, *Right Kind of Revolution*, 89.

25 Kilford, *Other Cold War*, 149–57.

26 Charles K. Magee, "Evaluation of US A.I.D. Technical Assistance for Water Storage Facilities: 1957–1964," 1 October 1964, 1, LAC, RG 17, box 14, file 630/FG4, vol. 2.

27 Ibid., 4.

28 Amy L.S. Staples, *The Birth of Development: How the World Bank, Food and Agriculture Organization, and World Health Organization Changed the World, 1945–1965* (Kent, OH: Kent State University Press, 2006), 64–66.

29 "Plan of Operations, United Nations Special Fund Project in Ghana," n.d., 2, in *Land and Water Surveys: Northern and Upper Regions (F.A.O-U.N Special Fund Project) [1962–67]*, BL, EAP541/1/1/246, https://eap.bl.uk/archive-file/EAP541-1-1-246.

30 "Memorandum to B.H. Kristjanson, Acting Assistant Deputy Minister, from M.J. Fitzgerald, Director," 21 February 1963, LAC, RG 17, box 14, file 630/FG4, vol. 1.

31 Donaghy, "'Reasonably Well-Organized.'" For an earlier and different interpretation, see Keith Spicer, *A Samaritan State? External Aid in Canada's Foreign Policy* (Toronto: University of Toronto Press, 1966), 94–95.

32 W.R. Martin, EAO, to High Commissioner for Canada, 14 February 1961, in "AID TO AFRICA – General Approach," LAC, RG 74, box 578, file 36-9GH-1, part 1.

33 Canada, House of Commons Standing Committee on External Affairs, *Minutes of Proceedings*, 24th Parliament, 4th Session, Meeting 7, 1961, https://parl.canadiana.ca/view/oop.com_HOC_2404_4_1/198.

34 H.O. Moran, Director General of EAO, to High Commissioner for Ghana, 28 March 1961, in "AID TO AFRICA – GHANA," LAC, RG 74, box 578, file 36-9GH-1, part 1. This concern is in tune with the findings of David R. Morrison, "The Choice of Bilateral Aid Recipients," in *Canadian International Development Assistance Policies: An Appraisal*, ed. Cranford Pratt (Montreal/Kingston: McGill-Queen's University Press, 1994), 125–26.

35 Spicer, *A Samaritan State?* 103.

36 "Confidential Memorandum, M.J. Fitzgerald (Director) to S.C. Barry (Deputy Minister of Agriculture, Ottawa)," 25 November 1963, LAC, RG 17, box 14, file 630/FG4, vol. 1.

37 "Agriculture in Ghana," 3, LAC, RG 17, box 14, file 630/FG4, vol. 1.

38 M.J. Fitzgerald, W.L. Foss, and K. Kristjanson to H.O. Moran, Director General, External Aid Office, 22 November 1963, LAC, RG 17, box 14, file 630/FG4, vol. 1.

39 Ibid.
40 "Confidential Report on Trip to Ghana by M.J. Fitzgerald, W.L. Foss, and Dr. Kris Kristjanson," draft, LAC, RG 17, box 14, file 630/FG4, vol. 1.
41 Frank Shefrin, Department of Agriculture, to M.J. Fitzgerald, 30 November 1964, LAC, RG 17, box 14, file 630/FG4, vol. 2.
42 N.L. Iverson to J.G. Watson, 9 November 1966, in "Policy on Extension of Terms of Service," LAC, RG 17, box 35, file 928.11/FG4, vol. 1.
43 "History and Geographical Location," LAC, RG 17, box 35, file 928.1/FG4-4, vol. 1.
44 P.J. Berthelet, C.A. L'Ami, and N.L. Iverson, "PFRA in Ghana: Report on Ghana-Canada Irrigation Development Project, 1965–1970," December 1971, LAC, RG 17, box 36, file 630/FG4, vol. 2S.
45 C.A. L'Ami to N.L. Iverson, 12 February 1969, in "Proposed Ghana-Canada Agreement, Annex Excerpts," LAC, RG 17, box 35, file 928.11/FG4, vol. 1.
46 External Aid Office, *Annual Review, 1966–67* (Ottawa: Department of External Affairs, 1967), 10.
47 Webster, "Foreign Policy," 166; Molly Kane, "Canada and the Third World: Development Aid," in *Canada and the Third World: Overlapping Histories*, ed. Karen Dubinsky, Sean Mills, and Scott Rutherford (Toronto: University of Toronto Press, 2016), 94. On similar assumptions beyond Canada, see Westad, *Global Cold War*, 74, 92.
48 H.O. Moran, Director General, to S.C. Barry, Deputy Minister of Agriculture, n.d., LAC, RG 17, box 14, file 630/FG4, vol. 3.
49 M.J. Fitzgerald, Director, to F.G. Wagner, Chief Administration Division, 26 November 1965, LAC, RG 17, box 14, file 630/FG4, vol. 3.
50 Doug J. Porter, "Scenes from Childhood: The Homesickness of Development Discourses," in *Power of Development*, ed. Jonathan Crush (London: Routledge, 1995), 69.
51 M.J. Fitzgerald (PFRA Director) to M.L. Dewan (Deputy Chief, Special Fund Operations, FAO, UN), 9 November 1964, LAC, RG 17, box 14, file 630/FG4, vol. 2.
52 M.J. Fitzgerald to Hodson, EAO, 5 January 1965, LAC, RG 17, BAN 1998-00888-6(a), box 14, file 630/FG4, vol. 2.
53 "Memorandum from C.A. L'Ami to N.L. Iverson," 8 November 1968, LAC, RG 17, box 36, file 928.1/FG4, vol. 1.
54 Handwritten letter from John to "Gang," 20 December 1965, LAC, RG 17, box 14, file 630/FG4, vol. 3.
55 D.J. Thiessen (PFRA Associate Director) to I.A. Hodgson, 28 February 1963, LAC, RG 17, box 14, file 630/FG4, vol. 1.
56 Project Engineer Iverson to Chief Engineer Watson, 30 June 1966, LAC, RG 17, box 14, file 630/FG4, vol. 3.
57 "Inflow to Reservoir," LAC, RG 17, BAN 1998-00888-6(a), box 35, file 928.1/FG4-4, vol. 1.
58 J.G. Watson to W.M. Berry and L.K. Szojka, 29 March 1968, LAC, RG 17, box 36, file 928.1/FG4, vol. 1.
59 Robert Ankrah, "General," LAC, RG 17, box 35, file 928.1/FG4-4, vol. 1.
60 Nick Cullather, *The Hungry World: America's Cold War Battle against Poverty in Asia* (Cambridge, MA: Harvard University Press, 2010), 8, 70; Latham, *Right Kind of Revolution*, 109–20.
61 Mark. W. Charlton, "Continuity and Change in Canadian Food Aid," in *Canadian International Development Assistance: An Appraisal*, ed. Cranford Pratt, 55–86 (Montreal/Kingston: McGill-Queen's University Press, 1994); Mark W. Charlton, *The Making of*

Canadian Food Aid Policy (Montreal/Kingston: McGill-Queen's University Press, 1992); Ian MacPherson and John Herd Thompson, "An Orderly Reconstruction: Prairie Agriculture in World War Two," in *Canadian Papers in Rural History* 4 (1984): 28–29.

62 N.L. Iverson, "Recommendations Regarding Extension of Ghana-Canada Irrigation Development Program," 1, LAC, RG 17, box 36, file 928.1/FG4, vol. 1.

63 N.L. Iverson to J.G. Watson, 30 June 1966, LAC, RG 17, BAN 1998-00888-6(a), box 14, file 630/FG4, vol. 3; "Report on PFRA Program Ghana," LAC, RG 17, box 36, file 630/FG4, vol. 2S.

64 N.L. Iverson to J.G. Watson, 10 February 1966, LAC, RG 17, box 36, file 928/1 FG4, vol. 1.

65 "History and Geographical Location," LAC, RG 17, box 35, file 928.1/FG4-4, vol. 1.

66 "Report on PFRA Program Ghana," 2, LAC, RG 17, box 36, file 630/FG4, vol. 2S.

67 J.G. Watson to N.L. Iverson, 26 [month illegible] 1966, LAC, RG 17, box 36, file 928.1/FG4, vol. 1.

68 N.L. Iverson to W.M. Berry, 29 March 1968, LAC, RG 17, box 36, file 928.1/FG4, vol. 1.

69 N.L. Iverson to K.M. Lamb, 8 October 1966, LAC, RG 17, box 36, file 928.1/FG4, vol. 1.

70 "Hydrology," LAC, RG 17, box 36, file 928.1/FG4, vol. 1.

71 N.L. Iverson to J.G. Watson, 9 November 1965, LAC, RG 17, box 36, file 928.1/FG4, vol. 1.

72 William M. Adams, *Wasting the Rain: Rivers, People, and Planning in Africa* (London: Earthscan, 1992), 101.

73 C.F. Bentley, "Agriculture, and Aid for It, in Development," July 1968, 7, copy in possession of the author.

74 Kwame Arhin, *The Political Systems of Ghana: Background to Transformations in Traditional Authority in the Colonial and Post-colonial Periods* (Accra: Historical Society of Ghana, 2002); Steve Tonah, "Conflicts and Consensus between Migrant Fulani Herdsmen and Mamprusi Farmers in Northern Ghana," in *Ghana's North: Research on Culture, Religion, and Politics of Societies in Transition,* ed. Franz Kröger and Barbara Meier (Frankfurt: Peter Lang, 2003), 80–81; Carola Lentz, *Land, Mobility, and Belonging in West Africa* (Bloomington: Indiana University Press, 2013); Sean Hawkins, *Writing and Colonialism in Northern Ghana: The Encounter between the LoDagaa and "the World on Paper"* (Toronto: University of Toronto Press, 2002).

75 Lentz, *Land, Mobility,* 21.

76 Benjamin Kunbuor, "Multiple Layers of Land Rights and 'Multiple Owners': The Case of Land Disputes in the Upper West Region of Ghana," in *Ghana's North: Research on Culture, Religion, and Politics of Societies in Transition,* ed. Franz Kröger and Barbara Meier, 101–28 (Frankfurt: Peter Lang, 2003).

77 Christian Lund, *Local Politics and the Dynamics of Property in Africa* (Cambridge, UK: Cambridge University Press, 2009), 156.

78 Ibid., 172–73.

79 Alexis B. Tengan, *Hoe-Farming and Social Relations among the Dagara of Northwestern Ghana and Southwestern Burkina Faso* (Frankfurt: Peter Lang, 2000), 227.

80 Handwritten letter from John to "Gang," 20 December 1965, LAC, RG 17, box 14, file 630/FG4, vol. 3.

81 Jack Goody, "'Kalabule' and the Death of African Socialism," in *Ghana's North: Research on Culture, Religion, and Politics of Societies in Transition,* ed. Franz Kröger and Barbara Meier (Frankfurt: Peter Lang, 2003), 16–19.

82 Project Engineer C.A. L'Ami to Project Manager N.L. Iverson, 16 May 1968, LAC, RG 17, box 12, file 170.1-1, vol. 1.

83 M.J. Fitzgerald to J.G. Watson and F.G. Wagner, 27 July 1965, LAC, RG 17, box 14, file 630/FG4, vol. 3.
84 M.J. Fitzgerald, "Report on Visit to Ghana, 15–22 May 1965," 26 May 1965, LAC, RG 17, box 14, file 630/FG4, vol. 2.
85 "Report on PFRA Program Ghana," LAC, RG 17, box 36, file 630/FG4, vol. 2S.
86 Director General, External Aid Office, "Supplemental Food Supplies for Advisers and Teachers Going to Ghana," LAC, RG 17, box 14, file 630/FG4, vol. 3.
87 "Memorandum of Understanding between the Government of Canada and the Government of Ghana for the Provision of Assistance for Irrigation Development," 26 January 1966, 3, LAC, RG 17, box 36, file 928.1/FG4, vol. 1.
88 M.J. Fitzgerald, "Report on Visit to Ghana, 15–22 May 1965," 26 May 1965, LAC, RG 17, box 14, file 630/FG4, vol. 2.
89 K. Kristjanson to M.J. Fitzgerald, 31 October 1963, LAC, RG 17, box 14, file 630/FG4, vol. 1.
90 C.A. L'Ami to N.L. Iverson, 12 February 1969, LAC, RG 17, box 36, file 928.1/FG4, vol. 1.
91 "Report on PFRA Program Ghana," LAC, RG 17, box 36, file 630/FG4, vol. 2S.
92 Ibid.
93 Ibid.
94 K.O. Saddlemyer to F.G. Wagner, 22 February 1967, LAC, RG 17, box 14, file 630/FG4, vol. 3; "Re: Import Privilege," 13 March 1969, LAC, RG 17, box 36, file 928.1/FG4, vol. 1.
95 C.A. L'Ami to N.L. Iverson, 12 February 1969, LAC, box 36, file 928.1/FG4, vol. 1.
96 N.L. Iverson to D.A. Holser, 18 January 1966, LAC, RG 17, box 35, file 928.11/FG4, vol. 1.
97 C.E. Tagoe to M.J. Fitzgerald, 19 December 1964, LAC, RG 17, box 14, file 630/FG4, vol. 2.
98 N.L. Iverson to J.G. Watson, 11 April 1967, LAC, RG 17, box 36, file 928.1/FG4, vol. 1.
99 M.J. Fitzgerald to A.B. Connelly, 26 February 1969, LAC, RG 17, box 36, file 928.1/FG4, vol. 1.
100 W.K. Dobson, "Training Requirements for Irrigation in Ghana," 26 March 1969, LAC, RG 17, box 36, file 928.1/FG4, vol. 1.
101 W.K. Dobson to M.F. Maurice Strong, Director General, Canadian International Development Agency, 26 January 1969, LAC, RG 17, box 36, file 928.1/FG4, vol. 1.
102 F.G. Wagner to J.G. Watson, 3 November 1966, LAC, RG 17, box 35, file 928.11/FG4, vol. 1.
103 W.K. Dobson, "Training Requirements for Irrigation in Ghana," 26 March 1969, LAC, RG 17, box 36, file 928.1/FG4, vol. 1.
104 "Report on PFRA Program Ghana," LAC, RG 17, box 36, file 630/FG4, vol. 2S.
105 Kilford, *Other Cold War,* 149–57.
106 J.E. Beamish to M.J. Fitzgerald, 16 October 1968, LAC, RG 17, box 36, file 928.1/FG4, vol. 1.
107 "Memorandum from C.A. L'Ami to N.L. Iverson," 8 November 1968, LAC, RG 17, box 36, file 928.1/FG4, vol. 1; J.E. Beamish to M.J. Fitzgerald, 16 October 1968, LAC, RG 17, box 36, file 928.1/FG4, vol. 1.
108 J.E. Ako-Nai to J.G. Watson, 6 April 1968, LAC, RG 17, box 36, file 928.1/FG4, vol. 1; "Memorandum on Policy and Organization for the Development of Irrigation in Ghana," 10, LAC, box 36, file 928.1/FG4, vol. 1.
109 "Training Requirements for Irrigation in Ghana," LAC, RG 17, box 36, file 928.1/FG4, vol. 1. See also Patrick A. Twumasi, "Colonialism and International Health: A Study on Social Change in Ghana," *Social Sciences and Medicine* 2, 15B (1981): 150.
110 J.E. Beamish to M.J. Fitzgerald, 16 October 1968, LAC, RG 17, box 36, file 928.1/FG4, vol. 1.
111 "Report on PFRA Program Ghana," LAC, RG 17, box 36, file 630/FG4, vol. 2S.

112 C.A. L'Ami to N.L. Iverson, 12 February 1969, LAC, RG 17, box 35, file 928.11/FG4, vol. 1.

113 David Webster, *Fire and the Full Moon: Canada and Indonesia in a Decolonizing World* (Vancouver: UBC Press, 2009), 158.

114 Kane, "Canada and the Third World," 96.

115 "Memorandum from C.A. L'Ami to N.L. Iverson," 12 February 1969, LAC, RG 17, box 35, file 928.11/FG4, vol. 1.

116 W.K. Dobson to Fitzgerald, Director PFRA, 26 January 1969, LAC, RG 17, box 36, file 928.1/FG4, part 1.

117 "Memorandum from C.A. L'Ami to N.L. Iverson," 8 November 1968, LAC, RG 17, box 36, file 928.1/FG4, vol. 1.

118 T.M. Pallas, Capital Assistance Division, CIDA, "Irrigation Project Ghana: Report on Survey of Project," March 1969, 17, LAC, RG 17, box 14, file 630/FG4, vol. 1S.

119 C.A. L'Ami, "Addendum to Letter," 16 May 1968, LAC, RG 17, box 35, file 928.11/FG4, vol. 1; "Message from CIDA to Accra, Ghana," 18 July 1969, LAC, RG 17, box 11, file 102.1/FG4, vol. 1.

120 David R. Morrison, *Aid and Ebb Tide: A History of CIDA and Canadian Development Assistance* (Waterloo, ON: Wilfrid Laurier University Press, 1998), 73; David Webster and Greg Donaghy, "Introduction," in *A Samaritan State Revisited: Historical Perspectives on Canadian Foreign Aid*, ed. Greg Donaghy and David Webster (Calgary: University of Calgary Press, 2019), 9.

121 Charles C. Hughes and John M. Hunter, "Disease and 'Development' in Africa," *Social Sciences and Medicine* 3, 4 (1970): 443–93.

122 John M. Hunter, "Elephantiasis: A Disease of Development in North East Ghana," *Social Sciences and Medicine* 35, 5 (1992): 627–45.

123 John M. Hunter, "Past Explosion and Future Threat: Exacerbation of Red Water Disease (Schistosomiasis haematobium) in the Upper Region of Ghana," *GeoJournal* 5, 4 (1981): 307.

124 The 1949 study is referenced in Joseph N. Lanoix, "Relation between Irrigation Engineering and Bilharziasis," *Bulletin of the World Health Organization* 18, 5–6 (1958): 1101–35.

125 World Health Organization Expert Committee, *Simulium and Onchocerciasis in the Northern Territories of the Gold Coast* (Geneva: World Health Organization, 1956), 42. See also G. Crisp, *Simulium and Onchocerciasis in the Northern Territories of the Gold Coast* (London: H.K. Lewis, 1956).

126 N.L. Iverson to F.W. Dawes, 12 July 1968, LAC, RG 17, box 35, file 928.11/FG4, vol. 1.

127 Will Langford, *The Global Politics of Poverty in Canada: Development Programs and Democracy, 1964–1979* (Montreal/Kingston: McGill-Queen's University Press, 2021), 7.

128 Langford, *Global Politics*, 212–43.

129 Hughes and Hunter, "Disease and 'Development,'" 443, 481.

Chapter 7: Hope and Disappointment

1 A.H. Bunting, "Preface," in *Change in Agriculture*, ed. A.H. Bunting (London: Gerald Duckworth, 1970), xi.

2 Tina Loo, *Moved by the State: Forced Relocation and Making a Good Life in Postwar Canada* (Vancouver: UBC Press, 2109); Will Langford, *The Global Politics of Poverty in Canada: Development Programs and Democracy, 1964–1979* (Montreal/Kingston: McGill-Queen's University Press, 2020).

3 Scott Rutherford, *Canada's Other Red Scare: Indigenous Protest and Colonial Encounters during the Global Sixties* (Montreal/Kingston: McGill-Queen's University Press, 2020), 10, 62–82; Karen Dubinsky, Catherine Krull, Susan Lord, Sean Mills, and Scott Rutherford, eds., *New World Coming: The Sixties and the Shaping of Global Consciousness* (Toronto: Between the Lines, 2009).

4 Loo, *Moved by the State,* 7, 205–7.

5 Dimitry Anastakis and P.E. Bryden, "Introduction," in *Framing Canadian Federalism: Historical Essays in Honour of John T. Saywell,* ed. Dimitry Anastakis and P.E. Bryden (Toronto: University of Toronto Press, 2009), 3.

6 "Expanded Research Post-war Period, Experimental Farms Service" 2, Library and Archives Canada (LAC), RG 17, acc. 1991-92/086, box 002, file 142.5, vol. 2. Although not indicated on the document itself, Archibald's authorship is specified in a previous document in the same file. See Wm. Dickson, Secretary, Department of Agriculture Committee on Reconstruction, to Mr. Geo. Spence, Director, Prairie Farm Rehabilitation, 21 August 1944, LAC, RG 17, acc. 1991-92/086, box 002, file 142.5, vol. 2.

7 George Spence, "Post-war Projects for the Prairies," *The Engineering Journal,* February 1945, 76–78, Provincial Archives of Saskatchewan (PAS), GR 80, VIII, 21.

8 L.B. Thomson, PFRA Director, to Marler, 2 January 1953, Provincial Archives of Alberta, PR0228, PR1975.0040/0127b.

9 Meredith McKittrick, "Industrial Agriculture," in *A Companion to Global Environmental History,* ed. J.R. McNeill and Erin Stewart Mauldin, 411–31 (Chichester, UK: Wiley-Blackwell, 2012).

10 C.G.E. Downing, "Mechanization," in Canada, Department of Northern Affairs and National Resources, *Resources for Tomorrow: Conference Background Papers,* vol. 1, 83–92 (Ottawa: Queen's Printer, 1961).

11 W.M. Drummond and W. Mackenzie, *Progress and Prospects of Canadian Agriculture,* ed. Royal Commission on Canada's Economic Prospects (Ottawa: Queen's Printer 1957), 247.

12 Canada, Senate, Special Committee on Land Use in Canada, *Minutes of Proceedings,* vol. 1, no. 7, 24th Parliament, 4th Session, 22 March 1961, https://parl.canadiana.ca/view/oop.com_SOC_2404_4_1/214.

13 Murray Knuttila, "From the National Policy to Continentalism and Globalization: The Shifting Context of Canadian Agricultural Policies," in *Fighting for the Farm: Rural America Transformed,* ed. Jane Adams (Philadelphia: University of Pennsylvania Press, 2002), 67.

14 Canada, Senate, Special Committee on Land Use in Canada, *Minutes of Proceedings,* vol. 1, no. 4, 26th Parliament, 1st Session, 12 December 1963, https://parl.canadiana.ca/view/oop.com_SOC_2601_3_1/115.

15 C.E.S. Franks, "The Senate and Its Reform," *Queen's Law Journal* 12, 3 (1987): 454–72.

16 Canada, Senate, Special Committee on Land Use in Canada, *Minutes of Proceedings,* vol. 1, no. 4, 26th Parliament, 1st Session, 12 December 1963, https://parl.canadiana.ca/view/oop.com_SOC_2601_3_1/109.

17 Canada, Senate, Special Committee on Land Use in Canada, *Minutes of Proceedings,* vol. 1, no. 7, 22nd Parliament, 5th Session, 28 March 1957, https://parl.canadiana.ca/view/oop.com_SOC_2205_1_1/255.

18 Canada, Senate, Special Committee on Land Use in Canada, *Minutes of Proceedings,* vol. 1, no. 6, 22nd Parliament, 5th Session, 21 March 1957, https://parl.canadiana.ca/view/oop.com_SOC_2205_1_1/216.

19 Canada, Senate, Special Committee on Land Use in Canada, *Minutes of Proceedings*, vol. 1, no. 4, 22nd Parliament, 5th Session, 7 March 1957, 109, https://parl.canadiana.ca/view/oop.com_SOC_2205_1_1/127.
20 Canada, Senate, Special Committee on Land Use in Canada, *Minutes of Proceedings*, vol. 1, no. 4, 22nd Parliament, 5th Session, 7 March 1957, 102, https://parl.canadiana.ca/view/oop.com_SOC_2205_1_1/129.
21 Denis Smith, *Rogue Tory: The Life and Legend of John G. Diefenbaker* (Toronto: Macfarlane, Walter and Ross, 1995), 224; P.E. Bryden, *Planners and Politicians: Liberal Politics and Social Policy, 1957–1968* (Montreal/Kingston: McGill-Queen's University Press, 1997), 23–24.
22 Smith, *Rogue Tory*, 224–27.
23 André Magnan, *When Wheat Was King: The Rise and Fall of the Canada-UK Grain Trade* (Vancouver: UBC Press, 2016), 64–67; Tom Kent, *A Public Purpose: An Experience of Liberal Opposition and Canadian Government* (Montreal/Kingston: McGill-Queen's University Press, 1988), 31–32.
24 Raymond Blake, "Regional and Rural Development Strategies in Canada: The Search for Solutions," in *Collected Research Papers of the Royal Commission on Renewing and Strengthening Our Place in Canada* (St. John's, NL: Royal Commission on Renewing and Strengthening Our Place in Canada, 2003), 199, https://www.exec.gov.nl.ca/royalcomm/default.html.
25 Anthony G.S. Careless, *Initiative and Response: The Adaptation of Canadian Federalism to Regional Economic Development* (Montreal/Kingston: McGill-Queen's University Press, 1977), 7.
26 Canada, *Bill C-77: An Act to Provide for the Rehabilitation of Agricultural Lands and the Development of Rural Areas in Canada*, 1st Reading, 24th Parliament, 4th Session, 23 March 1961, https://parl.canadiana.ca/view/oop.bills_HOC_2404_1/707.
27 Shannon Stunden Bower, "Tools for Rational Development: The Canada Land Inventory and the Canada Geographic Information System in Mid-Twentieth Century Canada," *Scientia Canadensis* 40, 1 (2018): 44–75; Matt Dyce and Graeme Wynn, "Mapping Canadian Nature and the Nature of Canadian Mapping," in *Mapping Nature across the Americas*, ed. Kathleen A. Brosnan and James R. Akerman, 239–69 (Chicago: University of Chicago Press, 2021).
28 W.B. Baker, "The Rehabilitation Process," in *Rural Rehabilitation Policies: An Exploration of Goals, Values, and Alternatives: A Report on the First of Three Symposiums on the Problems of Organization for Rural Development and Rehabilitation* (Saskatoon: Centre for Community Studies, University of Saskatchewan, 1965), 2.
29 Canada, Senate, Special Committee on Land Use in Canada, *Minutes of Proceedings*, vol. 1, no. 4, 26th Parliament, 1st Session, 12 December 1963, https://parl.canadiana.ca/view/oop.com_SOC_2601_3_1/135.
30 M.J. Fitzgerald, PFRA Director, to C.J. Anderson, General Manager, Eastern Irrigation District, 9 May 1963, Eastern Irrigation District Office Files.
31 Director of Rehabilitation to E.A.W.R. McKenzie, Indian Agent, Crooked Lake Agency, 20 June 1939, PAS, GR 80, VI, file 11m.
32 H.C. Riesen, PFRA Regional Engineer, to G.N. Munro, PFRA Chief Engineer, 30 May 1957, LAC, RG 17, acc. 1991-92/086, box 14, file 622/G15, vol. 1.
33 J.E. Beamish, Chief, Water Development Service, to R.A. Clark, Regional Director of Indian Affairs, 17 June 1966, LAC, RG 17, acc. 1991-92/086, box 14, file 622/G15-4, vol. 2.

There is an inconsistency in the initials of Clark's name, which appear as "R.A." here and as "F.A." in the other cited correspondence.

34 F.A. Clark, Regional Director of Indian Affairs, to PFRA, "RE: Water Storage on Saskatchewan Indian Reservations," 28 April 1966, LAC, RG 17, acc. 1991-92/086, box 14, file 622/G15-4, vol. 2. Although the typed letter indicates Clark as the author, it is signed by someone else.

35 Ibid.

36 M.J. Fitzgerald, Director, to J.E. Beamish, Chief Water Development Service, 9 May 1966, LAC, RG 17, acc. 1991-92/086, box 14, file 622/G15-4, vol. 2.

37 J.E. Beamish to F.A. Clark, 17 June 1966, LAC, RG 17, acc. 1991-92/086, box 14, file 622/G15-4, vol. 2.

38 R.C. Whitton, Acting Chief, PFRA Water Development Service, to R.M. Connelly, Regional Director, Indian Affairs Branch, 17 April 1969, LAC, RG 17, acc. 1991-92/086, box 14, file 622/G15-4, vol. 2; J.E. Beamish, Chief, PFRA Water Development Service, to J.G. Watson, PFRA Director, "Subject: Assistance to Indian Bands," 27 August 1971, LAC, RG 17, acc. 1991-92/086, box 14, file 622/G15-4, vol. 2.

39 J.E. Beamish, Chief, PFRA Water Development Service, to J.G. Watson, PFRA Director, "Subject: Assistance to Indian Bands," 27 August 1971, LAC, RG 17, acc. 1991-92/086, box 14, file 622/G15-4, vol. 2; R.C. Whitton, Superintendent, PFRA Water Development Division, to Regional Supervisors and All District Officers, 28 June 1971, LAC, RG 17, acc. 1991-92/086, box 14, file 622/G15-4, vol. 2.

40 J.G. Watson, Director of PFRA, to E.C. Aquilina, Assistant Deputy Minister, Western Region, 30 August 1971, LAC, acc. 1991-92/086, box 14, file 622/G15-4, vol. 2.

41 "Community Projects Indian Reservations," 29 June 1971, LAC, RG 17, acc. 1991-92/086, box 14, file 622/G15-4, vol. 2.

42 Department of Regional Economic Expansion, "PFRA Small Water Development and Community Pasture Programs: A Consolidated Report," 30 March 1972, 14, LAC, RG 17, acc. 1991-92/086, box 5, file 520.8, vol. 01(S).

43 H.J. Hargrave, "The Prairie Farm Rehabilitation Administration, Canada," in *Change in Agriculture,* ed. A.H. Bunting (London: Gerald Duckworth, 1970), 473.

44 "Reserve Pastures Proving Boom to Western Bands," *Indian Record,* March 1968, 15.

45 Department of Regional Economic Expansion, "PFRA Small Water Development and Community Pasture Programs: A Consolidated Report," 30 March 1972, 69, LAC, RG 17, acc. 1991-92/086, box 5, file 520.8, vol. 01(S).

46 "PFRA Programs for Agricultural Development on Indian Lands," LAC, RG 17, acc. 1991-92/086, box 14, file 622/G15, vol. 2.

47 ARDA Meeting at Kehewin, 19 September 1968, LAC, RG 10, MIKAN no. 2308018, box 308, file 701/19_2_9, vol. 1; "Reserve Pastures Proving Boom to Western Bands," *Indian Record,* March 1968, 15.

48 Department of Regional Economic Expansion, "PFRA Small Water Development and Community Pasture Programs: A Consolidated Report," 30 March 1972, 68, LAC, RG 17, acc. 1991-92/086, box 5, file 520.8, vol. 01(S).

49 "Reserve Pastures Proving Boom to Western Bands," *Indian Record,* March 1968, 15.

50 ARDA Meeting at Kehewin, 19 September 1968, LAC, RG 10, MIKAN no. 2308018, box 308, file 701/19_2_9, vol. 1.

51 Department of Regional Economic Expansion, "PFRA Small Water Development and Community Pasture Programs: A Consolidated Report," 30 March 1972, 68, LAC, RG 17, acc. 1991-92/086, box 5, file 520.8, vol. 01(S).
52 Ibid., 68–70.
53 Ibid., 69.
54 Ibid., 77.
55 Peggy Martin-McGuire, *First Nation Land Surrender on the Prairies, 1896–1911* (Ottawa: Indian Claims Commission, 1998); Keith D. Smith, *Liberalism, Surveillance, and Resistance: Indigenous Communities in Western Canada, 1877–1927* (Edmonton: Athabasca University Press, 2009); Sarah Carter, *Lost Harvests: Prairie Indian Reserve Farmers and Government Policy* (Montreal/Kingston: McGill-Queen's University Press, 1990).
56 Careless, *Initiative and Response,* 72.
57 Kent, *Public Purpose,* 420.
58 Careless, *Initiative and Response,* 73–74.
59 Ibid., 88. See also Christo Aivalis, *The Constant Liberal: Pierre Trudeau, Organized Labour, and the Canadian Social Democratic Left* (Vancouver: UBC Press, 2018), 70; Langford, *Global Politics,* 279.
60 Careless, *Initiative and Response,* 86; Donald J. Savoie, *Regional Economic Development: Canada's Search for Solutions,* 2nd ed. (Toronto: University of Toronto Press, 1992), 41–42.
61 Canada, Department of Regional Economic Expansion, *Annual Report 1968/69* (Ottawa: Department of Regional Economic Expansion, 1969), 1.
62 Department of Regional Economic Expansion, "PFRA Small Water Development and Community Pasture Programs: A Consolidated Report," 30 March 1972, i, LAC, RG 17, acc. 1991-92/086, box 5, file 520.8, vol. 01(S).
63 R.W. Allen, Assistant City Engineer, Regina, to George Spence, Director of Rehabilitation, 22 August 1944, LAC, RG 17, acc. 1991-92/086, box 2, file 142.5, vol. 2.
64 L.B. Thomson, "Municipal Water Supplies," 23 September 1954, Glenbow Western Research Centre (GWRC), Irrigation Research Project (W.L. Jacobson) Collection (C0048), file M-3761-204.
65 Prairie Farm Rehabilitation Administration, "Proposal to Reorganize Components of PFRA to Establish a Soil and Water Conservation Branch an Amalgamated Construction Service," March 1980, 3, LAC, acc. 1991 92/086, RG 17, box 2, file 170.3C1, vol. 01(S).
66 Department of Regional Economic Expansion, "PFRA Small Water Development and Community Pasture Programs: A Consolidated Report," 30 March 1972, i, LAC, RG 17, acc. 1991-92/086, box 5, file 520.8, vol. 01(S).
67 Careless, *Initiative and Response,* 129–38.
68 Kent, *Public Purpose,* 428; Careless, *Initiative and Response,* 190.
69 Department of Regional Economic Expansion, Prairie Farm Rehabilitation Administration, "Cost Recovery PFRA Land Use Program," October 1978, 48–49, LAC, RG 17, acc. 1991-92/086, box 6, file 520.802, vol. 01(S).
70 "Cost Recovery, PFRA Land Use Program," 4, LAC, RG 17, acc. 1991-92/86, box 6, file 520.802, vol. 1.
71 "PFRA Pasture Program Evaluation," April 1978, LAC, RG 17, acc. 1991-92/086, box 6, file 520.802, vol. 1; PFRA Land Use Service, "Report on Recommended 1980–81 Community

Pasture Fees," August 1979, 6–7, LAC, RG 17, acc. 1991-92/086, box 6, file 520.802, vol. 02(S).

72 "Cost Recovery, PFRA Land Use Program," LAC, RG 17, acc. 1991-92/86, box 6, file 520.802, vol. 1.

73 Department of Regional Economic Expansion, Prairie Farm Rehabilitation Administration, "Cost Recovery PFRA Land Use Program," October 1978, 231, LAC, RG 17, acc. 1991-92/086, box 6, file 520.802, vol. 01(S).

74 Ibid., 234.

75 Jean Chrétien to Don Jamieson, Minister of Regional Economic Expansion, 3 April 1975, in ibid., 249.

76 "Study Outline, Evaluation of PFRA Community Pasture Program," revised 27 June 1978, LAC, RG 17, acc. 1991-92/086, box 6, file 502.802, vol. 1.

77 "Request for Authority, 1980–81, Grazing Fee Schedule – PFRA Community Pastures," September 1979, LAC, RG 17, acc. 1991-92/086, box 6, file 520.802, vol. 2; Prairie Farm Rehabilitation Administration, *Prairie Farm Rehabilitation Administration Annual Report, 1979–1980* (Ottawa: Department of Regional Economic Expansion, 1981), 11–13.

78 F.G. Wagner to Harry M. Hill, Director General, PFRA, 13 December 1979, LAC, RG 17, acc. 1991-92/086, box 6, file 520.8020, vol. 2.

79 Ibid.

Conclusion

1 Letter from W.M. Jones, PFRA 50th Anniversary Committee Chair, to various, 14 September 1982, Library and Archives Canada (LAC), RG 17, acc. 1991-92/086, box 19, file 661.506.

2 Ibid.

3 Ibid.

4 "Briefing Note for the Minister, Coordination of Environment Canada and PFRA Immediate and Long-Term Objectives," 18 May 1983, LAC, RG 17, acc. 1991-92/086, box 003, file 170.8, vol. 1; Harry M. Hill, PFRA Director General, to J.P. Connell, Agriculture Deputy Minister, 7 March 1983, LAC, RG 17, acc. 1991-92/086, box 003, file 170.8, vol. 1. On the elimination of DREE, see Donald J. Savoie, "The Toppling of DREE and Prospects for Regional Development," in *Regional Development Revisited*, ed. Donald J. Savoie, 1–15 (Moncton, NB: Canadian Institute for Research on Regional Development, 1992).

5 William J. Carlyle, "The Decline of Summerfallow on the Canadian Prairies," *Canadian Geographer* 41, 3 (1997): 271; C.A. Campbell, R.P. Zentner, P. Basnyat, R. DeJong, R. Lemke, R. Desjardins, and M. Reiter, "Nitrogen Mineralization under Summer Fallow and Continuous Wheat in the Semiarid Canadian Prairie," *Canadian Journal of Soil Science* 88, 5 (2008): 681–96.

6 Donald G. Wetherell, with Elise A. Corbet, *Breaking New Ground: A Century of Farm Equipment Manufacturing on the Canadian Prairies* (Saskatoon: Fifth House, 1993), 115.

7 Garry Lawrence Fairbairn, *Will the Bounty End? The Uncertain Future of Canada's Food Supply* (Saskatoon: Western Producer Prairie Books, 1984), 31.

8 Carlyle, "Decline of Summerfallow," 268.

9 James H. Gray, *Men against the Desert* (Saskatoon: Western Producer Prairie Books, 1967), 72.

10 Carlyle, "Decline of Summerfallow," 270. See also Suren Kulshreshtha and Gary G. Storey, "Soil Conservation Practices," in *Atlas of Saskatchewan,* 2nd ed., ed. Ka-iu Fung, 239–41 (Saskatoon: University of Saskatchewan, 1999).

11 Joshua Nygren, "A 'Plow to Save the Plains': Conservation Tillage on the North American Grasslands, 1938–1973," in *The Greater Plains: Rethinking a Region's Environmental Histories,* ed. Brian Frehner and Kathleen A. Brosnan, 202–29 (Lincoln: University of Nebraska Press, 2021); Philip J. Nelson, "To Hold the Land: Soil Erosion, Agricultural Scientists, and the Development of Conservation Tillage Techniques," *Agricultural History* 71, 1 (1997): 71–90.

12 Carlyle, "Decline of Summerfallow," 272; Canada, Standing Senate Committee on Agriculture, Fisheries and Forestry, *Soil at Risk: Canada's Eroding Future* (Ottawa: Parliament of Canada, 1984), 22; E.R. Pidgeon, *How Specific Federal Policies May Impact on Prairie Soil and Moisture Conservation* (Ottawa: Agriculture Canada, 1984).

13 Carlyle, "Decline of Summerfallow," 272; Wendy Simpson-Lewis, Ruth McKechnie, and V. Neimanis, *Stress on Land in Canada* (Ottawa: Canadian Government Publishing Centre, 1983), 253.

14 Cited in Fairbairn, *Will the Bounty End?* 30n10.

15 D.A. Rennie and J.G. Ellis, *The Shape of Saskatchewan* (Saskatoon: Institute of Pedology, University of Saskatchewan, 1978), 59.

16 Lana Awada, C. Wayne Lindwall, and Bernie Sonntag, "The Development and Adoption of Conservation Tillage Systems on the Canadian Prairies," *International Soil and Water Conservation Research* 2, 1 (2014): 51.

17 Ibid., 51; Lana Awada, "The Adoption of Conservation Tillage Innovation on the Canadian Prairies" (PhD diss., Bioresource Policy, Business, and Economics, University of Saskatchewan, 2012), 37.

18 Awada, Lindwall, and Sonntag, "Development and Adoption," 52–53; Awada, "Adoption of Conservation," 26.

19 Awada, Lindwall, and Sonntag, "Development and Adoption," 53. On Monsanto, see Bartow J. Elmore, *Seed Money: Monsanto's Past and Our Food Future* (New York: W.W. Norton, 2021). Note that Monsanto was bought out by Bayer in 2018.

20 Awada, Lindwall, and Sonntag, "Development and Adoption," 53.

21 Ibid.; Adrian A. Seaborne, "Crop Diversification in Canada's Breadbasket: Land Use Changes in Saskatchewan's Agriculture," *Geography* 82, 2 (2001): 153–55.

22 Awada, "Adoption of Conservation"; Alan Hall, "Adoption of Conservation Tillage: An Understanding of the Social Contexts," in *Farm Communities at the Crossroads: Challenge and Resistance,* ed. Harry P. Diaz, JoAnn Jaffe, and Robert Stirling, 267–85 (Regina: Canadian Plains Research Centre, University of Regina, 2003); C. Wayne Lindwall and Bernie Sonntag, eds., *Landscapes Transformed: The History of Conservation Tillage and Direct Seeding* (Saskatoon: Knowledge Impact in Society, 2010).

23 Prairie Farm Rehabilitation Administration, "Proposal to Reorganize Components of PFRA to Establish a Soil and Water Conservation Branch an Amalgamated Construction Service," March 1980, esp. ch. 4, "Shortcomings of Present PFRA Soil and On-Farm Water Conservation Activities," LAC, RG 17, acc. 1991-92/086, box 2, file 170.3C1, vol. 01(S).

24 Carlyle, "Decline of Summerfallow," 274. For more information on the characteristics of Canadian agriculture in the 1970s, see Agriculture Canada, *Orientation of Canadian Agriculture: A Task Force Report,* vol. 1, part A, *A Review of the Canadian Agriculture and Food Complex – The System* (Ottawa: Agriculture Canada, 1977).

25 Canada, House of Commons, Standing Committee on Regional Development, *Minutes of Proceedings,* vol. 1, no. 4, 31st Parliament, 1st Session, 20 November 1979, https://parl.canadiana.ca/view/oop.com_HOC_3101_17_1/194.

26 Canada, House of Commons, Standing Committee on Regional Development, "Appendix RD-3: Notes for a Statement by the Honourable Elmer Mackay, Minister of Regional Economic Expansion," in *Minutes of Proceedings,* vol. 1, no. 4A, 31st Parliament, 1st Session, 20 November 1979, https://parl.canadiana.ca/view/oop.com_HOC_3101_17_1/217.

27 Prairie Farm Rehabilitation Administration, "Proposal to Reorganize Components of PFRA to Establish a Soil and Water Conservation Branch an Amalgamated Construction Service," March 1980, LAC, RG 17, acc. 1991-92/086, box 2, file 170.3C1, vol. 01(S).

28 Ibid., 69.

29 Margaret R. Biswas and Asit K. Biswas, "Preface," in *Desertification: Associated Case Studies Prepared for the United Nations Conference on Desertification,* ed. Margaret R. Biswas and Asit K. Biswas (Oxford: Pergamon, 1980), vii. For a critical analysis of what happened in the Sahel in this period, see Roy H. Behnke and Michael Mortimore, eds., *The End of Desertification? Disputing Environmental Change in the Drylands* (Heidelberg: Springer, 2016), esp. part 1.

30 M. Anderson and L. Knapik, *Agricultural Land Degradation in Western Canada: A Physical and Economic Overview* (Ottawa: Regional Development Branch, Agriculture Canada, 1984), 2; Food and Agriculture Organization of the United Nations, *World Soil Charter* (November 1982).

31 Lester R. Brown, "Conserving Soils," in *State of the World 1984: A Worldwatch Institute Report on Progress Toward a Sustainable Society,* ed. Linda Starke, 53–73 (New York: W.W. Norton, 1984).

32 Lester R. Brown and Edward C. Wolf, *Soil Erosion: Quiet Crisis in the World Economy* (Washington, DC: Worldwatch Institute, 1984), 22. For more about Lester R. Brown, see Lester R. Brown, *Breaking New Ground: A Personal History* (New York: W.W. Norton, 2013).

33 Brown and Wolf, *Soil Erosion,* 41–44.

34 Prairie Farm Rehabilitation Administration, *Prairie Farm Rehabilitation Administration 50th Anniversary Seminar: Proceedings* (Regina: Department of Agricultural Economics and Farm Management, University of Manitoba, 1985), 37–38.

35 Prairie Farm Rehabilitation Administration, Soil and Water Conservation Branch, "Land Degradation and Soil Conservation Issues on the Canadian Prairies: An Overview," unpublished draft (Ottawa: Agriculture Canada, 1982).

36 Prairie Farm Rehabilitation Administration, Soil and Water Conservation Branch, *Land Degradation and Soil Conservation Issues on the Canadian Prairies* (Ottawa: Agriculture Canada, 1983), ii.

37 Ibid., ix. There was uncertainty about rates of salinity documented here, although there was consensus that the prospects were worrying. On the uncertainty, see Anderson and Knapik, *Agricultural Land Degradation,* 17–20.

38 Prairie Farm Rehabilitation Administration, Soil and Water Conservation Branch, *Land Degradation,* x.

39 Ibid.

40 Ibid., 1. This circumstance was also recognized in other publications, including Anderson and Knapik, *Agricultural Land Degradation,* 1–7; R.L. Halstead and L. Parker, "Research Strategies," in *In Search of Soil Conservation Strategies in Canada: Conference Proceedings,*

April 1, 2, 3, 1986, ed. D.W. Anderson, 137–52 (Ottawa: Agricultural Institute of Canada, 1987).

41 Prairie Farm Rehabilitation Administration, Soil and Water Conservation Branch, *Land Degradation,* 275.

42 Anderson and Knapik, *Agricultural Land Degradation,* 3.

43 S.C. Lok, *United States Department of Agriculture Soil Conservation Activities on the U.S. Great Plains: Lessons for Agriculture Canada on the Canadian Prairies* (Ottawa: Regional Development Branch, Agriculture Canada, 1984), 1.

44 Canada, Standing Senate Committee on Agriculture, Fisheries and Forestry, *Soil at Risk,* vii.

45 Fairbairn, *Will the Bounty End?*

46 L.A. Leskiw and C.F. Bentley, *Sustainability of Farmed Lands: Current Trends and Thinking* (Ottawa: Minister of Supply and Services Canada, 1985), 18.

47 Science Council of Canada, *A Growing Concern: Soil Degradation in Canada* (Ottawa: Minister of Supply and Services, 1986), 7.

48 D.W. Anderson, ed., *In Search of Soil Conservation Strategies in Canada, April 1, 2, 3, 1986: Conference Proceedings* (Ottawa: Agricultural Institute of Canada, 1987), iii.

49 "PFRA Anniversary Committee Meeting, Meeting 11, 14 August 1984," LAC, RG 17, acc. 1991-92/086, box 18, file 661.501.

50 "Chronological Review of Events in Development of Anniversary Film," 20 February 1985, LAC, RG 17, acc. 1991-92/086, box 19, file 661.503.

51 Prairie Farm Rehabilitation Administration, *Prairie Farm Rehabilitation Administration 50th Anniversary,* Foreword, n.p.

52 A.M. Runciman, "Chairman's Remarks," in Prairie Farm Rehabilitation Administration, *Prairie Farm Rehabilitation Administration 50th Anniversary,* 1.

53 Harry M. Hill, "PFRA – Future Challenges," in Prairie Farm Rehabilitation Administration, *Prairie Farm Rehabilitation Administration 50th Anniversary,* 76.

54 Ibid., 77.

55 Ibid., 78.

56 Ibid., 81.

57 John F. Conway, *The Rise and Fall of the New West: A History of a Region in Confederation* (Toronto: James Lorimer, 2014), 224–25.

58 Grace Skogstad, *Internationalization and Canadian Agriculture: Policy and Governing Paradigms* (Toronto: University of Toronto Press, 2008), 59.

59 Murray Knuttila, *Eroding a Way of Life: Neoliberalism and the Family Farm* (Regina: University of Regina Press, 2023), 125–94.

60 Awada, "Adoption of Conservation," 12; Jim Warren, "The 'Min Till' Revolution and the Culture of Innovation," in *Vulnerability and Adaptation to Drought: The Canadian Prairies and South America,* ed. Harry P. Diaz, Margot Hurlbert, and Jim Warren (Calgary: University of Calgary Press, 2016), 108–9.

61 Awada, "Adoption of Conservation," 44; Warren, "'Min Till' Revolution," 124–25.

62 Prairie Farm Rehabilitation Administration, *The Prairie Farm Rehabilitation Administration (PFRA) Soil Conservation Activity Report for 1986–87 and 1987–88* (Ottawa: Agriculture Canada, 1988), 5; Katherine Strand, "How to Make the Desert Bloom: An Ethnographic and Historical Account of Dryland Agriculture Within Palliser's Triangle" (PhD diss., Anthropology, McGill University, 2021), 214–15.

63 Prairie Farm Rehabilitation Administration, *1985 Report PFRA Tree Nursery* (Ottawa: Agriculture Canada, 1985), 1.

64 Murray Fulton, "Foreword," in *Landscapes Transformed: The History of Conservation Tillage and Direct Seeding,* ed. C. Wayne Lindwall and Bernie Sonntag (Saskatoon: Knowledge Impact in Society, 2010), xi.

65 Awada, "Adoption of Conservation." See also Awada, Lindwall, and Sonntag, "Development and Adoption," 59–61.

66 Lana Awada, Richard S. Gray, and Cecil Nagy, "The Benefits and Costs of Zero Tillage RD&E on the Canadian Prairies," *Canadian Journal of Agricultural Economics* 64, 3 (2016): 427–28; Awada, Lindwall, and Sonntag, "Development and Adoption."

67 Lana Awada, Cecil Nagy, and Peter W.B. Phillips, "Contribution of Land Use Practices to GHGs in the Canadian Prairies Crop Sector," *PLOS ONE* 16, 2 (2021): e0260946, https://doi.org/10.1371/journal.pone.0260946.

68 Awada, Gray, and Nagy, "Benefits and Costs," 417–18.

69 Diogo Soares, Liliana Silva, Sofia Duarte, Angelina Pena, and André Pereira, "Glyphosate Use, Toxicity and Occurrence in Food," *Foods* 10, 11 (2021): 2785, https://doi.org/10.3390/foods10112785; Islam Md. Meftaul, Kadiyala Venkateswarlu, Rajarathnam Dharmarajan, Prasath Annamalai, Md. Asaduzzaman, Aney Parven, and Mallavarapu Megharaj, "Controversies over Human Health and Ecological Impacts of Glysophate: Is It to Be Banned in Modern Agriculture?" *Environmental Pollution* 263, part A (2020): 114372, https://doi.org/10.1016/j.envpol.2020.114372; Charles M. Benbrook, "How Did the US EPA and IARC Reach Diametrically Opposed Conclusions on the Genotoxicity of Glyphosate-Based Herbicides?" *Environmental Sciences Europe* 31, 2 (2019), https://doi.org/10.1186/s12302-018-0184-7; John M. DeSesso, Amy Lavin Williams, and Richard Reiss, "Conflicting Views on the Potential Carcinogenicity of Glyphosate: How Did We Get Here and What Should We Do?" *Journal of Public Health and Emergency* (2017), http://dx.doi.org/10.21037/jphe.2017.09.03; Jose V. Tarazona, Daniele Court-Marques, Manuela Tiramani, Hermine Reich, Rudolf Pfeil, Frederique Istace, and Federica Crivellente, "Glyphosate Toxicity and Carcinogenicity: A Review of the Scientific Basis of the European Union Assessment and Its Differences with IARC," *Archives of Toxicology* 91 (2017): 2723–43, https://link.springer.com/article/10.1007/s00204-017-1962-5; Kathryn Z Guyton, Dana Loomis, Yann Grosse, Fatiha El Ghissassi, Lamia Benbrahim-Tallaa, Neela Guha, Chiara Scoccianti, Heidi Mattock, and Kurt Straif, on behalf of the International Agency for Research on Cancer Monograph Working Group, "Carcinogenicity of Tetrachlorvinphos, Parathion, Malathion, Diazinon, and Glyphosate," *Lancet Oncology* 16, 5 (2015): 490–91, http://dx.doi.org/10.1016/S1470-2045(15)70134-8.

70 Warren, "'Min Till' Revolution," 128–29.

71 Annie Shattuck, "Generic, Growing, Green? The Changing Political Economy of the Global Pesticide Complex," *Journal of Peasant Studies* 48, 2 (2021): 231–53.

72 Michel Gertler, JoAnne Jaffe, and Mary A. Beckie, "Duelling Discourses of Sustainability: Neo-conventional and Organic Farming on the Canadian Prairies," in *Contested Sustainability Discourses in the Agrifood System,* ed. Douglas H. Constance, Jason T. Konefal, and Maki Hatanaka, 163–87 (London: Routledge, 2018). On neoliberalism in Canadian agriculture, see also Elizabeth Moore, "The New Direction of Federal Agricultural Research in Canada: From Private Good to Public Gain?" *Journal of Canadian Studies* 37, 3 (2002): 112–34.

73 Katherine Strand, "From Partner to Consumer: The Changing Role of Farmers in the Public Agricultural Research Process on the Canadian Prairies," in *In Defense of Farmers: The Future of Agriculture in the Shadow of Corporate Power*, ed. Jane Gibson, Sara Alexander, and John K. Hansen, 249–87 (Lincoln: University of Nebraska Press, 2019).

74 Harry P. Diaz and Robert Stirling, "Degradation of Farm Work in the Canadian Prairies," in *Farm Communities at the Crossroads: Challenge and Resistance*, ed. Harry P. Diaz, Joann Jaffe, and Robert Stirling (Regina: Canadian Plains Research Centre, University of Regina, 2003), 31–43. See also Greg Argue, Bob Stirling, and Polo Diaz, "Agricultural Chemicals and Agri-business," in *Farm Communities at the Crossroads: Challenge and Resistance*, ed. Harry P. Diaz, Joann Jaffe, and Robert Stirling, 207–22 (Regina: Canadian Plains Research Centre, University of Regina, 2003).

75 Wilhelm C. Peekhaus, *Resistance Is Fertile: Canadian Struggles on the BioCommons* (Vancouver: UBC Press, 2013).

76 Eda Kranakis, "Percy Schmeiser, Roundup Ready© Canola, and Canadian Agricultural Modernity," in *Made Modern: Science and Technology in Canadian History*, ed. Edward Jones-Imhotep and Tina Adcock, 216–48 (Vancouver: UBC Press, 218).

77 Elmore, *Seed Money*, 277.

78 Emily Eaton, *Growing Resistance: Canadian Farmers and the Politics of Genetically Modified Wheat* (Winnipeg: University of Manitoba Press, 2013).

79 Prairie Farm Rehabilitation Administration, *Prairie Agricultural Landscapes: A Land Resource Review* (Ottawa: Agriculture and Agri-Food Canada, 2000). For a later publication that also includes an environmental emphasis, see Agriculture and Agri-Food Canada, Agri-Environment Services Branch, *PFRA 1935 – AESB 2010: 75 Years* (Ottawa: Departmental Publications Service, 2010).

80 Laura Rance, "More Than A Name," *Manitoba Co-operator*, 16 April 2009.

81 Department of Regional Economic Expansion, "PFRA Small Water Development and Community Pasture Programs: A Consolidated Report," 30 March 1972, 23, LAC, RG 17, acc. 1991-92/086, box 5, file 520.8, vol. 01(S).

82 Ibid., 51–52.

83 Ibid., 48–49.

84 Ibid., 8.

85 Ian MacLachlan, *Kill and Chill: Restructuring Canada's Beef Commodity Chain* (Toronto: University of Toronto Press, 2002), 53–87.

86 Department of Regional Economic Expansion, "PFRA Small Water Development and Community Pasture Programs: A Consolidated Report," 30 March 1972, 70, LAC, RG 17, acc. 1991-92/086, box 5, file 520.8, vol. 01(S).

87 Will Langford, *The Global Politics of Poverty in Canada: Development Programs and Democracy, 1964–1979* (Montreal/Kingston: McGill-Queen's University Press, 2020), 273.

88 Prairie Farm Rehabilitation Administration, Soil and Water Conservation Branch, *Land Degradation*, 118.

89 Hill, "PFRA – Future Challenges," 78.

Bibliography

Archival Sources

Bancroft Library, Oral History Centre

Walter E. Packard, "Land and Power Development in California, Greece, and Latin America," vol. 2, interview by Willa Klug Baum, Berkeley, California, 1970.

James C. Scott, "James C. Scott: Agrarian Studies and Over 50 Years of Pioneering Work in the Social Sciences," interview by Todd Holmes, Berkeley, California, 2020.

British Library

Endangered Archives Programme, Tamale Region – Records from Northern Regional Administration, 1909–1988 (EAP541/1)

Eastern Irrigation District Office Files

Gabriel Dumont Institute of Native Studies and Applied Research

Virtual Museum of Métis History and Culture

Glenbow Western Research Centre, University of Calgary

Alfred Rawlins fonds (F1527)

Calgary Herald fonds (F0358)

Irrigation Research Project (W.L. Jacobson) Collection (C0048)

Paul L. Farnalls fonds (F0748)

Library and Archives Canada

Canadian International Development Agency fonds (RG 74)

Central Registry Files of Inland Waters Branch (RG 89)

Department of Agriculture Records (RG 17)

Department of Indian Affairs Records (RG 10)

Evelyn and Lawrence Cherry Papers (MG 31-D 173)
John Woodruff (C-007819)
National Film Board fonds (RG 53)
Privy Council Office (RG 2)

Provincial Archives of Alberta
Alberta Federation of Agriculture fonds (PR0228)
Legislative Assembly of Alberta fonds (GR1976.0206)

Provincial Archives of Saskatchewan
Accession 1382 (Photo R)
Department of Agriculture Records (GR 6, GR 6-2, GS 44)
George Spence Papers (GR 80)
Great Depression on the Prairies Oral History Project (R-18 to R-33)
James G. Gardiner fonds (F 65)
Saskatchewan Rivers Development Association Oral History Project (R-A1266 to R-A1273, R-A1662, R-A1663)
Saskatchewan Rivers Development Association Records (GR 212)
T.C. Douglas Papers (F 117)

University of Alberta Archives
Travis W. Manning Papers (UAA-1983-123)

University of Calgary Archives and Special Collections
James H. Gray fonds (F0060)
University of Calgary Digital Collections

University of Lethbridge Library Digitized Collections
Agriculture and Agri-Food Canada, Lethbridge Research Center Photo Collection
Alberta Parks – Southern Region Herbarium

Newspapers and Magazines

Alberta Report
Brandon Sun
Equinox
Georgia Straight
Hill Times
Indian Record
Lethbridge Herald
Maclean's Magazine
Manitoba Co-operator
National Observer
Prince Albert Daily Herald
Regina Leader-Post
Saskatoon StarPhoenix
The Sheaf
Western Producer
Winnipeg Free Press

Other Sources

Abu, Razak, and Maureen G. Reed. "Adaptation through Bricolage: Indigenous Responses to Long-Term Social-Ecological Change in the Saskatchewan River Delta, Canada." *Canadian Geographer* 62, 4 (2018): 437–51.

Abu, Razak, Maureen G. Reed, and Timothy D. Jardine, "Using Two-Eyed Seeing to Bridge Western Science and Indigenous Knowledge Systems and Understand Long-Term Change in the Saskatchewan River Delta, Canada." *International Journal of Water Resources Development* 36, 5 (2020): 757–76.

Adams, William M. *Wasting the Rain: Rivers, People, and Planning in Africa.* London: Earthscan, 1992.

Adese, Jennifer, and Chris Andersen, eds. *A People and A Nation: New Directions in Contemporary Métis Studies.* Vancouver: UBC Press, 2021.

Agbemabiese, Lawrence, and John Byrne. "Commodification of Ghana's Volta River: An Example of Ellul's Autonomy of Technique." *Bulletin of Science, Technology and Society* 25, 1 (2005): 17–25.

Agriculture and Agri-Food Canada, Agri-Environment Services Branch. *PFRA 1935 – AESB 2010: 75 Years.* Ottawa: Departmental Publications Service, 2010.

Agriculture Canada. *Orientation of Canadian Agriculture: A Task Force Report.* Vol. 1, part A, *A Review of the Canadian Agriculture and Food Complex – The System.* Ottawa: Agriculture Canada, 1977.

Ahenakew, Barry. *âtayôhkewina: Mōstos-awāsis asiniy Buffalo Child Stone.* Regina: All Nations Hope Network, 2019.

–. "The Story of Buffalo Child Stone, Part I." *Saskatchewan Archaeological Society Newsletter* 30, 4 (2009): 117–20.

–. "The Story of Buffalo Child Stone, Part II." *Saskatchewan Archaeological Society Newsletter* 31, 1 (2010): 21–23.

Ahenakew, Beth, and Stan Hardlotte. *Cree Legends.* Vol. 2. Saskatoon: Saskatchewan Indian Cultural College, 1973.

Aivalis, Christo. *The Constant Liberal: Pierre Trudeau, Organized Labour, and the Canadian Social Democratic Left.* Vancouver: UBC Press, 2018.

Alberta. *A Report on the Rehabilitation of the Dry Areas of Alberta and Crop Insurance, 1935–1936.* Edmonton: King's Printer, 1936.

–. *Report of the Survey Board for Southern Alberta.* 1922.

Alberta Co-operative Sugar Beet Growers Association. *Submission to the Royal Commission on Dominion-Provincial Relations.* Lethbridge, AB: Alberta Co-operative Sugar Beet Growers Association, 1938.

Anastakis, Dimitry, and P.E. Bryden. "Introduction." In *Framing Canadian Federalism: Historical Essays in Honour of John T. Saywell,* ed. Dimitry Anastakis and P.E. Bryden, 3–14. Toronto: University of Toronto Press, 2009.

Andersen, Chris. *"Métis": Race, Recognition, and the Struggle for Indigenous Peoplehood.* Vancouver: UBC Press, 2014.

Anderson, C.H. *A History of Soil Erosion by Wind in the Palliser Triangle of Western Canada.* Ottawa: Research Branch, Department of Agriculture, 1975.

Anderson, Carl J. "'This Land Must Be Good for Some Kind of Farming ... ': Dominion Lands Policy, Drought and Agricultural Rehabilitation in Southwestern Saskatchewan, 1908–1935." MA thesis, History, University of Regina, 2008.

Anderson, D.W., ed. *In Search of Soil Conservation Strategies in Canada: Conference Proceedings, April 1, 2, 3, 1986.* Ottawa: Agricultural Institute of Canada, 1987.

Anderson, Jennifer. "The Pro-Soviet Message in Words and Images: Dyson Carter and Canadian 'Friends' of the USSR." *Journal of the Canadian Historical Association* 18, 1 (2007): 179–206.

Anderson, Kym, ed. *The Political Economy of Agricultural Price Distortions.* Cambridge, UK: Cambridge University Press, 2010.

Anderson, M., and L. Knapik. *Agricultural Land Degradation in Western Canada: A Physical and Economic Overview.* Ottawa: Regional Development Branch, Agriculture Canada, 1984.

Anderson, Peter Grant. "Field Experiments: Critical Historical Geographies of Canada's Central Experimental Farm, 1886–1938." PhD diss., Geography, Queen's University, 2017.

Andrews, Evan J. "Environmental Justice and Dam Management: A Case Study in the Saskatchewan River Delta." MA thesis, Environment and Sustainability, University of Saskatchewan, 2015.

Andrews, Evan J., Maureen G. Reed, Timothy D. Jardine, and Toddi A. Steelman. "Damming Knowledge Flows: POWER as a Constraint on Knowledge Pluralism in River Flow Decision-Making in the Saskatchewan River Delta." *Society and Natural Resources* 31, 8 (2018): 892–907.

Anstey, T.H. *One Hundred Harvests: Research Branch, Agriculture Canada, 1886–1986.* Ottawa: Supply and Services Canada, 1986.

Arbuthnott, Katherine, and Josef K. Schmutz. "PFRA Community Pastures: History and Drama of a Prairie Commons." *Saskatchewan Notes* (Canadian Centre for Policy Alternatives), April 2013, 1–8, https://policyalternatives.ca/sites/default/files/uploads/publications/Saskatchewan%20Office/2013/04/SKnotes_PFRA_0.pdf.

Archer, John H. *Saskatchewan: A History.* Saskatoon: Western Producer Prairie Books, 1980.

Argue, Greg, Bob Stirling, and Polo Diaz. "Agricultural Chemicals and Agri-business." In *Farm Communities at the Crossroads: Challenge and Resistance,* ed. Harry P. Diaz, Joann Jaffe, and Robert Stirling, 207–22. Regina: Canadian Plains Research Centre, University of Regina, 2003.

Arhin, Kwame. *The Political Systems of Ghana: Background to Transformations in Traditional Authority in the Colonial and Post-colonial Periods.* Accra, Ghana: Historical Society of Ghana, 2002.

Armstrong, Christopher, Matthew Evenden, and H.V. Nelles. *The River Returns: An Environmental History of the Bow.* Montreal/Kingston: McGill-Queen's University Press, 2009.

Arrington, Leonard J. *Beet Sugar in the West: A History of the Utah-Idaho Sugar Company, 1891–1966.* Seattle: University of Washington Press, 1966.

Asay, Kay H. "Breeding Strategies in Crested Wheatgrass." In *Crested Wheatgrass: Its Values, Problems, and Myths: A Symposium,* ed. Kendall L. Johnson, 53–57. Logan: Utah State University, 1986.

Awada, Lana. "The Adoption of Conservation Tillage Innovation on the Canadian Prairies." PhD diss., Bioresource Policy, Business, and Economics, University of Saskatchewan, 2012.

Awada, Lana, Richard S. Gray, and Cecil Nagy. "The Benefits and Costs of Zero Tillage RD&E on the Canadian Prairies." *Canadian Journal of Agricultural Economics* 64, 3 (2016): 417–38.

Awada, Lana, C. Wayne Lindwall, and Bernie Sonntag. "The Development and Adoption of Conservation Tillage Systems on the Canadian Prairies." *International Soil and Water Conservation Research* 2, 1 (2014): 47–65.

Awada, Lana, Cecil Nagy, and Peter W.B. Phillips. "Contribution of Land Use Practices to GHGs in the Canadian Prairies Crop Sector." *PLOS ONE* 16, 2 (2021): e0260946. https://doi.org/10.1371/journal.pone.0260946.

Backhouse, Constance. *Colour-Coded: A Legal History of Racism in Canada, 1900–1950.* Toronto: University of Toronto Press, 1999.

Baker, W.B. "The Rehabilitation Process." In *Rural Rehabilitation Policies: An Exploration of Goals, Values, and Alternatives: A Report on the First of Three Symposiums on the Problems of Organization for Rural Development and Rehabilitation,* 1–6. Saskatoon: Centre for Community Studies, University of Saskatchewan, 1965.

Balkwill, Daniel M. "The Prairie Farm Rehabilitation Administration and the Community Pasture Program, 1937–1947." MA thesis, History, University of Saskatchewan, 2002.

Bankes, Nigel, and Elizabeth Bourget. "Apportionment of the St. Mary and Milk Rivers." In *Water without Borders? Canada, the United States, and Shared Waters,* ed. Emma S. Norman, Alice Cohen, and Karen Bakker, 159–78. Toronto: University of Toronto Press, 2013.

Barkwell, Lawrence J. *The Metis Homeland: Its Settlements and Communities.* Winnipeg: Louis Riel Institute, 2016.

–. *20th Century Métis Displacement and Road Allowance Communities in Manitoba.* Winnipeg: Louis Riel Institute, 2016. https://www.metismuseum.ca/media/document.php/149555.

Barnetson, Bob. "The Regulatory Exclusion of Agricultural Workers in Alberta." *Just Labour: A Canadian Journal of Work and Society* 14 (2009): 50–74.

Barron, F. Laurie. *Walking in Indian Moccasins: The Native Policies of Tommy Douglas and the CCF.* Vancouver: UBC Press, 1997.

Bartlett, Richard H. "Hydroelectric Power and Indian Water Rights." *Prairie Forum* 14, 2 (1989): 177–93.

Bavington, Dean. *Managed Annihilation: An Unnatural History of the Newfoundland Cod Collapse.* Vancouver: UBC Press, 2010.

Beattie, James, and Ruth Morgan. "Engineering Edens on This 'Rivered Earth'? A Review Article on Water Management and Hydro-Resilience in the British Empire, 1860s–1940s." *Environment and History* 23, 1 (2017): 39–63.

Beaulieu, Alain. "Une histoire instrumentalisée: réflexions sur l'usage du passé dans les revendications autochtones." In *Vert, le droit? Conférence des juristes de l'État 2009,* 349–71. Cowansville, QC: Éditions Yvon Blais, 2009. Translated as "An Instrumentalized History: Reflections on the Use of the Past in Aboriginal Claims." https://www.academia.edu/5129408/An_Instrumentalized_History_Reflections_on_the_Use_of_the_Past_in_Aboriginal_Claims.

Behnke, Roy H., and Michael Mortimore, eds. *The End of Desertification? Disputing Environmental Change in the Drylands.* Heidelberg: Springer, 2016.

Benbrook, Charles M. "How Did the US EPA and IARC Reach Diametrically Opposed Conclusions on the Genotoxicity of Glyphosate-Based Herbicides?" *Environmental Sciences Europe* 31, 2 (2019). https://doi.org/10.1186/s12302-018-0184-7.

Benidickson, Jamie. "The Evolution of Canadian Water Law and Policy: Securing Safe and Sustainable Abundance." *McGill Journal of Sustainable Development Law* 13, 1 (2017): 59–104.

Bentley, C.F. "Agriculture, and Aid for It, in Development." July 1968. Copy in possession of the author.

Beres, Brian L., L.M. Dosdall, David K. Weaver, Hector A. Cárcamo, and D.M. Spaner. "Biology and Integrated Management of Wheat Stem Sawfly and the Need for Continuing Research." *Canadian Entomologist* 143, 2 (2011): 105–25.

Berger, Thomas R. *Northern Frontier, Northern Homeland: The Report of the Mackenzie Valley Pipeline Inquiry.* Ottawa: Minister of Supply and Services Canada, 1977.

Bergson, Lorrie, comp. *Somebody Had To Do It! A Collection of Stories and Poetry from PFRA Community Pastures.* Winnipeg: n.p., 1995.

Berkman, Richard, and W. Kip Viscusi. *Damming the West.* New York: Penguin, 1973.

Berry, Kate A., and Sue Jackson. "The Making of White Water Citizens in Australia and the Western United States: Racialization as a Transnational Project of Irrigation Governance." *Annals of the American Association of Geographers* 108, 5 (2018): 1354–69.

Bicentennial Committee of Cumberland House. *A History of Cumberland House ... as Told by Its Own Citizens, 1774 to 1974.* Cumberland House, SK: Bicentennial Committee of Cumberland House, 1974.

Billington, David P., and Donald C. Jackson. *Big Dams of the New Deal Era: A Confluence of Engineering and Politics.* Norman: University of Oklahoma Press, 2006.

Binnema, Theodore (Ted), and Melanie Niemi. "'Let the line be drawn now': Wilderness, Conservation, and the Exclusion of Aboriginal People from Banff National Park in Canada." *Environmental History* 11, 4 (2006): 724–50.

Biswas, Margaret R., and Asit K. Biswas. "Preface." In *Desertification: Associated Case Studies Prepared for the United Nations Conference on Desertification,* ed. Margaret R. Biswas and Asit K. Biswas, vii–ix. Oxford: Pergamon, 1980.

–, eds. *Desertification: Associated Case Studies Prepared for the United Nations Conference on Desertification.* Oxford: Pergamon, 1980.

Bivar, Venus. "Agricultural High Modernism and Land Reform in Postwar France." *Agricultural History* 93, 4 (2019): 636–55.

Blake, Raymond. "Regional and Rural Development Strategies in Canada: The Search for Solutions." In *Collected Research Papers of the Royal Commission on Renewing and Strengthening Our Place in Canada,* 189–227. St. John's, NL: Royal Commission on Renewing and Strengthening Our Place in Canada, 2003. https://www.exec.gov.nl.ca/royalcomm/default.html.

Bligh, E.G. "Mercury Contamination in Fish." In *A Summary of Material Presented at the Twentieth Annual Institute for Public Health Inspectors.* Winnipeg: Department of Health and Social Development, 1970.

Bocking, Stephen. "The Politics of Endangered Species: A Historical Perspective." In *Politics of the Wild: Canada and Endangered Species,* ed. Karen Beazley and Robert Boardman, 119–36. Don Mills, ON: Oxford University Press, 2001.

Boone, Catherine. *Political Topographies of the African State: Territorial Authority and Institutional Choice.* Cambridge, UK: Cambridge University Press, 2003.

Bracken, John. *Crop Production in Western Canada.* Winnipeg: Grain Growers' Guide, 1920.

–. *Dry Farming in Western Canada.* Winnipeg: Grain Growers' Guide, 1921.

–. *The Rehabilitation of the Drought Area: An Address Delivered by the Honourable John Bracken before the Canadian Club of Winnipeg, October 25th, 1934.* Winnipeg: Manitoba Department of Agriculture, 1934.

Brado, Edward. *Cattle Kingdom: Early Ranching in Alberta.* Surrey, BC: Heritage House, 2004.

Brantley, Ben. "Review/Theater: Faith Healer; From 3 Versions of a Shared Past, a Vision of Memory's Power." *New York Times,* 26 April 1994.

Brassard, Brooke. "Thirsty Land into Springs of Water: Negotiating a Place in Canada as Latter-Day Saints, 1887–1947." PhD diss., Religious Studies, University of Waterloo, 2018.

Breen, David. *The Canadian Prairie West and the Ranching Frontier, 1874–1924*. Toronto: University of Toronto Press, 1983.

Brennan, Bill. *How the West Was Written: The Life and Times of James H. Gray*. Calgary: Fifth House, 2006.

Britnell, George Edwin. "The Rehabilitation of the Prairie Wheat Economy." *Canadian Journal of Economics and Political Science* 3, 4 (1937): 508–29.

–. *The Wheat Economy*. Toronto: University of Toronto Press, 1939.

Britnell, George Edwin, and Vernon Fowke. *Canadian Agriculture in War and Peace, 1935–1950*. Stanford, CA: Stanford University Press, 1962.

Broadfoot, Barry. *Years of Sorrow, Years of Shame: The Story of the Japanese Canadians in World War II*. Toronto: Doubleday, 1977.

Brown, Lester R. *Breaking New Ground: A Personal History*. New York: W.W. Norton, 2013.

–. "Conserving Soils." In *State of the World 1984: A Worldwatch Institute Report on Progress toward a Sustainable Society*, ed. Linda Starke, 53–73. New York: W.W. Norton, 1984.

Brown, Lester R., and Edward C. Wolf. *Soil Erosion: Quiet Crisis in the World Economy*. Washington, DC: Worldwatch Institute, 1984.

Bryden, P.E. *Planners and Politicians: Liberal Politics and Social Policy, 1957–1968*. Montreal/Kingston: McGill-Queen's University Press, 1997.

Buckley, Eve E. *Technocrats and the Politics of Drought and Development in Twentieth-Century Brazil*. Chapel Hill: University of North Carolina Press, 2017.

Buckley, Helen. *From Wooden Ploughs to Welfare: Why Indian Policy Failed in the Prairie Provinces*. Montreal/Kingston: McGill-Queen's University Press, 1992.

Bunting, A.H. "Preface." In *Change in Agriculture*, ed. A.H. Bunting, xi–xii. London: Gerald Duckworth, 1970.

–, ed. *Change in Agriculture*. London: Gerald Duckworth, 1970.

Burnett, J. Alexander. *A Passion for Wildlife: The History of the Canadian Wildlife Service*. Vancouver: UBC Press, 2003.

Burns, Robert. "To a Mouse, on Turning Her Up in Her Nest with the Plough, November, 1785." In *Poems, Chiefly in the Scottish Dialect*, 138–40. Kilmarnock: John Wilson, 1786. https://archive.org/details/bim_eighteenth-century_poems-chiefly-in-the-sc_burns-robert_1786.

Calibre Consultants Inc. *Environmental Effects of Major Hydro-Electric Projects*. Saskatoon: Saskatchewan Energy Conservation and Development Authority, 1994.

Campbell, C.A., R.P. Zentner, P. Basnyat, R. DeJong, R. Lemke, R. Desjardins, and M. Reiter. "Nitrogen Mineralization under Summer Fallow and Continuous Wheat in the Semiarid Canadian Prairie." *Canadian Journal of Soil Science* 88, 5 (2008): 681–96.

Campbell-Miller, Jill. "Encounter and Apprenticeship: The Colombo Plan and Canadian Aid in India, 1950–1960." In *A Samaritan State Revisited: Historical Perspectives on Canadian Foreign Aid*, ed. Greg Donaghy and David Webster, 27–52. Calgary: University of Calgary Press, 2019.

Canada. *Annual Report of the Minister of Agriculture for the Dominion of Canada for the Year Ended March 31, 1941*. Ottawa: Department of Agriculture, 1941.

–. *Report of the Royal Commission on Aboriginal Peoples*. Vol. 1, *Looking Forward, Looking Back*. Ottawa: Queen's Printer, 1996. https://publications.gc.ca/site/eng/9.819007/publication.html.

–. *Report of the Royal Commission on the South Saskatchewan River Project*. Ottawa: Queen's Printer, 1952. https://publications.gc.ca/site/eng/9.827922/publication.html.

Canada, Commission of Conservation. *Conservation of Soil Fertility and Soil Fibre*. Report of a conference held at Winnipeg, Manitoba, 14–16 July 1920. Ottawa: Thomas Mulvey, 1920.

–. *Report of the First Annual Meeting*. Ottawa: Commission of Conservation, 1910.

–. *Report of the Third Annual Meeting*. Ottawa: Commission of Conservation, 1912.

Canada, Department of Northern Affairs and National Resources. *Resources for Tomorrow: Proceedings of the Resources for Tomorrow Conference Held in Montreal, Oct. 23–28, 1961*. Vol. 3. Ottawa: Queen's Printer, 1962.

Canada, Department of Regional Economic Expansion. *Annual Report 1968/69*. Ottawa: Department of Regional Economic Expansion, 1969.

Canada, Division of Entomology, Science Service. *The Wheat Stem Sawfly Situation in Manitoba, Saskatchewan, and Alberta for 1942*. Ottawa: Department of Agriculture, 1942.

Canada, Federal Task Force on Agriculture. *Canadian Agriculture in the Seventies: Report of the Federal Task Force on Agriculture*. Ottawa: Queen's Printer, 1969.

Canada, Royal Commission on Canada's Economic Prospects. *Final Report*. Ottawa: Queen's Printer, 1957.

Canada, Standing Senate Committee on Agriculture, Fisheries and Forestry. *Soil at Risk: Canada's Eroding Future*. Ottawa: Parliament of Canada, 1984.

Canadian Dam Association. *Dams in Canada – 2019*. Ottawa: Canadian Dam Association, 2019. https://cda.ca/publications/dams-in-canada-2019.

CanMap Content Suite v2021.3. Markham, ON: DMTI Spatial, 2021. https://abacus.library.ubc.ca/dataset.xhtml?persistentId=hdl:11272.1/AB2/ZGQDCJ.

CanVec Series [Admin., Land, Hydro]. Ottawa: Natural Resources Canada, 2019. https://open.canada.ca/data/en/dataset/306e5004-534b-4110-9feb-58e3a5c3fd97.

Cardinal, Harold, and Walter Hildebrandt. *Treaty Elders of Saskatchewan: Our Dream Is That Our Peoples Will One Day Be Clearly Recognized as Nations*. Calgary: University of Calgary Press, 2000.

Careless, Anthony G.S. *Initiative and Response: The Adaptation of Canadian Federalism to Regional Economic Development*. Montreal/Kingston: McGill-Queen's University Press, 1977.

Carlisle, Kathleen. *Fiery Joe: The Maverick Who Lit Up the West*. Regina: University of Regina Press, 2017.

Carlyle, William J. "The Decline of Summerfallow on the Canadian Prairies." *Canadian Geographer* 41, 3 (1997): 267–80.

–. "Rural Population Change on the Canadian Prairies." *Great Plains Research* 4, 1 (1994): 65–87.

Carrière, Réal. "Kikicîtowek Insiniwuk: Nehinuw Governance in Nehinuw Terms." PhD diss., Policy Studies, Ryerson University, 2018.

Carter, Sarah. *Imperial Plots: Women, Land, and the Spadework of British Colonialism on the Canadian Prairies*. Winnipeg: University of Manitoba Press, 2016.

–. *Lost Harvests: Prairie Indian Reserve Farmers and Government Policy*. Montreal/Kingston: McGill-Queen's University Press, 1993.

Charlton, Mark W. "Continuity and Change in Canadian Food Aid." In *Canadian International Development Assistance: An Appraisal*, ed. Cranford Pratt, 55–86. Montreal/Kingston: McGill-Queen's University Press, 1994.

–. *The Making of Canadian Food Aid Policy*. Montreal/Kingston: McGill-Queen's University Press, 1992.

Christensen, Deanna. *Ahtahkakoop: The Epic Account of a Plains Cree Head Chief, His People, and Their Struggle for Survival, 1816–1896.* Altona, MB: Friesens, 2000.

Christian, Janice M., and Scott D. Wilson. "Long-Term Ecosystem Impacts of an Introduced Grass in the Northern Great Plains." *Ecology* 80, 7 (1999): 2397–407.

Clark, W. Leland. "The Location of Experimental Farms and Illustration Stations: An Agricultural or Political Consideration?" In *The Developing West: Essays on Canadian History in Honor of Lewis H. Thomas,* ed. John E. Foster, 203–18. Edmonton: University of Alberta Press, 1983.

Clarke, M.A. and M.F.G. Cleary. "Sugarbeet." In *Encyclopedia of Food Sciences and Nutrition,* 2nd ed., ed. Benjamin Caballero, Luiz C. Trugo, and Paul M. Finglas, 5651–56. Cambridge, MA: Academic, 2003.

Cole, Robert. "The Historic Sites and Monuments Board of Canada's Representation of Indigenous History from 1945 to 1982." MA thesis, History, University of Ottawa, 2017.

Coleman, Daniel. *White Civility: The Literary Project of English Canada.* Toronto: University of Toronto Press, 2006.

Colpitts, George. "Fish and Game Associations in Southern Alberta, 1907–1928." *Alberta History* 42, 4 (1994): 16–26.

–. *Game in the Garden: A Human History of Wildlife in Western Canada to 1940.* Vancouver: UBC Press, 2003.

–. *Pemmican Empire: Food, Trade, and the Last Bison Hunts in the North American Plains, 1780–1882.* Cambridge, MA: Cambridge University Press, 2015.

–. "'Victuals to Put into our Mouths': Environmental Perspectives on Fur Trade Provisioning Activities at Cumberland House, 1775–1782." *Prairie Forum* 22, 1 (1997): 1–19.

Committee on Saskatchewan River Delta Problems. *Resources, Development and Problems of the Saskatchewan River Delta.* Regina: Saskatchewan Water Resources Commission, 1972.

Committee on Western Water Problems. "Report of Committee on Western Water Problems." *The Engineering Journal* 23, 3 (1940): 127.

–. "Report of the Committee on Western Water Problems." *The Engineering Journal* 24, 5 (1941): 222–23.

Conway, John F. *The Rise and Fall of the New West: A History of a Region in Confederation.* Toronto: James Lorimer, 2014.

Cook, Ramsay. *The Regenerators: Social Criticism in Late Victorian English Canada.* 2nd ed. Toronto: University of Toronto Press, 2016.

Craig, Béatrice. *Backwoods Consumers and Homespun Capitalists: The Rise of a Market Culture in Eastern Canada.* Toronto: University of Toronto Press, 2009.

"Cree Names of Cree-Speaking Communities." Creeliteracy.org, 6 November 2017. http://creeliteracy.org/2017/11/06/indigenous-mapping-workshop-2017-supporting-cree-as-a-21st-century-language/.

Criddle, Norman. "The Western Wheat-Stem Sawfly in Canada." *Report of the Entomological Society of Ontario* 36 (1922): 18–21.

Crisp, G. *Simulium and Onchocerciasis in the Northern Territories of the Gold Coast.* London: H.K. Lewis, 1956.

Crosby, Alfred W. *Ecological Imperialism: The Biological Expansion of Europe, 900–1900.* 2nd ed. Cambridge, UK: Cambridge University Press, 2004.

Crowson, Belinda. *Southern Alberta's Sugar-Coated History: The Sugar Beet Industry.* Lethbridge, AB: Lethbridge Historical Society, 2013.

Cullather, Nick. *The Hungry World: America's Cold War Battle against Poverty in Asia.* Cambridge, MA: Harvard University Press, 2010.

Dale, Janis E. "Focus Study 5.2: Soils of Saskatchewan." In *Saskatchewan: Geographical Perspectives,* ed. Bernard D. Thraves, M.L. Lewry, Janis E. Dale, and Hansgeorg Schlichtmann, 94–98. Regina: Canadian Plains Research Centre, University of Regina, 2007.

Danysk, Cecilia. *Hired Hands: Labour and the Development of Prairie Agriculture, 1880–1930.* Toronto: McClelland and Stewart, 1995.

–. "'Showing These Slaves Their Class Position': Barriers to Organizing Prairie Farm Workers." In *Building beyond the Homestead: Rural History on the Prairies,* ed. David C. Jones and Ian MacPherson, 163–77. Calgary: University of Calgary Press, 1985.

Daschuk, James. *Clearing the Plains: Disease, Politics of Starvation, and the Loss of Indigenous Life.* Regina: University of Regina Press, 2013.

–. "A Dry Oasis: The Canadian Plains in Late Prehistory." *Prairie Forum* 34, 1 (2009): 1–29.

Davidson, Gerald T. "An Interdisciplinary Approach to the Role of Climate in the History of the Prairies." In *Toward Defining the Prairies: Region, Culture, and History,* ed. Robert A. Wardhaugh, 101–19. Winnipeg: University of Manitoba Press, 2001.

Davies, Kirk W., Chad S. Boyd, and Aleta M. Nafus. "Restoring the Sagebrush Component in Crested Wheatgrass–Dominated Communities." *Rangeland Ecology and Management* 66, 4 (2013): 472–78.

Davis, Diana K. *The Arid Lands: History, Knowledge, Power.* Cambridge, MA: MIT Press, 2016.

–. *Resurrecting the Granary of Rome: Environmental History and French Colonial Expansion in North Africa.* Athens: Ohio University Press, 2007.

Dawson, C.A. *Group Settlement: Ethnic Communities in Western Canada.* Toronto: Macmillan, 1936.

Dawson, Peter C. "Seeing Like an Inuit Family: The Relationship between House Form and Culture in Northern Canada." *Inuit Studies* 30, 2 (2006): 113–35.

Diaz, Harry P., and Robert Stirling. "Degradation of Farm Work in the Canadian Prairies." In *Farm Communities at the Crossroads: Challenge and Resistance,* ed. Harry P. Diaz, Joann Jaffe, and Robert Stirling, 31–43. Regina: Canadian Plains Research Centre, University of Regina, 2003.

de Loë, Rob C. "Return of the Feds, Part I: The St. Mary Dam." *Canadian Water Resources Journal* 22, 1 (1997): 25–34.

–. "Stability and Change in Southern Alberta Water Management." PhD diss., Geography, University of Waterloo, 1994.

de Vecchi, Vittorio G.M. "Science and Scientists in Government, 1878–1896 – Part II." *Scientia Canadensis* 9, 2 (1985): 97–113.

den Otter, A.A. "Adapting the Environment: Ranching, Irrigation, and Dry Land Farming in Southern Alberta, 1880–1914." *Great Plains Quarterly* 6, 3 (1986): 171–89.

–. *The Philosophy of Railways: The Transcontinental Railway Idea in British North America.* Toronto: University of Toronto Press, 1997.

Desbiens, Caroline. *Power from the North: Territory, Identity, and the Culture of Hydroelectricity in Quebec.* Vancouver: UBC Press, 2013.

DeSesso, John M., Amy Lavin Williams, and Richard Reiss. "Conflicting Views on the Potential Carcinogenicity of Glyphosate: How Did We Get Here and What Should We Do?" *Journal of Public Health and Emergency* (2017). http://dx.doi.org/10.21037/jphe.2017.09.03.

Dewing, Rolland. *Regions in Transition: The Northern Great Plains and the Pacific Northwest in the Great Depression.* Lanham, MD: University Press of America, 2006.

Dirschl, H.J., A.S. Goodman, and M.C. Dennington. *Land Capability for Wildlife Production and Utilization in the Western Saskatchewan River Delta.* Regina: Saskatchewan River Delta Development Committee, 1967.

Donaghy, Greg. "'Reasonably Well-Organized': A History of Early Aid Administration." In *A Samaritan State Revisited: Historical Perspectives on Canadian Foreign Aid,* ed. Greg Donaghy and David Webster, 53–72. Calgary: University of Calgary Press, 2019.

Dotterweich, Markus. "The History of Human-Induced Soil Erosion: Geomorphic Legacies, Early Descriptions and Research, and the Development of Soil Conservation – A Global Synopsis." *Geomorphology* 201 (2013): 1–34.

Downing, C.G.E. "Mechanization." In Canada, Department of Northern Affairs and National Resources, *Resources for Tomorrow: Conference Background Papers,* vol. 1, 83–92. Ottawa: Queen's Printer, 1961.

Dreisziger, N.F. "The Canadian-American Irrigation Frontier Revisited: The International Origins of Irrigation in Southern Alberta, 1885–1909." *Historical Papers/Communications historiques* 10, 1 (1975): 211–29.

Drummond, W.M., W.J. Anderson, and T.C. Kerr. *A Review of Agricultural Policy In Canada.* Ottawa: Agricultural Economics Research Council of Canada, 1966.

Drummond, W.M., and W. Mackenzie. *Progress and Prospects of Canadian Agriculture.* Ed. Royal Commission on Canada's Economic Prospects. Ottawa: Queen's Printer, 1957.

Dubinsky, Karen, Catherine Krull, Susan Lord, Sean Mills, and Scott Rutherford, eds. *New World Coming: The Sixties and the Shaping of Global Consciousness.* Toronto: Between the Lines, 2009.

Dummitt, Christopher. *The Manly Modern: Masculinity in Postwar Canada.* Vancouver: UBC Press, 2007.

Dunlap, Thomas. *Nature and the English Diaspora: Environment and History in the United States, Canada, Australia, and New Zealand.* Cambridge, UK: Cambridge University Press, 1999.

Dunsworth, Edward. "Green Gold, Red Threats: Organization and Resistance in Depression-Era Ontario Tobacco." *Labour/Le Travail* 79 (2017): 105–42.

Dwyer, Don D. "Setting the Stage for the Crested Wheatgrass Symposium." In *Crested Wheatgrass: Its Values, Problems and Myths: Symposium Proceedings,* ed. Kendall L. Johnson, 1–2. Logan: Utah State University, 1986.

Dyce, Matt, and Graeme Wynn. "Mapping Canadian Nature and the Nature of Canadian Mapping." In *Mapping Nature across the Americas,* ed. Kathleen A. Brosnan and James R. Akerman, 239–69. Chicago: University of Chicago Press, 2021.

Dyck, Erika, and Alex Deighton. *Managing Madness: Weyburn Mental Hospital and the Transformation of Psychiatric Care in Canada.* Winnipeg: University of Manitoba Press, 2017.

Dyck, Ian G. "Eighty-One Years of Archaeology in the Saskatchewan Museum of Natural History." *Saskatchewan Archaeology* 8 (1987): 15–42.

Eagle, John A. *The Canadian Pacific Railway and the Development of Western Canada, 1896–1914.* Montreal/Kingston: McGill-Queen's University Press, 1989.

Eaton, Emily. *Growing Resistance: Canadian Farmers and the Politics of Genetically Modified Wheat.* Winnipeg: University of Manitoba Press, 2013.

Eisler, Dale. *Rumours of Glory: Saskatchewan and the Thatcher Years.* Edmonton: Hurtig, 1987.

Ekbladh, David. *The Great American Mission: Modernization and the Construction of an American World Order.* Princeton, NJ: Princeton University Press, 2009.

–. "'Mr. TVA': Grass-Roots Development, David Lilienthal, and the Rise and Fall of the Tennessee Valley Authority as a Symbol for US Overseas Development, 1933–1973." *Diplomatic History* 26, 3 (2002): 335–74.

Ellis, J.H. *The Pasquia Land Settlement Project Interim Report No. 1.* Winnipeg: Department of Mines and Natural Resources, 1956.

Elmore, Bartow J. *Seed Money: Monsanto's Past and Our Food Future.* New York: W.W. Norton, 2021.

Ens, Gerhard, and Joe Sawchuk. *From New Peoples to New Nations: Aspects of Métis History and Identity from the Eighteenth to the Twenty-First Centuries.* Toronto: University of Toronto Press, 2015.

Elofson, Warren. *Cowboys, Gentlemen and Cattle Thieves: Ranching on the Western Frontier.* Montreal/Kingston: McGill-Queen's University Press, 2000.

–. *Frontier Cattle Ranching in the Land and Times of Charlie Russell.* Montreal/Kingston: McGill-Queen's University Press, 2004.

–. *So Far and Yet So Close: Frontier Cattle Ranching in Western Canada and the Northern Territory of Australia.* Calgary: University of Calgary Press, 2015.

–. *Somebody Else's Money: The Walrond Ranch Story, 1883–1907.* Calgary: University of Calgary Press, 2009.

Escobar, Arturo. *Encountering Development: The Making and Unmaking of the Third World.* Princeton, NJ: Princeton University Press, 1995.

Evans, Clinton L. *The War on Weeds in the Prairie West: An Environmental History.* Calgary: University of Calgary Press, 2002.

Evans, Simon. *The Bar U: Canadian Ranching History.* Calgary: University of Calgary Press, 2004.

Evenden, Matthew. "Precarious Foundations: Irrigation, Environment, and Social Change in the Canadian Pacific Railway's Eastern Section, 1900–1930." *Journal of Historical Geography* 32, 1 (2006): 74–95.

External Aid Office. *Annual Review, 1966–67.* Ottawa: Department of External Affairs, 1967.

Eyford, Ryan. *White Settler Reserve: New Iceland and the Colonization of the Canadian West.* Vancouver: UBC Press, 2016.

Fairbairn, Garry Lawrence. *Will the Bounty End? The Uncertain Future of Canada's Food Supply.* Saskatoon: Western Producer Prairie Books, 1984.

Farish, Matthew, and P. Whitney Lackenbauer. "High Modernism in the Arctic: Planning Frobisher Bay and Inuvik." *Journal of Historical Geography* 35, 3 (2009): 517–44.

Fehr, Florence, and C.A.R. Dennis. *Investigations into the Use and Health Hazard of Mercury in Saskatchewan.* Regina: Prairie Institute of Environmental Health, 1975.

Finkel, Alvin. *Working People in Alberta: A History.* Edmonton: Athabasca University Press, 2021.

Fitzgerald, Deborah. *Every Farm a Factory: The Industrial Ideal in American Agriculture.* New Haven, CT: Yale University Press, 2003.

Fleury, George. *Kanawayihtamaahk li taan paassii – Preserving Our Past: Ste. Madeleine, Manitoba.* Winnipeg: Louis Riel Institute, 2016.

Food and Agriculture Organization of the United Nations. *World Soil Charter*. November 1982.

Fooks, Georgia Green. *Prairie Prisoners: POWs in Lethbridge during Two World Wars.* Lethbridge, AB: Lethbridge Historical Society, 2002.

Foran, Max. *Trails and Trials: Markets and Land Use in Alberta Beef Cattle Industry, 1881–1948.* Calgary: University of Calgary Press, 2003.

Foster, Janet. *Working for Wildlife: The Beginning of Preservation in Canada.* 2nd ed. Toronto: University of Toronto Press, 1998.

Fowke, Vernon. *Canadian Agricultural Policy: The Historical Pattern.* Toronto: University of Toronto Press, 1946.

–. "Economic Effects of the War on the Prairie Economy." *Canadian Journal of Economics and Political Science* 11, 3 (1945): 373–87.

–. *The National Policy and the Wheat Economy.* Toronto: University of Toronto Press, 1957.

Franks, C.E.S. "The Senate and Its Reform." *Queen's Law Journal* 12, 3 (1987): 454–72.

"Free Vector World and Country Maps." https://freevectormaps.com/.

Freeman, Linda. *The Ambiguous Champion: Canada and South Africa in the Trudeau and Mulroney Years.* Toronto: University of Toronto Press, 1997.

Freer, O. "Development of Community Pastures in Saskatchewan under PFRA." *Canadian Cattlemen,* September 1938, 82, 89.

Friel, Brian. *Faith Healer.* London/Boston: Faber and Faber, 1980.

–. "Faith Healer." In *Collected Plays: Volume Two,* 361–410. Oldcastle, Ireland/London: Gallery Press/Faber and Faber, 2016.

Friesen, Gerald. *The Canadian Prairies: A History.* Toronto: University of Toronto Press, 1984.

–. "2005 Presidential Address of the CHA: Space and Region in Canadian History." *Journal of the Canadian Historical Association* 16, 1 (2005): 1–22.

Fujiwara, Aya. "Informal Internment: Japanese Canadian Farmers in Southern Alberta, 1941–1945." In *Civilian Internment in Canada: Histories and Legacies,* ed. Rhonda L. Hinther and Jim Mochoruk, 167–79. Winnipeg: University of Manitoba Press, 2020.

–. "Japanese-Canadian Internally Displaced Persons: Labour Relations and Ethno-religious Identity in Southern Alberta, 1942–1953." *Labour/Le Travail* 69 (2012): 63–89.

Fuller, Les. "Chernozemic Soils of the Prairie Region of Western Canada." *Prairie Soils and Crops Journal* 3 (2010): 37–45.

Fulton, Murray. "Foreword." In *Landscapes Transformed: The History of Conservation Tillage and Direct Seeding,* ed. C. Wayne Lindwall and Bernie Sonntag, ix–xiv. Saskatoon: Knowledge Impact in Society, 2010.

Garland, S.W., and S.C. Hudson. *Government Involvement in Agriculture: A Report Prepared for the Federal Task Force on Agriculture.* Ottawa: Queen's Printer, 1968.

Gavloski, J., and S. Meers. "Arthropods of Cereal Crops in Canadian Grasslands." In *Arthropods of Canadian Grasslands,* vol. 2, *Inhabitants of a Changing Landscape,* ed. K.D. Floate, 217–37. Ottawa: Biological Survey of Canada, 2011.

Gertler, Michel, JoAnne Jaffe, and Mary A. Beckie. "Duelling Discourses of Sustainability: Neo-conventional and Organic Farming on the Canadian Prairies." In *Contested Sustainability Discourses in the Agrifood System,* ed. Douglas H. Constance, Jason T. Konefal, and Maki Hatanaka, 163–87. London: Routledge, 2018.

Gilbert, Jess. "Low Modernism and the Agrarian New Deal: A Different Kind of State." In *Fighting for the Farm: Rural America Transformed,* ed. Jane Adams, 129–46. Philadelphia: University of Pennsylvania Press, 2003.

–. *Planning Democracy: Agrarian Intellectuals and the Intended New Deal.* New Haven, CT: Yale University Press, 2015.

Gilpin, John F. *Quenching the Prairie Thirst: A History of the Magrath Irrigation District, Raymond Irrigation District, Taber Irrigation District, St. Mary Irrigation District.* Altona, MB: Friesens, 2000.

Giraud, Marcel. *The Métis in the Canadian West.* Vol. 2. Trans. Michel Woodcock. Edmonton: University of Alberta Press, 1986.

Girard, Michel. *L'écologisme retrouvé: essor et déclin de la Commission de la conservation du Canada.* Ottawa: University of Ottawa Press, 1988.

Glenn, John Elmer. "The Role of Government Legislation, Policy and Agency Activity in Irrigation Development: The Cypress Hills Area, 1888–c. 1968." MA thesis, Geography, University of Calgary, 1969.

Goody, Jack. "'Kalabule' and the Death of African Socialism." In *Ghana's North: Research on Culture, Religion, and Politics of Societies in Transition,* ed. Franz Kröger and Barbara Meier, 11–19. Frankfurt: Peter Lang, 2003.

Goulet, Keith Napoleon. "Land and Colonization: A Nehinuw (Cree) Perspective." PhD diss., History, University of Regina, 2021.

Goulet, Linda M., and Keith Napoleon Goulet. *Teaching Each Other: Nehinuw Concepts and Indigenous Pedagogies.* Vancouver: UBC Press, 2014.

Goulet, Trish. "Revitalizing Cree Legal Traditions: Cumberland House and Pelican Narrows." LLM thesis, University of Manitoba, 2013.

Gray, James H. *Men against the Desert.* Saskatoon: Western Producer Prairie Books, 1967.

–. *The Winter Years: The Depression on the Prairies.* Toronto: Macmillan of Canada, 1966.

Green, Derek J., Mark Duffy, David M. Janz, Keven McCullum, Gary Carrière, and Timothy D. Jardine. "Historical and Contemporary Patterns of Mercury in a Hydroelectric Reservoir and Downstream Fishery: Concentration Decline in Water and Fishes." *Archives of Environmental Contamination and Toxicology* 71, 2 (2016): 157–70.

Green Party of Canada. *Honest. Ethical. Caring. Leadership: Election Platform 2019.* Ottawa: Green Party of Canada, 2019. https://fipa.bc.ca/wp-content/uploads/2019/10/platform_2019_en_web_update_09-16.pdf.

–. *Platform 2021: Green Future, Life with Dignity, Just Society.* Ottawa: Green Party of Canada, 2021. https://www.numerade.com/notes/directory/school/22/courses/245821/files/1697325.

Grove, Richard H. *Green Imperialism: Colonial Expansion, Tropical Island Edens, and the Origins of Environmentalism.* Cambridge, UK: Cambridge University Press, 1995.

Guyton, Kathryn Z., Dana Loomis, Yann Grosse, Fatiha El Ghissassi, Lamia Benbrahim-Tallaa, Neela Guha, Chiara Scoccianti, Heidi Mattock, and Kurt Straif, on behalf of the International Agency for Research on Cancer Monograph Working Group. "Carcinogenicity of Tetrachlorvinphos, Parathion, Malathion, Diazinon, and Glyphosate." *Lancet Oncology* 16, 5 (2015): 490–91. http://dx.doi.org/10.1016/S1470-2045(15)70134-8.

Hall, Alan. "Adoption of Conservation Tillage: An Understanding of the Social Contexts." In *Farm Communities at the Crossroads: Challenge and Resistance,* ed. Harry P. Diaz,

JoAnn Jaffe, and Robert Stirling, 267–85. Regina: Canadian Plains Research Centre, University of Regina, 2003.

–. "Canadian Agricultural Policy: Liberal, Global, and Sustainable." In *Fighting for the Farm: Rural America Transformed,* ed. Jane Adams, 209–28. Philadelphia: University of Pennsylvania Press, 2003.

Hall, D.J. *Clifford Sifton: A Lonely Eminence, 1901–1929.* Vancouver: UBC Press, 1985.

–. *From Treaties to Reserves: The Federal Government and Native Peoples in Territorial Alberta, 1870–1905.* Montreal/Kingston: McGill-Queen's University Press, 2015.

Halstead, R.L., and L. Parker. "Research Strategies." In *In Search of Soil Conservation Strategies in Canada: Conference Proceedings, April 1, 2, 3 1986,* ed. D.W. Anderson, 137–52. Ottawa: Agricultural Institute of Canada, 1987.

Hanson, Eric J. *Financial History of Alberta, 1905–1950.* Calgary: University of Calgary Press, 2003.

Harding, William M. "The Royal Commission on Agriculture and Rural Life." In *Dignity and Growth: Citizen Participation in Social Change: Essays in Honor of W.B. "Bill" Baker,* ed. Harold R. Baker, James A. Draper, and Brett T. Fairbairn, 49–62. Calgary: Detselig Enterprises, 1991.

Hargrave, H.J. "The Prairie Farm Rehabilitation Administration, Canada." In *Change in Agriculture,* ed. A.H. Bunting, 471–78. London: Gerald Duckworth, 1970.

Hargreaves, Mary W.M. *Dry Farming in the Northern Great Plains: Years of Readjustment.* Lawrence: University Press of Kansas, 1993.

Harrison, J.T., and D.T. Waite. *Mercury Survey of the Saskatchewan River System in Saskatchewan.* Ottawa: Environment Canada, 1988.

Hart, David. *The Volta River Project: A Case Study in Politics and Technology.* Edinburgh: Edinburgh University Press, 1980.

Hartley, William G. "Mormon Sugar in Alberta: E.P. Ellison and the Knight Sugar Factory." *Journal of Mormon History* 23, 2 (1997): 1–29.

Hawkins, Sean. *Writing and Colonialism in Northern Ghana: The Encounter between the LoDagaa and "the World on Paper."* Toronto: University of Toronto Press, 2002.

Hays, D.W. "Economic Development for Irrigable Lands." *The Engineering Journal* 24, 5 (1941): 232–35.

Hays, Samuel P. *Conservation and the Gospel of Efficiency.* 1959. Reprint, Pittsburgh: University of Pittsburgh Press, 1999.

Heaman, Elsbeth. *Tax, Order, and Good Government: A New Political History of Canada, 1867–1917.* Montreal/Kingston: McGill-Queen's University Press, 2017.

Hecky, R.E., D.J. Ramsey, R.A. Bodaly, and N.E. Strange. "Increased Methylmercury Contamination in Fish in Newly Formed Freshwater Reservoirs." In *Advances in Mercury Toxicology,* ed. Tsuguyoshi Suzuki, Nobumasa Imura, and Thomas W. Clarkson, 33–53. New York: Springer, 1991.

Hedges, James B. *Building the Canadian West: The Land and Colonization Policies of the Canadian Pacific Railway.* New York: Russell and Russell, 1971.

Heinmiller, B. Timothy. "The Boundary Waters Treaty and the International Joint Commission in the St. Mary–Milk Basin." In *The First Century of the International Joint Commission,* ed. Daniel Macfarlane and Murray Clamen, 143–64. Calgary: University of Calgary Press, 2020.

Henderson, Darcy C., and M. Anne Naeth. "Multi-scale Impacts of Crested Wheatgrass Invasion in Mixed-Grass Prairie." *Biological Invasions* 7, 4 (2005): 639–50.

Heron, Barbara. *Desire for Development: Whiteness, Gender, and the Helping Imperative.* Waterloo, ON: Wilfrid Laurier University Press, 2007.

Herriot, Trevor. *River in a Dry Land: A Prairie Passage.* Toronto: Stoddart, 2000.

–. *Towards a Prairie Atonement.* Regina: University of Regina Press, 2016.

Hill, Harry M. "PFRA – Future Challenges." In Prairie Farm Rehabilitation Administration, *Prairie Farm Rehabilitation Administration 50th Anniversary Seminar: Proceedings,* 75–82. Regina: Department of Agricultural Economics and Farm Management, University of Manitoba, 1985.

Himour, Bradley David. "An Archaeological Reconnaissance of the Lake Diefenbaker Region in South Central Saskatchewan." MA thesis, Archaeology, University of Saskatchewan, 1997.

Hind, Henry Youle. *Reports of Progress Together with a Preliminary and General Report, on the Assiniboine and Saskatchewan Exploring Expedition: Made under Instructions from the Provincial Secretary, Canada.* Toronto: J. Lovell, 1859.

Hisey, Forrest, Melissa Heppner, and Andrea Olive. "Supporting Native Grasslands in Canada: Lessons Learned and Future Management of the Prairie Pastures Conservation Area (PPCA) in Saskatchewan." *Canadian Geographer* 66, 4 (2022): 683–95.

Hodge, Joseph Morgan. *Triumph of the Expert: Agrarian Doctrines of Development and the Legacies of British Colonialism.* Athens: Ohio University Press, 2007.

–. "Writing the History of Development (Part 2: Longer, Deeper, Wider)." *Humanity: An International Journal of Human Rights, Humanitarianism, and Development* 7, 1 (2016): 125–74.

Hodgetts, J.E., William McCloskey, Reginald Whitaker, and V. Seymour Wilson. *The Biography of an Institution: The Civil Service Commission of Canada, 1908–1967.* Montreal/Kingston: McGill-Queen's University Press, 1972.

Hoeppner, Kenneth. *The Ordinary Genius: A Life of Arnold Platt.* Edmonton: University of Alberta Press, 2007.

Hogue, Michel. *Metis and the Medicine Line: Creating a Border and Dividing a People.* Chapel Hill: University of North Carolina Press, 2015.

Holleman, Hannah. *Dust Bowls of Empire: Imperialism, Environmental Politics, and the Injustice of "Green" Capitalism.* New Haven, CT: Yale University Press, 2018.

Holliday, N.J. "Norman Criddle: Pioneer Entomologist of the Prairies." *Manitoba History* 51 (2006): 8–15.

Horn, Michiel. *The Great Depression of the 1930s in Canada.* Ottawa: Canadian Historical Association, 1984.

Hove, Jon Olav. "The Volta River Project and Decolonization, 1945–1957: The Rise and Fall of an Integrated Aluminum Project." In *Aluminum Ore: The Political Economy of the Global Bauxite Industry,* ed. Robin S. Gendron, Mats Ingulstad, and Espen Storli, 185–210. Vancouver: UBC Press, 2013.

Hubbard, Tasha. "The Call of the Buffalo: Exploring Kinship with the Buffalo in Indigenous Creative Expression." PhD diss., English, University of Calgary, 2016.

Hughes, Charles C., and John M. Hunter. "Disease and 'Development' in Africa." *Social Sciences and Medicine* 3, 4 (1970): 443–93.

Hunter, John M. "Elephantiasis: A Disease of Development in North East Ghana." *Social Sciences and Medicine* 35, 5 (1992): 627–45.

–. "Past Explosion and Future Threat: Exacerbation of Red Water Disease (Schistosomiasis haematobium) in the Upper Region of Ghana." *GeoJournal* 5, 4 (1981): 305–13.

Hurt, R. Douglas. *Problems of Plenty: The American Farmer in the Twentieth Century.* Chicago: Ivan R. Dee, 2002.

Independent Committee of Inquiry. *Report of an Independent Committee of Inquiry Established to Examine the Conditions of Migrant Workers in the Sugar Beet Industry in Alberta.* Edmonton: Department of Lands and Mines, 1970.

Ingram, Darcy. "Governments, Governance, and the 'Lunatic Fringe': The Resources for Tomorrow Conference and the Evolution of Environmentalism in Canada." *International Journal of Canadian Studies* 51 (2015): 69–96.

–. *Wildlife, Conservation, and Conflict in Quebec, 1840–1914.* Vancouver: UBC Press, 2013.

Innes, Robert Alexander. *Elder Brother and the Law of the People: Contemporary Kinship and Cowessess First Nation.* Winnipeg: University of Manitoba Press, 2013.

–. "Multicultural Bands on the Northern Plains and the Notion of 'Tribal' Histories." In *Finding a Way to the Heart: Feminist Writings on Aboriginal and Women's History in Canada,* ed. Robin Brownlie and Valerie J. Korinek, 122–45. Winnipeg: University of Manitoba Press, 2012.

Insects Unlocked Project, University of Texas at Austin. https://hdl.handle.net/2152/69920.

Ivie, Michael A. "On the Geographic Origin of the Wheat Stem Sawfly (Hymenoptera: Cephidae): A New Hypothesis of Introduction from Northeastern Asia." *American Entomologist* 47, 2 (2001): 84–97.

Ivie, Michael A., and Alexey G. Zinovjev. "Discovery of the Wheat Stem Sawfly (CEPHUS CINCTUS NORTON) (HYMENOPTERA: CEPHIDAE) in Asia, with the Proposal of a New Synonymy." *Canadian Entomologist* 128, 2 (1996): 347–48.

Iwaasa, David B. "The Japanese in Southern Alberta, 1941–45." *Alberta History* 24, 3 (1976): 5–19.

–. "The Mormons and Their Japanese Neighbours." *Alberta History* 53, 1 (2005): 7–11.

Jackson, Jeremy B.C., Karen E. Alexander, and Enric Sala, eds. *Shifting Baselines: The Past and Future of Ocean Fisheries.* Washington, DC: Island, 2011.

Jackson, Jeremy B.C., Michael Xavier Kirby, Wolfgang H. Berger, Karen A. Bjorndal, Louis W. Botsford, Bruce J. Bourque, Roger H. Bradbury, Richard G. Cooke, Jon Erlandson, James A. Estes, Terence P. Hughes, Susan M. Kidwell, Carina B. Lange, Hunter S. Lenihan, John M. Pandolfi, Charles H. Peterson, Robert S. Steneck, Mia J. Tegner, and Robert R. Warner. "Historical Overfishing and the Recent Collapse of Coastal Ecosystems." *Science,* 27 July 2001, 629–38.

Jarrell, Richard A. "Hind, Henry Youle." In *Dictionary of Canadian Biography,* vol. 13. http://www.biographi.ca/en/bio/hind_henry_youle_13E.html.

Johnson, Eldon. "The Saskatchewan Archaeological Society – A History." *Saskatchewan Archaeology* 8 (1987): 3–13.

Johnson, Kendall L. "Foreword." In *Crested Wheatgrass: Its Values, Problems and Myths: Symposium Proceedings,* ed. Kendall L. Johnson, vii. Logan: Utah State University, 1986.

Jones, David C. "The Canadian Prairie Dryland Disaster and the Reshaping of 'Expert' Farm Wisdom." *Journal of Rural Studies* 1, 2 (1985): 135–46.

–. *Empire of Dust: Settling and Abandoning the Prairie Dry Belt.* Edmonton: University of Alberta Press, 1987.

–. "Schools and Social Disintegration in the Alberta Dry Belt of the Twenties." *Prairie Forum* 3, 2 (1978): 1–20.

–, ed. *"We'll all be buried down here": The Prairie Dryland Disaster, 1917–1926.* Calgary: Historical Society of Alberta, 1986.

Jones, Esyllt. *Radical Medicine: The International Origins of Socialized Health Care in Canada.* Winnipeg: ARP Books, 2019.

Jones, Tim E.H. *Archaeological Resource Management in Saskatchewan: An Overview.* Regina: Government of Saskatchewan, Department of Culture and Youth, 1978.

Jones, Tim E.H., Muriel Carlson, and T.R. Smith. "People, Potsherds and Projectile Points: Pondering the Saskatoon Archaeological Society's Past." In *Out of the Past: Sites, Digs and Artifacts in the Saskatoon Area,* ed. Urve Linnamae and Tim E.H. Jones, 7–23. Saskatoon: Saskatoon Archaeological Society, 1988.

Jones, Tim E.H., and Lorne Lepp. "Glacial Erratics Enduring Reminder of Ice Age." *Saskatchewan Archaeological Society Newsletter* 23, 1 (2002): 16–17.

Josephson, Paul R. *Industrialized Nature: Brute Force Technology and the Transformation of the Natural World.* Washington, DC: Island, 2002.

Juillet, Luc, and Ken Rasmussen. *Defending a Contested Ideal: Merit and the PSC of Canada, 1908–2008.* Ottawa: University of Ottawa Press, 2008.

Kane, Molly. "Canada and the Third World: Development Aid." In *Canada and the Third World: Overlapping Histories,* ed. Karen Dubinsky, Sean Mills, and Scott Rutherford, 88–119. Toronto: University of Toronto Press, 2016.

Keeling, Arn. "A Dynamic, Not a Static Conception: The Conservation Thought of Roderick Haig-Brown." *Pacific Historical Review* 71, 2 (2002): 239–68.

Keeling, Arn, and Robert McDonald. "The Profligate Province: Roderick Haig-Brown and the Modernizing of British Columbia." *Journal of Canadian Studies* 36, 3 (2001): 7–23.

Kelly, John Joseph. "The Prisoner of War Camps in Canada, 1939–1947." MA thesis, History, University of Windsor, 1976.

Kelly, L.V. *The Range Men: Pioneer Ranchers of Alberta.* Toronto: W. Briggs, 1913.

Kenny, James L., and Andrew Secord. "Engineering Modernity: Hydroelectric Development in New Brunswick, 1945–1970." *Acadiensis* 39, 1 (2010): 3–26.

Kent, Tom. *A Public Purpose: An Experience of Liberal Opposition and Canadian Government.* Montreal/Kingston: McGill-Queen's University Press, 1988.

Kerber, Jenny. "Pulling up Roots: Border-Crossing and Migrancy on Southern Alberta's Irrigation Frontier." *Dalhousie Review* 90, 1 (2010): 47–60.

Ketchell, Shelly Ikebuchi. "Carceral Ambivalence: Japanese Canadian 'Internment' and the Sugar Beet Programme during WWII." *Surveillance and Society* 7, 1 (2009): 21–35.

Kheraj, Sean. "A History of Oil Spills on Long-Distance Pipelines in Canada." *Canadian Historical Review* 101, 2 (2020): 161–91.

Kilford, Christopher R. *The Other Cold War: Canada's Military Assistance to the Developing World, 1945–1975.* Kingston, ON: Canadian Defence Academy Press, 2010.

Killan, Gerald. *Protected Places: A History of Ontario's Provincial Parks System.* Toronto: Dundurn, 1993.

Killan, Gerald, and George Warecki. "The Algonquin Wildlands League and the Emergence of Environmental Politics in Ontario, 1965–1974." *Environmental History Review* 16, 4 (1992): 1–27.

Kirk, D.W. *The Bow River Irrigation Project Part 1.* Ottawa: Department of Agriculture, 1955.

Kirk, L.E., T.M. Stevenson, and S.E. Clarke. *Crested Wheat Grass.* Ottawa: Department of Agriculture, 1934.

Kirk-Greene, Anthony H.M. "Canada in Africa: Sir Percy Girouard, Neglected Colonial Governor." *African Affairs* 83, 331 (1984): 207–39.

Kirk-Greene, Anthony H.M., Suzann Buckley, and John E. Flint. "Taking Canada into Partnership in 'The White Man's Burden': The British Colonial Service and the Dominion Selection Scheme of 1923." *Revue canadienne des études africaines/Canadian Journal of African Studies* 15, 1 (1981): 33–54.

Klassen, Stan, and John Gilpin. "Alberta Irrigation in the Old and New Millenium." *Canadian Water Resources Journal* 24, 1 (1999): 61–69.

Knowles, R.P. *Crested Wheat Grass.* Ottawa: Department of Agriculture, 1956.

Knuttila, Murray. *Eroding a Way of Life: Neoliberalism and the Family Farm.* Regina: University of Regina Press, 2023.

–. "From the National Policy to Continentalism and Globalization: The Shifting Context of Canadian Agricultural Policies." In *Fighting for the Farm: Rural America Transformed,* ed. Jane Adams, 47–74. Philadelphia: University of Pennsylvania Press, 2002.

Komori, Jane. "The Canadian 'War of the Two Sugars': Homegrown Sugar Beets and the Racial Stratification of Labour." *Historical Materialism: Research in Critical Marxist Theory* 31, 3 (2023): 252–75.

Kondolf, G.M. "Hungry Water: Effects of Dams and Gravel Mining on River Channels." *Environmental Management* 21 (1997): 533–51.

Kopas, Paul. *Taking the Air: Ideas and Change in Canada's National Parks.* Vancouver: UBC Press, 2007.

Korinek, Valerie J. *Prairie Fairies: A History of Queer Communities and People in Western Canada, 1930–1985.* Toronto: University of Toronto Press, 2018.

Kranakis, Eda. "Percy Schmeiser, Roundup Ready© Canola, and Canadian Agricultural Modernity." In *Made Modern: Science and Technology in Canadian History,* ed. Edward Jones-Imhotep and Tina Adcock, 216–48. Vancouver: UBC Press, 2019.

Kuiper, E. "Sediment Transport and Delta Formation." *Journal of the Hydraulics Division* 86, 2 (1960): 55–68.

Kulshreshtha, Suren, George Pearson, Brant Kirychuk, and Rick Gaube. "Distribution of Public and Private Benefits on Federally Managed Community Pastures in Canada." *Rangelands* 30, 1 (2008): 3–11.

Kulshreshtha, Suren, and Gary G. Storey. "Soil Conservation Practices." In *Atlas of Saskatchewan,* 2nd ed., ed. Ka-iu Fung, 239–41. Saskatoon: University of Saskatchewan, 1999.

Kunbuor, Benjamin. "Multiple Layers of Land Rights and 'Multiple Owners': The Case of Land Disputes in the Upper West Region of Ghana." In *Ghana's North: Research on Culture, Religion, and Politics of Societies in Transition,* ed. Franz Kröger and Barbara Meier, 101–28. Frankfurt: Peter Lang, 2003.

Laforge, Julia M.L., Vanessa Corkal, and Aaron Cosbey. *Farming the Future: Agriculture and Climate Change on the Canadian Prairies.* Winnipeg: International Institute for Sustainable Development, 2021. https://www.iisd.org/publications/report/farming-future-agriculture-and-climate-change-canadian-prairies.

Laforge, Julia M.L., and Stéphane M. McLachlan. "Environmentality on the Canadian Prairies: Settler-Farmer Subjectivities and Agri-environmental Objects." *Antipode* 50, 2 (2017): 359–83.

Laforge, Julia M.L., and Robert McLeman. "Social Capital and Drought-Migrant Integration in 1930s Saskatchewan." *Canadian Geographer* 57, 4 (2013): 488–505.

Laliberte, Ronald F. "The 'Grab-a-Hoe' Indians: The Canadian State and the Procurement of Aboriginal Labour for the Southern Alberta Sugar Beet Industry." *Prairie Forum* 31, 2 (2006): 305–23.

–. "Why Move Aboriginal Labour In and Then Out? The Transition of Migrant Labour from Aboriginal to Mexican Workers in Southern Alberta's Sugar Beet Industry." PhD diss., Sociology, University of Calgary, 2007.

Laliberte, Ronald F., and Vic Satzewich. "Native Migrant Labour in the Southern Alberta Sugar-Beet Industry: Coercion and Paternalism in the Recruitment of Labour." *Canadian Review of Sociology and Anthropology* 36, 1 (1999): 65–85.

Lamontagne, Myrna L. *D'Amour: An Era of Change.* Altona, MB: Friesens, 1983.

Langford, Will. "Gerald Sutton Brown and the Discourse of City Planning Expertise in Vancouver, 1953–1959." *Urban Studies Review* 41, 2 (2013): 30–41.

–. *The Global Politics of Poverty in Canada: Development Programs and Democracy, 1964–1979.* Montreal/Kingston: McGill-Queen's University Press, 2020.

Lanoix, Joseph N. "Relation between Irrigation Engineering and Bilharziasis." *Bulletin of the World Health Organization* 18, 5–6 (1958): 1101–35.

Larsen, Laura. "The Public Good and Private Business of the Crow Rate: Prairie Grain Handling and Transportation Policy." PhD diss., History, University of Saskatchewan, 2020.

Latham, Michael. *The Right Kind of Revolution: Modernization, Development, and U.S. Foreign Policy from the Cold War to the Present.* Ithaca, NY: Cornell University Press, 2011.

Latour, Bruno. "Visualisation and Cognition: Drawing Things Together." in *Knowledge and Society: Studies in the Sociology of Culture Past and Present,* vol. 6, ed. Henrika Kuklick and Elizabeth Long, 1–40. Greenwich, CT: Jai, 1986.

Leahey, A. "Soil Surveys and Soil Research." *C.S.T.A. Review* 23 (December 1939): 10–13.

Lee, Lawrence B. "Dominion Ditches and British Columbia Canals: A History of the Western Canada Irrigation Association." *Journal of the West* 7 (1968): 31–40.

Lemmen, Donald, and Lisa Dale-Burnett. "The Palliser Triangle." In *Atlas of Saskatchewan,* 2nd ed., ed. Ka-iu Fung, 41. Saskatoon: University of Saskatchewan, 1999.

Lentz, Carola. *Land, Mobility, and Belonging in West Africa.* Bloomington: Indiana University Press, 2013.

Leonard, Frank. "'Eighth Wonder of the World': The Cariboo Wagon Road as British Columbia's First Megaproject." *Journal of the Canadian Historical Association* 27, 1 (2016): 169–200.

Lesica, Peter, and Thomas H. DeLuca. "Long-Term Harmful Effects of Crested Wheatgrass on Great Plains Grassland Ecosystems." *Journal of Soil and Water Conservation* 51, 5 (1996): 408–9.

Lesieur, Vincent, Jean-François Martin, David K. Weaver, Kim A. Hoelmer, David R. Smith, Wendell L. Morrill, Nassera Kadiri, Frank B. Peairs, Darren M. Cockrell, Terri L. Randolph, Debra K. Waters, and Marie-Claude Bon. "Phylogeography of the Wheat Stem Sawfly, *Cephus cinctus* Norton (Hymenoptera: Cephidae): Implications for Pest Management." *PLOS ONE* 11, 12 (2016): e0168370. https://doi.org/10.1371/journal.pone.0168370.

Leskiw, L.A. and C.F. Bentley. *Sustainability of Farmed Lands: Current Trends and Thinking.* Ottawa: Minister of Supply and Services Canada, 1985.

Li, Lin, Pouya Sabokruhie, and Karl-Erich Lindenschmidt. "Dam-Induced Riverbed Degradation in the Saskatchewan River Delta." *Land Degradation and Development* 35, 2 (2024): 772–83.

Liberal Party of Canada. *Forward. For Everyone.* Ottawa: Liberal Party of Canada, 2021. https://liberal.ca/wp-content/uploads/sites/292/2021/09/Platform-Forward-For-Everyone.pdf.

–. *Forward: A Real Plan for the Middle Class.* Ottawa: Liberal Party of Canada, 2019. https://2019.liberal.ca/wp-content/uploads/sites/292/2019/09/Forward-A-real-plan-for-the-middle-class.pdf.

Lindwall, C. Wayne, and Bernie Sonntag, eds. *Landscapes Transformed: The History of Conservation Tillage and Direct Seeding.* Saskatoon: Knowledge Impact in Society, 2010.

Lodge, Robert W. "Complementary Grazing Systems for Sandhills of the Northern Great Plains." *Journal of Range Management* 16, 5 (1963): 240–44.

Loewen, Royden. *Diaspora in the Countryside: Two Mennonite Communities and Mid-Twentieth-Century Rural Disjuncture.* Toronto: University of Toronto Press, 2006.

–. "Rurality, Ethnicity, and Gender Patterns of Cultural Continuity During the 'Great Disjuncture' in the R.M. of Hanover, 1945–1961." *Journal of the Canadian Historical Association* 4, 1 (1993): 161–82.

Lok, S.C. *United States Department of Agriculture Soil Conservation Activities on the U.S. Great Plains: Lessons for Agriculture Canada on the Canadian Prairies.* Ottawa: Regional Development Branch, Agriculture Canada, 1984.

Loo, Tina. "High Modernism, Conflict, and the Nature of Change in Canada." *Canadian Historical Review* 97, 1 (2016): 34–58.

–. "Making a Modern Wilderness: Conserving Wildlife in Twentieth-Century Canada." *Canadian Historical Review* 82, 1 (2001): 91–121.

–. *Moved by the State: Forced Relocation and Making a Good Life in Postwar Canada.* Vancouver: UBC Press, 2019.

–. "People in the Way: Modernity, Environment, and Society on the Arrow Lakes." *BC Studies,* 142–43 (2004): 161–96.

–. *States of Nature: Conserving Canada's Wildlife in the Twentieth Century.* Vancouver: UBC Press, 2006.

Loo, Tina, and Meg Stanley. "An Environmental History of Progress: Damming the Peace and Columbia Rivers." *Canadian Historical Review* 92, 3 (2011): 399–427.

Lorenz, Russell J. "Introduction and Early Use of Crested Wheatgrass in the Northern Great Plains." In *Crested Wheatgrass: Its Values, Problems, and Myths: A Symposium,* ed. Kendall L. Johnson, 9–20. Logan: Utah State University, 1986.

Lotz, Jim. "The Beginning of Community Development in English-Speaking Canada." In *Community Organizing: Canadian Experiences,* ed. Brian Wharf and Michael Clague, 15–28. Toronto: Oxford University Press, 1997.

Loveridge, D.M., and Barry Potyondi. *From Wood Mountain to the Whitemud: A Historical Survey of the Grasslands National Park Area.* Ottawa: National Historic Parks and Sites Branch, Parks Canada, 1983.

Luby, Brittany. *Dammed: The Politics of Loss and Survival in Anishinaabe Territory.* Winnipeg: University of Manitoba Press, 2020.

Lund, Christian. *Local Politics and the Dynamics of Property in Africa.* Cambridge, UK: Cambridge University Press, 2009.

Lytwyn, Victor P. *Muskekowuck Athinuwick: Original People of the Great Swampy Land.* Winnipeg: University of Manitoba Press, 2002.

M.A. Carson and Associates. *Sediment Issues in the Cumberland Lake Area, Saskatchewan River Delta Complex.* Regina: Water Resources Branch, Western and Northern Region, Inland Waters Directorate, Environment Canada, 1993.

MacCallum, Mary Jane, and Adele Perry. *Structures of Indifference: An Indigenous Life and Death in a Canadian City.* Winnipeg: University of Manitoba Press, 2018.

Macdougall, Brenda. "The Myth of Metis Cultural Ambivalence." In *Contours of a People: Metis Family, Mobility, and History*, ed. Nicole St-Onge, Carolyn Podruchny, and Brenda Macdougall, 422–64. Norman: University of Oklahoma Press, 2012.

–. *One of the Family: Metis Culture in Nineteenth-Century Saskatchewan.* Vancouver: UBC Press, 2010.

–. "Wahkootowin: Family and Cultural Identity in Northwestern Saskatchewan Metis Communities." *Canadian Historical Review* 87, 3 (2006): 431–62.

Macdougall, Brenda, Carolyn Podruchny, and Nicole St-Onge. "Introduction: Cultural Mobility and the Contours of Difference." In *Contours of a People: Metis Family, Mobility, and History*, ed. Nicole St-Onge, Carolyn Podruchny, and Brenda Macdougall, 3–21. Norman: University of Oklahoma Press, 2012.

MacEachern, G.A. *Retention of the Crow Rate and the Alberta Livestock Economy.* Ottawa: Agricultural Economics Research Council of Canada/Alberta Cattle Commission, 1978.

MacEwan, Grant. *Between the Red and the Rockies.* Toronto: University of Toronto Press, 1952.

–. *The Breeds of Farm Live-Stock in Canada.* Toronto: Thomas Nelson and Sons, 1941.

–. *The Feeding of Farm Animals.* Toronto: Thomas Nelson and Sons, 1945.

–. *Fifty Mighty Men.* Saskatoon: Western Producer Prairie Books, 1970.

Macfarlane, Daniel. "'A Completely Man-Made and Artificial Cataract': The Transnational Manipulation of Niagara Falls." *Environmental History* 18, 4 (2013): 759–84.

–. "Creating the St. Lawrence Seaway: Mobility and a Modern Megaproject." In *Moving Natures: Environments and Mobility in Canadian History*, ed. Ben Bradley, Jay Young, and Colin M. Coates, 127–49. Calgary: NiCHE–University of Calgary Press Environmental History Series, 2016.

–. "Negotiating High Modernism: The St. Lawrence Seaway and Power Project." In *Made Modern: Science and Technology in Canadian History*, ed. Edward Jones-Imhotep and Tina Adcock, 326–47. Vancouver: UBC Press, 2018.

–. *Negotiating a River: Canada, the US, and the Creation of the St. Lawrence Seaway.* Vancouver: UBC Press, 2014.

Macfarlane, Daniel, and Andrea Olive. "Whither Wintego: Environmental Impact Assessment and Indigenous Opposition in Saskatchewan's Churchill River Hydropower Project in the 1970s." *Canadian Historical Review* 102, 4 (2021): 620–46.

MacFarlane, David L. "Book Review: Report of the Royal Commission on the South Saskatchewan River Project, Ottawa, Queen's Printer and Controller of Stationery, 1952, pp. 423, xix." *Canadian Journal of Agricultural Economics* 1, 2 (1953): 31–34.

MacKenzie, G.L. "The St. Mary–Milk River Irrigation Project." *The Engineering Journal* 31, 9 (1948): 485–95.

MacLachlan, Ian. "The Historical Development of Cattle Production in Canada." Unpublished ms, 2006.

–. "Industrial Development of Lethbridge: A Geographer's Interpretation." Unpublished ms, 2004.

–. *Kill and Chill: Restructuring Canada's Beef Commodity Chain.* Toronto: University of Toronto Press, 2002.

Macpherson, Ian, and John Herd Thompson. "The Business of Agriculture: Prairie Farmers and the Adoption of 'Business Methods,' 1880–1950." In *The Prairie West: Historical Readings*, 2nd ed., ed. R. Douglas Francis and Howard Palmer, 475–96. Edmonton: Pica Pica, 1995.

–. "An Orderly Reconstruction: Prairie Agriculture in World War Two." *Canadian Papers in Rural History* 4 (1984): 11–32.

Magnan, André. *When Wheat Was King: The Rise and Fall of the Canada-UK Grain Trade.* Vancouver: UBC Press, 2016.

Marchildon, Gregory P. "Drought and Public Policy in the Palliser Triangle." In *Vulnerability and Adaptation to Drought: The Canadian Prairies and South America,* ed. Harry P. Diaz, Margot Hurlbert, and Jim Warren, 181–97. Calgary: University of Calgary Press, 2016.

–. "Institutional Adaptation to Drought and the Special Areas of Alberta, 1909–1939." *Prairie Forum* 32, 2 (2007): 251–71.

–. "The Prairie Farm Rehabilitation Administration: Climate Crisis and Federal-Provincial Relations during the Great Depression." *Canadian Historical Review* 90, 2 (2009): 275–301.

Marchildon, Gregory P., Suren Kulshreshtha, Elaine Wheaton, and Dave Sauchyn. "Drought and Institutional Adaptation in the Great Plains of Alberta and Saskatchewan, 1914–1939." *Natural Hazards* 45 (2008): 391–411.

Marchildon, Gregory P., Jeremy Pittman, and David J. Sauchyn, "The Dry Belt and Changing Aridity in the Palliser Triangle, 1895–2000." *Prairie Forum* 34, 1 (2009): 31–44.

Martin, Chester. *"The Natural Resources Question": The Historical Basis of Provincial Claims.* Winnipeg: King's Printer, 1920.

Massie, Merle, and Maureen G. Reed. "Cumberland House in the Saskatchewan River Delta: Flood Memory and the Municipal Response, 2005 and 2011." In *Climate Change and Flood Risk Management: Adaptation and Extreme Events at the Local Level,* ed. E. Carina H. Keskitalo, 150–89. Cheltenham, UK: Edward Elgar, 2013.

Mateos, Gisela, and Edna Suárez-Díaz. "Development Interventions: Science, Technology and Technical Assistance." *History and Technology* 36, 3–4 (2020): 293–309.

Mathieu, Saje. "North of the Color Line: Sleeping Car Porters and the Battle against Jim Crow on Canadian Rails, 1880–1920." *Labour/Le Travail* 47 (2001): 9–42.

Matsui, Kenichi. *Native Peoples and Water Rights: Irrigation, Dams, and the Law in Western Canada.* Montreal/Kingston: McGill-Queen's University Press, 2009.

Matthews, Robert O. "Canada and Anglophone Africa." In *Canada and the Third World,* ed. Peyton V. Lyon and Tareq Y. Ismael, 60–132. Toronto: Macmillan of Canada/Maclean-Hunter, 1976.

Martin, Chester. *"Dominion Lands" Policy.* Ed. Lewis H. Thomas. Toronto: McClelland and Stewart, 1973.

Martin, Thibault. "Hydro Development in Quebec and Manitoba: Old Relationships or New Social Contract?" In *Power Struggles: Hydro Development and First Nations in Manitoba and Quebec,* ed. Thibault Martin and Steven Hoffman, 19–37. Winnipeg: University of Manitoba Press, 2008.

Martin, Thibault, and Steven Hoffman, eds. *Power Struggles: Hydro Development and First Nations in Manitoba and Quebec.* Winnipeg: University of Manitoba Press, 2008.

Martin-McGuire, Peggy. *First Nation Land Surrender on the Prairies, 1896–1911.* Ottawa: Indian Claims Commission, 1998.

McHugh, Paul G. *Aboriginal Societies and the Common Law: A History of Sovereignty, Status and Self-Determination.* Oxford: Oxford University Press, 2005.

McLeod, Neal. *Cree Narrative Memory: From Treaties to Contemporary Times.* Saskatoon: Purich, 2007.

McKay, Ian. "The Canadian Passive Revolution, 1840–1950." *Capital and Class* 34, 3 (2010): 361–81.

–. "The Liberal Order Framework: A Prospectus for a Reconnaissance of Canadian History." *Canadian Historical Review* 81, 4 (2000): 616–45.

McKenzie, R.E. *Saskatchewan Institute of Agrologists, 1946–1970: An Account of the First 25 Years.* Saskatoon: Saskatchewan Institute of Agrologists, 1970.

McKercher, Asa, and Philip Van Huizen. "Introduction." In *Undiplomatic History: The New Study of Canada and the World,* ed. Asa McKercher and Philip Van Huizen, 3–29. Montreal/Kingston: McGill-Queen's University Press, 2019.

McKittrick, Meredith. "Industrial Agriculture." In *A Companion to Global Environmental History,* ed. J.R. McNeill and Erin Stewart Mauldin, 411–32. Chichester, UK: Wiley-Blackwell, 2012.

McLeman, Robert A. *Climate and Human Migration: Past Experiences, Present Challenges.* Cambridge, UK: Cambridge University Press, 2013.

McLeman, Robert A., Juliette Dupre, Lea Berrang Ford, James Ford, Konrad Gajewski, and Gregory P. Marchildon. "What We Learned from the Dust Bowl: Lessons in Science, Policy, and Adaptation." *Population and Environment* 35 (2013): 417–40.

McLeman, Robert A., Sam Herold, Zoran Reljic, Mike Sawada, and Daniel McKenney. "GIS-Based Modeling of Drought and Historical Population Change on the Canadian Prairies." *Journal of Historical Geography* 36, 1 (2010): 43–56.

McManus, Curtis R. *Happyland: A History of the "Dirty Thirties" in Saskatchewan, 1914–1937.* Calgary: University of Calgary Press, 2011.

McNeill, J.R., and Verena Winiwarter. "Breaking the Sod: Humankind, History, and Soil." *Science,* 11 June 2004, 1627–29.

–. "Soils, Soils Knowledge, and Environmental History." In *Soils and Societies: Perspectives from Environmental History,* ed. J R. McNeill and Verena Winiwarter, 1–6. Isle of Harris, UK: White Horse, 2006.

Meftaul, Islam Md., Kadiyala Venkateswarlu, Rajarathnam Dharmarajan, Prasath Annamalai, Md. Asaduzzaman, Aney Parven, and Mallavarapu Megharaj. "Controversies over Human Health and Ecological Impacts of Glysophate: Is It to Be Banned in Modern Agriculture?" *Environmental Pollution* 263, part A (2020): 114372. https://doi.org/10.1016/j.envpol.2020.114372.

Melnick, Loriena Pearl. "Fish, Food and the Fur Trade: The Use of Hudson's Bay Company's Post Journals for Moose Factory, Cumberland House, Edmonton House, Fort Athabasca, and Ile a la Crosse to Reconstruct the Provisioning of Fish, Fowl and Game, ca. 1777–1827." MA thesis, Native Studies, University of Alberta, 2018.

Meren, David. "'Commend me the Yak': The Colombo Plan, the Inuit of Ungava, and 'Developing' Canada's North." *Histoire sociale/Social History* 50, 102 (2017): 343–70.

Meyer, David, and Paul C. Thistle. "Saskatchewan River Rendezvous Centers and Trading Posts: Continuity in a Cree Social Geography." *Ethnohistory* 42, 3 (1995): 403–44.

Miescher, Stephan F. "Building the City of the Future: Visions and Experiences of Modernity in Ghana's Akosombo Township." *Journal of African History* 53, 3 (2012): 367–90.

–. "'Nkrumah's Baby': The Akosombo Dam and the Dream of Development in Ghana, 1952–1966." *Water History* 6, 4 (2014): 341–66.

–. "'No One Should Be Worse Off': The Akosombo Dam, Modernization, and the Experience of Resettlement in Ghana." In *Modernization as Spectacle in Africa,* ed. Peter

J. Bloom, Stephan F. Miescher, and Takyiwaa Manuh, 184–204. Bloomington: Indiana University Press, 2014.

Miescher, Stephan F., and Dzodzi Tsikata. "Hydro-Power and the Promise of Modernity and Development in Ghana: Comparing the Akosombo and Bui Dam Projects." *Ghana Studies* 12–13 (2009–10): 15–53.

Montgomery, David R. "Soil Erosion and Agricultural Sustainability." *Proceedings of the National Academy of Sciences* 104, 33 (2007): 13268–72. https://doi.org/10.1073/pnas.0611508104.

Moon, David. *The American Steppes: The Unexpected Russian Roots of Great Plains Agriculture, 1870s–1930s.* Cambridge, UK: Cambridge University Press, 2020.

Moore, Elizabeth. "The New Direction of Federal Agricultural Research in Canada: From Private Good to Public Gain?" *Journal of Canadian Studies* 37, 3 (2002): 112–34.

Morrison, Alli, and Iain Davidson-Hunt. *Opaskwayak Cree Nation Guide to the Wetlands of the Saskatchewan River Delta.* Winnipeg: Aboriginal Issues, 2012.

Morrison, David R. *Aid and Ebb Tide: A History of CIDA and Canadian Development Assistance.* Waterloo, ON: Wilfrid Laurier University Press, 1998.

–. "The Choice of Bilateral Aid Recipients." In *Canadian International Development Assistance Policies: An Appraisal,* ed. Cranford Pratt, 123–55. Montreal/Kingston: McGill-Queen's University Press, 1994.

Morton, Arthur S., and Chester Martin. *History of Prairie Settlement and "Dominion Lands" Policy.* Toronto: Macmillan, 1938.

Morton, W.L. "Seeing an Unliterary Landscape." In *Contexts of Canada's Past: Selected Essays of W.L. Morton,* ed. A.B. McKillop, 15–26. Montreal/Kingston: McGill-Queen's University Press, 1980.

Moynan, J.C., and M.J. Tinline. "Sub-Stations and Their Relation to Rehabilitation." *C.S.T.A. Review* 23 (December 1939): 78–84.

Murray, A.R. *An Analysis of Mercury Contamination in Fish from Northern Saskatchewan Lakes, 1969–1976.* La Ronge: Department of Northern Saskatchewan, 1978.

Neatby, Hilda. *The Politics of Chaos: Canada in the Thirties.* Toronto: Macmillan of Canada, 1972.

Nelles, H.V. *The Politics of Development: Forests, Mines, and Hydro-Electric Power in Ontario, 1849–1941.* 2nd ed. Montreal/Kingston: McGill-Queen's University Press, 2005.

Nelson, Philip J. "To Hold the Land: Soil Erosion, Agricultural Scientists, and the Development of Conservation Tillage Techniques." *Agricultural History* 71, 1 (1997): 71–90.

Nkrumah, Kwame. *Ghana: The Autobiography of Kwame Nkrumah.* 1957. Reprint, New York: International Publishers, 1971.

Norman, Emma S. *Governing Transboundary Waters: Canada, the United States, and Indigenous Communities.* London: Routledge, 2015.

Notzke, Claudia. *Aboriginal Peoples and Natural Resources in Canada.* Concord, ON: Captus University Publications, 1994.

Nygren, Joshua. "A 'Plow to Save the Plains': Conservation Tillage on the North American Grasslands, 1938–1973." In *The Greater Plains: Rethinking a Region's Environmental Histories,* ed. Brian Frehner and Kathleen A. Brosnan, 202–29. Lincoln: University of Nebraska Press, 2021.

Obosu-Mensah, Kwaku. *Ghana's Volta Resettlement Scheme: The Long-Term Consequences of Post-colonial State Planning.* San Francisco: International Scholars, 1996.

O'Donnell, Edward T. *Henry George and the Crisis of Inequality: Progress and Poverty in the Gilded Age.* New York: Columbia University Press, 2015.

O'Hagan, Michael. "Beyond the Barbed Wire Fence: POW Labour Projects in Canada during the Second World War." PhD diss., History, University of Western Ontario, 2020.

Okimāsis, Jean, and Arok Wolvengrey. *How to Spell It in Cree: The Standard Roman Orthography.* Oskana kā-asastēki: miywāsin ink, 2008.

Pailey, Robtel Neajai. "De-centering the 'White Gaze' of Development." *Development and Change* 51, 3 (2020): 729–45.

Palmer, A.E., "Irrigation in Western Canada: Its Possible Effect on Industry and Population." *The Engineering Journal* 31, 9 (1948): 497–98.

Palmer, Howard. "Nativism in Alberta, 1925–1930." *Historical Papers/Communications historiques* 9, 1 (1974): 183–212.

–. *Patterns of Prejudice: A History of Nativism in Alberta.* Toronto: McClelland and Stewart, 1982.

Parent, David. "Governing Metis Indigeneity: The Settler-Colonial Dispossession and Regulation of Metis in Mid-Twentieth Century Manitoba." PhD diss., Native Studies, University of Alberta, 2021.

Partners for the Saskatchewan River Basin. *From the Mountains to the Sea: The State of the Saskatchewan River Basin.* Saskatoon: Partners for the Saskatchewan River Basin, 2009.

Patel, Kiran Klaus. *The New Deal: A Global History.* Princeton, NJ: Princeton University Press, 2016.

Patrias, Carmela. "Race, Employment Discrimination, and State Complicity in Wartime Canada, 1939–1945." *Labour/Le Travail* 59 (2007): 9–41.

Pauly, D. "Anecdotes and the Shifting Baseline Syndrome of Fisheries." *Trends in Ecology and Evolution* 10, 10 (1995): 430.

Peekhaus, Wilhelm C. *Resistance Is Fertile: Canadian Struggles on the BioCommons.* Vancouver: UBC Press, 2013.

Pellant, Mike, and Cindy R. Lysne. "Strategies to Enhance Plant Structure and Diversity in Crested Wheatgrass Seedings." In *Sage-Grouse Habitat Restoration Symposium Proceedings,* comp. Nancy L. Shaw, Mike Pellant, and Stephen B. Monsen, 81–92. Fort Collins, CO: Forest Service, Rocky Mountain Research Station, US Department of Agriculture, 2005.

Perkin, Harold. "'The Condescension of Posterity': The Recent Historiography of the English Working Class." *Social Science History* 3, 1 (1978): 87–101.

Perry, Adele. *Aqueduct: Colonialism, Resources, and the Histories We Remember.* Winnipeg: ARP Books, 2016.

Peters, Evelyn, Matthew Stock, and Adrian Werner. *Rooster Town: The History of an Urban Métis Community, 1901–1961.* Winnipeg: University of Manitoba Press, 2018.

Peterson, Robert. "Soil Mechanics as Related to the PFRA Water Development Program." In *Proceedings of 1949 Civilian Soil Mechanics Conference,* 52–53. Ottawa: National Research Council of Canada, 1953. https://nrc-publications.canada.ca/eng/view/accepted/?id=3fb69faa-504b-413b-8d1f-3848c84da924.

Phillips, Sarah T. "Drylands, Dust Bowl, and Agro-technical Internationalism in Southern Africa." In *Transatlantic Rebels: Agrarian Radicalism in Comparative Context,* ed. Thomas Summerhill and James C. Scott, 265–97. East Lansing: Michigan State University Press, 2004.

–. *This Land, This Nation: Conservation, Rural America, and the New Deal.* New York: Cambridge University Press, 2007.

–. "Lessons from the Dust Bowl: Dryland Agriculture and Soil Erosion in the United States and South Africa, 1900–1950." *Environmental History* 4, 2 (1999): 245–66.

Pickersgill, J.W. *My Years with Louis St. Laurent: A Political Memoir.* Toronto: University of Toronto Press, 1975.

Pidgeon, E.R. *How Specific Federal Policies May Impact on Prairie Soil and Moisture Conservation.* Ottawa: Agriculture Canada, 1984.

Pietz, David. *The Yellow River: The Problem of Water in Modern China.* Cambridge, MA: Harvard University Press, 2015.

Pisani, Donald. *To Reclaim a Divided West: Water, Law, and Public Policy, 1848–1902.* Albuquerque: University of New Mexica Press, 1992.

Pitsula, James M. *Keeping Canada British: The Klu Klux Klan in 1920s Saskatchewan.* Vancouver: UBC Press, 2013.

Platt, A.W. "Breeding Wheat for Sawfly Resistance." *Canadian Geographical Journal* 33, 3 (1946): 138–41.

Pohorecky, Zenon Stephen. "Archaeology and Prehistory: The Saskatchewan Case." In *A Region of the Mind: Interpreting the Western Canadian Plains,* ed. Richard Allen, 47–72. Regina: Canadian Plains Studies Centre, University of Saskatchewan, 1973.

–. *Field Status Report on the South Saskatchewan Reservoir Archaeological Survey Covering the Period between July 8 and August 10, 1960.* Ottawa: National Museum of Canada, 1960.

–. *Report on the South Saskatchewan Reservoir Archaeological Survey, June–September, 1960.* Ottawa: National Museum of Canada, 1960.

Poirier, Valérie. "'L'autoroute est-ouest, c'est pas le progrès!': environnement et mobilisation citoyenne en opposition au projet d'autoroute est-ouest à Montréal en 1971." *Bulletin d'histoire politique* 23, 2 (2015): 66–91.

Pomeroy, John W., Dirk de Boer, and Lawrence W. Martz. *Hydrology and Water Resources of Saskatchewan.* Saskatoon: Centre for Hydrology, University of Saskatchewan, 2005.

Porter, Doug J. "Scenes from Childhood: The Homesickness of Development Discourses." In *Power of Development,* ed. Jonathan Crush, 63–86. London: Routledge, 1995.

Potyondi, Barry. *In Palliser's Triangle: Living in the Grasslands, 1850–1930.* Saskatoon: Purich, 1995.

Prairie Farm Rehabilitation Administration. *Annual Report on Prairie Farm Rehabilitation and Related Activities, 1959–1960.* Ottawa: Department of Agriculture, 1960.

–. *Annual Report on Prairie Farm Rehabilitation and Related Activities, 1961–1962.* Ottawa: Department of Agriculture, 1962.

–. *Eleventh Annual Report on Activities under the Prairie Farm Rehabilitation Act for the Fiscal Year Ended March 31, 1946.* Ottawa: Department of Agriculture, 1946.

–. *Full Development Possibilities in the Saskatchewan River Basin.* Regina: Hydrology Division, 1952.

–. *Handbook for the Classification of Irrigated Land in the Prairie Provinces.* Regina: Prairie Farm Rehabilitation Administration, 1964.

–. *1985 Report PFRA Tree Nursery.* Ottawa: Agriculture Canada, 1985.

–. *Prairie Agricultural Landscapes: A Land Resource Review.* Ottawa: Agriculture and Agri-Food Canada, 2000.

–. *Prairie Farm Rehabilitation Act: Annual Report of Activities, Year Ended March 31st, 1943.* Ottawa: Department of Agriculture, 1943.

–. *Prairie Farm Rehabilitation Administration Annual Report, 1979–1980.* Ottawa: Department of Regional Economic Expansion, 1981.

–. *Prairie Farm Rehabilitation Administration 50th Anniversary Seminar: Proceedings.* Regina: Department of Agricultural Economics and Farm Management, University of Manitoba, 1985.

–. *The Prairie Farm Rehabilitation Administration (PFRA) Soil Conservation Activity Report for 1986–87 and 1987–88.* Ottawa: Agriculture Canada, 1988.

–. *Report on Activities Conducted under the Prairie Farm Rehabilitation Act for the Fiscal Year Ending March 31, 1942.* Ottawa: Department of Agriculture, 1942.

–. *Report on Activities under the Prairie Farm Rehabilitation Act for the Fiscal Year Ending March 31, 1940.* Ottawa: Department of Agriculture, 1940.

–. *Report on Activities under the Prairie Farm Rehabilitation Act for the Year Ending March 31, 1945.* Ottawa: Department of Agriculture, 1945.

–. *Report on Prairie Farm Rehabilitation and Related Activities, 1952–53.* Ottawa: Department of Agriculture, 1953.

–. *Report on Prairie Farm Rehabilitation and Related Activities, 1954–55.* Ottawa: Department of Agriculture, 1955.

–. *Report of Proceedings under the Prairie Farm Rehabilitation Act for the Fiscal Year Ending March 31, 1937.* Ottawa: Department of Agriculture, 1937.

–. *Report on Proceedings under the Prairie Farm Rehabilitation Act for the Fiscal Year Ending March 31, 1938.* Ottawa: Department of Agriculture, 1938.

–. *Report on Proceedings under the Prairie Farm Rehabilitation Act for the Fiscal Year Ending March 31, 1941.* Ottawa: Department of Agriculture, 1941.

–. *Report on Progress under the Prairie Farm Rehabilitation Act for the Fiscal Year Ending March 31, 1939.* Ottawa: Department of Agriculture, 1939.

–. *Report of the Work Conducted under the Prairie Farm Rehabilitation Act for the Fiscal Year 1935–36.* Ottawa: Department of Agriculture, 1936.

–. *Shelterbelt Centre: History of the Tree Nursery, 1901–1993.* Ottawa: Agriculture Canada, 1993.

Prairie Farm Rehabilitation Administration, Soil and Water Conservation Branch. *Land Degradation and Soil Conservation Issues on the Canadian Prairies.* Ottawa: Agriculture Canada, 1983.

–. "Land Degradation and Soil Conservation Issues on the Canadian Prairies: An Overview." Unpublished draft. Ottawa: Agriculture Canada, 1982.

Price, David H. Cold War Anthropology: the CIA, the Pentagon, and the Growth of Dual Use anthropology. Durham, NC: Duke University Press, 2016.

–. Cold War Deceptions: The Asia Foundation and the CIA. Seattle: University of Washington Press, 2024.

Provincial Archives of Alberta. *An Administrative History of the Government of Alberta, 1905–2005.* Edmonton: Priority Printing, 2006.

Qualman, Darrin, with the National Farmers Union. *Tackling the Farm Crisis and the Climate Crisis: Transformative Strategy for Canadian Farms and Food Systems.* Saskatoon: National Farmers Union, 2019.

Quiring, David M. *CCF Colonialism in Northern Saskatchewan: Battling Parish Priests, Bootleggers, and Fur Sharks.* Vancouver: UBC Press, 2004.

–. "From the Bush to the Village in Northern Saskatchewan: Contrasting CCF Community Development Projects." *Journal of the Canadian Historical Association* 17, 1 (2006): 151–78.

Ray, Arthur J. *The Canadian Fur Trade in the Industrial Age.* Toronto: University of Toronto Press, 1990.

Ray, Arthur J., J.R. Miller, and Frank J. Tough. *Bounty and Benevolence: A History of Saskatchewan Treaties.* Montreal/Kingston: McGill-Queen's University Press, 2000.

Regular, Keith W. *Neighbours and Networks: The Blood Tribe in the Southern Alberta Economy, 1884–1939.* Calgary: University of Calgary Press, 2009.

Reid, Escott. "The Saskatchewan Liberal Machine before 1929." *Canadian Journal of Economics and Political Science* 2, 1 (1936): 27–40.

Rein, Paula Fay. "These Changing Conditions: A Study of the Saskatchewan Royal Commission on Agriculture and Rural Life." MA thesis, History, University of Regina, 1994.

Reisner, Marc. *Cadillac Desert: The American West and Its Disappearing Water.* New York: Viking Penguin, 1986.

Rennie, D.A., and J.G. Ellis. *The Shape of Saskatchewan.* Saskatoon: Institute of Pedology, University of Saskatchewan, 1978.

Report of Commission Appointed in 1936 to Inquire into the Various Phases of Irrigation Development in Alberta. Lethbridge, AB: Lethbridge Herald, 1937. https://archive.org/details/P006001.

Richtik, James M. "Mapping Land for Agriculture in Western Canada." *Great Plains Quarterly* 5, 4 (1985): 236–48.

Riegert, Paul W. *From Arsenic to DDT: A History of Entomology in Western Canada.* Toronto: University of Toronto Press, 1980.

–. *Outbreaks of Grasshoppers and Control Campaigns in Alberta, 1939–1980.* Regina: Rampeck, 1999.

Riesen, H.G., and E. Kuiper. *Report: Saskatchewan River Reclamation Project.* Ottawa: Prairie Farm Rehabilitation Administration, Department of Agriculture, 1956.

Robin, Libby. "Ecology: A Science of Empire?" In *Ecology and Empire: Environmental History of Settler Societies,* ed. Libby Robin and Tom Griffiths, 63–75. Edinburgh: Keele University Press, 1997.

Robins, Joseph G., and Kevin B. Jensen. "Breeding of the Crested Wheatgrass Complex (*Agropyron* spp.) for North American Temperate Rangeland Agriculture and Conservation." *Agronomy* 10, 8 (2020): 1134. https://doi.org/10.3390/agronomy10081134.

Robinson, Danielle. "Modernism at a Crossroad: The Spadina Expressway Controversy in Toronto, Ontario, ca. 1960–1971." *Canadian Historical Review* 92, 2 (2011): 295–322.

Ross, Corey. *Ecology and Power in the Age of Empire: Europe and the Transformation of the Tropical World.* Oxford: Oxford University Press, 2017.

Ross, Norman M. *Tree-Planting on the Prairies of Manitoba, Saskatchewan and Alberta.* Ottawa: Dominion Experimental Farms, Department of Agriculture, 1933.

Rothermund, Dietmar. *The Global Impact of the Great Depression, 1929–1939.* London: Routledge, 1996.

Roy, Patricia. *The Triumph of Citizenship: The Japanese and Chinese in Canada, 1941–1967.* Vancouver: UBC Press, 2007.

Roy, Patricia, J.L. Granatstein, Masako Lino, and Hiroko Takamura. *Mutual Hostages: Canadians and Japanese during the Second World War.* Toronto: University of Toronto Press, 1990.

Rozum, Molly. *Grasslands Grown: Creating Place on the U.S. Northern Plains and Canadian Prairies.* Lincoln: University of Nebraska Press, 2021.

Rudin, Ronald. *Against the Tides: Reshaping Landscape and Community in Canada's Maritime Marshlands.* Vancouver: UBC Press, 2021.

–. *Kouchibouguac: Removal, Resistance, and Remembrance at a Canadian National Park.* Toronto: University of Toronto Press, 2016.

Runciman, A.M. "Chairman's Remarks." In Prairie Farm Rehabilitation Administration, *Prairie Farm Rehabilitation Administration 50th Anniversary Seminar: Proceedings*, 1–4. Regina: Department of Agricultural Economics and Farm Management, University of Manitoba, 1985.

Russell, Benjamin. *Report on Surface Water Supplies and Water Power of Alberta: Their Present and Ultimate Uses.* Alberta: n.p., 1948.

Russell, Dale R. *Eighteenth-Century Western Cree and Their Neighbours.* Ottawa: Canadian Museum of Civilization, 1991.

Russell, Edmund P. *Evolutionary History: Uniting History and Biology to Understand Life on Earth.* New York: Cambridge University Press, 2011.

–. "'Speaking of Annihilation': Mobilizing for War against Human and Insect Enemies, 1914–1945." *Journal of American History* 82, 4 (1996): 1505–29.

Russell, Peter A. "The Far-from-Dry Debates: Dry Farming on the Canadian Prairies and the American Great Plain." *Agricultural History* 81, 4 (2007): 493–521.

–. *How Agriculture Made Canada: Farming in the Nineteenth Century.* Montreal/Kingston: McGill-Queen's University Press, 2012.

Rutherford, Scott. *Canada's Other Red Scare: Indigenous Protest and Colonial Encounters during the Global Sixties.* Montreal/Kingston: McGill-Queen's University Press, 2020.

Safarian, A.E. *The Canadian Economy in the Great Depression.* 3rd ed. Montreal/Kingston: McGill-Queen's University Press, 2009.

Sammons, Olivia N. "Leaving Ste. Madeleine: A Michif Account." *Canadian Journal of Native Studies* 33, 2 (2013): 149–64.

Sandlos, John. "From the Outside Looking In: Aesthetics, Politics, and Wildlife Conservation in the Canadian North." *Environmental History* 6, 1 (2001): 6–31.

–. *Hunters at the Margin: Native People and Wildlife Conservation in the Northwest Territories.* Vancouver: UBC Press, 2007.

–. "Nature's Nations: The Shared Conservation History of Canada and the USA." *International Journal of Environmental Studies* 70, 3 (2013): 358–71.

–. "Not Wanted in the Boundary: The Expulsion of the Keeseekoowenin Ojibway Band from Riding Mountain National Park." *Canadian Historical Review* 89, 2 (2008): 189–221.

Sangster, Joan. "Presidential Address: Confronting Our Colonial Past: Reassessing Political Alliances over Canada's Twentieth Century." *Journal of the Canadian Historical Association* 28, 1 (2017): 1–43.

–. *Transforming Labour: Women and Work in Postwar Canada.* Toronto: University of Toronto Press, 2010.

Saskatchewan. *Forty-Third Annual Report of the Department of Agriculture of the Province of Saskatchewan for the Twelve Months Ended April 30, 1948.* Regina: King's Printer, 1948.

–. *Report of the Royal Commission of Inquiry into Farming Conditions.* Regina: J.W. Reid, King's Printer, 1921.

Saskatchewan, Royal Commission on Agriculture and Rural Life. *Crop Insurance.* Regina: Government of Saskatchewan, 1956.

–. *Farm Income.* Regina: Government of Saskatchewan, 1957.

–. *The Scope and Character of the Investigation.* Regina: Government of Saskatchewan, 1955.

Saskatchewan Irrigation Projects Association. *Time to Irrigate.* Vol. 2, *The Economic, Social and Environmental Benefits of Expanding Irrigation in Saskatchewan.* Regina: Clifton Associates, 2008.

Saskatchewan Water Corporation. *History of South Sask. River Irrigation Project.* Moose Jaw: Operations Division, Irrigation Services, Saskatchewan Water Corporation, 1987.

Satzewich, Vic. *Racism and the Incorporation of Foreign Labour: Farm Labour Migration to Canada since 1945.* London: Routledge, 1991.

Sauchyn, David. "Prairie Climate Trends and Variability." In *The New Normal: The Canadian Prairies in a Changing Climate,* ed. David Sauchyn, Harry P. Diaz, and Suren Kulshreshtha, 32–40. Regina: Canadian Plains Research Centre Press, 2021.

Sauchyn, David, and Samantha Kerr. "Canadian Prairies Drought from a Paleoclimate Perspective." In *Vulnerability and Adaptation to Drought: The Canadian Prairies and South America,* ed. Harry P. Diaz, Margot Hurlbert, and Jim Warren, 39–58. Calgary: University of Calgary Press, 2016.

Sauder, P.M. *Irrigation in Southern Alberta.* Edmonton: Department of the Environment, Government of Alberta, n.d.

Savoie, Donald J. *Regional Economic Development: Canada's Search for Solutions.* 2nd ed. Toronto: University of Toronto Press, 1992.

–. "The Toppling of DREE and Prospects for Regional Development." In *Regional Development Revisited,* ed. Donald J. Savoie, 1–15. Moncton, NB: Canadian Institute for Research on Regional Development, 1992.

Seaborne, Adrian A. "Crop Diversification in Canada's Breadbasket: Land Use Changes in Saskatchewan's Agriculture." *Geography* 82, 2 (2001): 151–58.

Seaborne, Adrian A., and R.L. Blackwell. "Patterns of Irrigation Development in the South Saskatchewan River Basin." *Prairie Forum* 18, 1 (1993): 97–115.

Seamans, H.L. "Insect Surveys in the Rehabilitation Program." *C.S.T.A. Review* 23 (December 1939): 99–101.

Schlegel, John P. *The Deceptive Ash: Bilingualism and Canadian Policy in Africa, 1957–1971.* Washington, DC: University Press of America, 1978.

Schmalz, Charles L. "The Second Raymond Sugar Factory: U&I Sugar's Canadian Venture 1925–1931." *Alberta History* 64, 2 (2014): 2–9.

Schmalzer, Sigrid. *"Red Revolution, Green Revolution": Scientific Farming in Socialist China.* Chicago: University of Chicago Press, 2016.

Schreiner, John. *The Refiners: A Century of BC Sugar.* Vancouver: Douglas and McIntyre, 1989.

Schrepfer, Susan, and Philip Scranton. *Industrializing Organisms: Introducing Evolutionary History.* New York: Routledge, 2003.

Schwartz, Charles. *The Search for Stability.* Toronto: McClelland and Stewart, 1959.

Science Council of Canada. *A Growing Concern: Soil Degradation in Canada.* Ottawa: Minister of Supply and Services, 1986.

Scott, James C. "High Modernist Social Engineering: The Case of the Tennessee Valley Authority." In *Experiencing the State,* ed. Lloyd I. Rudolph and John Kurt Jacobsen, 3–52. New Delhi: Oxford University Press, 2006.

–. *Seeing Like a State: How Certain Schemes to Improve the Human Condition Have Failed.* New Haven, CT: Yale University Press, 1998.

Shattuck, Annie. "Generic, Growing, Green? The Changing Political Economy of the Global Pesticide Complex." *Journal of Peasant Studies* 48, 2 (2021): 231–53.

Shaw, A.M., and Grant MacEwan. "An Experiment in Beef Production in Western Canada." *Scientific Agriculture* 19, 4 (1938): 177–98.

Showers, Kate Barger. *Imperial Gullies: Soil Erosion and Conservation in Lesotho.* Athens: Ohio University Press, 2005.

Silverstein, Ben. "Patrick Wolfe (1949–2016)." *History Workshop Journal* 82, 1 (2016): 315–23.

Simpson-Lewis, Wendy, Ruth McKechnie, and V. Neimanis. *Stress on Land in Canada.* Ottawa: Canadian Government Publishing Centre, 1983.

Sims, Daniel. "Dam Bennett: The Impacts of the W.A.C. Bennett Dam and Williston Lake Reservoir on the Tsek'ehne of Northern British Columbia." PhD diss., History, University of Alberta, 2017.

Skogstad, Grace. *Internationalization and Canadian Agriculture: Policy and Governing Paradigms.* Toronto: University of Toronto Press, 2008.

–. *The Politics of Agricultural Policy-Making in Canada.* Toronto: University of Toronto Press, 1987.

Skovron, Wyatt Mark. "A People's Commission? High Modernism, Direct Democracy and Rural Life, 1952–57." MA thesis, History, Simon Fraser University, 2011.

Smith, David E. "James G. Gardiner: Political Leadership in the Agrarian Community." In *Swords and Ploughshares: War and Agriculture in Western Canada,* ed. R.C. Macleod, 220–39. Edmonton: University of Alberta Press, 1993.

–. *Prairie Liberalism: The Liberal Party in Saskatchewan, 1905–1971.* Toronto: University of Toronto Press, 1975.

Smith, Denis. *Rogue Tory: The Life and Legend of John G. Diefenbaker.* Toronto: Macfarlane, Walter and Ross, 1995.

Smith, Keith D. *Liberalism, Surveillance, and Resistance: Indigenous Communities in Western Canada, 1877–1927.* Edmonton: Athabasca University Press, 2009.

Smith, Norman. "Evolution of Upper SRD Following the 1870's Evulsion and Subsequent Geomorphic Effects of E.B. Campbell Dam." In *Saskatchewan River Delta Symposium: Past, Present and Future, April 1–3, 2008, Saskatoon, Saskatchewan: Proceedings,* 29. Saskatoon: Partners for the Saskatchewan River Basin, 2008.

Smith, Norman, Galina S. Morozova, Marta Pérez-Arlucea, and Martin R. Gibling. "Dam-Induced and Natural Channel Changes in the Saskatchewan River below the E.B. Campbell Dam, Canada." *Geomorphology* 269 (2016): 186–202.

Smith, R.F. "History and Current Status of Irrigation in Alberta." *Canadian Water Resources Journal* 3, 1 (1978): 6–18.

Sneddon, Christopher. *Concrete Revolution: Large Dams, Cold War Geopolitics, and the US Bureau of Reclamation.* Chicago: University of Chicago Press, 2015.

Soares, Diogo, Liliana Silva, Sofia Duarte, Angelina Pena, and André Pereira. "Glyphosate Use, Toxicity and Occurrence in Food." *Foods* 10, 11 (2021): 2785. https://doi.org/10.3390/foods10112785.

Spence, C.C., B.H. Kristjanson, and J.L. Anderson. *Farming in the Irrigation Districts of Alberta.* Ottawa: Minister of Agriculture, 1947.

Spence, George. "Submission by Dr. George Spence." In Canada, *Report of the Royal Commission on the South Saskatchewan River Project,* 318–29. Ottawa: Queen's Printer, 1952. https://publications.gc.ca/site/eng/9.827922/publication.html.

–. *Survival of a Vision.* Ottawa: Department of Agriculture, 1967.

Spence, George, and John Vallance. "Organization of the P.F.R.A. for Water Conservation and Resettlement." *C.S.T.A. Review* 23 (December 1939): 29–31.

Spicer, Keith. *A Samaritan State? External Aid in Canada's Foreign Policy.* Toronto: University of Toronto Press, 1966.

St. Mary and Milk Rivers Water Development Committee. *Report on Further Storage and Irrigation Works Required to Utilize Fully Canada's Share of International Streams in Southern Alberta.* Ottawa: Department of Mines and Resources, 1942.

Stanger-Ross, Jordan, ed. *Landscapes of Injustice: A New Perspective on the Internment and Dispossession of Japanese Canadians.* Montreal/Kingston: McGill-Queen's University Press, 2020.

Stanger-Ross, Jordan, with Kaitlin Findlay, Eiji Okawa, Yasmin Railton, Josh van Es, and Trevor Wideman. "Introduction." In *Landscapes of Injustice: A New Perspective on the Internment and Dispossession of Japanese Canadians,* ed. Jordan Stanger-Ross, 3–50. Montreal/Kingston: McGill-Queen's University Press, 2020.

Stapleford, E.W. *Report on Rural Relief in the Prairie Provinces due to Drought Conditions and Crop Failures in Western Canada.* Ottawa: Minister of Agriculture, 1939.

Staples, Amy L.S. *The Birth of Development: How the World Bank, Food and Agriculture Organization, and World Health Organization Changed the World, 1945–1965.* Kent, OH: Kent State University Press, 2006.

Statistics Canada. *Ecological Land Classification, 2017.* Ottawa: Minister of Industry, 2018. https://www.statcan.gc.ca/en/subjects/standard/environment/elc/elc2017.

Stephens, D.M. "The Saskatchewan River and Manitoba's Problem." In Canada, *Report of the Royal Commission on the South Saskatchewan River Project,* 343–48. Ottawa: Queen's Printer, 1952. https://publications.gc.ca/site/eng/9.827922/publication.html.

Stewart, A. "The Prairie Farm Rehabilitation Programme." *Canadian Journal of Economics and Political Science* 5, 3 (1939): 310–24.

Stone, Christopher D. *Should Trees Have Standing? Law, Morality, and the Environment.* 3rd ed. Oxford: Oxford University Press, 2010.

Stonechild, Blair. *Buffy Sainte-Marie: It's My Way.* Markham, ON: Fifth House, 2012.

St-Onge, Nicole, and Carolyn Podruchny. "Scuttling along a Spider's Web: Mobility and Kinship in Metis Ethnogenesis." In *Contours of a People: Metis Family, Mobility, and History,* ed. Nicole St-Onge, Carolyn Podruchny, and Brenda Macdougall, 59–92. Norman: University of Oklahoma Press, 2012.

Strand, Katherine. "How to Make the Desert Bloom: An Ethnographic and Historical Account of Dryland Agriculture within Palliser's Triangle." PhD diss., Anthropology, McGill University, 2021.

–. "From Partner to Consumer: The Changing Role of Farmers in the Public Agricultural Research Process on the Canadian Prairies." In *In Defense of Farmers: The Future of Agriculture in the Shadow of Corporate Power,* ed. Jane Gibson, Sara Alexander, and John K. Hansen, 249–87. Lincoln: University of Nebraska Press, 2019.

Stunden Bower, Shannon. "Irrigation Infrastructure, Technocratic Faith, and Irregularities of Vision: Canada's Prairie Farm Rehabilitation Administration in Ghana, 1965–1970." *Agricultural History* 93, 2 (2019): 311–40.

–. "Strip Farming and the Wheat Stem Sawfly on the Canadian Prairies, 1930s–1940s." *Folklore* 41, 3 (2020): 4–8.

–. "Tools for Rational Development: The Canada Land Inventory and the Canada Geographic Information System in Mid-Twentieth Century Canada." *Scientia Canadensis* 40, 1 (2018): 44–75.

–. *Wet Prairie: People, Land, and Water in Agricultural Manitoba.* Vancouver: UBC Press, 2011.

Sumner, Arthur K., Jadu G. Saha, and Young W. Lee. "Mercury Residues in Fish from Saskatchewan Waters with and without Known Sources of Pollution – 1970." *Pesticides Monitoring Journal* 6, 2 (1972): 122–25.

Sunahara, Ann Gomer. *The Politics of Racism: The Uprooting of Japanese Canadians during the Second World War.* Toronto: James Lorimer, 1981.

Swidler, Eva-Maria. "The Social Production of Soil." *Soil Science* 174, 1 (2009): 2–8.

Tarazona, Jose V., Daniele Court-Marques, Manuela Tiramani, Hermine Reich, Rudolf Pfeil, Frederique Istace, and Federica Crivellente. "Glyphosate Toxicity and Carcinogenicity: A Review of the Scientific Basis of the European Union Assessment and Its Differences with IARC." *Archives of Toxicology* 91 (2017): 2723–43. https://link.springer.com/article/10.1007/s00204-017-1962-5.

Taylor, H.J. *To Plant the Prairies and the Plains: The Life and Work of Niels Ebbesen Hansen.* Mount Vernon, VA: Bios, 1941.

Tengan, Alexis B. *Hoe-Farming and Social Relations among the Dagara of Northwestern Ghana and Southwestern Burkina Faso.* Frankfurt: Peter Lang, 2000.

Thomas, Lewis H. "Introduction to the Carleton Library Edition." In Chester Martin, *"Dominion Lands" Policy,* ed. Lewis H. Thomas, ix–xviii. Toronto: McClelland and Stewart, 1973.

Thompson, E.P. *The Making of the English Working Class.* London: Victor Gollancz, 1963.

Thompson, John Herd. *Forging the Prairie West.* Toronto: Oxford University Press, 1998.

Thompson, John Herd, and Ian MacPherson. "'How You Gonna Get 'Em Back to the Farm': Writing the Rural/Agricultural History of the Prairie West." Paper presented at the Western Canadian Studies Conference, Saskatoon, Saskatchewan, 23 October 1987.

Thompson, John Herd, and Allen Seager. *Canada 1922–1939: Decades of Discord.* Toronto: McLelland and Steward, 1985.

–. "Workers, Growers and Monopolists: The 'Labour Problem' in the Alberta Beet Sugar Industry during the 1930s." *Labour/Le Travail* 3 (1978): 153–74.

Thomson, Don W. *Skyview Canada: A Story of Aerial Photography in Canada.* Ottawa: Department of Energy, Mines and Resources, 1975.

Thomson, L.B. *Brief to the Royal Commission on Canada's Economic Prospects.* Ottawa: Department of Agriculture, 1955.

Tillotson, Shirley. *Contributing Citizens: Modern Charitable Fundraising and the Making of the Welfare State, 1920–1966.* Vancouver: UBC Press, 2008.

Toews, Owen. *Stolen City: Racial Capitalism and the Making of Winnipeg.* Winnipeg: ARP Books, 2018.

Tonah, Steve. "Conflicts and Consensus between Migrant Fulani Herdsmen and Mamprusi Farmers in Northern Ghana." In *Ghana's North: Research on Culture, Religion, and Politics of Societies in Transition,* ed. Franz Kröger and Barbara Meier, 79–99. Frankfurt: Peter Lang, 2003.

Tough, Frank J. *"As Their Natural Resources Fail": Native Peoples and the Economic History of Northern Manitoba, 1870–1930.* Vancouver: UBC Press, 1996.

–. "'The World's Largest Muskrat Ranch': The Summerberry Muskrat Rehabilitation Project, 1935–1965." *Meridian,* Spring–Summer 2008, 17–24. https://publications.gc.ca/collections/collection_2008/cpc-ccap/R102-4-2008-1E.pdf.

Tsikata, Dzodzi. *Living in the Shadow of the Large Dams: Long-Term Responses of Downstream and Lakeside Communities of Ghana's Volta River Project.* Leiden: Brill, 2006.

Tucker, Richard P. "Containing Communism by Impounding Rivers: American Strategic Interests and the Global Spread of High Dams in the Early Cold War." In *Environmental Histories of the Cold War,* ed. J.R. McNeill and Corinna R. Unger, 139–64. Washington, DC: Cambridge University Press, 2010.

Turner, Chris. *The War on Science: Muzzled Scientists and Wilful Blindness in Stephen Harper's Canada.* Vancouver: Greystone Books, 2013.

Twumasi, Patrick A. "Colonialism and International Health: A Study on Social Change in Ghana." *Social Sciences and Medicine* 2, 15B (1981): 147–51.

Tyrchniewicz, Allen, and Art Wilson. *Sustainable Development for the Great Plains Policy Analysis: Focusing Sustainable Development on Agriculture.* Winnipeg: International Institute for Sustainable Development, 1994.

Valverde, Mariana. "Seeing Like a City: The Dialectic of Modern and Premodern Ways of Seeing in Urban Governance." *Law and Society Review* 45, 2 (2011): 277–312.

Van Huizen, Philip. "Building a Green Dam: Environmental Modernism and the Canadian-American Libby Dam Project." *Pacific Historical Review* 79, 3 (2010): 418–53.

Vaness, Brenda M., and Scott D. Wilson. "Impact and Management of Crested Wheatgrass (*Agropyron cristatum*) in the Northern Great Plains." *Canada Journal of Plant Science* 87, 5 (2007): 1023–28.

Vernon, Karina. *The Black Prairie Archive: An Anthology.* Waterloo, ON: Wilfrid Laurier University Press, 2020.

Vogel, Kenneth P. "Humans, Climate, and Plants: The Migration of Crested Wheatgrass and Smooth Bromegrass to the Great Plains of North America." In *Biological Resources and Migration,* ed. Dietrich Werner, 35–45. Berlin: Springer, 2004.

Vogel, Kenneth P., and John Hendrickson. "History of Grass Breeding for Grazing Lands in the Northern Great Plains of the USA and Canada." *Rangelands* 41, 1 (2019): 1–16.

Voisey, Paul. "A Mix-Up over Mixed Farming: The Curious History of the Agricultural Diversification Movement in a Single Crop Area of Southern Alberta." In *Building beyond the Homestead: Rural History on the Prairies,* ed. David C. Jones and Ian MacPherson, 179–205. Calgary: University of Calgary Press, 1985.

–. *Vulcan: The Making of a Prairie Community.* Toronto: University of Toronto Press, 1988.

von Heyking, Amy. "Teaching Prairie Pasts in 20th-Century Alberta and Saskatchewan Schools." *Prairie History* 12 (2023): 5–18.

Vreeman, T.S., and A.A. Fantino. *The Economics of Agricultural Chemical Use in Prairie Agriculture: Productivity and Environmental Impacts.* Edmonton: Alberta Agricultural Research Institute, 1994.

Waiser, Bill. *Saskatchewan: A New History.* Calgary: Fifth House, 2005.

Waldram, James B. *Cumberland House and the E.B. Campbell Dam: An Economic Impact Study.* Thunder Bay, ON: Centre for Northern Studies, Lakehead University, 1989.

–. *As Long as the Rivers Run: Hydroelectric Development and Native Communities in Western Canada.* Winnipeg: University of Manitoba Press, 1993.

Walker, Barrington. "Finding Jim Crow in Canada, 1789–1967." In *A History of Human Rights in Canada: Essential Issues,* ed. Janet Miron, 81–98. Toronto: Canadian Scholars' Press, 2009.

–. "Immigration Policy, Colonization, and the Development of a White Canada." In *Canada and the Third World: Overlapping Histories,* ed. Karen Dubinsky, Sean Mills, and Scott Rutherford, 37–59. Toronto: University of Toronto Press, 2016.

Walker, James W. St.G. *"Race," Rights and the Law in the Supreme Court of Canada.* Toronto/Waterloo, ON: Osgoode Society for Canadian Legal History/Wilfrid Laurier University Press, 1997.

Wall, Derek. *The Commons in History: Culture, Conflict, and Ecology.* Cambridge, MA: MIT Press, 2014.

Wallace, Lew E. "Field-Plot Tests of Chemicals for Wheat Stem Sawfly Control." *Journal of Economic Entomology* 55, 1 (1962): 908–12.

Wallach, Bret. "Physical Environment." In *Encyclopedia of the Great Plains,* ed. David J. Wishart, 611–18. Lincoln: University of Nebraska Press, 2004.

Wandel, Johanna, Harry P. Diaz, Jim Warren, Monica Hadarits, Margot Hurlbert, and Jeremy Pittman. "Drought and Vulnerability: A Conceptual Approach." In *Vulnerability and Adaptation to Drought: The Canadian Prairies and South America,* ed. Harry P. Diaz, Margot Hurlbert, and Jim Warren, 16–21. Calgary: University of Calgary Press, 2016.

Wandel, Johanna, and Gregory P. Marchildon. "Institutional Fit and Interplay in a Dryland Agricultural Social-Ecological System in Alberta, Canada." In *Adaptive Capacity and Environmental Governance,* ed. Derek Armitage and Ryan Plummer, 179–95. Berlin: Springer-Verlag Berlin, 2010.

Ward, Norman, and David Smith. *Jimmy Gardiner: Relentless Liberal.* Toronto: University of Toronto Press, 1990.

Wardhaugh, Robert A. "James G. Gardiner, Land Policy, and Dominion-Provincial Relations." MA thesis, History, University of Saskatchewan, 1990.

–. *Mackenzie King and the Prairie West.* Toronto: University of Toronto Press, 2000.

Warecki, George. *Protecting Ontario's Wilderness: A History of Changing Concepts and Preservation Politics, 1927–1973.* New York: Peter Lang, 2000.

Warkentin, John. "Water and Adaptive Strategies in Settling the Canadian West." *Manitoba Historical Society Transactions,* series 3, no. 28 (1971–72). http://www.mhs.mb.ca/docs/transactions/3/waterstrategies.shtml.

Warren, Jim. "The 'Min Till' Revolution and the Culture of Innovation." In *Vulnerability and Adaptation to Drought: The Canadian Prairies and South America,* ed. Harry P. Diaz, Margot Hurlbert, and Jim Warren, 107–32. Calgary: University of Calgary Press, 2016.

Warren, Jim, and Harry P. Diaz. *Defying Palliser: Stories of Resilience from the Driest Region of the Canadian Prairies.* Regina: Canadian Plains Research Centre Press, 2012.

Wearing, Joseph. *The L-Shaped Party: The Liberal Party of Canada, 1958–1980.* Toronto: McGraw-Hill Ryerson, 1981.

Weaver, John C. *The Great Land Rush and the Making of the Modern World, 1650–1900.* Montreal/Kingston: McGill-Queen's University Press, 2003.

Webb, Walter P. *The Great Plains.* Lincoln: University of Nebraska Press, 1931.

Webster, David. "Developing the World in Canada's Image: Hugh Keenleyside and Technical Assistance." In *A Samaritan State Revisited: Historical Perspectives on Canadian*

Foreign Aid, ed. Greg Donaghy and David Webster, 73–99. Calgary: University of Calgary Press, 2019.

–. *Fire and the Full Moon: Canada and Indonesia in a Decolonizing World.* Vancouver: UBC Press, 2009.

–. "Foreign Policy, Diplomacy, and Decolonization." In *Canada and the Third World: Overlapping Histories,* ed. Karen Dubinsky, Sean Mills, and Scott Rutherford, 155–92. Toronto: University of Toronto Press, 2016.

Webster, David, and Greg Donaghy. "Introduction." In *A Samaritan State Revisited: Historical Perspectives on Canadian Foreign Aid,* ed. Greg Donaghy and David Webster, 1–20. Calgary: University of Calgary Press, 2019.

Westad, Odd Arne. *The Global Cold War: Third World Interventions and the Making of Our Times.* Cambridge, UK: Cambridge University Press, 2005.

Westover, H.L., and George A. Rogler, *Crested Wheatgrass.* Washington, DC: United States Department of Agriculture, 1941. https://digital.library.unt.edu/ark:/67531/metadc1567/m1/1/.

Wetherell, Donald G., with Elise A. Corbet. *Breaking New Ground: A Century of Farm Equipment Manufacturing on the Canadian Prairies.* Saskatoon: Fifth House, 1993.

Whitaker, Reginald. *The Government Party: Organizing and Financing the Liberal Party of Canada, 1930–58.* Toronto: University of Toronto Press, 1977.

White, Clinton O. *Power for a Province: A History of Saskatchewan Power.* Regina: University of Regina, 1976.

White, Richard. "Urban Renewal Revisited: Toronto, 1950 to 1970." *Canadian Historical Review* 97, 1 (2016): 1–33.

White, Sarah C. "Thinking Race, Thinking Development." *Third World Quarterly* 23, 3 (2002): 407–19.

Widstoe, John A. *An Examination into the Conditions on the Lethbridge Northern Irrigation District.* Edmonton: J.W. Jeffery, King's Printer, 1925.

Williams, C.M. (Red). "Always the Bridesmaid: The Development of the Saskatchewan Beef Production System." Part 2, "Historical Highlights and Integral Factors." *Saskatchewan History* 44, 2 (1992): 68–76.

Willpacker, James J., Collin A. Eagles-Smith, Michelle A. Lutz, Michael T. Tate, Jesse M. Lepak, and Joshu T. Ackerman. "Reservoirs and Water Management Influence Fish Mercury Concentrations in the Western United States and Canada." *Science of the Total Environment* 568 (2016): 739–48.

Wilson, Jeremy. "For the Birds? Neoliberalism and the Protection of Biodiversity in British Columbia." *BC Studies,* 142–43 (2004): 241–77.

Wilson, M.L., W.H. Fairfield, and L.C. Charlesworth. *Report of Commission Appointed to Report on the Lethbridge Northern and Other Irrigation Districts in Alberta.* Edmonton: Government of Alberta, 1930. https://open.alberta.ca/publications/1551414.

Wishart, David J., ed. *Encyclopedia of the Great Plains.* Lincoln: University of Nebraska Press, 2004.

Wolfe, Patrick. *Settler Colonialism and the Transformation of Anthropology: The Politics and Poetics of an Ethnographic Event.* London/New York: Cassell, 1999.

Wood, David. *Places of Last Resort: The Expansion of the Farm Frontier into the Boreal Forest in Canada, c. 1910–1940.* Montreal/Kingson: McGill-Queen's University Press, 2006.

Woolford, Andrew, and Jeff Benvenuto. "Canada and Colonial Genocide." *Journal of Genocide Research* 17, 4 (2015): 373–90.

World Health Organization Expert Committee. *Simulium and Onchocerciasis in the Northern Territories of the Gold Coast.* Geneva: World Health Organization, 1956.

Worster, Donald. *Rivers of Empire: Water, Aridity and the Growth of the American West.* New York: Pantheon Books, 1985.

Younging, Gregory. *Elements of Indigenous Style: A Guide for Writing by and about Indigenous Peoples.* Edmonton: Brush Education, 2018.

Youngman, Raymond. "Government of Canada Community Pastures." *Journal of Range Management* 4, 6 (1951): 382–85.

Zeilig, Ken, and Victoria Zeilig. *Ste. Madeleine: Community without a Town, Metis Elders in Interview.* Winnipeg: Pemmican, 1987.

Zelko, Frank. *Make It a Green Peace! The Rise of Countercultural Activism.* Oxford: Oxford University Press, 2013.

Index

Note: "(f)" after a page number indicates a figure

Adams, William M., 132
Africa (drought), 165
agricultural colonization. *See* prairie agricultural settlement; settler colonialism
Agricultural Improvement Associations (AIAs), xix–xx, 30–31, 32, 38
Agricultural Institute of Canada, 147–48, 167
Agricultural Rehabilitation and Development Act (ARDA), 146, 149–50
Agri-Environment Services, 4
Alberta Railway and Irrigation Company, 47
Anastakis, Dimitry, 146
Anishinaabeg Nation, 10
Ankrah, Robert, 130, 140
Archibald, E.S., 120–22, 146, 230*n*6
Aswan Dam, 141
Auld, E.H., 38
Awada, Lana, 169

Balkwill, Daniel, 63
Bayer chemical company, 170, 235*n*19
B.C. Sugar, 53
Beamish, J.E., 138–39, 151
Beckie, Mary A., 170
beet farming. *See* sugar beet farming
Beet Workers Industrial Union, 53
Benidickson, Jamie, 86
Bennett, R.B., 25
Bentley, C.F., 132, 167
Berger, Thomas, 117
Better Farming Commission, 24, 25–26
Big Rock Committee, 109–10
Bivar, Venus, 34, 191*n*110
Boone, Catherine, 123
Boundary Waters Treaty (1909), 56–57
Bracken, John, 22, 23–24, 25–26, 76
Bradley, W.J., 77
Britnell, George Edwin, 5
Brook, Vicki, 109
Brown, Lester R., 165
Bryden, P.E., 146
Burns, Robert, xx, xxi, 176*n*22

Calder, Viola, 31
Canada Geographic Information System, 149
Canada Land Inventory, 149
Canada Water Agency, 3, 177*n*2
Canadian Environmental Advisory Council, 167

Canadian Farm Resilience Administration, 3
Canadian Federation of Agriculture, 147–48, 167
Canadian International Development Agency (CIDA), 139–40
Canadian New Deal, 25
Canadian North West Irrigation Company, 44
Canadian Pacific Railway, 44
Canadian Prairies: about, 20–21(f); drylands, 20–21(f), 22–26; map, 21(f); precipitation rates, 58, 164; soil degradation, 161–71; soil zones, 11–12(f), 183*n*57. *See also* prairie agricultural settlement
Canadian Society of Soil Science, 167
Canadian Society for Technical Agriculturalists, 148
Canadian Wheat Board, 162
Careless, Anthony G.S., 155, 156
Chaboyer, Rene, 118
Charlesworth, L.C., 33
Chrétien, Jean, 157
Churchill River Basin, 117
Clark, F.A., 151, 232*n*34
climate change, xx–xxi, 3, 17
Cold War, 120, 123–24, 130–31
Colpitts, George, 107
Commission on Conservation, 23–24
Committee on Lands, 23
Committee on Saskatchewan River Delta Problems, 116
Community Pastures Program, 61–80; about, 15, 26, 61–62; analysis, 79–80; assessment, 173; biodiversity challenges, 78–79, 80; capacity, 156; conservation, 66; crested wheatgrass, xx, 76–77(f), 78–79, 156, 207*n*85; Crow Rate, 65; on Crown Lands, 64; expansion, 151–54; farmer displacement, 64; federal farm assistance legislation and eligibility, 73–75; fencing, 68–69(f), 70, 152(f); government policy challenges, 73–76, 79–80; grazing associations annual meetings, 70(f)–71; high vs low modernism, 68, 72, 79; Indigenous vs non-Indigenous benefits, 104–6, 151–54, 157; livestock raising, 9, 68–69(f), 72, 153(f), 173; locations, 62, 63–66(f), 202*n*3; Métis removal from, 104–6; objectives, 157; on-reserve pasture program, 151–54; pasture creation, 64–67(f), 68, 104, 203*nn*17–18; pasture improvement program funding, 156; pasture managers, 71; policy shift, 156–58; popularity of, 69; promotion of, 64–68; relief policies and price supports, 75; side benefits, 157; soil conservation techniques, 68; statistics, 64, 66–67(f), 68; on sub-marginal lands, 62–63, 68, 75, 104; unsettlement goals, 62–68; user fees, 70, 152, 156–58; women, 71. *See also* Indigenous land dispossession and displacement; Prairie Farm Rehabilitation Administration (PFRA)
conservation. *See* soil conservation
Cook, Ramsey, 51–52
Co-operative Commonwealth Federation (CCF), 94
Cowessess Reserve, 150, 152, 152(f)–53(f)
Craig, Béatrice, xvii–xviii
Cree: Nehinuwuk Nation, Kaminstigominuhigoskak/Cumberland House, 10, 102, 112(f)–113, 115–18, 215*n*6, 219*n*91; nēhiyawak Nation, 10, 101, 102, 182*n*53, 215*n*6; Opaskwayak Nation, 112, 219*n*89; Sweetgrass Nation, 109, 111
crested wheatgrass *(Agropyron cristatum)*, xx, 76–77(f), 78–79, 207*n*85
Criddle, Norman, 36
Crow Rate, 65
Cumberland House Cree (Kaminstigominuhigoskak [Nehinuwuk Nation]), 10, 102, 112(f)–113, 115–18, 215*n*6, 219*n*91
Cumberland Lake, 114

Dakota Nation, 10
Danysk, Cecilia, 49
Daschuk, James, 13
de Boer, Dirk, 114
Deighton, Alex, 8

DeLuca, Tom, 78
Department of Agriculture, 76, 146, 161, 166
Department of Indian Affairs and Northern Development (DIAND), 150–51
Department of Regional Economic Expansion (DREE), 154–55, 161, 173
Diaz, Harry P., 170
Diefenbaker, John, 97, 98, 110, 148–49
District Experimental Sub-Stations, 27–28(f), 29–31
Dobson, Frank J., 124, 126
Dobson, W.K., 137–38, 139–40
Dominion Experimental Stations, 28(f), 37, 42, 76
Dominion Lands Act (1872), 13
Dominion Lands Policy, 179*n*32
Dominion Range Experiment Station, 76
Dominion Water and Power Bureau, 57
Donaghy, Greg, 121, 125
Donald, Dwayne, 217*n*44
drought, 14, 17, 27, 164–65
dry farming, 22
drylands, 20–21(f), 22–26
Ducks Unlimited, 113
Dyck, Erika, 8

E.B. Campbell Dam, 114, 115, 116–18, 220*n*100
Egypt (Aswan Dam), 141
Ellis, J.G., 163, 166
Elmore, Bartow, 170
Engineering Institute of Canada, 56
Ewing Report (Justice Albert Ewing), 53
Experimental Farms Service: cultural work, 40; directors, 146; farming techniques, 13, 26, 30, 37, 58; sugar beet farming, 48; tree nurseries, 25
External Aid Office (EAO), 125, 127, 139

Fairbairn, Garry Lawrence, 167
fairway crested wheatgrass *(Agropyron cristatum)*, 76
farming techniques: adjustments and failures, 4, 21–26; chemical pesticides and herbicides, 39, 163, 169–70, 235*n*19; conservation tillage, 169–70; dry farming, 22; economic losses, 168; experimental demonstration stations, 27–28(f), 29–31; genetic engineering, 170; later seeding, 38; neo-conventional farming, 170; postwar agricultural industrialization, 162–63; soil conservation, 15, 23–26, 68, 169; strip farming, 15, 20, 29(f)–30, 37–38; summerfallow, 22, 23–24, 29, 161–64; technological advances, 163–64; trash cover, 29, 161, 162; zero tillage, 169. *See also* irrigation; prairie agricultural settlement; Prairie Farm Rehabilitation Administration (PFRA)
Farstad, C.W., 38
Ferguson, Harley B., 85, 91
Fineday, Sidney, 109, 110
Fineday, Wes, 106
Fitzgerald, M.J., 125–26, 150
Fleury, George, 104, 105
Fleury, Norman, 106
Florizone, Richard, 3
Food and Agriculture Organization (FAO), 120, 125, 129, 165
Forestry Nursery Stations, 25
Foss, W.L., 126
Fouillard, Benoit, 104
Fouillard, Lazare, 105
Fowke, Vernon, 5, 19, 206*n*79
François-Finlay Dam, 117
Friesen, Gerald, 6
Fujiwara, Aya, 199*n*75
Fulton, Murray, 169
fur trade, 11–12, 113

Gaherty, G.A., 90, 91
Galt, Alexander, 22
Gardiner, James Garfield: about, 26; community pastures program, 61, 64; large water development project, 87, 88, 89–90, 94; patronage, 35; settlement mistakes, 178*n*12; small water development projects, 31
Gardiner Dam, 81–82(f), 97–98(f), 108, 114, 116
George, Henry, 51–52

Gertler, Michael, 170
Ghana: about, 122; agricultural cultural practices, 133; colonialism, 122–23; food production, 131, 141; foreign relations, 123–24; government, 122–24, 138; hoe-farming, 133; international development assistance beginnings, 125–28; land rights, 132–33; linguistic and cultural groups, 132; livestock statistics, 125; map, 121(f); northern vs southern development, 123; racism, 123; standards of living, 123; water supply history, 124–25, 126; work ethic and racialized conceptions of, 133–34
Ghana (water conservation project), 120–43; about, 16, 121; analysis of, xii–xiii, 142–43; Canadian vs Ghanaian parallels, 131–32; critiques of, 139–40; dam construction, 122; dam sites proposals, 131; evaluation of, 137–42; Ghanaian employees, 129–30(f); Ghanaian staff qualifications, 138–39; health effects, 141–42; hydrometric records, 129; information challenges, xiii, 129–32; infrastructure degradation, 139; local vs expert knowledge, 16, 122; "package" projects, 139; recommendations and agreement, 126–27; small dams assessment, 137; staff challenges, 129–32, 137–38; stream-flow data, 129; training and supervision, 137–38; withdrawal, 140–42. *See also* Prairie Farm Rehabilitation Administration (PFRA)
Ghana (water conservation project) Canadians in: aid vs consulting, 139; Canadian vs Ghanaian power dynamics, 134(f); deployment, 128(f)–132; foodstuffs importation, 135; health and medical care, 135–36; housing conditions, 135, 136; living conditions, 134–36; morale, 136–37; staff applications, 128–29; staff family, 128(f); twinning arrangements, 127, 138; withdrawal, 140–42
Gilbert, Jess, xix, 15, 19–20, 35, 75
Goody, Jack, 133
Gordon Commission, 146
Goulet, Keith Napoleon, 112–13, 116–17, 118, 215*n*6
Goulet, Trish, 115
Grand Rapids Dam, 114
grasses: brome, 38, 76; crested wheatgrass *(Agropyron cristatum)*, 76–77(f), 78–79, 207*n*85; fairway crested wheatgrass, 76
Gray, James H., 5–6, 7, 19, 30, 162
Great Depression, 3, 5, 24, 35, 69, 104
Great Plains, 20–21(f), 22
Green Party of Canada, 3, 17, 177*n*1
Greene, J.J., 110
Gregory, Dick, 109
Griffin, Augustus, 51

Hamilton, Alvin, 98
Hargrave, Bert, 164
Hargrave, H.J., 144, 151
Herriot, Trevor, xvi, xviii, 100, 106, 111
high modernism: about, 7–8, 181*n*40; vs low modernism, xviii–xix, 19–20, 34–35, 40, 68, 72, 191*n*110; Prairie Farm Rehabilitation Administration, xviii–xix, 7–8, 19–20, 33–35, 40, 68, 72, 79, 181*n*40, 184*n*7
Hill, Harry M., 158, 165, 168, 174
Hind, Henry Youle, 83, 107
Historic Sites and Monuments Board of Canada, 109–10
historical scholarship: bygone contingency, xvi; labour history, xviii, 176*n*16; usable past, 175*n*9
Hogg, Dr. T.H., 90, 91
Holleman, Hannah, 23, 100
Hope, E.C., 73–74
Hubbard, Trevor, 106, 107
Hudson's Bay Company, 113
Hughes, Charles C., 141, 142–43
Hunter, John M., 141, 142–43
Hunter, William E., 57
Hutterite communities, 57
hydroelecticity projects. *See* South Saskatchewan Regional Plan (SSRP)

Indian Residential School System, 13, 107
Indigenous land dispossession and displacement, 100–119; agricultural land

limitations (road allowances), 103, 104, 105; analysis, xv, 118–19; "clearing the plains," 12–13; food insecurity and poverty, xii, 105–6, 107; interviews about removal, 105–6; natural gas pipelines effects, 117; vs non-Indigenous removal avoidance, 105, 106; on-reserve water development program, 150–51; onto reserve lands, 103, 107–8; pasture program barriers, 151–54; redress efforts, 117–18; residential school system, 13, 107; river delta development harms, 116–18; river delta sovereignty, 118; scrip system, 103; taxation as dispossession, 105. *See also* Community Pastures Program; settler colonialism; Ste. Madeleine community (Métis); *individual names of nations*
Indigenous peoples: kinship ties, 10–11; labour racialization, 16, 45–46(f), 58; Traditional Stories principles, 106–7. *See also individual names of nations*
Inninewak Nation, 10
Inquiry into Farming Conditions (1921), 24
international development assistance. *See* Ghana (water conservation project)
International Institute for Sustainable Development, 3, 17
internment camps, 55–56
irrigation: advocacy groups, 93–94, 212*n*59, 212*n*61; capitalist investment in, 22, 42, 44, 47; challenges, 42, 47–48, 56–57; costs, 44, 48; districts, 43, 47–48, 50–51; environmental impacts, 47, 113–14; expansion, 99; farmer cooperatives, 42–43, 47; government investment, 24, 42, 47–54, 57, 59; health hazards, 141–42; historical map of, 52(f), 53; legislation, 22, 47; muskrat activity, 47; recommendations, 48, 49–50, 51; salinity, 47; statistics, 87, 99; sugar beet farming, 15, 43, 45(f), 56–57; water rights treaty, 56–57. *See also* farming techniques; Prairie Farm Rehabilitation Administration (PFRA)
Irrigation District Act (1915), 47
Iverson, N.L., 129, 131, 132, 137, 140, 141–42
îyârhe Nakodabi Nation, 10

Jaffe, JoAnn, 170
Japanese people: internment, 54–56; labour racialization, 45–46, 54–55(f), 56, 69, 199*n*75
Jensen, Christian, 51
Jones, David C., 6, 23
Jones, Esyllt, 8
Josephson, Paul, 88

Kahkewistahaw Reserve, 152
Kainai Nation (Blood Tribe), 10, 45, 57
Kaminstigominuhigoskak (Cumberland House Cree/Nehinuwuk Nation), 10, 102, 112(f)–113, 115–18, 215*n*6, 219*n*91
Kane, Molly, 139
Kennedy, John F., 124
Kerber, Jenny, 59
Kerr, Samantha, 14
King, William Lyon Mackenzie, 19, 26
Kirk, L.E., 76
Knight Sugar Factory, 44, 45, 47
Knuttila, Murray, 6
Korinek, Valerie, 8
Kristjanson, Kris, 126, 135

Laing, Arthur, 110
Lake Diefenbaker, 81, 82(f), 99, 108, 111
Lakota Nation, 10
L'Ami, C.A., 139, 140
Land Utilization Board (LUB), 63–64, 75
Langford, Will, 94, 142, 145, 174
Latham, Michael E., 122, 123–24
Latour, Bruno, xii
Lesica, Peter, 78
Leskiw, L.A., 167
Lethbridge Northern Irrigation District (LNID), 47–48
Liberal Party of Canada: patronage interests, 35–36, 191*n*117, 192*n*122; PFRA endorsement, 3, 17, 177*n*2
Lilienthal, David, 90
Loewen, Royden, 10
Lok, S.C., 166

Loo, Tina, 145, 150, 181*n*40
low modernism: vs high modernism, xviii–xix, 19–20, 34–35, 40, 68, 72, 191*n*110
Lowdermilk, Walter C., 123
Lower Inventories for Tomorrow (LIFT) program, 162, 163
Luby, Brittany, 101
Lund, Christian, 133

Mackay, Elmer, 165
MacKenzie, G.L., 91, 108
Mackenzie Valley Pipeline Inquiry, 117
Maclean's Magazine, 77
MacPherson, Ian, 6, 9
Magee, Charles K., 125
Magrath Irrigation District, 50–51
Marchildon, Gregory P., 6, 63
Maritime Marshland Reclamation Act, 35, 59, 184*n*7
Martin, Chester, 4
Martz, Lawrence W., 114
Matthews, G.D., 37
Mayer-Oakes, William J., 108
McHugh, Paul, xvi
McKay, Ian, xiv, 40
McManus, Curtis, 6, 23
McNeill, J.R., 23
Meek Commission (Victor Meek), 57
Menzies, June and Merril, 148
Métis community: projects funding limitations, 151; racism against, 102–5; Red River settlement, 102. *See also* Indigenous peoples; Ste. Madeleine community (Métis)
Milk River, 56–57
Mistasiniy (Mistaseni/Mistusinne/Buffalo Child Stone): about, 101, 106–11, 217*n*44; archaeological survey report, 108–9, 217*n*52; cairn, 111; community fracture, 109–11; erratic boulder, 107; flooding and destruction of, 108–11, 118; preservation advocacy, 109–10; relocation costs, 109; as sacred place, 101, 106–7
Mistusinne Cairn, 111
modernism: about, 7–8, 181*n*40; high vs low modernism, xviii–xix, 19–20, 34–35, 40, 68, 72, 191*n*110
Moe, Scott, 99
Monsanto chemical company, 163, 170, 235*n*19
Moran, H.O., 125–26
Morton, W.L., xiv
muskrats, 113

Nakawe (Saulteaux Nation), 10
Nakota Nation, 10
National Farmers Union, 3, 17
natural gas pipelines, 117
Nehinuwuk Nation (Kaminstigominuhigoskak/Cumberland House Cree), 10, 102, 112(f)–113, 115–18, 215*n*6, 219*n*91
nēhiyawak (Cree Nation), 10, 101, 102, 182*n*53, 215*n*6
New Deal (US), 35
Nipawin Hydroelectric Station, 117
Nkrumah, Kwame, 122–24, 138
Nollet, Isidore Charles, 96
North Saskatchewan River, 11

Ochapowace Reserve, 152
Opaskwayak (Cree Nation), 112, 219*n*89

Packard, Walter, 51
Pallas, T.M., 140
Palliser John, 14
Palliser's Triangle, 14
Palmer, Asael E., 42, 44, 194*n*1
Palmer, Howard, 46, 49
Parent, David, 105
Patterson, William John, 178*n*12
Pearce, William, 83, 209*n*5
Peekhaus, Wilhelm, 170
PFRA. *See* Prairie Farm Rehabilitation Administration (PFRA)
Phillips, Sarah T., 34
Piikani Nation, 10
Pohorecky, Zenon, 108–9
Pollock, J.N., 56
Pomeroy, John W., 114
Porter, Doug J., 127
Potyondi, Barry, 6, 179*n*32
prairie agricultural settlement: adjustments to, 4, 21–26; capitalist investment in,

22, 42, 44, 47; chemical revolution, 9–10; as colonization, 10–13, 20–23, 42, 44, 171–72; crises, 22–26, 187*n*28; drought, 14, 17, 27, 164–65; dry farming, 22; drylands impacts, 20–21(f), 22–26; ecological consequences, xix–xx; economic conditions and government policy, 24; environmental historians, 23; historians, 4–10, 23; intensification, 9; liberal order framework, xiv–xv; mechanical revolution, 9–10; mistakes of, 4–7, 178*n*12, 178*n*15; precipitation rates, 14, 24–25; promotion of, 13; Special Areas, 24; "the great land rush," 12–13, 62. *See also* Canadian Prairies; farming techniques; Prairie Farm Rehabilitation Administration (PFRA)

Prairie Farm Assistance Act (PFAA), 62, 73–75, 206*n*79

Prairie Farm Rehabilitation Administration (PFRA): about, 3–4; activity types, 27–36; agricultural adjustment, 74–76, 86; agricultural colonization, 171–72; agricultural improvement associations, 30–31, 32; analysis of, xi–xii, 14, 17, 39–41, 118–19, 158–59, 171–74; anniversary, 160, 167–68, 174; annual reports, 30, 35, 63, 202*n*3, 203*nn*17–18; assessments of, 4–7, 32, 178*n*12, 178*n*15; beginnings and early years, xiv, 18–41; climate change, xx–xxi, 3, 17; conservation tillage promotion, 169–70; contemporary context, 17; criticisms of, 32; directors (*see* Fitzgerald, M.J.; Hargrave, Bert; Hill, Harry M.; Spence, George; Thomson, L.B.); district experimental sub-stations, 27–28(f), 29–31; dominion experimental stations, 28(f), 37, 42; economic surveys, 33–34, 35, 62–63, 75; elimination of, 3, 4, 178*n*7; environmental context, xix–xx, 10–14, 15, 25, 171–72; expansion, 26, 58–59; farming techniques (wheat stem sawfly), 36–37(f), 38–39, 40; federal vs regional authority, 156–57, 164; film about, 168; final years, 170–71; future, 168, 174; geographic boundaries, 26–27(f), 189*n*63; grasses (brome) distribution, 38, 76; high vs low modernism approach, xviii–xix, 7–8, 19–20, 33–35, 40, 68, 72, 79, 181*n*40, 184*n*7; historical context, xiii, 10–14, 15; hydrometric surveys, 33; Indigenous engagement, 145; inequalities patterns, 59–60; influence and significance, 144, 145–50; international development assistance, 120–22, 125, 127, 138–39; jurisdiction, 63, 79; "as a laboratory for experiments in federalism," xiii, 158; land evaluation guidebook, 131; legislation, 25, 26, 149; low modernism efforts, 31–32; mandate, xiv, 20; on-reserve pasture program, 151–54; on-reserve water development program, 150–51; organizational goals, 9; patronage role, 20, 35–36, 192*n*122; political endorsement of, 3, 177*nn*1–2; postwar agricultural industrialization, 146–47; power and privilege, 60; promotional speaking tours, 18–19, 89; regional transformation, 9, 171–74; rehabilitation schemes case studies, 144; research efforts, 32–34; restructuring, 40–41; settlement mistakes response, 4–7, 178*n*12, 178*n*15; settler colonial inequalities, xii, xiv, xv–xvi; shift, xiii, 145, 154–59, 160–61; small water development programs, 31, 173; soil conservation techniques, 15, 25–26, 169–70; soil surveys, 32–33(f); soil and water conservation programs, 165–71; strip farming promotion, 15, 20, 29(f)–30, 37–38; summary report (dam proposal), 86–87; transnational, 8; urban vs rural water development reservoir programs, 155–56; West vs East orientation (rural vs urban), 155. *See also* Community Pastures Program; farming techniques; Ghana (water conservation project); irrigation; prairie agricultural settlement; South Saskatchewan Regional Plan (SSRP)

Qu'Appelle River Dam, 81, 82(f), 97, 108

Quiring, David, 113

Railways Agreement, 48–49
Rance, Laura, 171
Rawlins, Alfred, 32
Red River, 11–12
Red River settlement, 102
Regular, W. Keith, 45–46
Rennie, D.A., 163, 166
Rescue Wheat, 39
residential school system, 13, 107
Retlaw Agricultural Improvement Association, 32
Richardson, B.T., 91
Riel, Louis, 102
Robertson, James W., 23
Rogers, B.T., 53
Rowell-Sirois Commission, 146
Royal Commission on Aboriginal Peoples, 118–19
Royal Commission on Agriculture and Rural Life (RCARL), 94–96, 147
Royal Commission on Canada's Economic Prospects, 74–75, 92, 146
Royal Commission on Dominion-Provincial Relations, 146
Royal Commission on the South Saskatchewan River Project, 90–92, 93–94, 212*n*56
Rudin, Ronald, 35, 184*n*7

Sainte-Marie, Buffy, 109
Sakimay Reserve, 152, 152(f)–53(f)
Saskatchewan Institute of Agrologists, 5–6
Saskatchewan River Delta: alteration of, 113; chlor-alkali plants, 114, 220*n*103; committee study report, 116; conservation efforts, 113; erosion, 115; fish contamination, 116; Indigenous sovereignty, 118; industrial development and Indigenous harms, xx, 116–18; infrastructure development consequences, xx, 111–12(f), 113–18; map, 101(f); methylmercury, 115–16; sedimentation processes, 114–15; waterflow variations and wildlife effects, 114–15
Saskatchewan River watershed (North and South): dams and reservoirs, 81–82(f), 97–98(f), 108, 111, 114–18, 220*n*100; hydroelectricity generation, 89, 96, 97, 113–14; maps, 82(f), 101(f); North waterway, 11. *See also* South Saskatchewan Regional Plan (SSRP)
Saskatchewan Rivers Development Association (SRDA), 93–94, 212*n*59
Saskatoon Archaeological Society, 108–9
Sauchyn, Dave, 14
Science Council of Canada, 167
Scott, James C.: high modernism, xviii, 7, 8, 15, 19, 34; local vs state knowledge, 82–83; research efforts, 32; work with the Central Intelligence Agency, 180*n*37
Seager, Allen, 53
Seamans, H.L., 37
Second World War: farm labour needs, 9, 54–56, 69; livestock value, 66; postwar agricultural industrialization, 146–47, 162–63; postwar reconstruction, 69, 84, 120
Selby, John, 104
settler colonialism: capitalist expansion, xvii–xviii, 10–13, 23; fur trade, 11–12, 113; gender and racial inequality, 13, 16, 46; as regional redesign, 82–83, 87–88; as structure vs event, xvii; "the great land rush," 12–13, 62; usable past, 175*n*9; waterways impacts, 11–12, 115; white supremacy and racism, 9. *See also* Indigenous land dispossession and displacement
Shirrif, C., 37
Siksika Nation, 10
Silverstein, Ben, xvii
Skovron, Wyatt Mark, 95
small water development program, 31, 173
Smith, Lewis, 126
soil conservation, 15, 23–26, 68, 169–70
soil creation, 11
soil degradation: agricultural settlement effects, 23–24, 161–71; organic matter decline, 11, 23, 161, 163, 166; processes, 166; reports, 166–67; salinity, 47, 166, 236*n*37; soil drifting, 27, 37–38, 73, 77–78, 161; tillage, 39, 163, 169–70
soil surveys, 32–33(f)
soil zones, 11–12(f), 183*n*57

South Saskatchewan Regional Plan (SSRP), 81–99; about, 16; agricultural development commission, 94–96; analysis of, 99; archaeological survey report, 108–9; beginnings, 83–84; book about, 81–82, 83; consequences of, 111–18; construction, 97–98(f); costs, 87, 89, 97; criticisms of, 88–92; dam engineering, 85–86, 91; dam project reports, 89–90; dam site proposals, 84–86; endorsements, 92–98; expert vs political authority on, 88, 90–92; hydroelectricity generation, 89, 96, 97; local vs state knowledge, 82–83; multipurpose approach, 86–88, 89; public consultation, 95; reconsiderations, 88–92; as regional redesign, 82–83, 87–88; royal commission on, 90–92, 93–94, 212*n*56; water conservation association, 93–94, 212*n*59. *See also* irrigation; Prairie Farm Rehabilitation Administration (PFRA); Saskatchewan River watershed (North and South)
Sparrow, H.O., 167
Special Areas, 24
Special Committee on Land Use, 147–48
Spence, George: about, 18–19; agricultural rehabilitation advocacy, 5, 58, 146; community pastures, 106; farming crisis inquiries, 24; Indigenous projects support, 150–51; livestock quality, 71; speaking tours, 18–19, 89; Ste. Madeleine population as "squatters," 104, 105; water development project advocate, 16, 57, 88, 89, 93–94; water development project book, 81–82, 83, 89
Spence-Sales, Harold, 148
St. Laurent, Louis, 88, 90, 91, 92, 97
St. Mary Dam, 57, 85
St. Mary River, 56–57
Stanger-Ross, Jordan, 54
Ste. Madeleine community (Métis): displacement and dispossession, xv–xvi, 100, 102–6, 118–19, 172–73; disrespect towards, 105, 106; as "forty or fifty squatters," 104; interviews about removal, 105–6; population, 103. *See also* Indigenous peoples; Métis community
Stirling, Robert, 170
Stonechild, Blair, 109
strip farming, 15, 20, 29(f)–30, 37–38
Strong, Maurice, 140
Stunden Bower, Shannon: on high vs low modernism, xviii–xix; "as a laboratory for experiments in federalism," xii; multi-facted approach, xi–xii, xiv
sugar beet farming: challenges, 44–45; child labour, 194*n*1; early years, 43–47; farming areas, 43, 194*n*3; fertilizers, 44, 48; irrigation infrastructure, 15, 43, 45(f), 56–57; labour racialization, xv–xvi, 15, 43, 45–46(f), 53–55(f), 56, 58, 172, 199*n*75; labour shortages, 48, 54; labour wages, 53; labour-intensive harvesting, 44–45; migrant labour, 48–49; prisoners of war labour, 54–56; processing plants, 44, 48, 53; productivity, 58; unions, 53; wartime, 54–56; water supply shortages, 56–57
Sugar Beet Growers Association, 48–49, 54, 56, 197*n*41
Summerberry Muskrat Rehabilitation Project, 113, 114
summerfallow, 22, 23–24, 29, 161–64
Supplementary Public Works Construction Act (1935), 25
Sweetgrass Cree Nation, 109, 111

Tanzania, 142
Tengan, Alexis B., 133
Thompson, E.P., xviii, 176*n*16
Thompson, John Herd, 6, 9, 40, 53
Thomson, L.B.: about, 89–90; soil conservation, 66, 168; water management, 92, 155, 212*n*56
Tobin Reservoir, 114, 115, 116
Tough, Frank, 113, 114
trash cover, 29, 161, 162
tree nurseries, 25
tree planting, 169
Trudeau, Pierre, 145, 154–55, 164
Tsuut'ina Nation, 10
Tufts, William B., 94

United States: engineering, 85–86, 91; overseas irrigation projects, 126; soil degradation, 167
University of Reading (agriculture science seminar), 144
urban growth poles, 155
Utah-Idaho Sugar Company, 48, 53

Venne, Joe, 103–4
Voisey, Paul, 65
Volta Dam, 124–25
Volta River Authority, 124, 126

Wagner, F.G., 158
Waiser, Bill, 96, 111, 178*n*15
Waldram, James, 117
water conservation and development management: associations, 93–94, 212*n*59; drought remediation programs, 165–66; E.B. Campbell Dam, 114, 115, 116–18, 220*n*100; Egypt (Aswan Dam), 141; François-Finlay Dam, 117; Gardiner Dam, 81–82(f), 97–98(f), 108, 114, 116; Grand Rapids Dam, 114; hydrometric surveys, 33; Lake Diefenbaker, 81, 82(f), 99, 108, 111; large projects (*see* Ghana [water conservation project]; South Saskatchewan Regional Plan [SSRP]); legislation, 25; on-reserve, 150–51; Qu'Appelle River Dam, 81, 82(f), 97, 108; small projects, 31, 173; St. Mary Dam, 57, 85; Tobin Reservoir, 114, 115, 116; urban vs rural, 155–56; Volta Dam, 124–25. *See also* irrigation
Weaver, John, 12–13, 93
Webster, David, 121
wheat: crop damage, xix–xx, 25, 36–39; grasshopper damage, 25; pesticides and herbicides, 39; plant breeding research, 39; precipitation rates, 24–25; prices and surpluses, 24, 162, 168; rescue wheat, 39
wheat stem sawfly *(Cephus cinctus):* educational campaigns against, 38–39; grasses (brome) attractant, 38; infestation, xix–xx, 36–37(f), 38–39; pesticides and herbicides against, 39; strip farming, 36–37(f), 38; wheat plant breeding research, 39
Widstoe, Dr. John A., 42, 48, 90, 91
William Pearce Stockwatering Project, 209*n*5
Wilson, M.L., 49–50, 51
Winiwarter, Verena, 23
Wolf, Edward C., 165
Wolfe, Patrick, xvii
Wood, David, 6
World Health Organization (WHO), 141
World Soil Charter, 165
Worldwatch Institute, 165

Younging, Gregory, 106

Zeilig, Ken, 105
Zeilig, Victoria, 105
zero tillage, 169

NATURE | HISTORY | SOCIETY

Claire Elizabeth Campbell, *Shaped by the West Wind: Nature and History in Georgian Bay*

Tina Loo, *States of Nature: Conserving Canada's Wildlife in the Twentieth Century*

Jamie Benidickson, *The Culture of Flushing: A Social and Legal History of Sewage*

John Sandlos, *Hunters at the Margin: Native People and Wildlife Conservation in the Northwest Territories*

William J. Turkel, *The Archive of Place: Unearthing the Pasts of the Chilcotin Plateau*

Greg Gillespie, *Hunting for Empire: Narratives of Sport in Rupert's Land, 1840–70*

James Murton, *Creating a Modern Countryside: Liberalism and Land Resettlement in British Columbia*

Stephen J. Pyne, *Awful Splendour: A Fire History of Canada*

Sharon Wall, *The Nurture of Nature: Childhood, Antimodernism, and Ontario Summer Camps, 1920–55*

Hans M. Carlson, *Home Is the Hunter: The James Bay Cree and Their Land*

Joy Parr, *Sensing Changes: Technologies, Environments, and the Everyday, 1953–2003*

Liza Piper, *The Industrial Transformation of Subarctic Canada*

Jamie Linton, *What Is Water? The History of a Modern Abstraction*

Dean Bavington, *Managed Annihilation: An Unnatural History of the Newfoundland Cod Collapse*

J. Keri Cronin, *Manufacturing National Park Nature: Photography, Ecology, and the Wilderness Industry of Jasper*

Shannon Stunden Bower, *Wet Prairie: People, Land, and Water in Agricultural Manitoba*

Jocelyn Thorpe, *Temagami's Tangled Wild: Race, Gender, and the Making of Canadian Nature*

Sean Kheraj, *Inventing Stanley Park: An Environmental History*

Darcy Ingram, *Wildlife, Conservation, and Conflict in Quebec, 1840–1914*

Caroline Desbiens, *Power from the North: Territory, Identity, and the Culture Hydroelectricity in Quebec*

Daniel Macfarlane, *Negotiating a River: Canada, the US, and the Creation of the St. Lawrence Seaway*

Justin Page, *Tracking the Great Bear: How Environmentalists Recreated British Columbia's Coastal Rainforest*

Ryan O'Connor, *The First Green Wave: Pollution Probe and the Origins of Environmental Activism in Ontario*

John Thistle, *Resettling the Range: Animals, Ecologies, and Human Communities in British Columbia*

Jessica van Horssen, *A Town Called Asbestos: Environmental Contamination, Health, and Resilience in a Resource Community*

Nancy B. Bouchier and Ken Cruikshank, *The People and the Bay: A Social and Environmental History of Hamilton Harbour*

Carly A. Dokis, *Where the Rivers Meet: Pipelines, Participatory Resource Management, and Aboriginal-State Relations in the Northwest Territories*

Jonathan Peyton, *Unbuilt Environments: Tracing Postwar Development in Northwest British Columbia*

Mark R. Leeming, *In Defence of Home Places: Environmental Activism in Nova Scotia*

Jim Clifford, *West Ham and the River Lea: A Social and Environmental History of London's Industrialized Marshland, 1839–1914*

Michèle Dagenais, *Montreal, City of Water: An Environmental History*

David Calverley, *Who Controls the Hunt? First Nations, Treaty Rights, and Wildlife Conservation in Ontario, 1783–1939*

Jamie Benidickson, *Levelling the Lake: Transboundary Resource Management in the Lake of the Woods Watershed*

Daniel Macfarlane, *Fixing Niagara Falls: Environment, Energy, and Engineers at the World's Most Famous Waterfall*

Angela V. Carter, *Fossilized: Environmental Policy in Canada's Petro-Provinces*

Stéphane Castonguay, *The Government of Natural Resources: Science, Territory, and State Power in Quebec, 1867–1939*

Ronald Rudin, *Against the Tides: Reshaping Landscape and Community in Canada's Maritime Marshlands*

Andrew Watson, *Making Muskoka: Tourism, Rural Identity, and Sustainability, 1870–1920*

Printed and bound in Canada by Friesens
Set in Garamond by Artegraphica Design Co. Ltd.
Copy editor: Robert Lewis
Proofreader: Sophie Pouyanne
Indexer: Margaret de Boer
Cover designer: Alexa Love
Cover images: *top:* Summer round-up in a community pasture, R-B8299, Provincial Archives of Saskatchewan; *bottom:* Aerial photograph of Lake Diefenbaker, Information Services Corporation, Saskatchewan.

